Teach them their identity and their purpose!

— Russell M. Nelson

## I AM A CHILD OF GOD

We live in a world that can cause us to forget who we are. Our experiences can influence incorrect views of our self that have the capacity to create ongoing struggles. While many of us acknowledge our relationship to God, we tend to still see our self in terms of worthlessness, being helpless, unimportant or unlovable and highly self-conscious about our bodies. The incorrect beliefs we hold about our self impact many aspects of our ongoing earthly experience. This book will assist in getting rid of incorrect beliefs and have us draw into a correct view of who each of us really are. Man is indeed the literal offspring of God. If we would believe and live by this truth our perception would dictate purpose, as we would come to see ourselves as capable, acceptable and incredibly designed. One day you will see Him again and when you do, you will see a Being with whom you long have been acquainted and in whose image you have been made.

## HEALTHY-ESTEEM: A MATTER OF BELIEF

By: Lawrence A. Bradley, M.A. LMFT

# ACKNOWLEDGEMENTS

I would like to offer a special thanks to everyone that helped with this project, especially those that have encouraged me and provided feedback. Many of those so encouraging have been a number of past Program Participants who are now living life with joy and purpose. As I worked with clients, inevitably most knew of many others that struggle with sensing their worth and having confidence in face of life's challenges. Several of my past clients inquired if I ever thought of putting The Program into a book or manual, so that they could share this information more effectively.

I would also like to thank all those that read the manuscript and offered important critiques. At times I found it difficult to translate what I do in my office and put it in a self-help book. So I appreciate those that are acquainted with my approach and for their important suggestions in developing a text that others could follow and come to a better understanding and appreciation for their true identity. One of the more frequent comments I heard was that while much of the material taught in this book are things participants have known, it was how things were connected that allowed participants to develop a tangible, never fading view of them self. The stabilizing of individual worth and identity was the missing link for those that had struggled for so long.

Finally, to Vicki Walker for providing a wonderful picture for the book cover. I like the picture because you can see in the process of sincere study, the Holy Ghost as a companion to facilitate understanding. Our Father in Heaven wants each of us to know of our relationship to Him, which when believed will work in us to become that which we were created to become. His announcement that we are His children and that He will never give up on us, is central to all the prophets have written.

Artist Website: www.vickiwalkerart.com

Author's Website: dixiefamilyskillscenter.com

# Table of Contents

"We become what we think about."

— Earl Nightingale

"Life is 10% what happens to me and 90% of how I react to it."

— Charles Swindoll

## PREFACE

In Meredith Wilson and Lacey Franklin's story, The Music Man, we find a con-artist by the name of Harold Hill, coming into a small town in Iowa, trying to create a problem where a problem doesn't actually exist. The intent of setting up the problem was so that Harold Hill could sell them a solution. He convinces the townsfolk that the local billiard parlor would lead to their children becoming disobedient, wasting time, and increasing deviancy. His solution was to have the community form a youth marching band, keeping the youth involved and away from the billiard parlor, but also wherein Harold Hill could sell band instruments and uniforms. Unlike the trumped up problems concocted in the musical, in our communities we do have growing problems. These are real and bear out in the statistics. Mental health issues are on the rise. Suicide, the perceived final escape, rose 31% from 2001 to 2017. Even in our small town paper appeared the following quote:

> As I am sure you know, our youth and adult suicide rate is increasing rapidly, and we are seeing an increase in the number of kids who report high depressive symptoms and suicide ideation, and an increasing number of youth who are self-harming as a coping strategy for their depression, loneliness, and other behavioral struggles. (Ivins Partners With Southwest Behavioral Health Center, Approves Annual Suicide Prevention Funding; St. George News, July 16, 2019)

Yes folks, there is a real problem! People are losing a sense of who they are and the purpose they have both here and in eternity. That loss of self is what is leading to the rise in the suicide statistics; as well as many other problems currently being experienced in society. The leading indicators of suicide in the U.S. have been identified as untreated mental health conditions, such as depression and anxiety, behavioral problems, impulsivity, low self-esteem, substance use and abuse, and legal issues brought on by instability and anti-social tendencies.

It sounds like an overwhelming amount of conditions to address if we expect to make a dent in the growing problems. If we are paying attention; those problems are not only growing larger but as the quote points out, they are also growing at an accelerated pace. But what if all of these prevailing indicators and issues actually only had a single source? What if all of these conditions were manifestations of just one single thing?

You are about to go on a journey of discovery, one that will have you understand the emerging science of Epigenetics and how this science should have us begin to look at our existence. Epigenetics is the science that has unlocked the door in helping us understand that all of the issues related to depression, anxiety, mood dysregulation; ADHD, low self-esteem, loneliness, isolation, anger, addiction, abuse, relationship struggles, fear of intimacy, unending cycles of poverty, obesity, negative attitudes, etc. are simply manifestations of what has come to be stored at the cellular level; especially what one has come to *believe* about them self. So profoundly convincing is the research, Bruce Lipton, a specialist in this field stated:

> The issue is who are we? We've been limited by our beliefs; our perceptions. If we believe we are a victim, we become a victim. Henry Ford said it. If you think you can or you think you can't, you're right. That's really where it comes down to...... we are very powerful people. Our belief systems empower us.
> (Epigenetics and Evolution: Bettering Yourself And Humanity, March 27, 2018)

In essence, how one sees them self has serious ongoing ramifications; as how one sees them self tends to steer their destiny. It is from these developed beliefs of self that affects chemical and enzymatic differences in cellular function. Belief formed in cells is influencing and shaping ongoing experience. So, how one sees them self, what one has come to believe about self will impact every other aspect of one's life, i.e. how we respond to stress, how we interact socially, our personal efforts, our goals and dreams, our view of the world, our belief about what others think of us, mental and physical health issues, relationship choices, etc. There is nothing more important than an understanding of how our self-perception shapes our ongoing experience.

Epigenetics has shifted our focus from looking at external reasons for our ongoing struggles and has us begin to recognize that the real reason for our ongoing difficulties is because of what is stored inside of us at the cellular level. Cells are living entities and they are influenced in their ongoing activity by what they have learned. Cellularly stored learning is never dormant. Cellularly stored learning is consistently sending signals that influence how we see ourselves. Self-perception becomes encoded upon DNA and stored in neural pathways and acts in a way that shapes our ongoing experience.

In laymen's terms, Epigenetics has us understand how cells function, which provides the insight as to how our current circumstances related to both mental and physical health issues got their footing. Each of us is made of approximately 100 trillion cells. Cells are designed to do one thing and they do this very well – they absorb our experience and our environment. If our cells have absorbed and stored incorrect information we will experience negative feedback in a host of different ways. The cellularly stored distortions that incorrect information form are discerned by ongoing, patternistic negative emotions and behaviors, whether these be social anxiety, fear of intimacy, depression, agitation, or explosive anger; feeling life is unfair, ongoing stress, fear of what others think about us, a general sense of shame, perfectionism, a feeling that one does not matter, an ongoing sense of helplessness, feeling like a failure, or that we are not deserving of good things, bi-polar and other mood dysregulation, anxiety, greater social isolation, addiction, arrogance, pride, cynicism, not taking responsibility, etc., and the list goes on and on.

While all of our environment and experience is affecting cellular health and activity, Epigenetic researchers made abundantly clear that the most impactful, single source of programming our cells incorrectly is our own mindset. Our mindset is an epigenetic signal of the environment which heavily influences so many aspects of our daily living. The old adage, 'As a man thinketh, so is he,' is now proven through the science of Epigenetics. Here is what we now know. Every minute of every day, our body is physically reacting, literally changing, in response to the thoughts that run through our mind.

It's been shown over and over again that just thinking about something causes our brain to release neurotransmitters, chemical messengers that open vital communication between cells and our nervous system. Neurotransmitters control virtually all of our body's functions, from hormones to digestion to feeling happy, sad, or stressed. Our cells bathe in the neurochemicals that are being released in relation to our thoughts, whereby our cells begin to take on the nature of what those chemicals suggest. Human thoughts and intentions are carried within our physiology as protein messengers; therefore every thought possesses the power and energy to transform perception, DNA performance, and our physical and mental health. Our cells are heavily influenced by the compositional medium of those neurochemicals released in connection with our thoughts.

## Thoughts Influence Neural Pathway Genesis

Expectancies and learned associations have been shown to change brain chemistry and circuitry. The thoughts we introduce to our cells will impact and shape real physiological and cognitive outcomes. If those thoughts are accurate then those outcomes are positive, but if our thoughts provide inaccurate information to our cells that will have a different outcome. Thoughts have an astonishing power to influence physiology.

What flows consistently and repetitively through our minds sculpts our brain in nearly permanent ways. Think of the thoughts of our mind as the movement of information through our nervous system, which on a physical level is all the electrical signals running back and forth, most of which is happening below our conscious awareness. As a thought travels through our brain, neurons fire together in distinctive ways based on the specific information being handled, and those patterns of neural activity actually change our neural structure. To keep things in perspective, your brain will produce more electrical signals in a day than all of the telephones in the world combined. That level of activity is greatly influencing both structure and function of our neurophysiology.

## Thoughts Program Cells

Our thoughts likewise program our cells. A thought is an electrochemical event which signals the release of a host of chemical and electrical particles, some in the form of neuro or polypeptides that look for receptor sites on cells. Each and every cell contains thousands and thousands of receptor sites and just as the word indicates, these sites are there to receive information. What docks in those receptor sites influences cell activity. If we are flooding our cells with incorrect information the daughter cells formed through mitosis will structurally change. These structural changes can lead to a host of physical and mental difficulties.

If we bombard our cells with polypeptides from negative thoughts, we are literally programming our cells to receive more of the same negative polypeptides in the future. What's even worse is that we lessen the number of receptors for positive peptides on the cells, making our self more inclined towards negativity.

## Thoughts Impact DNA Function

Our thoughts activate or deactivate genes. The rapidly growing field of Epigenetics is demonstrating clearly that we are an extension of our environment and experience. Our cells are constantly absorbing environmental signals, including the environmental signals of our thoughts. All environmental signals have the capacity to activate or deactivate gene programming. Genes can actually be switched on or off depending upon what information is being absorbed. Gene performance is directly tied to protein synthesis. What proteins are being manufactured by our DNA plays heavily upon our ongoing life experience. If you would like to know how powerful thoughts are as environmental signals, the research is indicating that 95 to 99% of all health issues are related to the negative thoughts we say to ourselves. That is because most health issues are directly influenced by stress and emotional states. These are an outgrowth of our negative thoughts and mindset. So if you are struggling with metabolic issues such as adrenal exhaustion, hypo or hyper-thyroidism, Hashimoto's disease, pituitary issues, high blood pressure, chemical or hormonal imbalances, inflammation, immune system abreactions, etc. many of these issues are a result of unhealthy DNA protein synthesis, which is being influenced by our mindset. The same is true of mental health issues. Our health, both physical and mental is significantly influenced by our thoughts and mindset.

Our life experience of absorbing environmental signals doesn't alter the genome we were born with, meaning the GENOTYPE. What changes is our genetic activity, meaning the hundreds of proteins, enzymes, and other chemicals that regulate our cells. These are referred to as the PHENOTYPE. Epigenetics is showing that our perceptions and thoughts impact the phenotype, but it is the phenotypal variances that is providing information to the genome, which then directly impacts gene expression. How our cells are being regulated is what is influencing DNA performance, which if you think about it, places us in the driver's seat. By changing our thoughts, we can influence and shape our own genetic readout.

We have a choice in determining what input our cells receive. The more positive or correct the input, the more positive or correct the output of our genes. Epigenetics is allowing lifestyle choices to be directly traced to the genetic level and is proving the mind-body connection irrefutable. At the same time, research into Epigenetics is also emphasizing how important positive mental self-care practices are because they directly impact, not just our mental health, but our physical health as well.

Our mindset is recognized by our body — right down to the genetic level, and the more we improve our mental habits, the more beneficial response we'll get from our body. We can't control many of the external events we experience in life; what we can control is our perception of such events. Our mindset acts in shaping neurological wiring; how our cells become programmed; and how our DNA is expressing itself. Providing our cells with correct information through correct perceptions will change our brain, cells, and genes, either eliminating or significantly decreasing mental and physical health issues. Our ongoing perception is directly linked to what we have come to believe about our self.

The Human Genome or the genetic material each of us have received from our parents may suggest less than desired outcomes. There can be much incorrect information passed on as inheritance. Gratefully, we live in an era of scientific discovery and we now know that even incorrect and unhealthy genetic passing *does not* have to determine human outcomes — it is our responses to our environment that actually determine the expression of our genes. Through increased consciousness of negative inherited beliefs or traits, we have the power to alter such inheritance. If we lack consciousness, if we are not self-aware we tend to react to our environment from the developed false beliefs either genetically received or through learned negativity. When we respond to our environment with negative patterns of self-defeating thoughts we begin to program our cells to believe things about our self that are not real. Our beliefs are organized as matter, which is why we perceive ourselves the way we do. Beliefs are largely formed through the repeated messages we tell ourselves, therefore our beliefs influence cellular performance and can alter our biology as they act on how matter becomes organized and stored at the cellular level. In understanding this truth, then it should begin having us recognize that we have the power through our mind to heal ourselves, increase our positive feelings, as we come to observe ourselves correctly. In seeing ourselves accurately leads to the restructuring of matter leading to the emotional states we desire. Every aspect of our lives can be improved with the right perspective and the intentional way we maintain that perspective.

There are different ways we can approach life. We can approach life from a place of fear and doubt or from a place of love and faith. Whichever one we choose will have its outcome. From fear and doubt we get cut off from our deep, positive emotions and allow anxiety, depression, insecurity and anger to take over our lives. When we allow ourselves to be taken over by negativity, we are putting ourselves in a mental-biological state of fear; inducing the survival mechanisms designed in us.

From love and faith we grow positively as human beings. The positive emotions such as love, affection, joy, confidence, and a will to improve that which is still lacking in us speaks to the truth of who each of us really are. If we have developed false beliefs through an impoverished mindset, and are experiencing more of the negative emotions, then when we change our beliefs, our emotional states will change. When that happens, we change our lives.

First we have to believe what is true about our self. Only then do we give ourselves the opportunity to live life with hope, assurance; peace of mind, confidence, motivation, happiness and empowerment. Bottom line, our cells do not question what we provide them, but they do care. That is because cells are intelligent; they already know who they are and what they need. The thousands of receptor sites on each cell are designed to absorb information from the environment. They are hoping to receive correct information. However, your cells will absorb whatever it is you provide them. That is what is meant by "our cells do not question what we provide them." However they do care! The capacity for cells to provide feedback based upon what they have absorbed is the key to learning how to live as happy individuals. An accurate view of our self, expressed in accurate thoughts about our self, even in the midst of the challenges our environment present to us, is the key to living life in an optimistic, confident and happy manner.

Our identity is our destiny and that is why I am bringing to the forefront what we have learned in the last ten years. I don't think that our growing understanding of who we are and how we are designed is a coincidence. I don't think our increasing knowledge through the field of Epigenetics is happenstance. I think it is directly connected to the circumstances we find ourselves in these latter days (D&C 88:78-80). There is so much going on in the world that is directly related to having us question our identity. It is critical that we have a correct vision of whose children we are, as being children of the Highest provides an insight of our destiny. As we lose sight of this grand truth, life's experience can influence incorrect identity. Our energy, our decisions, our progress, and our purpose are all impacted by our view of our self.

In dealing with the increasing host of social issues that are causing church members to struggle, a question was raised in a training meeting for general authorities, "How can we help those struggling with pornography?" While this social issue is one of exceeding importance, the question could have contained numerous endings, i.e., "How can we help those struggling with........ depression, anxiety, suicide ideation, family discord, spousal and child abuse, drug use, social media and gaming addiction, anger, low self-esteem, etc?" Elder Russell M. Nelson rose and counseled:

Teach them their identity and purpose!

Such insightful instruction when one begins to understand how we are designed. It is my belief that the research is catching up with the revelations about our identity. This book will try and keep that perspective. It will weave in and out of both secular and spiritual information in developing strength within the reader to become accepting of the truth of who they really are. It will inform the reader on how they are designed and more importantly, how to develop a correct belief of their identity, if they do find them self struggling in this area.

Most of all, the Program that unfolds in this book is specifically designed to get the reader to achieve healthy-esteem through his or her own insight and efforts. The power is within each of us to gain awareness of our true self. When we see ourselves accurately, confidence arises, purpose unfolds and the challenges of life are buffered as they become viewed with correct perspective. Each of us are powerful beings already. Faith is the power by which all things are brought to pass. We each possess it. That power increases when we believe the right things and do the right things. Joseph Fielding Smith taught:

> God is full of energy, and should we mortals stand in His presence, unless His spirit was upon us to protect us we would be consumed. That is how much energy there is in a celestial body. (Seek Ye Earnestly, Deseret Book, 1970, 275)

That is our design because we are His species. Our purpose is to become as He is. It is literally written in the DNA we have received from Him. When we come to know who we are we then know how to influence the power of faith to grow within us, until one day we will likewise shine in perfection and power:

> That which is of God is light; and he that receiveth light, and continueth in God, receiveth more light; and that light groweth brighter and brighter until the perfect day. (D&C 50:24)

I do not have an agenda for any of my readers. I am not trying to create some cookie-cutter outcome for those that go through the Program. I have learned that as individuals become accepting of their true self they become inspired to make happiness a way of life, which is the reason why I don't have any preconceived notions. I will promise that all who will sincerely do the homework assignments outlined in future chapters will come to find that they are incredibly designed and more powerful, important and acceptable than they have ever imagined. I have over six years of experience in watching others change the way they were living as they came to see their identity correctly. I have witnessed the reversal of many health issues, clients coming off of medications, pounds shed, improved economic success, marriages improved, families drawing closer, people that thought would always be alone finding their eternal companion, lives of sin changed, addictions defeated, miraculous opportunities materialize, life-long depression and anxiety replaced by peace of mind, hope and joy, improved attitudes, humble acceptance of personal challenges, becoming thankful for them rather than bitter; and deepening faith in God and His plan for each of us. I know the Lord knows you. It is not a coincidence that you are reading this book. It is a manifestation of His tender mercy for you as you have pleaded with Him to change the unhealthy way you have come to see yourself.

"Could we change our attitude, we should not only see life differently, but life itself would come to be different. Life would undergo a change of appearance because we ourselves had undergone a change of attitude."

— Katherine Mansfield

## INTRODUCTION

Within my practice and on my radio show I have asked a few hundred people what they believe Self-Esteem is. The answers are varied, which alone is evidence that there is so much that is misunderstood about this concept. It is that misunderstanding that has so many needlessly struggle. Clarity about concepts or even clarity about what words mean provides a foundation that allows us to view ourselves correctly, thus getting rid of distortions that interfere with living life more abundantly. Self-Esteem is difficult to conceptualize when it is viewed in isolation from other interactive concepts. Understanding Self-Esteem and the other interactive concepts combine in a way that develops a sense of who we are, but without a correct view of Self-Esteem and its partnering concepts we may develop a very distorted and unhealthy belief about ourselves. With this in mind, it has become increasingly clear to me, especially through the findings of Epigenetics that the individual struggles we experience are largely being influenced by the unhealthy beliefs we have formed in how we see ourselves. Nearly all problems can be broken down to what we believe, *especially* what we believe about ourselves. As a teaser, I will tell you forthrightly the reason for drawing this conclusion. We are made of matter and how matter is organized tells us what we are looking at. Our beliefs are organized as matter in our cells and it is that organization that sends signals, which has us view ourselves in whatever manner we do. If you are scratching your head at this moment, your understanding of this concept will increase as you move forward in the book.

Technology is profoundly changing our view of many aspects of our existence. In the realm of cellular biology, we now understand the constant absorbing cells do of our environment and experience and how cells form a conscious belief based upon our perception of those things. Those beliefs become stored both in neural pathways, as well as being encoded upon DNA. How neurons wire together and what gets inputted upon genetic material plays a vital role in how we experience life.

As I came to understand what the recent research was revealing, it created for me a better view of how to help others live beyond what they had become so accustomed to. Issues related to relationship discord, the inability to connect well emotionally, loneliness, impulsivity, perfectionism, inattention, procrastination, disorganization, anxiety, depression, fear of intimacy, self-deprecation, giving up, living far below our potential, withdrawal, social awkwardness, trauma, addiction and a host of other insecurities and negative self-perceptions, are largely formed in the associations we make about our environmental experiences and how those associations are stored as learning and memory. Learning has a vast capacity to be stored within us due to the 23 pairs of chromosomes that are found in almost every cell, as well as the trillions of neural connections that are made throughout our life time. I guess what I am saying is that we can no longer ignore our biological design and how that design continues to impact perception and belief, *especially* the beliefs we hold about ourselves. Let me emphasize what I am saying, as stated earlier, what we believe about ourselves has serious ongoing ramifications; how we see ourselves tends to be our destiny and that belief about self is stored at the cellular level as organized matter, which is the storehouse of learning and memory.

There is no one that reads this book that is not personally acquainted with someone that experiences something of what has been described above. Every one of us has personal experience with people, perhaps even ourselves that battle with some of the conditions previously highlighted. The problems and issues become, it seems, as ongoing evidence to us that our negatively held beliefs about ourselves are accurate. Without any new evidence to suggest otherwise, we just remain stuck; little improves, nothing changes, and so we go to a place of self-defeatism or to a place of self-inflation in order to deal with the negative daily struggle of unhealthy esteem with all of its accompanying negative feelings.

In an article written by Konstantin Eriksen, he summarized what we now profoundly can see through improved technology :

> Our beliefs can change our biology. We have the power to heal ourselves, increase our feelings of self-worth and improve our emotional state. Every aspect of our lives can be improved with the right intention.
>
> The worst thing we can do as thinking and feeling people is to get cut off from our deep, positive emotions and let fear and anger take over our lives. When we allow ourselves to be taken over by negativity, we are putting ourselves in a mental-biological state of fear akin to the fight or flight response.
>
> In order to grow positively as human beings, we need to express positive emotions such as love, affection, joy and a will to conquer ourselves and our own lives. When we change our beliefs, we change our emotional states. When that happens, we change our lives.
>
> First we have to believe. Only then do we give ourselves the opportunity to achieve. (The Science Of Epigenetics – How Our Minds Can Reprogram Our Genes, Wake Up World)

To a degree, the scriptures point to these problems of incorrectly held belief and how it shapes and influences ongoing emotional response and experience as is revealed in its many characters. Cain became so angry that he turned to murder as a means to manage that feeling. Laman and Lemuel were consistently miserable. They're complaining and murmuring, trying to control others; and at times thoughts of homicide were the behaviors they turned to; to somehow resolve the negative emotions they were experiencing. King Saul had become jealous and envious of the adoration David was receiving, and his angry feelings of losing his right to rule likewise led to behaviors of destruction to manage his negative emotions of no longer being in a position of power.

And then we have others, when likewise faced with difficult mortal experiences, seem to approach their trials with dignity and proper perspective. Abraham, faced with negative feelings of having to offer his beloved son, still raised his arm with knife in hand to end the mortal life of the son of his old age. Lehi, after having achieved what seemed like a comfortable lifestyle, journeyed many years in the wilderness, literally leaving behind objects of enormous wealth, enduring the hardships of a hostile environment. Job, though experiencing great difficulties never cursed God. Joseph being sold into Egypt, never considered revenge when finally meeting his brothers many years later.

What was the difference between those that endured well and those that did not? My answer to a large degree is how each saw themselves. What they believed about who they were influenced heavily their approach to the trials they each faced. Without going into each character just mentioned, I turn to Cain to reinforce this point. The underlying problem of Cain's inability to live with greater confidence stemmed largely from what he believed about himself. It seemed that Cain could not shake the distortion that his brother was preferred before him. It wouldn't have hardly mattered what came to Cain; the template that he was less loved, less favored than his brother Abel is what all of his environment and experience was being filtered through. When Cain's sacrifice was rejected - was to Cain just further evidence that his belief was correct, though we as outside observers would never draw that conclusion. Cain's sacrifice was rejected because he did not offer it in faith. Part of the evidence of that claim is that he did not follow the revealed manner of the sacrifice. But try and convince Cain of that was seemingly impossible, so strong was the distorted template of self imbedded in his learning and memory. Even God tried to reason with Cain, focusing on the emotion being displayed, "Cain, why are you so wroth and why has your countenance fallen. If you do well...." meaning if you follow the loving revelations, "your offerings will be accepted." Cain had never understood that God is no respecter of persons. He believed otherwise. Cain's distortion of self led to many difficulties that otherwise could have been avoided. When such deep doubts and insecurities form, it seems very difficult to reverse.

Much of Cain's approach to regulate the negative feelings arising from the distorted sense of self came from a place of self-inflation or grandiosity. "Who is the Lord that I should know him?" Ceasing to "listen any more to the voice of the Lord, neither to his brother Abel," "Rejecting the greater counsel, which was had from God;" and "giving heed to the voice of Satan rather than God's" are all manifestations of grandiosity. Rebellion and resistance are forms of self-inflation and evidence that a person does not see him or herself correctly. Cain's approach is not very different from many that grow up in religious homes and societies. Gospel oriented homes are trying to send the correct information, but many times the delivery ends up sending a different one. I sense that somehow in Cain's interpretation of his home, he believed that he was not as acceptable or good enough as others in his family. Such perception was likely formed through many experiences where he developed a strong template that drove so much of how he handled life.

An example of this phenomenon is highlighted in the following story. As I was working with a man on his path to seeing himself correctly, his increasing awareness allowed him to get a better view of what was occurring in the lives of his wife and children. His wife largely focused on the behaviors of her children and in doing so sent a strong message that their acceptability was derived through obedience. With one of the children, this ongoing view resulted in the daughter seeing herself as "bad," "not good enough," and other self deprecating beliefs. Her negatively held beliefs are what led to so many of the "meltdowns" experienced when her mother would tell her to do something. The client I was working with shared a lot of his own growing insight with his wife to assist her in understanding the meltdowns of their daughter. One particular night during the middle of one of her breakdowns, these devalued beliefs came pouring out of their daughter's mouth. She was heard verbalizing how she saw herself. "I am bad!" "I'll never be able to do anything right," all of these being mixed with an intense emotional sobbing. As the parents were watching the meltdown of their daughter, the husband pointed out to his wife and said, "Those things she is saying is how she really sees herself and that is the reason for her struggles."

Well, that is what this book is all about. It is about opening a door of how belief is formed in any of us. It is about how modern research reveals how belief and identity get shaped in all of us and how that belief influences the relationship we have with our self and how that belief shapes our ongoing experience. More importantly, it is about how to change belief and identity if the current one is not serving us well.

I sense that the central concept in helping others overcome the devastating effects of a poor self-image is found in simple truths that when discovered empowers us to lift ourselves out of our circumstances; freeing us from the daily struggle of self-concern and self-absorption. Once free, it is amazing to watch the transformation from self-interest and concern to having us seek to the interest of others. It is in these simple truths where real happiness and quality of life is built and maintained; in spite of what life throws at us. Coming to see what is actually true about ourselves puts all things into empowering perspective.

First off I will say with incredible confidence that our DNA informs us who we really are. When we align our perception with what the DNA Code tells us, then we become accepting of our real identity. When these simple, evidentiary truths become settled upon in the hearts and mind of any us, it provides incredible bearings on how to face life with optimism, hope, assurance, peace and happiness.

Many current trends interfere with discovering and accepting our real identity. Individual identity is under attack. In many arenas, the powers that be are raising a voice against identity. Sometimes that voice tells you life is not fair or that you are a victim to others that have more power, resources and wealth. Sometimes that voice says you are less or more than another because of your cultural background. Sometimes that voice will say you are what you feel about yourself. Sometimes that voice will have you denounce your body thus eliminating part of your identity. Sometimes the societal voice declares you are less than others because of certain mistakes you have made in life. Sometimes the voice of addiction convinces us we are worthless, etc. The vast manifestation of incorrect voices is leading to confusion and is impacting purpose and confidence in society.

There is no honest social researcher that would conclude that society is headed down the right track. The wrong track has been impacting society for successive generations. The decline has been so gradual yet so incredibly persistent that we find ourselves overwhelmed with what the incorrect voices have shaped our society, our families and our individuality to currently be. The uprising generation in large measure does not see themselves from a place of great self-confidence. Losing touch of whom each of us really are is a growing pandemic in the world. Because of this lost understanding, many arise every day in the mode of survival rather than in the mode of purpose. To the depth that we pursue our purpose depends on the depth to which we grasp our identity. These, in truth, are inseparable partners. Many falsely seek a sense of their identity, purpose and worth through the external achievements or objects available to us in this mortal condition. If these cannot be achieved or acquired, distraction, disassociation and denial become a wonderful companion in order to avoid the pain of seeing oneself as worthless, in whatever that capacity of worthlessness is defined. Sometimes that disassociation and denial comes in the form of telling ourselves we are something we are not. Such labels, we find may garner temporary attention, sympathy and acceptance from portions of society; which may act as incredible reinforcement of the false labels; yet in time, these false labels will come back to haunt us.

The purpose of this book is to get things worked out so that anyone can begin seeing them self as they really are. This book will clearly define what Self-Esteem is and just as importantly, what it is not. It will also explain how belief is formed in any of us and how to change anything in our self estimation that is distorted. A correct understanding of who we really are is essential if we are going to live with confidence, assurance, happiness, hope and peace. This world is filled with experiences, distractions and opportunities. The more we incorrectly focus on any of these, the easier it is to treat casually, then ignore, and even forget who we really are. My invitation is to come and learn correctly. In doing so, the promise is that you will straighten out the misconceptions that have you see yourself in a devalued way and transform your understanding so that happiness and confidence can become your constant companion.

"Don't spend your life believing a story about yourself that you didn't write that's been fed to you - that simply you've accepted, embedded and added to. Let the story go and there beneath is the real you...and your unique gifts, heart and path that await you."

— Rasheed Ogunlaru

It might look like I'm doing nothing, but at the cellular level I'm really quite busy

— Anonymous

THE BIOLOGY OF BELIEF – UNDERSTANDING THE TRENDS OF CURRENT RESEARCH

While I am classically trained as a Marriage and Family Therapist, I recognized that the biggest part of people feeling better came from their desire to do so, not necessarily by applying any therapeutic model. Some of that desire could be promoted by the formal training of a Counselor as he or she uses relationship building interventions such as listening, validating, transparency and rapport building – allowing the client to increase their sense of importance and being cared for. When one begins to experience that they do matter and that someone cares about them it provides for a healthier sense of self and therefore personal desire for change can get its footing. Yet there are many, no matter how wonderful the skills of the therapist, continue to produce no internal desire to create the differences that lead to abundant, joyful living.

Some of that "lacking of personal desire" may be due to a level of comfort in not having to be responsible for one's own care. You see this in family systems of co-dependency; the parent figure deriving purpose from helping the incapable child (or spouse) and the incapable, helpless child (or spouse) enjoying the benefits of being taken care of. It is an easy system for the incapable, helpless child (or spouse) to manipulate for his or her own comfort. Yet, that is not the core reason for the lack of desire. The core reason that desire is lacking is what the incapable, helpless child (or spouse) actually believes about him or herself. Inadequacy and helplessness would become the companion beliefs one forms when they have never exercised their own muscles in becoming self-sufficient. This belief has the capacity to be stored in what is called IMPLICIT MEMORY and once there, will constantly be broadcasting signals to the individual of how they should see themselves.

If individuals have developed a strong devalued belief or template of themselves, then desire struggles in both forming and maintaining within the individual. This becomes the precipice of the struggle, a precipice that every good Counselor recognizes as the primary cause of remaining stuck; of inconsistent attendance and eventually falling off from therapeutic care. In this scenario a dichotomy keeps lifting its head, the Counselor being able to see their struggling client as capable of overcoming and the client seeing him or herself as incapable. It is this core belief that prevents desire from emerging or sustaining in the client.

We now have a very good understanding of how belief of self forms in any of us and since it is belief that is the source of how one sees them self and how that belief continues to filter ongoing experiences, then perhaps the source is where we should shift our focus.

Whether we see life through spiritual understanding or just secular experience is not going to change the truth of what I just spoke of. We live in a day and age where technological advances are providing incredible insight on how our biological design continues to contribute to how we view ourselves, others, our ongoing experience and our environment. The research is becoming so clear, it is time to stop ignoring it and perhaps begin paying high attention as a means of increasing our sense of individual worth, our importance, our being acceptable, our being valued both of ourselves and others, as well as our vast capability.

To give you some sort of context, it is important to provide a little background to where we once were and where we are today in understanding the impact biological design has on the formation of our identity or how we characteristically see ourselves. I attended my undergrad studies back in the 1980's and early 1990's. It was during that time that a project was funded that cost billions of dollars, included hundreds of researchers from around the world and took nearly 15 years to complete. That project was titled, "Mapping the Human Genome." If you are not clear on what that means, in each of us, within our cells is genetic material that we received from our parents, 23 pairs of chromosomes, half coming from our mother and the other half coming from our father. They mapped those 23 pairs of chromosomal matter.

Here comes a question that I ask every person that I am explaining this to – Why did they map the human genome? While there were some financial reasons promoting the research, yet at a simplistic view, the answer is – because they could. Technology had improved to the point that we could now peer inside a single cell and see the structures of those cells. One of those structures is our DNA. When they got to those 23 pairs of chromosomes they realized that they there were comprised of 3.2 billion nucleic acid sequences. Try and map 3.2 billion of anything and you begin to realize that you are in for it. If you were to print all the 3.2 billion letters of the human genome, it would fill 100,000 pages of telephone directories, if that gives you some perspective. That is why the project took so long to complete. Let's keep putting things into context. That project was completed in 2003. At the time of writing this book, that was only 15 years ago. The information that began to emerge from that project was new information. The information that was emerging began having us look at our existence from a completely different viewpoint.

Part of that changing perspective was the recognition that the DNA Code is a mathematical formula that tells us who we are. How or where DNA came from is still a great mystery to secular focused minds, however Dr. Francis Collins who headed up the project stated once, "Whoever wrote the DNA Code is the greatest mathematician in the Universe." No man-made language has this kind of precise mathematical structure. DNA is a tightly woven, highly efficient language that follows extremely specific rules. Its alphabet, grammar and overall structure are ordered by a beautiful set of mathematical functions. That mathematical formula carries or has encoded in it a message.

This very book that you are reading is made of letters, words and sentences. It contains a message that means something. If you can read English, you can understand the message. What has allowed for the production of the message contained in this book is my own mind. Whatever medium I choose to convey the message does not change the message. Sometimes I convey the message in a workshop; sometimes across the radio, sometimes in my office through personal counseling; and of course here you see it written on a page. The medium does not change the message. If you can decipher the symbols it is being delivered in then you can understand the message. In considering the message written in our DNA, it is interesting to note that messages are always the product of a mind. Messages, languages and coded information never, ever come from anything else besides a mind. No one has ever produced a single example of a message that did not come from a mind. Dr. Collins emphatic statement is recognizing that DNA, with its encoded message, is the product of a Mind!

DNA is not merely a molecule. The proteins and chemicals that make up the DNA Molecule are arranged to form an intricate language in the exact same way letters are organized to form any language, including things like computer language. There were two messages that were decoded in the Mapping the Human Genome Project. The first of these was how DNA knew how to code in order to make proteins. Proteins are the foundation for any living organism. Without the DNA Code, proteins would never be made. In other words, proteins could never have formed simply from matter and energy. If energy were the catalyst then making a protein would be likened to lighting a dynamite stick under a pile of bricks and when the dust settles we have a perfectly constructed house, or a tornado going through a metal plant and afterwards finding a perfectly formed airplane. The rarity that DNA some how formed from an evolutionary process with a message written in mathematical code would be $10^{40,000}$. In comparison, it is estimated that there are $10^{20}$ number of grains of sand in the deserts and beaches of this world; the number of stars in the galaxy at $10^{22}$. It is the enormous complexity of the number of elements and the enormous subtlety of the ways the DNA Code operates that suggests that something having a Mind created it.

John C. Lennox, Professor of Mathematics and Fellow in Philosophy of Science at Oxford's Green Templeton College stated:

> ....the obvious conclusion that arises from reflecting on the reality that sciences like physics and biology have uncovered is that information and intelligence are fundamental to the existence of the universe and life and, far from being the end products of an unguided natural process starting with energy and matter, they are involved from the very beginning. In other words, the whole universe has the unmistakable signature of monumental design about it.

Why is it important to understand that DNA knows how to make proteins? Well proteins are what we are made of. Proteins are life; therefore the DNA Code is the message of life! It is estimated that we are made of about 250,000 different types of proteins; and what proteins are being manufactured plays a heavy role in how we see ourselves and how we are experiencing life.

In a simple example, imagine someone begins to feel a loss of energy. Perhaps they conclude that they have been working too hard and so they decide to take a couple of days off to recuperate. After those couple of days the individual begins to realize that that they are growing even wearier. They go to the doctor and the very first thing the doctor does is draw the blood of that individual. Why? Because the life is in the blood (Leviticus 17:11). The bio or protein markers of whatever is behind the individual's loss of energy is found in the blood. Perhaps in this case the protein markers reveal that the individual has cancer. Yes, our DNA knows how to make the proteins that lead to cancer. It knows how to make proteins that can lead to a host of issues that have us experience both physical and mental deficits. Yet, the DNA molecule also knows how to manufacture the proteins that lead to good health and well being. Decoding the message of protein synthesis was a phenomenal advancement. It is the almost unbelievable complexity of the arrangements of the letters arranged in the DNA Code, which are needed to produce life. That is the first thing that was decoded in the message contained within the mathematical code of our DNA.

The second message decoded was that genes are not randomly or spontaneously doing whatever they want to do. This is important because genes have responsibilities that affect our overall well being. If they are taking care of their responsibilities then things work really well at the physiological level. In this second message we decoded, it became clear there are mechanisms built in that put us into the driver's seat with how our genes are operating. In other word's we began to understand that there are controls that influence genetic activity and expression. These controls are largely based in the choices we make, as our ongoing choices are being registered at the cellular level. This is where I try to keep it very simple. Our cells have the capacity to receive both correct information and incorrect information because of who they are. When cells are receiving the correct information, it influences the activity of the DNA to perform optimally. That means that the DNA will manufacture the proteins that have us enjoy all aspects of our lives. Incorrect information to the cells, on the flip side, has us begin to experience many negatively skewed outcomes.

DNA contains the message of life and yet the quality of life may differ between individuals. Epigenetics has shown that the difference in quality of life is heavily influenced by our mind, especially the perceptions we form as a result of our ongoing experiences. One thing that seems to be pretty clear to even the simplest understanding of the genetic code is that DNA is a blueprint of information, a blueprint that is not static or dormant. A good portion of our DNA is informing us and is contributing to our self-perspective. For example, physical characteristics such as eye color, hair type, height, and body types are being informed by what is written in the DNA Code. Likewise mannerisms are being driven through DNA. Have you ever watched a family and noticed how the family members move, the cadence in their speech, the tone of their voice being so similar? Yeah, all DNA driven! The very fact that we are human is because the DNA Code informs us of that truth. But there is much more that may be written in the blueprint that drives the variances we experience from human to human.

In the nineteen–forties, Conrad Waddington, an English embryologist, hypothesized that cellular differentiation or how one cell takes on the identity of a neuron as opposed to a bone cell, muscle cell, skin cell, etc. is how environmental signals influence the DNA Code. For that to happen, Waddington concluded, an additional layer of information must exist within the cell – a layer that hovered, ghostlike, above the genome. This layer would carry the memory of the cell, recording its past and establishing its future, marking its identity and its destiny but permitting that identity to be changed if needed. He termed the phenomenon "epi-genetics" meaning "above or outside of genetics." Waddington's hypothesis was perhaps a little too inspired. No one had visualized a gene in the nineteen-forties, and the notion of a layer of information levitating above the genome was an abstraction built atop an abstraction, impossible to test experimentally. We now know cell identity or differentiation of cells is because a specific set of genes is turned "on" and another set of genes is turned "off." This is when we began to realize that the genome is not a static blueprint. The blueprint is dynamic. The selective activation or repression of genes allows an individual cell to acquire its identity and to perform its function.

In extension to this information, cells not only differ from one another in what they become by the activating – deactivating process of genes, but cellular performance is influenced in the same way. The question is what gets genes to turn on or turn off? It's simple, both the DNA Code and life experience acts on gene expression. From life experience, idiosyncratic events are recorded through idiosyncratic marks in our bodies. If you sequence the genomes of a pair of identical twins every decade for fifty years, you get the same sequence over and over. But if you sequence the epigenomes of a pair of twins you find substantial differences. The pattern of epigenetic marks on the epigenomes of their various cells, virtually identical at the start of the experiment, diverges over time. So, chance events – injuries, infections, infatuations, and every other environmental experience is what creates the different epigenetic marks in the epigenome, including our perceptions of those events.

The DNA code contains instructions needed to make proteins and molecules essential for our growth, development, and health, including our mental health. What proteins are manufactured is what contributes to cells healthy or unhealthy expression, which also contributes to healthy or unhealthy views of our self. The point of Epigenetics is that if we don't like what the blueprint suggests, the mind is the power that can redraw many aspects of the blueprint leading to better outcomes.

As an undergrad student in the Department of Psychology, every once in a while one of my professors would bring in the most recently published article of this ongoing research project. Now this is a bit simplified, but this is what I kept hearing. Choice is an illusion. Choice is not real. Mostly what is driving our experience is being driven by our inherited DNA. Therefore, if you hope to have a good life, you better hope you had parents that had good DNA! That becomes a moment of reflection doesn't it?

As a person that was raised with a religious doctrine called Agency, this idea that choice being illusory was a difficult one to accept, but I was not so myopic that I just dismissed what was being reported. I really wanted to understand why they were saying what they were saying. These early geneticists were recognizing something very real. DNA has a powerful capacity to influence the next generation by what is encoded upon it. This view of DNA operation and pre-eminence was named "The Central Dogma" by these early researchers. In a moment I will explain to you why they formed this view.

In Nature Neuroscience Magazine (December 1, 2013), appeared an article explaining how traumatic experiences imprinted upon DNA, was passed down for two successive generations.

In the study, mice were trained to fear the smell of acetophenone, a chemical that smells like fruit and almonds. The researchers paired the scent with electrical shocks to a foot of the mice being exposed. The mice eventually learned to associate the scent with pain creating obvious behavioral responses of shuddering whenever the scent was released.

While operant conditioning may be a viable explanation for the fear response, remember, we live in a time where through advanced technology we can map DNA. All of the mice in this research project had their DNA mapped prior to the experiment and then remapped after the project. It was discovered that on a single gene that the letters or nucleotides had rearranged their order. For the 'children' and 'grandchildren' that had likewise received this altered genetic trait, despite never having encountered acetophenone in their lives, the offspring exhibited the same behavior when acetophenone was introduced to their environment. These transgenerational epigenetic effects again were identifiable on a single gene. Along with many other similar research projects, it becomes evident that epigenetic alterations can and do influence successive generations.

Let me tell you about an article that I read in Scientific Journal in November of 2016. The article pointed out that Microsoft, along with the University of Washington had developed synthetic DNA. This article referenced, in order to provide some perspective, a mechanical pencil lead. The lead they referenced was the .05 lead – the fine lead. The researchers on this project reported that they had encoded upon the synthetic DNA of an area no larger than the surface of the tip of that lead, not the entire length – just the tip, several music videos and volumes of books, over 100,000 books. Now I understood where this article was leading to, though it never mentioned it. Technological firms were looking for a way to increase storage or memory and it is now very well understood, DNA is the material in the Universe that has the greatest capacity for storage and retrieval. I want you to stop and consider this. Many gaming systems, computers and smart-phones are coming with larger and larger capacity for storage. As technology improves, the capacity to utilize advancing technology has a price and that price is storage space and an enhanced ability to retrieve stored information. Interestingly they refer to storage capacity as *memory*. That idea is going to come into play as we proceed down this road.

In February 2017, I read a follow-up article to the one just referenced. In the follow-up article the researchers announced that they had now perfected the process of encoding upon and retrieving from synthetic DNA without any corruption. When one considers the current materials used in technology, one comes to understand that all the materials being utilized for storage and retrieval are susceptible to corruption. This is a technological advance.

Three weeks after I read the article in February, I came across another article. Here was the title of that article, "Will Your T.V. in the Future Have DNA in It?" Yes folks, it will – right along with many other products that will function better by improved capacity for storage and retrieval.

What I am getting ready to share with you I do so from a place of humility as I observed my own experience. I recognized that my religious beliefs, my psychology background and my pre-med training came together in a moment that allowed me to see some things that perhaps many would not have. In my cellular biology classes, I had come to learn that DNA is tightly wound upon itself. However, if you could entirely unfold the DNA, in just one of your cells, it would create a tower of material six feet tall! If you will do a little math and multiply that length by the nearly 100 trillion cells that contain our DNA, the genetic material in each of us would measure about twice the diameter of our solar system. That is a lot of genetic material to encode upon. But then the next aha moment occurred. Again, whether spiritually perceived or just viewing from a secular position, it became obvious that the experiences of life contribute to our understanding and learning. From a gospel perspective, we are told that our mortal probation was designed for us to come and have experience that we might learn to "taste the bitter in order to know to prize the good" (Moses 6:55). I then realized that if we could not retain the experience then learning could not occur. For example, if we spank a child trying to shape a better behavior, if the child could not retain the experience of the pain felt would the child ever learn? Well guess what? And this is the point, we are designed as cells and there is something these cells are doing every second of our existence; there is nothing you and I can do to stop it because our cells are designed to do this one thing and they do it very well. Our cells are absorbing our experience and our environment and then storing it as learning and *memory*. What we learn and store as memory in our cells is significantly influenced by our perception of that experience of the environment. We literally have the capacity to store our entire life experience, with all of its editorial perceptions due to the storage ability of DNA.

Let's return briefly to some of what the early geneticists were helping us to understand. As they peered on the DNA, they recognized that the information encoded in that material was constantly sending signals. There was observable energy emanating from the DNA molecule. The signals are somewhat subtle and we likely really never pay much attention at a high conscious level of what the signals are saying, nevertheless, the signals are real and never dormant. These signals shape somewhat how we characteristically see ourselves. The reason for this energy or the signaling that is constantly going on is because matter, which we are all made of, is comprised of energy.

To further impress upon your understanding of signaling, I would have you consider the impact and influence on our perspective to any signal we receive. We live in a very politically driven era. The growing problems in society are believed by some to be reversible through political policy. Hopefully your further understanding of what is written in this book will have you keep things in perspective. Yet, if I were to ask you to listen to Fox News Channel and nothing else for the next three months that signal will likely influence your perspective. If I then asked you, after those three months, to switch your viewing to CNN for three months that signal will also likely change how you see a few things. Signals are impactful and highly influential and all of us have signals being sent from our DNA. Providing an example of inherited parental signaling coming from our DNA may be anxiety. If somebody comes into a Counselor's office struggling with anxiety, a normal question the Counselor will ask is, which of the client's parents present with anxiety? The client usually has no difficulty in identifying which one. What is the explanation for this line of questioning?

In the thousands of brains that have been examined, it is pretty clear that a person struggling with anxiety has a brain that is wired differently and it functions differently than a brain from a person that does not struggle with anxiety. This unique wiring then could be considered a physical trait, as much as a physical trait as eye color, texture of hair, skin tone, shape of nose, etc. The unique wiring is information that is encoded upon DNA due to the individual's constant approach to life through fear and doubt. The manner of thinking associated with fear and doubt is information that becomes encoded upon DNA and like any physical characteristic, children that carry that DNA would have a propensity toward developing the same wiring. So let's see how this DNA signal then acts within the recipient. If I am an embryo developing in my parent and my brain begins to uniquely wire in the fashion my anxious parent is wired, that wiring begins to send signals on how I see myself – yes, even in embryo. So how does a person that struggles with anxiety see themselves? Typically insecure, worried about what others think of them; and to a degree incapable and/or unacceptable. If the baby is wired with this propensity, then it informs the child with those same held beliefs. To exacerbate the issue, if the embryo is growing inside of the anxious parent, the reinforcement of those signals becomes exponential in their influence. None of this information is meant to create guilt, it is simply informing on what we now understand about how belief begins to take shape in each of us.

Well, if our inherited DNA was the only factor that led to how we experience ourselves, we would all be doomed because there is no such thing as a perfect parent as there can be numerous negative transgenerational epigenetic markers being passed down. Let us continue the story then. In 2002, one year prior to the completion of Mapping the Human Genome, a group of these geneticists began to see something that turned the field of science upside down. These researchers began to recognize that choice is real and was playing a significant role in how DNA performed, how it altered its expression and how parental signaling could be changed or turned off. These alterations are again what researchers refer to as the phenotype of the DNA recorded on the epigenome.

This discovery was made when the researchers asked themselves an honest question about the DNA they were mapping. DNA is encapsulated by a band of protein called histones. The early researchers would simply remove this protein in order to get to the DNA itself and without understanding what this band of protein was for, they made the conclusions they made, meaning "The Central Dogma" that it was all being driven by DNA. But, as the researchers began to pay attention to this band of protein they recognized that DNA is heavily influenced by this protein band. I might interject an idea right now, so as to build a basis of understanding in my reading audience. Proteins are not only the basis for life they are also the carrier of messages and information within cells and between cells. We have approximately 250,000 different proteins in our body. What proteins are interacting with DNA makes a difference in what gets encoded upon DNA, and remember, what gets encoded upon DNA continually broadcasts signals that shapes within us perception or belief, including what we believe about ourselves.

Signals are highly influential. The things we read, listen to, and do all act as signals that influence our beliefs, especially the beliefs we have about our self. Another way to conceptualize the power of environmental signals is to think of the radio in your car. Whatever station you are tuned into is a signal. Many times we will not like what the signal is bringing to us and so the design of the radio is such that we can change the signal by pushing another button. Sometimes we can't find any signals that we like and we turn to the master knob and completely cut-off all of the signals. Likewise, when we do find a radio station we do like we may actually turn up the volume! That is what this group of genetic researchers uncovered. This is the great message discovered in decoding the message written in our DNA. The choice of what individuals wanted their cells to absorb from the environment could literally begin to alter how DNA informed us, talked to us, expressed itself and performed, or in other words the signals that are always present and coming from our DNA. The science that emerged from this research is called Epigenetics. "Epi" means above or outside of. So now you can hear what this science is saying. "No, actually there is more to DNA's functioning than what is inherited from parents. There are things outside of us that also influence DNA functioning." The cell is designed to absorb environment and experience; and what it absorbs influences the epigenome, which in turn plays a significant part in how we see our self, others and the world in general. Because technology has so improved this is what we now know:

> To grasp the reality of life as it has been revealed by molecular biology, we
> must magnify a cell a thousand million times until it is twenty kilometers in
> diameter and resembles a giant airship large enough to cover a great city like
> London or New York. What we would then see would be an object of
> unparalleled complexity and *adaptive* design. On the surface of the cell we

would see millions of openings, like the port holes of a vast space ship, opening and closing to allow a continual stream of materials to flow in and out. If we were to enter one of these openings we would find ourselves in a world of supreme technology and bewildering complexity... (Michael Denton, *Evolution: A Theory in Crisis*, London: Burnett Books, 1985, p. 328)

These materials outside that they are referring to are the environmental signals that influence cell function and in consistent exposure are absorbed and stored as learning and memory. Let's take a look at what the Epigeneticists mean. Sunshine is an environmental signal that is absorbed by cells. People that have low energy or perhaps depression are influenced in a more positive way when the sunshine contributes to the formation of Vitamin D. Vitamin D helps lift lower moods. When someone's mood lifts, how do they see themselves, in a more positive or more negative way? Of course more positive; the choice to go out and be in the sun is exactly that – a choice. Nutrition is an environmental signal that is absorbed by cells. There are ninety (90) essential elements that cells utilize to function at optimal levels. When cells are receiving the correct elements how do we feel? That is correct, we feel better. And if we feel better and we are sensing a healthy energy level then how does it shape how we see ourselves? Again, we see ourselves in a more positive way. The foods we eat are a choice. We do have the power to provide correct information to our cells.

Is lead paint in a bedroom absorbed by the cells of the individual that lives in that room? Yes, the properties contained within paint eventually migrate their way to the surface and then are released into the air. As a person breaths in air that contains toxins, those toxins are absorbed by their cells and lead paint is toxic to our cells and therefore we may begin to experience physical symptoms that may alter how we see ourselves. Choosing to live in a room that contains toxins is a choice. Do our cells absorb a toxic relationship? Yes they do! If I am continually involved with a person that is cruel, insensitive, abusive, controlling, neglectful, etc, that person is part of my environment and my cells are absorbing that experience. It does so in large measure by the thoughts we tell ourselves because of being viewed and treated so poorly. Our relationships are choices. We are going to come back to this idea in a moment, but be assured that our cells are designed to absorb our experience and environment and depending on what information they receive will influence heavily one's perception, one's health, one's expression of DNA and ultimately, one's belief about their identity. This is not the old argument of Nature vs. Nurture; this is recognizing and understanding how nature and nurture combine in a way that shapes personal belief in us, meaning what we actually believe about ourselves.

The Epigeneticists wanted us to know one thing however, and it was this; of all of the environmental signals our cells absorb, the one that has the greatest impact on how we see ourselves are our own thoughts. From a secular position, researchers do not understand the origin of a thought but they do know that thoughts are converted into proteins, called neuropeptides or polypeptides and these polypeptides are conveyed to our cells. Remember, proteins are the carrier of messages. Depending upon what proteins accesses cells has everything to do with what our cells will learn, how they will perform, and what signals are being activated from DNA. DNA can express itself in healthy or unhealthy ways. I think most of us would enjoy having the signals that come from healthy DNA expression.

To further appreciate the process we are speaking of and to give us greater insight to the heavy influence cellular learning has on our perception of ourselves, let me get into a basic definition of learning and memory, because that is how cells store our absorbing of experience and environment. Learning in its simplest definition is when two brain cells connect to one another. This is called the Law of Associative Memory and we can only learn if we are associating at least two things together. Associative learning is a principle that states that ideas and experiences reinforce each other and can be mentally linked to one another. In keeping it simple, our brains were not designed to encode or recall information in isolation; instead we group information together into one associative memory. The stronger the links or grouping; the more indelible the impact upon belief and perception.

Memory is simply stored learning. There are several types of memory that form within us, but to keep to the subject, let me just talk about two. To introduce the first type, just answer the following questions:

1) Where were you born?
2) Can you remember the name of an elementary school you attended?
3) Out of your academic career, no matter how long or short, can you recall the name of at least one of your teacher's?
4) What city are you currently in? What is the address of your home?
5) Who was the 16th President of the United States?

This 5th question, about 50% answer quickly. However, the rest usually pause, go inside of their head and begin looking for the information and then declare, "I don't know." I point out that it was obvious that they did try and retrieve the information. I then remind them that since learning is associative, that if the 16th President of the United States is stored in them perhaps they just need another association. I then add, "The Civil War." Almost all state "Abraham Lincoln." For those that still struggle with the answer, I draw a mental picture by saying, "Tall Top Hat and Long Beard," which the remaining then say, "Abraham Lincoln." To understand the varying replies, some have stored Abraham Lincoln being more associated as a number, to some a historical event and to some a picture. The point is, if Abraham Lincoln is stored as memory in anyone, then with enough associations that person would be able to retrieve the information.

I then ask one more question:

1) Give me one memory when you were 11 years old?

Again, depending upon the strength of the association of being 11 and recalling a memory the person may require an association – I say 6th Grade. At that the individual starts speaking about a memory at that age. The memory I am playing with is what is called Explicit Memory. It is basically data recall and autobiographical memory. But herein lies the intuitive question; could any of that information been given had it not been stored inside the individual? The answer is obvious and important to stop and consider. I hope you are beginning to see something about our design. We do store our experience within us as learning and memory. Cellularly stored learning is real.

The next type of memory I want my clients to understand is called Implicit Memory. This type of memory is formed through repetition – the things we do over and over and over again. However, continual exposure to something so repetitive reduces our awareness of its presence.

A good example of this reduced awareness is walking. Walking is something that is learned. It makes up a portion of our Implicit Memory. We have walked so many times we no longer pay attention to it. If we have understood the definition of learning then I can ask, what does *walking* look like in the brain? Correct, it looks like a bunch of neurons connected to each other. These connections have a long term association with one another, so much so, that the strong neural pathway formed allows walking to be an automatic response in us. Walking is so well learned that we don't have to pay much attention to it and in fact we don't. When any of us inched to the side of our bed this morning, none of us asked, "Now how do I walk again?" Without any thought we left our bed and walked. With that example alone can we begin to appreciate the power of Implicit Learning and Memory? It is incredibly powerful. Some experts have concluded that 90% plus of everything we do is being driven by Implicit Memory. To demonstrate the power of Implicit Memory, Implicit Memory processes 40 million bits of information per second, while Explicit Memory processes about 40 bits per second. Trust me, we are at the mercy of this powerful Implicit Memory and so it is very important to be highly aware of what we store as Implicit Learning and Memory. As you begin to see the application of Implicitly stored Learning and Memory, it is not something to get upset about. In fact, we should be grateful for this design as we would become miserable if we actually had to produce high consciousness with everything we do. Unfortunately, there are things that can become stored in Implicit Memory that are not accurate, which may lead to ongoing negative patterns in our life without our awareness what drives such patterns.

Over time, Implicit Memory has us become blind to the obvious. We swim in a sea of implicit consciousness, like a fish swims in water. And like a fish that has become oblivious to its aqueous environment, we have become dulled to the ubiquity of consciousness. We no longer give high attention to how we have come to see ourselves; we just daily act out the memorized self. In returning to the idea that learning and memory can be influenced by even the thoughts we tell ourselves it then becomes obvious that perceptual identity; (i.e.; how I see myself), can be shaped by our internal conversations. These ongoing internal conversations create what I call the memorized self. The memorized self then responds to environment in very patternistic or procedural ways. Let me provide a few examples of how the internal conversation we have with ourselves shapes our belief about ourselves. In the examples, please notice the associations being formed between thoughts, the meaning we attach to those thoughts, the emotions growing out of the thought with its associated meaning; and the reactive behavior trying to manage the negative emotions experienced. Finally notice the general beliefs that begin to form and shape within an individual that consistently and repetitively talks to themselves in this manner.

Example #1" The Problem – Parents emotionally manipulate a child by withdrawing love when the child has made a choice that goes against the family standards or values.

Thought: I am only acceptable when I do things the way my parents want me to
Meaning: I don't think there is much good about me
Emotion: Hurt, sadness, inadequate
Behavior: Withdraw, stuff things, become a bit rebellious

Belief(s): Unlovable

Example #2 The Problem – A young lady has just broken up with a third boyfriend. All three of the boyfriends lied to her or betrayed her in some way.

Thought: I am vulnerable
Meaning: I can't trust anyone
Emotion: Fear, anger, ambivalent
Behavior: Closed book, avoid, divert attention away

Belief(s): Helpless, Unlovable

Example #3 The Problem – An extremely overweight husband was just caught looking at pornography by his wife.

Thought: I am bad
Meaning: This person will eventually leave me
Emotion: Fear, anger, apathy
Behavior: Seek negative attention, be a victim, try and win the argument

Belief(s): Unlovable, Negative Body Image

Example #4 The Problem – A person struggling with social anxiety and who does not have any close friends.

Thought: I am not good enough or I am worthless
Meaning: If you knew me you wouldn't want much to do with me
Emotion: Guarded, anxiety, depression
Behavior: Do nothing, isolate myself

Belief(s): Unlovable

Example#5 The Problem – An overweight teen

Thought: I am ugly. I am disgusting
Meaning: No one will ever want me
Emotions: Depression, loneliness
Behavior: Binge/Eat unhealthy

Belief(s): Helpless, Unlovable, Negative Body Image

These internal conversations go on all the time throughout life. You may notice bits and pieces of them, but are rarely ever paying attention to all of the associations being formed. They work within us in a way that shapes our view of ourselves. When these become so highly associated and they do so through repetition, we become less responsive to life's events and more reactive, because this is now on auto-pilot. This is how the memorized self forms. In other words, our belief about ourselves becomes formed by the repeated messages we tell ourselves, therefore our belief is stored in Implicit Memory and now we are filtering life's ongoing events through that Implicit Belief. Implicit memory is stored below the threshold of awareness and becomes highly procedural or reactive. It is the consciousness we become oblivious to and yet has us view ourselves the way we do.

If you will forgive me, I would like to repeat what I wrote in the Preface of this book as it will likely make much more sense now that I have given examples of the Internal Conversation in relation to our perception of our environment and experience. Thoughts are an epigenetic signal of the environment which heavily influences so many aspects of our daily living. Here is what we now know. Every minute of every day, your body is physically reacting, literally changing, in response to the thoughts that run through your mind and what general belief developed and shaped in you by the associations you make in relation to those thoughts.

Current technology allows us to see the neuropeptides or polypeptides released into our blood stream, which formed because of our thoughts. Just thinking about something causes your brain to release neurotransmitters, chemical messengers that open vital communication between cells and your nervous system. Neurotransmitters control virtually all of your body's functions, from hormones to digestion to feeling happy, sad, or stressed. Our cells bathe in the neurochemicals that are being released in relation to our thoughts. Human thoughts and intentions are carried within our physiology as protein messengers; therefore every thought possesses the power and energy to transform the beliefs we hold about ourselves, due to the perceptions we have about our ongoing experience and environment. The information carried by the neuropeptide or polypeptide also impacts DNA performance, which affects our physical and mental health. Our cells are heavily influenced by the compositional medium of those neurochemicals released in connection with our thoughts.

Expectancies and learned associations have been shown to change brain chemistry and circuitry. The thoughts we introduce to our cells will impact and shape real physiological and cognitive outcomes. If those thoughts are accurate then those outcomes are positive, but if our thoughts provide inaccurate information that will have a different outcome. Thoughts have an astonishing power to influence physiology.

A mental picture I like to draw for people is observing metal being cut by a torch. The amount of energy being exerted is what changes the organization of matter of the metal. Likewise, the energy of our thoughts with all of their associations flows consistently and repetitively through our minds and sculpts our brain in nearly permanent ways, just as the energy of the torch changes the metal it is directed toward. Think of the thoughts of our mind as the movement of information through our nervous system, which on a physical level is all the electrical signals running back and forth, most of which is happening below our conscious awareness. As a thought travels through our brain, neurons fire together in distinctive ways based on the specific information being handled, and those patterns of neural activity actually change our neural structure.

Our thoughts likewise program our cells. A thought is an electrochemical event which signals the release of a host of chemical and electrical particles, in the form of long amino acid chains called neuropeptides or polypeptides. These amino acid chains then look for receptor sites on cells. Each and every cell contains hundreds of thousands, if not millions of receptor sites and just as the word indicates, these sites are there to receive information. What docks in those receptor sites influences cell activity. If we are flooding our cells with incorrect information the daughter cells formed through mitosis will structurally change. These structural changes can lead to a host of physical and mental difficulties.

If we bombard our cells with polypeptides from negative thoughts, we are literally programming our cells to receive more of the same negative polypeptides in the future. What's even worse is that we lessen the number of receptors for positive peptides on the cells, making our self more inclined towards negativity. Daughter cells formed through mitosis can either be healthier, meaning more receptor sites allowing for more positive input; or unhealthier, meaning more receptor sites that are designed to receive more negative input.

Our thoughts also have the power to activate or deactivate genes. The rapidly growing field of Epigenetics is demonstrating clearly that we are an extension of our environment and experience. Our cells are constantly absorbing environmental signals, including the environmental signals of our thoughts. All environmental signals have the capacity to activate or deactivate gene programming. Genes can actually be switched on or off depending upon what information is being absorbed. Most physical and mental health issues are related to the negative thoughts we say to ourselves. That is because most of health issues are directly influenced by stress and emotional states. These are an outgrowth of our negative thoughts and mindset.

Your life experience of absorbing environmental signals doesn't alter the genes you were born with. Your DNA is the Genotype. You will always be human! What changes is your genetic activity, meaning the hundreds of proteins, enzymes, and other chemicals that regulate your cells. These changes are referred to as the Phenotype. Epigenetics is showing that our perceptions and thoughts impact biological controls, which, if you understand this, places us in the driver's seat. By changing our thoughts, we can influence and shape our own genetic readout. We can redraw the blueprint.

Cells already know who they are and what they need. Their identity is written in the message of the DNA Code. We have a choice in determining what input our cells receive. The more positive or correct the input based upon their identity; the more positive or correct the output of our genes. Epigenetics is allowing lifestyle choices to be directly traced to the genetic level and is proving the mind-body connection irrefutable. At the same time, research into Epigenetics is also emphasizing how important positive mental self-care practices are because they directly impact our mental and physical health.

Our mindset is recognized by our body — right down to the genetic level, and the more we improve our mental habits, the more beneficial response we'll get from our body. We can't control many of the external events we experience in life, which, up to this point have all acted in shaping the neurological wiring of the brain; how our cells have become programmed; and how our DNA is expressing itself. However, we do have the power in this moment and going forward to increase consciousness of our internal conversations and choose correct perspective and behavior, which will change our brain, cells, and genes.

Folks, thoughts are a product of our mind. Thoughts are converted into protein messengers and these thoughts get absorbed into our cells. Just like any other environmental signal, what we allow our cells to absorb will one day be communicated back to us by our cells. Our negative thoughts about ourselves will result in many difficult negative emotions. Those negative emotions are the cells informing us what we gave them. But because we have said these negative thoughts to ourselves so many times they have become IMPLICIT, they are on automatic drive; we hardly even pay attention to or are even aware of what we say to ourselves about ourselves. The collective thoughts combined with the other negative associations found in the internal conversation then shape within us personal belief, meaning what we believe about ourselves. To change such entrenched learning will require real intentional intervention. This is not difficult but does require real and consistent effort.

Since the field of Epigenetics has us understand that our perceptions of self, stored as belief, is what is driving our emotional states, then one important thing to consider when looking at belief, is that it is possible for us as humans to believe things that are accurate or true, but it is also possible to believe things that are inaccurate or not true. Let me give an example. If I were to ask you what 2 + 2 equals, you would say 4. Well, what if I believe 2 + 2 equals 7? Since it is possible to believe things that are not true; and I did believe 2 + 2 equals 7, how do you think my career as a CPA would go, or how about my math or science career? You would tell me that there are going to be a lot of problems in any of those careers if I did believe 2 + 2 = 7. And there is my point. Many times we can look at the ongoing difficulties of life as evidence that there may be something in our own personal belief system that is distorted or completely untrue.

Well, what if we have formed a very unhealthy view of ourselves. What if there are distortions in the belief that has shaped in us due to repetitive negative internal conversations? How might we detect that such distortions do exist? In large measure, implicitly held distortions are discerned by ongoing, patternistic negative emotions and behaviors, whether these be social anxiety, fear of intimacy, depression, agitation, or explosive anger; feeling life is unfair, ongoing stress, fear of what others think about us, a general sense of shame, perfectionism, a feeling that one does not matter, an ongoing sense of helplessness, feeling like a failure, bi-polar and other mood dysregulation, greater social isolation, addiction; relationship discord, cynicism, bad attitude, cycles of poverty, weight issues, and the list goes on and on. If any of these are part of the reader's experience, then the inevitable question is, "If what drives these ongoing negative, patternistic emotions and behaviors is being driven by distortions in my implicit, personal belief system then how do I change or fix them?" In other words, how do you change something that you can hardly even see?

## QUANTUM THEORY - THE SCIENCE OF THE SCIENCES

Quantum Theory provides us the answer to that question. For those readers who may not have a good background in Quantum Physics, let me talk about science in general so that we can begin to appreciate how Quantum Theory made its place in the sciences. For the most part, the science that we learn in our educational studies is the science that largely describes the macroscopic physical universe. Electricity, magnetism, gravity, time, light and space are all aspects of the physical universe. We now understand these concepts so well that we have written mathematical formulas to describe the laws associated with them. These mathematical formulas provide a clear "cause and effect" allowing us to predict, to plan, and to solve. That is good, because if there was no order and all of these concepts were merely occurring on a random basis, we would be miserable.

As time has advanced so has technology and that improved technology allows us to see in the opposite direction. Rather than having our attention focused on the large macroscopic physical universe, we can now go down and see things at atomic levels and even further, subatomic levels. This is the level of energy and this is the realm of Quantum Science. The subatomic levels are those levels of which electrons, protons and neutrons are comprised. These subatomic particles have been given names based upon shape and function, such as quarks, neutrinos, bosons, etc. We could see that these particles of energy were heavily involved in how atoms or matter combined, organized and behaved, but there came a moment of great discouragement for the researchers. In trying to understand the microscopic or subatomic physical operations, when the same mathematical formulas developed explaining the large macroscopic, physical universe were inserted into the subatomic world, it all fell apart because the formulas did not work at these smaller levels.

Quantum Physics, which had been around since the early 1900's, had never found its home, until technology had advanced to the stages of highly specialized microscopes. Quantum Physics provides us information that has us begin to grasp what is occurring at these microscopic levels, what influences energy and matter, and how to get the outcomes we are looking for. I hope that my explanation of things to this point have been simple enough to give us understanding, as well as deepening interest to explore further. If you have no real background in Quantum Theory, I am going to keep things simple and will do so by explaining three laws of this science. If we can understand these three laws, our whole perspective is enhanced on our existence. They are as follows:

1) The Law of Entanglement
2) All Matter has Potential
3) The Law of the Observer

Entanglement simply means that everything is connected, though some things have deeper or more well-defined associations. The subatomic level that Quantum Theory addresses is the level of energy and energy can become associated, or linked with other forms or particles of energy. Once these associations occur, they will continue to influence one another, even if geographically one particle of energy distances itself from the other particle of energy it has become associated with. Regardless of distance, as soon as new information is given to one particle of energy, the other particles of energy; it has made previous associations with, will also be immediately impacted. The *Law of Entanglement* is to understand how one simple thing impacts or influences another thing at the level of energy. This process of grouping can begin with something as simple as a thought. A thought is detected as energy. A thought is carried as an electrical impulse within neural pathways. Likewise, a thought is converted to protein messengers. Protein itself is formed of energy and these protein messengers are absorbed into cells impacting or influencing the energy of the cell.

Quantum Theory says that because we are all comprised of energy, we are all connected or entangled. Therefore, what if our thoughts are filled with assumption? Would we likely interact with another person differently because we believe we know their motives? Does that interaction then resonate negatively in the person we are making assumptions about? Does our energy in any way influence their energy?

But more to the point, what if our thoughts are filled with distortions and untruthful judgments about our own worth, capacity, and importance? Would such thinking, due to being entangled with the rest of our physiology, lead to genetic mutations, abnormal rates of stress hormones within our blood stream, inflammation or other immune system abreactions, or even metabolic issues that may lead to deteriorating health? Is the mind and body entangled with each other?

A negative self-image or identity, meaning how and what we believe about ourselves has been shaped through long term associations of negative self-talk, the negative meanings we place on those thoughts, the negative emotions that have become faithful companions to our thoughts and meanings, and finally our reactive behavior that becomes the go to, in order to nullify or better manage the negative emotions that have become so prevalent and persistent partners to our daily experience.

Once things have become associated, according to this law, the rapidity of how one association communicates with another association can occur, in theory, faster than the speed of light. This might explain why so much of our ongoing experience is so repetitive, patternistic and procedural. The properties and description contained within Quantum Theory concerning the Law of Entanglement may be a secular perspective of what many of us know as the Light of Christ. The Light of Christ is a Divine Power that emanates from the presence of God and fills the immensity of space. It is what allows Him to be in all things, and through all things, and above all things, and round about all things, to be in the midst of all things, which giveth life to all things and is the law by which all things are governed. This Light or Divine Power is a manifestation of God's Omniscience by which He comprehends all things, as all things are before Him. All things are by Him and of Him. (D&C 88:6-13, 41). The secular language found in Quantum Theory appears in agreement with what has been revealed about the Light of Christ (John 1:4-5,9; D&C 93:2).I cannot think of better language as is revealed in the scriptures to describe what the Quantum Theorists call the Law of Entanglement

Returning to the examples of how belief is shaped through the internal conversations we have is significant to understanding how The Law of Entanglement operates within our cells and experience. With that said, let me be very clear on what The Law of Entanglement is not saying. It is not saying that once these unhealthy associations have been formed you are doomed. What the law is saying is that if you can change or provide new information to one of the associations, because of entanglement, the other associations can likewise be influenced in how they would have normally responded. This should give every person hope that change is always available to us.

So, if we truly understand what the Law of Entanglement is suggesting, if through awareness we can change just one aspect of our long term associations, will the other associated aspects be impacted to likewise change? And if I no longer hold true the long-term associations would I then see myself differently? The answer is obvious and should give us hope that things can be different.

The second law speaks to the nature of matter itself. It states clearly that all matter has potential. Potential to do what? To organize, shape and behave in various ways. The very next question that should be addressed is – what then is matter? Matter is everything or better said, everything is made of matter (with maybe a few exceptions?). A lot of my clients answering this question simply say, "It is stuff." I personally like that answer. Matter is the building blocks of the entire universe. The same "stuff" is found everywhere. There have been many recent articles from Quantum Theorists and other researchers that definitively assure us that we are made of the stars. What we are composed of is the same thing stars and planets are made of. We and the stars are comprised of about 97% of the same atoms of matter.

Hydrogen is the one element of matter we find the most of in the Universe. If Hydrogen correctly entangles or associates with Oxygen, we will get water. If it entangles correctly with Nitrogen we will get ammonia, with Carbon, methane gas. Matter has the potential to organize in seemingly innumerable ways. How it organizes is how we know what we are looking at or how we perceive things. All matter has potential to organize with other elements of matter.

Here is a reminder that will likely assist the reader in understanding how our physiology influences our ongoing experience and how our beliefs about are self become organized. At a fundamental level, energy and matter are interchangeable. While we look physical, we are energy, which is important to understand when we begin to deal with the negative emotions related to shame, shame being an unhealthy or distorted view of ourselves. Energy is what influences atomic associations. How atoms combine is the fundamental understanding of entanglement; and again, how matter combines or organizes has us understand what something is. Our mind is the energy that our cells are paying attention to. Our mind is what generates our perception of our ongoing experiences and largely does so in how we perceive ourselves in relation to that ongoing experience. The energy of our perception is shaping the matter we are made of and how matter becomes organized is how we perceive what things are. In a nutshell, our perception can shape either correct or incorrect views of who we are, meaning our perception influences how matter is organized within us.

Largely you and I are made of Carbon, Oxygen, Hydrogen and Nitrogen; though pick up a handful of dirt and analyze it and it too is largely made of Carbon, Oxygen, Hydrogen and Nitrogen (Ecclesiastes 12:7).   When viewing dirt and then viewing human beings it is clear that the way matter is organized and behaves is vastly different between the two. So what gets matter to organize, shape or behave in any way that it does? What allows the elements to express itself in so many varied ways? What is the influencing power that acts on matter to get it to become? What allows matter to take on so many forms?

I have a son who has a degree in physics, with a minor in astronomy, mathematics and computer science. One day I asked him, "Joel, this universe is filled with matter unorganized." He replied, "It is dad." I then asked, "What gets matter to organize?" He answered and said, "Energy! There are various manifestations of energy in the universe which act on matter that get it to organize." He paused and then added, "And apparently the energy of our mind is contributing to the organization of matter." What my son was alluding to was the third law of Quantum Theory, or the *Law of the Observer*.

Matter is largely influenced in how it organizes; shapes and behaves based upon how it is acted upon. Observing is one way that matter is brought into organization. Matter actually knows when it is being observed and it is influenced by the intentions of the observer. This concept is wrapped in the third law, called the Law of the Observer. There are a couple of simple examples I can turn to in order for the reader to wrap their head around this third law. I have six children, each being made of matter. When they are in my presence and they know I can see them they act one way; yet I have heard plenty of stories on other ways they act when I am not observing them.

Another way to understand this phenomenon is in the experience and messages we believe we are receiving in our childhood years on how significant others see us. This can begin as early as embryonic development when the growing fetus is picking up on the signals of his or her mother of not being wanted. It can occur with absent, uninvolved, or very busy parents. How does a child begin to assess how the parents view him or her based upon the parent's limited interaction? Or what about the childhood experience of being consistently criticized or being interacted with in a negative way? How does the child begin to see him or herself based upon that ongoing scenario? What if the child grows up in a home where the parents don't get along producing the inability to be emotionally regulated at school as a result? How does the ongoing experience of not being able to pay attention, focus or comprehend begin to shape how the child sees his or her ability? What about children that grow up in a home organized around addiction? Does the child begin to believe that the substance is more valuable than them self? Of course, if the home environment is filled with hope, optimism, and the parents have formed a truthful, healthy perspective of their own self, such parents provide an environment that allows the child to be seen as important, valued and capable. These are but a few examples of many that assist us in understanding how we interpret our ongoing experience through the lens of how we believe others see or observe us.

I have sat with many adult clients discussing this truth and then watched the client take hold of the concept and immediately begin connecting dots of their own childhood experience with how they were still seeing themselves, even well into adulthood! It is a very interesting phenomenon, yet a realistic explanation for how one develops a view of themselves.

As I began to comprehend this third law, I had some of my spiritual informing trickle to the surface. In the Lord's University, meaning the Temple, we realize that God is highly aware of the matter that exists in the Universe. To His Beloved Son, God directs attention to the unorganized and chaotic matter. "Look" Jehovah is told and through the observing of the matter, that which is in a chaotic and unorganized state, Jehovah is invited to organize into a world, as had been accomplished, from a mortal perspective, innumerable times before (Moses 1:31; John 1:3). The Temple is one place where the organizing principle is taught. What may seem like an unimportant event in the instruction of the Endowment may actually be a very important instructive moment.

In our current understanding, whatever is determined to be accomplished, successful outcomes are directly related to the power of the mind and its ability to solve, to reason, to concentrate and to observe. There is absolute power in the mind. Successful outcomes are associated with intent, desire and will, which increases when we are able to see things and understand correctly. As correct awareness increases, likewise empowerment increases as a benefit in having us accomplish that which we are engaged in accomplishing. This characteristic is the same quality being described in the Abrahamic account where we are told, "......... and there is nothing that the Lord thy God shall take in his heart to do but what he will do it" (Abraham 3:17). The empowerment is named 'Faith' and each of possess this power to a degree. Faith is the first great governing principle, which has power, dominion and authority over all things. By faith all things exist, are upheld and changed.

If you have ever created anything, you took of materials (all materials are made up of the basic building blocks found throughout the universe) and combined, fastened, and formed them in a way that your mind conceived it could. This ability to picture an end result is the difference between the details of the finished product. When we stop long enough and observe something, that observation has the power to change the outcome. A simple example of this process is when we choose to observe a situation positively instead of negatively. Whichever attitude we choose to see the situation through will produce a different outcome. This law is what we want to utilize in order to get the outcome we picture in our identity. In application to what this book is trying to get the reader to understand is the mind is producing the energy that has our atoms or matter associate in the way they do.

It is important to understand these three laws as we move forward. Nature seems to function according to these laws. To further expound the relevance of Quantum Theory, we turn to the Creation Drama. The modern western world has largely lost track of this ancient festival and gathering, where communities would meet annually to act out the glorious aspects of the creation of this earth. Through song, dance and theater, the participants would celebrate and remember each epoch of the creative process. The singular feature of all ancient Creation Dramas is to understand how order is developed out of disorder. I imagine very few that are reading this book has familiarized themselves sufficiently with these ancient practices to understand the vital insight I am going to share from a spiritual perspective, however many that are associated with the Latter Day Saints are acquainted with this element. The Creation Drama is part of the ceremony that Latter Day Saints enjoy when they attend the Temple. One of the rooms, this body of people congregate in is called the Creation Room. Here, through cinematic observing, the participants learn how the ordered cosmos was formed out of chaos and particularly how this celestial orb upon which we dwell was created.

It may be difficult to surmise, but as previously stated, the word "matter" is a concept of focus in the unfolding of the mystery being taught in the Creation Room. In the film, we hear the Great God of the Universe instruct His Son to "Look" upon the matter unorganized for the purpose of taking it from a place of disorganization to organize it into a world as they had done many times before.  In the Abrahamic account of the Creation we read that the once disorganized matter was being organized in the manner desired by the Gods:

> "And the Gods *watched* those things which they had ordered until they
> obeyed." (Abraham 4:18; Italics placed for emphasis)

There is that word again, "watch," "look," "examine;" "see," "visualize," and "observe." The Gods watched the things they had ordered. What had they ordered? The matter that was unorganized. How long did they watch it for?  Until it had become what they desired it to become. As stated before, nature seems to function according to the laws of Quantum Theory and this account from the scriptures describing the Creation seems to support the laws we are introducing.

Why is this important? The answer comes when you begin to understand the nature of a thought. A thought is matter. And since learning is defined in terms of association then thoughts, whether fully realized or not become associated with meanings, emotions and behaviors. These associations then shape within us a belief about ourselves. Repeated messages become stored in Implicit Memory and even encoded upon our DNA. So well learned are these repeated associations that we no longer pay much attention to them; they are kind of on automatic drive; they become procedural. Since matter is influenced in how it behaves and organizes by how it is being observed then it appears that becoming better observers of the thoughts we tell ourselves and the sequential responses that form learning and belief within us, perhaps we can get our disorganized, chaotic beliefs to become ordered in a way that reveals our true self, our true identity and our true potential.

As we raise our consciousness, we become less affected by negative experiences and negative environmental signals. If we go about not observing things correctly, we are going to be impacted by every negative external influence. As we become fully conscious of our true identity the outside stuff becomes irrelevant. The reason being is that our true nature of being God's children allows us to grow the power of faith within us. As the power of faith grows we face all manner of challenges more realistically. We begin to take notice that a correct observance of who we really are allows us to handle challenges effectively. When the power of faith is fully developed it is at that moment we have become like our Heavenly Parents. In this state of being, there is nothing outside of us that is more powerful than what is inside of us.

When we become honest observers of how belief is formed, then it becomes abundantly clear that the early years of life play the most pivotal role in ongoing experiences. When we begin by looking at the child's developing neural system, it should become evident quickly that these processes are not just coming together due to some genetic blueprint alone, no, it should be clear that the environment we are providing is acting on the development, sequencing, and strong associations being formed.

Because of the sequential development of the brain and its tremendous malleability early in life, early life experiences play a remarkable role in shaping how the brain functions; how implicit memory functions. Early experiences create a cascade, or sequential set of cognitive, emotional, social, and physiological templates that we carry around with us, and use as we go through life. If you have traumatic experiences early on when the neural systems that are responsible for the fear response are developing, this will create pervasive hypersensitivity to threats, to challenges, to all kinds of things. We certainly know that high risk children, who come from chronic chaotic environment's literally change their baseline responsivity to every single cue. These patternistic responses form and become encoded into *implicit memory* that results in reactivity to any cue. These are state memories; meaning cellularly stored learning, not just merely cognitive memories.

The developing neural associations that are occurring in our young children are a product of "signaling" that each of us is so sensitive to. Signaling is that process either genetically or environmentally that continues to impose itself on us throughout life and in doing so strengthens our self-concept or weakens it, depending upon how well we are observing the signals. Children lack the capacity to view things from a mature adult's perspective; from a high place of consciousness, hence the reason personal belief about one's identity is so largely attached to the formative years. Children make too many incorrect observations of their experiences. Parents know this because many times as their children turn into adults and begin to share their perspective of their growing, developing years, parents are surprised by how their children perceived so many events differently than the parent did.

A good portion of that signaling also comes from the internal responses (the internal conversation) we experience when our environment shapes the opportunities to either have reoccurring positive or negative intrapersonal feedback. In all of my dealing with the host of issues mental health counselors deal with on a regular basis, it has been unequivocally my experience that most symptoms of the various diagnosis have a magical way of disappearing as individuals begin taking greater responsibility for their circumstances, especially their thoughts. That greater individual effort to work on the etiology and formation of these negative symptoms and be personally responsible for the outcome someone is seeking is the KEY to living more abundantly.

So, it is time to stop overlooking our physiology. It is time to stop ignoring the vital role our 100 trillion cells play in our ongoing self-perception. Cells absorb whatever we allow them to. Whatever we allow our cells to absorb, ONE DAY our cells will speak back to us and declare what they have become based upon whether we were good observers or not. Elder Bruce R. McConkie appears to have alluded to this principle when he taught:

> In a real though figurative sense, the book f life is the record of the acts of men, as such record is written in their own bodies. It is the record engraven on the very bones, sinews and flesh (all made of cells)...... When the book of life is opened on the Day of Judgment, men's bodies will show what law they have lived. With this in mind, the promised prize or reward is not jus what we get, but what we become. Becoming like Christ becomes its own reward. (Mormon Doctrine, 97)

Our cells have the capacity to fulfill the measure of their creation (Ephesians 4:13, 23-24). They will do so when we begin to pay higher attention to what information we allow our cells to absorb. The cliché's or wisdom literature that points to the reality that we are what we eat, or as a man thinketh, so is he, has been confirmed by modern research. I think it is now very safe to say that the research has caught up to the revelations.

As I have looked at this research, I believe I can safely say that the issues that so many needlessly struggle with are largely determined by what has been stored in Implicit Memory, especially one's belief about them self. Remember, Implicit Memory is literally matter organized. This explains why so many relationships struggle. Many couples that come and see me about what they think are "couple problems" actually are individual implicit belief problems they trigger in one another. Same is true when parents are so easily triggered by their children. As each person in this relationship goes through the process of becoming better observers of their own interpretation of ongoing experience, those unhealthy beliefs are transformed into very realistic and healthy views of one's self, hence no more triggering, no more hurt, no more negative, patternistic reactions. What were once thought to be "couple problems" were actually individual problems, and now that these have been corrected, the couple enjoys the relationship for what healthy people bring to one another.

Thankfully it appears that implicit belief can be changed by becoming better observers, especially becoming better observers of the internal conversations we all have based upon ongoing experience. In time and through your own observing effort, you will come to see yourself truthfully and accurately. When we are able to see who we truly are is when we receive the power to become who we are truly meant to be. We are told that God is love (1 John 4:8). If being His children then we too have the capacity to be love as well. Those that operate from this correct perspective continually filter the incoming signals accurately, but for those that see themselves less than love filter ongoing signals that go against their very nature. In the

Addiction Recovery Manual, published by LDS Social Services, this idea that what we believe about ourselves shapes our ongoing experience is taught in the following manner:

> As you do your inventory, look beyond your past behaviors and examine the thoughts, feelings and beliefs that led to your behavior. Your thoughts, feelings and beliefs are actually the roots of your addictive behaviors. Unless you examine all your tendencies toward fear, pride, resentment, anger, self-will, and self-pity, your abstinence will be shaky at best. You will continue with your original addiction or switch to another one. Your addiction is a symptom of other causes and conditions. (Step 4, Pg 21)

It is clear that incorrect perceptions are precursors to the emotions related to fear, pride, resentment, anger, self-will and self pity. These ongoing negative and intrusive emotional experiences developed because the person did not observe many of life's events through the perspective of love (Moroni 7:45-47). Their incorrect perceptions are the catalyst to those ongoing negative emotions.

In Step 6 there is more insight to how developing a perspective through love has us come to our self:

> As the process of coming unto Christ takes hold in your heart, you will find the false beliefs that fueled negative thoughts and feelings gradually replaced by truth. (Step 6, Pg 35)

Those that truly come unto Christ begin to take on His very nature. When His quality of love increases in us, the personal beliefs we hold about ourselves begin to change and we see ourselves correctly.

So to wrap up what this chapter is saying, our personal view of our self is the source of living happy or miserable, confident or insecure. What we believe about ourselves has serious ongoing ramifications. How we see ourselves tends to be our destiny. Our mindset; our thoughts are recognized by our body — right down to the genetic level. If our thoughts and mindset has us see ourselves as broken or devalued in some way the body responds in negative emotional and behavioral patterns. Our Implicit Memory was shaped over years of life experience, experience that many times we have no cognitive memory of. There is no way for us to control what has happened in the past, so trying to always figure out the "Why" is less important than figuring out what we have come to "Believe" about ourselves because of the "Why." WHY is the wrong question; how many times do we hear in the counseling office, "Why me?" or "Why did this happen to me?" The better question is WHAT. What have I come to believe about myself because of the why?

How we evaluated the circumstances of our varied experiences is what has shaped the brain we have today, how our cells have become programmed, and why certain genes have been switched on or off. It will never be in revisiting the circumstances where personal growth is achieved. It will be in visiting what we have come to believe about ourselves and utilizing the power of the mind going forward to choose our perspective and behavior, which will change our brain, cells, and genes to conform to our truthful self. The mind is designed to be the master of the body!  Healthy and accurate belief stored at the cellular level continues to unfold what we were designed to become.

# SELF-ESTEEM
## There is only one way to build it correctly

(Worth - We think of Value/$)

Evidence of Inherent Worth
1. Priceless
2. Strangers
3. Laws
4. Empathy
5. Personal Atonement

a. Worth is a constant
b. There is nothing
you can do that
will add to or
diminish from it
c. Everyone's is the same

LIFE

Experiences
Growth
Relationships
Performance

To develop the *confidence* that
one day we can <u>take care of</u>
<u>ourselves</u> and possibly others.

Confidence Scale
1. Physical       6
2. Mental         7
3. Social         5
4. Spiritual      8
5. Emotional      4
6. Intellectual   9

| 1) Inherent Worth | 2) Sufficient Love |
|---|---|

Inherit = To be given something;       Sufficient = Adequate
        no requirement on our part;
        usually in connection with relationship.

1)

Incorrect way to build esteem. **This is the
method for building shame. Shame is debilitating**

2)

<u>Two Things Necessary to Grow in Healthy-Esteem</u>
1. A person must believe they are deserving of the          2. Personally effective
   outcomes associated with personal effectiveness

**NOTE:** The foregoing chart will be referenced in the discussion of this chapter.

After the explanation of how belief is formed and stored at the cellular level, the question becomes, how does someone go from a place of insecure or unhealthy functioning to the place of secure and confident functioning if the belief stored drives insecurity? The answer to this question is to be found in two simple concepts. The first of these is:

1.  The person has to begin operating from correct information

The second is:

2.  They have to begin to practice those things that support and maintain a healthy, confident self-perception.

So, it is not just knowing something, it is also doing something and doing it again and again until it becomes second nature. Tentative efforts to learn correctly, as well as putting forth minimal effort to organize your behavior around what you are learning will lead to tentative outcomes. If either one of these concepts is not being implemented then the secure, healthy-self will still be found lacking. For those of you that are not "doers" but "hearers" only, if you think that just knowing something will create the changes you are looking for, I can tell you it won't (James 2: 17). Faithful doing also works in developing and maintaining a correct and confident perspective.

How long do humans go on suffering with self-doubt and insecurity waiting for someone else to assume responsibility for their needs? For many, way too long! It simply cannot be approached in this way. God, in His kingdom requires a healthy balance in growing the power of faith within us. He expects our own efforts in developing that power and desires that until fully developed we support, encourage and lift one another. But ultimately, Heavenly Father will not do for us what we can and should do for ourselves.

With that point being made, I would like to begin with the concept of operating from correct information. One of the great dilemmas of humans is that they do not always understand what words or concepts mean. They repeat them and use these words and concepts in sentences, but never come to fully understand their meaning. They confuse too many concepts. They take one concept and make it another. Or they take one concept and have it impact another when it should not. Let's begin the journey of making things clear and seeing things for what they really are; or in other words, let's start operating from correct information.

Self-esteem is a misunderstood concept. When you ask someone to explain self-esteem you get varied answers. The answers appear to tap into a sense of what self-esteem is, but none ever fully clarify the concept. For example, "It is how one feels about them self;" or "It's how someone sees their worth," or "It is how others see me." These are just a few of the responses I have heard to the posed question, none of which provide any bearings for the person to strengthen that which seems to be so volatile at times.

Whatever self-esteem really is, one way people try and quantify it is in terms of "high" or "low, "That person has really *high* self-esteem," or "That person seems to have *low* self esteem." Like the difficulty with understanding what self-esteem is, viewing self-esteem in ambiguous terms as high or low also deepens the struggle of getting a grasp conceptualizing correctly what self-esteem is.

I would like to introduce an idea, perhaps a better way to quantify self esteem. In doing so alone will begin to bear light on what it is we are looking at when considering this concept. The diagram below will help in our increasing understanding of this concept.

| Unhealthy | Healthy | Unhealthy |
|---|---|---|
| Esteem | Esteem | Esteem |
| (Role) | | (Role) |

Realistic Sense of Both
Strengths and Limitations

←——————————————————————————————→

VICTIM                                                          GRANDIOSITY

When I look at self esteem, I look at in terms of Healthy Esteem or Unhealthy Esteem. The bi-lateral arrow drawn represents a spectrum of self-esteem. On this spectrum, Healthy Esteem keeps itself centered. Unhealthy Esteem tends to plays out on the edges of the spectrum.

What is Healthy Esteem? People with Healthy Esteem are able to recognize the good things about themselves. They are aware of their strengths and utilize these to see themselves in a more realistic and confident perspective. These strengths may emerge in terms of social confidence, or maybe academic ability. Some are inclined to music; others may appear to have an intrinsic gift toward athleticism or leadership, it may be as simple as having a good work ethic; or just common sense, as well as many other positive attributes or characteristics. Whatever these strengths are, a person with healthy esteem recognizes them, appreciates them and many times develop purpose around them. But a person that has Healthy Esteem also recognizes there is room for improvement and development. In other words, healthy esteem individuals recognize their limitations. They are realistic that they have flaws, imperfections, and underdeveloped potential. But this is what the person with Healthy Esteem never does; he or she never turns his or her limitations into a definition of their identity. When they see those areas that are in need of improvement they estimate that there is something in their power to begin making the changes that will take those weaknesses and develop them to become stronger, resulting in being more confident and charactered individuals.

Those that operate from Unhealthy Esteem go through life operating from two roles. It is these roles that are the outward evidence of an inward struggle. One of those roles is GRANDIOSITY. Grandiosity is an inflated sense of self. It is seeing one's self in a far better way than what is reality. Let's talk about some examples of how grandiosity may be displayed. The bully is grandiose. He or she has a difficult time seeing them self in a good way unless they can appear smarter, stronger, or better than others. Their approach is to put someone else down in order to get the false sense of importance. Grandiosity shows up in every form of anti-responsibility, such as, blaming others, excuse making, rationalizations, minimization of one's own contribution to ongoing problems, accusing others, getting angry, full deceptions, partial truths, and an unwillingness to see good in others. That unwillingness may show up in forms of gossiping, persuasive blaming and other forms of undermining someone else's character. When a person argues and argues to prove he or she is right is a form of grandiosity. So also is the person that constantly makes other's aware of the good things they do, i.e., "Hey did you see what I did?" We can see grandiosity in relationships, when a well-intended spouse may approach their companion and point out to his or her sweetheart a certain behavior that, if stopped, would lead to greater happiness. When approached, the grandiose partner will cut-off the well-intended spouse and immediately flip the conversation and start mentioning all of the inadequacies of their spouse to divert attention away from being focused on. Grandiosity also rears its ugly head in our relationship with God when we keep telling Him he needs to change His ways and begin to do things the way we want to do them; or by simply denying His perfections.

The other role is that of the VICTIM. The victim is willing to admit that things may not be going so well, yet their mantra is, "But it is not my fault!" This is the Lehi principle, of knowing we can either act or be acted upon (2 Nephi 2:26). Victims choose the latter. Examples of this victim mentality, "If so and so wouldn't have done that, I wouldn't even be here today" or "If the economy wouldn't have tanked, I wouldn't be in so much debt" or "My parent's did not give me the tools to succeed in life," or "My teacher doesn't like me," or "I don't know why he (or she) is so abusive towards me" or "He always apologizes after he hurts me," or............ and the list goes on and on. The victim lacks energy and determination. They don't follow through, they give up and procrastinate. Such individuals cannot empower themselves because they believe what is outside of them is more powerful than what is inside of them. Such individuals develop a mental template that they are destined to be acted upon. Such individual's give others control of over how they think, feel and behave.

One of the discerning means of detecting Unhealthy-Esteem is in the way such people approach relationships. Those that operate from Unhealthy-Esteem tend to view relationships more by what they can get from others or how other's relationships are affecting them. That approach is in direct proportion to the roles being played out.

The roles of GRANDIOSITY and VICTIM act as a powerful strategy and whether fully conscious of why they choose to play out on the edges of Unhealthy Esteem, the roles provide the mechanism of one key thing......... not having to look at one's own limitations. The reason this is central to the purpose of the roles is because individual's that do go around with Unhealthy Esteem at one point in their life experience turned their limitations into a definition of their identity. In doing so, the negative feelings that have had a long-term association with defining themselves in a devalued manner have become problematic, intrusive and at times overwhelming. With their hyper-focus on their emotions they have learned how to regulate those emotions by denying that they have any problems (GRANDIOSITY), or by denying that they have any control (VICTIM). One of the big problems with this approach is that these roles can become so strongly fixed within the individual they have a hard time seeing it. One of the other problems is that those who enter into relationships with Unhealthy Esteemed individuals many times begin to develop their own insecurities because of the way Unhealthy Esteemed individuals interact with them.

One night, I received a call from a church leader and he said that he had an emergency. A member of his congregation, a well educated, successful professional was found under his desk at his office, curled up, weeping with a gun in his mouth. When I met with this man it was evident that he had developed the unhealthy belief of "I am not good enough" in his implicit memory. After the second session, the man was able to find hope that he could change that identity. In discussing Epigenetics, the client could better understand how environment plays a significant part in how belief gets shaped and stored within us. He recognized that it is not the environment specifically that creates these unhealthy beliefs, but the perception one chooses of the ongoing environmental experience. One of the examples I give of environmental influence is being in a toxic relationship. This seemed to spark some interest in him and I believe he began to reflect on his own marriage in connection with what I was teaching. He stated that he would like to have his wife come in and hear these things I was educating him about.

By my second session, I have the client reflect on aspects of their life and provide a number between one and ten on how they think they are doing in those different areas. This client's wife gave herself a ten in each category (GRANDIOSITY), the first and only time I ever had a client do so. The husband reacted to her scoring. His eyes got wide, he turned and looked at her and then said, "Oh my goodness. I could never see this before." The husband began to understand how his "I am not good enough" belief had shaped within his implicit memory. He began to see how toxic his wife was. Since she was always perfect, always right, then that left him in an inferior position. Such perception led to the "I am not good enough" template. That was the last session she attended. Her GRANDIOSITY would not allow her to accept any responsibility for the deterioration of the marriage. In two weeks, she announced she was moving to another State in order to gain control of the counseling her husband was getting. Unhealthy Esteem runs rampant in the human population.

I hope this description of Healthy Esteem and Unhealthy Esteem provides a better perception of what we are beginning to introduce. It is my intent in your own self-reflection of these aspects that you have not taken it as criticism; but simply useful observing in gauging your own self-esteem on the spectrum. President Ezra Taft Benson in his hallmark address, "Beware of Pride," speaks more intimately of the Unhealthy-Esteem roles in terms of the pride from the top looking down and the pride of the bottom looking up. For increasing awareness, I invite everyone to review President Benson's remarks. Likewise, I reflect on the scripture found in Ether 12:27 as it relates to understanding Healthy Esteem. In the weaknesses or limitations each of us possesses, those weaknesses are there to get us into a relationship with God. A healthy relationship with Him mandates that we humble ourselves, meaning that we become submissive and teachable. It will be in that mindset that we will begin to see things as He sees them and in doing so will transform those weaknesses into strengths.

So how does someone, who is operating more from Unhealthy Esteem, begin to make the changes to have them move toward the center of the spectrum, to the place of Healthy Esteem? As mentioned prior, the answer is found in two concepts. The first is that the person has to begin operating from correct information. The second is that the person has to begin doing things that develop and maintain a healthy sense of them self. It is never enough to just know something, it also requires doing something. When we begin to incorporate both aspects, they act synergistically in changing implicitly held negative belief into a correct identity that has us approach life realistically and with confidence.

Let's return now to Self-Esteem and see if we can't begin making sense of this oft misunderstood concept. First off, whatever it is, have you ever noticed its volatility? Have you noticed how it seems to change or move around? One day you tend to experience greater confidence and happiness in who you are and other days you don't even want to face the day because of feeling insecure in yourself? Here then is a very insightful question. This thing that seems to move around so much, can it ever stabilize? Was it meant to always be in flux or can it become stable? I think it can stabilize and if it can, there must be a way to build it in order to do so.

## BUILDING SELF-ESTEEM

I personally like this analogy of building, as in my younger years I was in the construction trades. I was a contractor and so I knew quite a bit about good construction vs. the short-cuts so many take that leads to problems in the structure down the road. If there was one thing that became clear to me over and over again in dealing with a host of repairs was the importance of having a very good foundation. Many issues I was called out on to inspect were things like dynamic cracking in exterior walls, joints failing and structures sinking. Some would wonder if their stucco or plaster was failing or if the compound used in their joints was defective. My answer to such questions many times was simply this, "No, your foundation has shifted, which is now causing stress in the structure above."

Self-esteem is very much the same way. Without a sure foundation, self-esteem will always be susceptible to shifting. It will always be viewed as something that is in jeopardy as life's difficult winds blow against us. There are two foundation stones that have to get put into place if self-esteem is going to stabilize; and until these foundation stones get into place, life will continue to convince us that our value is at risk. I will visit these foundation stones in a moment but I would like you to view the diagram found at the beginning of this chapter as I want you to focus on the structure at the center, meaning the triangle. This triangle represents life; your life; my life; everybody's life. In life, would you agree that everyone is having experiences? Would you agree that everyone is programmed for growth, whether that is emotional, physical, developmental, social, etc? Would you agree that everyone has to deal with relationships? And finally, would you agree that every person goes around doing something? Doing something is what I have labeled as "performance." We are all going around performing.

Since everyone is doing the same stuff, is there a purpose to all of it? I believe there is. I believe that life and all of the similar stuff we do as humans has a very singular purpose. That purpose is to develop confidence, but this is a very specific type of confidence. It is the confidence that assures us that one day we can take care of ourselves; and if we have learned how to take care of ourselves, then possibly we can assist in taking care of others or teaching them how to take care of themselves.

There is a truism to this idea of what I am presenting and every parent that is reading this book knows what I am talking about. Every time we have a child, somewhere in the back of our mind is this thought, "I hope by the time this child reaches 18 to 20 years of age that he or she has developed enough confidence to go out and take care of them self." So from just the face of the statement we recognize some substance to what I am suggesting. The question at this point then is, "What does it mean to take care of ourselves?"

There are six core areas where humans take care of themselves. In the diagram, those core areas are listed. 1. Physically, 2. Mentally, 3. Socially, 4. Spiritually, 5. Emotionally ; and 6. Intellectually. Let's briefly take a look at each and see if we can take a general assessment of these core areas to see how well we are taking care of our self.

Physically – Each of us have physical needs. We need shelter, food and clothing. We also have a physical body and the better we learn to take care of it then the likelihood we will experience life in a more positive way. If we were to put taking care of ourselves physically on a scale of 1 to 10, a ten may look like this......... I never worry about taking care of my physical needs because I make so much money everything is already paid for. I own my home outright; my cars are completely paid off. I have no debt; in fact I have thousands of dollars coming into my accounts every single month and there is no end to that stream. I make an annual insurance premium payment and I make monthly utility payments, other than that it is all paid for. I also go to the gym three days a week; play a little golf and tennis between and I eat healthy. I am a TEN. What's a ONE? Think of an infant. On that scale, what number would you assign yourself; again this is just on you. Do not include any contribution from a spouse or parent.

**Place your number here _____**

Mentally – Mentally is about what I am saying to myself about myself. A person that is a TEN speaks to them self this way...... I know that I am capable. When life brings it difficulties, I know that with enough consistent effort and gathering of the correct resources that I can meet the challenges of life and overcome. I am also realistic and recognize that I will make mistakes. But I believe in resiliency, which says that I can honestly evaluate those mistakes that led to failing, learn from them and pick myself up and keep moving forward. I believe that I matter, that I am useful, that I have purpose, that I am acceptable and wanted, etc. A person that is a ONE......... "Um, yeah, if you knew me you probably wouldn't want much to do with me. Life's hard, I can't do this."

**Place your number here _____**

Socially – No human does well alone. People that are a TEN socially, understanding this truth, have developed a social scaffold that allows them to stay connected with others for the purpose of receiving those good things that we enjoy by doing so; such as, creating memories, forming emotional bonds, having someone to listen to us and understand us, combining with someone else to build unity and strength in meeting the challenges and experiencing the rewards of life, etc. A person that is a TEN has developed social skills and graces which allow him or her to engage with others with confidence. Such people do not experience social anxiety. A person that is a TEN also knows the difference between healthy and unhealthy relationships and desires and works toward that end of having healthy relationships by incorporating principles, such as faith, prayer respect, love, forgiveness, compassion, work and wholesome recreational activities. A person that is a ONE........... "Um, yeah, I do better alone. Yeah, I'm OK by myself. Friends? Yes I have friends. Every time I get online to game, those that show up to play with me, those are my friends. Yes, talking to others is important, that is why I text my mother two hundred times a month."

**Place your number here _____**

Spiritually – I believe in the dual nature of man. As the Prophet Job declared, "But there is a spirit in man: and the inspiration of the Almighty giveth them understanding" (Job 32:8). This spiritual side of us, just like any other part, needs attention and nurturing. One of the main ways we sense we are doing well spiritually is by the calming emotions such as peace, hope, assurance, happiness and love we experience. It seems that all of mankind seeks these emotions. Some may find them by being in contact with nature or through forms of meditation. Some turn to self-help books or inspirational authors, but since my objective in this book is to teach about our true identity, I suggest that these feelings can be our constant companion when we come to realize that there is a God in the Universe who knows each of us personally and wants the best for us and that because we are literally His children. As we reflect sincerely on this relationship, it begins to have us recognize our incredible potential (Genesis 1:27), yet we know that our potential will never be fully realized until we form a relationship with Him. It will only be through a correct relationship with Heavenly Father that we will obtain the power to become what we were designed to become. It is from Him that we receive inspiration, power and gifts, all of which are necessary in order to fulfill the measure of our creation. None of us will ever do it on our own. With this truth in mind, the people that are TENS spiritually are those that have developed the habits that maintain this relationship. I think one of those TEN spiritual habits is just changing our attitude. Instead of walking around focusing on the negative of a situation, we can focus on being grateful for even the smallest of blessings and being content with what we have been allotted. I think getting out of ourselves once in awhile and investing our time and resources into another person, not to be counted, but because we love them is a good TEN spiritual habit. I think meditation is a powerful habit that can unfold incredible insight to our ongoing growth and development spiritually. Many times this self reflection comes from studying and applying the scriptures to ourselves. For those that prepare properly for the Sacrament is involved in this habit as they reflect on their own standing before the Lord and their fellowman (Matthew 5:23-24). I think it is difficult to have a good relationship with anyone unless you are communicating with them. So the habit of prayer or "always having a prayer in your heart" is a TEN spiritual habit. Finally, if we really want to know the nature and character of God, because we have the potential to be like Him, we might just pick up a book once in awhile that has been written by someone that has met Him to give us a correct perspective of Him and what we can become. A TEN spiritually is manifest when one has built his or her own testimony of God and of His revealed principles.

What is a ONE spiritually? "There is no God. Life is a fluke. When we die it all goes out of existence, therefore I am going to get whatever I can get while I am here, by whatever means I can get it."

**Place your number here _____**

Emotionally – We humans have these things called emotions. A person that is a TEN emotionally knows where emotions come from, and because they know where emotions come from, when they are feeling a negative emotion they are able to quickly regulate it appropriately.... where the negative emotion never becomes overwhelming or intrusive.

A person that is a ONE emotionally? They do not understand the source of emotions and have become hyper focused on the negative emotions that invade and consume their thoughts. They think through their emotions, they are run by their emotions; their emotions are running and dictating their choices, their day; their belief about themselves. They use negative emotions as evidence that they are broken, not important; not good enough and a host of other self-defeating, devaluating beliefs.

**Place your number here _____**

Intellectually – Taking care of ourselves intellectually is not the same thing as taking care of ourselves mentally. Remember, taking care of ourselves mentally is about what we are saying to ourselves about ourselves. Taking care of ourselves intellectually is in response to recognizing that we are designed to learn.

Those that are a TEN intellectually then have made a commitment to be a life-long learner. This process may be as simple as learning a new hobby, like flying a helicopter or it may be more challenging like mastering a field of science. People that have adopted the attitude of ongoing informing read, they digest articles in magazines or research journals. They read about political theory, theological development, or even financial strategies. They may travel to learn of other cultures or languages. They may purchase a telescope someday and begin looking at the stars trying to figure out how all that works. They watch shows on nature and the earth's environment or history. They may learn how to play a musical instrument. They are constantly digesting information and increasing their knowledge.

What is a ONE intellectually? "What's a book?" is there mantra.

**Place your number here _____**

The numbers you have selected for your self are those represented in the diagram on the right side of the triangle. Obviously yours may be different. Now let's discuss what these numbers represent. The first thing they represent is that the numbers you assigned yourself is a snapshot. This is how you are currently assessing your confidence in the areas listed. However, if I ask you have these numbers ever been different at times in your life, you are going to answer, "Yes." So, these numbers move! What then is the influencing power on what gets these numbers to move? At this point I ask my clients to consider two areas. The first I call EXTERNAL influences and the second I call INTERNAL processes. Let me lay an idea of EXTERNAL influences. Life comes at us. There are so many things that are out of our control. Economic decline, a natural disaster, the closing of a business that we may be employed at, betrayal, crimes committed against us, etc. I think certainly these EXTERNAL influences can push at these numbers to a degree. But still, is it more of the EXTERNAL influences or perhaps more of our own INTERNAL processes? The vast majority of clients conclude it is INTERNAL processes.

If the moving of these numbers is indeed largely associated with our own INTERNAL processes, or in other words, if you believe you truly have the power to move these numbers upwards, then we could ask some questions that would verify that understanding. As you look at the numbers you recorded, pick some of the lower ones and ask yourself the following questions. What would I start doing..... What would I stop doing......... or, What would I do differently to get that number to increase? Here is an example utilizing the above referenced diagram.

"You are a 5 socially. We are not looking for a 10. But if you believe you have the power to improve that number and just simply start moving it toward a 6, What would you start doing.... What would you stop doing.... What would you do differently?" The answer may be, "I would start doing more things with others rather than sit home as often as I do." OR "Rather than being on my phone so much, I am going to put it away when I am with others." After the client answers the question, I just simply reinforce what they are saying....... "So you believe by getting out more rather than sitting at home and by putting your phone away when you are with others will get that number to move in the right direction?" The client then answers yes.

I then pick one or two more areas and ask the same questions, each time the client concluding that they do have power to move the numbers upward; increasing their confidence. I then ask this poignant question, "Who then has the power of moving these numbers?" Every time, the client concludes that the power is within them. I then add, "I don't want you to ever forget that! We are here to understand and operate from correct information. Each of us has the power to take better care of ourselves in each of the areas described any time we decide to" That is correct information!

This important discussion then leads my introducing what self-esteem really is. Self-esteem, more than anything else, is the level of confidence we are experiencing in how well we are taking care of ourselves. Some parts of our self-esteem may be filled with greater confidence than other areas, but in a general sense, self-esteem is directly related to the confidence we are experiencing in these different areas that we are responsible for improving if we expect to experience life in a better way. With this clear understanding, then I say it is OK that some of the areas are underdeveloped, because as long as the person recognizes the power is within them to improve in any of the areas then it is just a matter of them doing so.

As we seek to improve these numbers and enjoy the greater confidence from doing so, what we are really experiencing is faith's growing power within us. The power of God is named FAITH (Hebrews 11:1,3). We being His literal offspring are endowed with the same power, though it not being fully developed. When our confidence improves then this power is growing within us. Faith is power. And where there is power, there is faith; and where there is no power, there is no faith. Faith is to have confidence in something that has not yet come into fruition, something that has not yet been realized, yet can be. Faith then motivates action to bring about what is observed can be. It is taking passive faith, what we observe can be; and turning it into active faith by putting into operation those things necessary to get it to come to pass. It is in faith's growing power that we get an idea and growing sense of our true identity.

The Foundation Stone – SUFFICIENT LOVE

Yet earlier I stated that even knowing we have the power to improve our confidence in these areas, it will never stabilize until we get the foundation stones into place. The first of these foundation stones I have called INHERENT WORTH; the other I have labeled SUFFICIENT LOVE. Let's first explore SUFFICIENT LOVE.

The word sufficient does not mean perfect, which is good news for us because we do not need to experience perfect love in order to receive the benefits of this concept. The word sufficient suggests to us that there is an adequacy level that provides enough in its performance allowing us to form correct understanding. Sufficient love is to receive a consistent nurturing of our basic needs, with likely a sprinkling in of our wants.

As humans, we are constantly sending signals out into the environment with the hopes that such signals will be responded to in a favorable manner. Perhaps we want someone to listen to us, or spend time with us. Maybe we are concerned about something that requires help. Maybe we need a hug or some other form of reassurance. Maybe we are looking for encouragement in making a choice. These and a host of other signals when responded to in a consistent nurturing manner, is when we are experiencing SUFFICIENT LOVE.

Let's consider this from the perspective of an infant. Babies have needs; they get hungry, they get soiled, they get tired and bored. But how does the baby go about changing its own diaper or fixing its own meal or avoid boredom? The obvious answer is that others provide these for the young one. In infancy, SUFFICIENT LOVE is experienced when there is maximum comfort coupled with minimum inconsistency. While parents are the frontline in meeting these needs, it is important to ask the question, "How do the parents know what and when to provide nurturing to their infants?" The answer is clear, most times the parents nurturing is activated by the child's sounds, whether that is whimpering, crying or fussing, etc. These are signals that are sent out into the environment and how the parent's respond to that signal has everything to do whether the child is experiencing SUFFICIENT LOVE.

Since my program is centered in identity, meaning what one comes to believe about him or herself, there are three important attributes that emerge in the identity of anyone that is experiencing SUFFICIENT LOVE. The first of these is TRUST. This consistent nurturing provides an environment where the developing human can begin to trust in others as well as begin to trust in one's self. How important is trust if we are going to experience life in a more realistic and happy manner? Trust is vital in the development of identity. The second attribute that emerges in the identity of those experiencing SUFFICIENT LOVE is a SENSE OF CONTROL. Even an infant develops this attribute because their signals are very distinguishable based upon the need they are expressing. If others are discerning the babies signals, then certainly that would provide a sense of control. How important is it to have a sense of control if we are going to go live life in a good way? The third attribute that emerges in the identity of the child is a SENSE THAT THEY MATTER; that others see them in a good and acceptable way.

Why does this have to be a foundation stone? Because if we cannot trust, if we don't have a sense of control or if we don't believe that we matter, we will never produce the emotional energy to go and take better care of ourselves. In essence, the inconsistent meeting of our signals, meaning our needs and wants robs us of self-empowerment.

I am going to tell you a big story, it is a true story, but it is a big story that supports this concept we are talking about. Many years ago, I was a therapist at a residential youth program. One day I received a new client, Justin, fifteen years old. His adoptive parents brought him to our program because Justin had just burned down the "family business barn." This was not the little red barn in the backyard where the lawnmower was kept. The family business was to provide housing, training, healthcare and breeding of horses. Many were thoroughbreds, the $250,000.00 type of horses and Justin torched that facility and many of the horses did not make it out. It was also discovered that Justin had been inappropriate with a younger niece and when Justin would go to school, well he would go to school but he never turned in any work. He would just sit out the day either sleeping, or daydreaming or doodling. I ask the question, "Does it seem like Justin is doing very well at 15?" The answer is obvious!

Upon handing Justin over to our care, the parent's left me with a file folder that contained varying reports on Justin. Some of these were academic and school counseling related, others from previous treatments, but there was one report that as I began to peruse it, had me believe that I was looking at the source of Justin's struggles. Strangely enough, this report was written by a Highway Patrolman. In the officer's report, it was indicated that while out patrolling on the I-15, that the officer's attention was caught by a "light flickering with intensity," some distance off of the highway. What created the curiosity in the officer was that he could not discern the source of that light and so he left the highway to investigate what he saw. When the officer arrived at the location he believed where the light originated, the only thing he could see that may have been the source was an old car that was abandoned out on the desert floor; a few yards from the road.

We have all seen these cars, bullet holes in them, glass broken, upholstery ruined by UV rays, dents, flat tires, etc. What possibly could an old car like that do with light flickering with intensity that the officer saw? I think all of us have been blinded by reflection of sun rays off of cars, either their windshields or chrome. Yet, I am with you, "Was this really the source of the light?" When you hear the rest of the story, I would like to think I know what that Source was. The officer's report continued, "I suddenly received the strongest impression to get out of my car and go look in that car," and when the patrolman did, he found Justin, 15 months old, abandoned in that car. When Justin was taken to the hospital and the healthcare check-up was given, it was discovered that Justin's body was filled with parasites that were eating him alive.

I ask the important question – for the first 15 months of Justin's life, did he experience SUFFICIENT LOVE? If you have understood what I spoke of earlier in this book then it becomes clear that Justin's cells, absorbing his early-life experience, stored that early-life experience in a way that was still sending signals to him well into his adolescence. You may be asking, but what about his adoptive parents? Wouldn't 14 years have made a difference in how Justin saw himself? First of all, let me repeat, the earlier-life experiences, meaning between in-utero and seven years of age play a more substantial role in forming identity than at any other time in our life. These state memories form strong templates through which we continue to filter life's events through. Like most of us as parents, Justin's adoptive parents were well intended. They would have had no idea that Justin's state-memory template was incorrectly interpreting their interactions with him. Let me help you understand what I am saying. Justin's dad was a successful businessman. He was very much a hard-working cowboy kind of guy. In his mind, he believed that he would teach Justin how to work hard and that through hard work Justin would be able to develop confidence in his life. Sounds reasonable correct? Unless you had a strong devalued template like Justin did. You see, when dad would ask Justin to do something, sometimes Justin would hesitate or refuse to perform. Dad would give him a swift kick in the rear to get him moving – a very cowboy way of doing things. It worked for him when his dad would give him a little boot, so certainly it would work for Justin. However, if your template is one already filled with a devalued view of yourself, what does a boot in the rear really mean? Correct, it is just further evidence of that devalued template. At times when Justin would put forth some effort, like a normal parent, dad would point out Justin didn't follow exactly what dad had asked him to do. What does pointing out these incorrect outcomes look like through a strong devalued template? Correct, it is just further evidence of that devalued template.

Mom was likewise a wonderful woman, but to a degree she believed Justin had already suffered enough in his life; so whenever Justin would signal some distress, mom was quickly there to alleviate that distress by usually doing for Justin what he should have been learning to do for himself. What does a person who already believes that they are powerless experience when their mother continues to do everything for them? Correct, it just reinforces that one is not capable.

What is the point of this whole story about Justin? Justin's early life experience was absent of SUFFICIENT LOVE, which shaped in Justin a distorted template. Some of the very key attributes of a healthy view of one's self were missing. Justin had difficulty trusting others and him self. Justin believed he was incapable; helpless and therefore absent of control. Justin's depression, not just when I met him, but throughout his life was evidence to him that he did not matter. If a person cannot trust, if they do not believe they have any control and if they don't perceive themselves as one that matters, they will never produce the power to go and take better care of them self. Can you see why SUFFICIENT LOVE has to be part of our foundation?

One day I was listening to the Dennis Prager Show. I do not recall the guest's name, but he was a professor at UCLA and a clinical psychologist. He made a comment that struck me as it related to this topic we are discussing. He said that many people do not get good starts to life. Sometimes they are unfortunate in having parents that do not engage and interact from this SUFFICIENT LOVE principle. He then said, "That is why it is good to get to know God and believe in Him, because He is a good parent that understands our needs and wants and interacts with us in a consistent manner. Whatever we may have missed from our imperfect, mortal parents, because He is perfect, He knows how to give abundantly."

While God invites us to come and learn of Him and to consider His ways, not too far on that road of invitation we discover that He asks us to love Him with all of our heart, might, mind and strength. The truth is that He does the same for each of us (1 John 4:19). Sometimes SUFFICIENT LOVE is best experienced when we finally accept Him, not only as our God, but more importantly, as our Father.

Elder Neal A. Maxwell taught us about God's love for us and a little bit about our responsibility to love Him:

> "Too often we behave as if we were in massive competition with others for God's love. But we have His love, unconditionally and universally; it is our love for Him that remains to be proven." (Even As I AM, Pg 63)

The Foundation Stone – INHERENT WORTH

Now let's turn to INHERENT WORTH. Here is another concept that humans struggle understanding. Like self-esteem, they read about it, they use it in conversations, they may even sing songs or hymns that teach about it, but never fully coming to an understanding of what it really is.

When one looks at the word INHERENT, it is obvious that it is the same word as INHERIT. The word INHER means to receive. So what does it mean to inherit something? To inherit means to receive something as a gift and is typically in connection with a relationship.

So do you hear what this foundation stone is suggesting? Our worth is an inheritance, a gift because of a relationship. We will discuss that relationship in more depth later. Now I want you to affix your eyes to the "ENT" ending. This "ENT" ending is helping us understand a quality of this worth and that it is likewise a *fixed* quality. That is what the "ENT" ending means. Not only did we receive our worth as a gift based upon a relationship, but it is also a *fixed* quality.

There are three fixed characteristics or attributes to this worth we are talking about:

- 1st - Our worth is a constant. What that means is that it will never go away. We can always count on it being there. It is reliable;
- 2nd - There is nothing any of us will ever do that will add to that worth or take away from that worth – NOTHING!
- 3rd - Your worth, my worth and everyone else's worth is equal. It is exactly the same.

These are the fixed characteristics or attributes of INHERENT WORTH, which helps us see its quality.

Since the foundation is essential if self-esteem is ever going to stabilize, when you look at these two foundation stones you begin to recognize that they get put into place by different methods. SUFFICIENT LOVE is established as a good foundation when we experience it. But the only way INHERENT WORTH is put into place is when we come to believe it. So, how does anyone come to believe anything? The answer to that question is, we believe things when we have had enough evidence to suggest to our mind that we can believe it.

Let's then begin to look at some evidence for INHERENT WORTH. When we think of worth we think of some sort of value. In returning to the previous diagram, we are now focused on the left side of the triangle. At the top we see this concept of Value/$ as a heading. Below that heading are five significant evidences of this worth, labeled as 1) Priceless; 2) Strangers; 3) Laws; 4) Empathy; and 5) Personal Atonement.

The Evidence of Inherent Worth – PRICELESS

Parental love is one of the most profound evidences of INHERENT WORTH. This can be tricky though for some clients as their own personal experience with their parents may have not sent the correct message. However, for the most part, I will ask a client (Yes, even my adult clients) to call one of their parents and ask them the following question, "Mom (or dad), if someone came to you and offered you anything this world has to offer in terms of its wealth and resources, what would you take in exchange for me?" The answer has always been, "I would not take anything. There is nothing more valuable than you." That has created a number of tender moments in my office.

For those clients that have children I will ask them what they would take in exchange for their child; again the answer is always they wouldn't take anything. Some times I will press the issue...... "If I could give you all of the oil fields in the world are you sure you wouldn't exchange your child for that? Can you think about how different your life would be if you owned all of the oil fields?" Still the answer is the same; they won't take any thing this world has to offer in terms of its resources and wealth in exchange for that precious child. I then add either; "Your parents have made you a MasterCard commercial – you are priceless." or "You have made your child a MasterCard commercial – (he or she) is priceless." This is the beginning of building evidence that worth is inherent. When we pause and ask our self this type of question we begin to peer at reality and sense the truth of INHERENT WORTH

The Evidence of Inherent Worth – STRANGERS

If I go home and my house is on fire, I am not waiting on the curb. But there is not one of my neighbors that would question my behavior. It is obvious my behavior is being driven by the deep bonds that I have with those that abide with me in my home; and yet my behavior may be putting me at incredible risk even to the extent that I might lose my own life in the process. But again, no one is going to question my behavior. This brings us then to an interesting question because we see this same type of behavior where people will put themselves in harm's way, even many times losing their life to help someone they don't even know.; someone they have never met before. How do we explain that behavior? Why would someone risk their own life for someone they have never even met?

I think there can be various reasons to explain such behavior, but I still believe there has to be a core reason. Let me explain what I mean about various reasons verses a core reason. Everyone that knows me knows I eat at Taco Bell. There are various reasons why I eat there. I may be hungry, or it is convenient because it is located close to my office. It is relatively inexpensive. I like how the food tastes. Perhaps my favorite, there is no clean-up. Just flip the tray into the trash and leave. Yet none of these reasons are core enough to explain my behavior of going to Taco Bell. Here is the core reason I eat at Taco Bell - I would have to believe that there is going to be food there when I arrive, otherwise I would never go. Can you see how core that reason is and how it differs from the various reasons?

So what is the core reason why strangers risk their own life to help someone they do not know? I believe the core reason is that they must sense the worth of the individual otherwise I don't think they ever would do it. Would that make sense to you? Good! We are just building evidence so that we can come to believe in the concept of INHERENT WORTH.

The Evidence of Inherent Worth – LAWS

This is another big story. It is a true story, but it is a big story. I am using it to drive the evidence that supports the truth of INHERENT WORTH.

Many years ago there were two ladies. Both were senior citizens. Each was in their 80's. These ladies were friends and they lived together in a home located in Bel Air, California. If you have ever seen "The Fresh Prince of Bel Air" then you know that Bel Air is an upscale neighborhood; lots of money. Bel Air is right next to Beverly Hills.

When I was reading the Los Angeles Times article concerning these two ladies, the article spoke about their wealth. One of the representations of that wealth was their cars. One of the ladies drove a nice Mercedes Benz, the other a nice Cadillac. But the article further pointed out that these women had gone out and purchased a third car. This car was kind of a clunker – not much to look at; and the women never drove that car.

The two women were going around to the homeless population in Los Angeles, befriending many in this population. What I mean by befriending is that they were getting to know some of these homeless people so well that they were able to collect some interesting information about them; things like full birth names, birth places, birth dates, social security numbers and mother's maiden names. Most will recognize that such information is required in financial transactions. After the women had collected enough information they were going to insurance companies and taking out Life Insurance Policy's on these homeless people. If you know anything about life insurance then you know that there's a two-year window, where if a person dies in the first two years of that policy being issued; the insurance company takes a little harder look at the death. In fact there are some things the insurance company won't even pay out on in those two years. Suicide committed within the first two years is one of those things.

In process of discovery for trial, there was a spreadsheet uncovered on these ladies' computer at there home. In one column was listed the homeless people's names. In another column was recorded the Insurance Company from which the policy had been underwritten. In the next column was the value of that insurance policy if the homeless person died; and finally in the adjacent column at the top was recorded, "2 YR" meaning two year. In this column were just a bunch of dates and sometime after that date would arrive, the women would hire the same man to drive that old clunker car to run over the homeless person to kill them so that they could collect on the insurance policy. The women were convicted. At trial it was discovered that these women, along with the driver were serial killers. They had been doing this for over 20 years.

Upon returning to the judge on the day of sentencing, the judge told these ladies that they would spend the rest of their natural lives in prison. He further informed them that there would be no possibility for parole and then emphasized their consequence by telling them that they would die while in prison. The women objected verbally in court to the sentence, asking why the sentence was so harsh seeing that these were just homeless people. As I read the LA Times article, it only reports what the judge did at this moment. He did not get angry, he did not act in any hostile way toward the two women; he simply reached in to his pocket pulling out a twenty dollar bill and asked the ladies to declare in open court the value of that bill. Both ladies stated that it was worth twenty dollars. The judge then took the next few moments and he began to really alter how that bill appeared. He tore at it, he wrote on it, he crumpled it, stomped on it, had it become soiled by the dirt in a nearby potted plant. He really defaced this bill. He then unfolded it to the ladies and in its obvious altered state asked the ladies to once again declare the value of the bill. The ladies stated that it was still worth twenty dollars. The judge then said, "Ladies life has a way of beating us up, crumpling us and tearing at us, but it will never change our value." He then went on to tell the women that his judgment was based in the laws that were written in the books and that the law was very clear about one thing, it does not matter if you are rich or poor, the color of your skin, the culture or belief system you espouse. The law looks beyond all those factors and simply declares that all life is equal in the eyes of the law. Can the laws then be added as evidence that INHERENT WORTH is real?

The Evidence of Inherent Worth – EMPATHY

Have you ever experienced empathy? That is such a funny design built within each of our capacity. The idea that we can go deep enough into the experience of another person that we can actually begin to feel what it is they are experiencing. The only thing that comes out of that experience is that we sense the worth of the individual; otherwise, what would be the purpose of such an experience? Empathy alone can be evidence of INHERENT WORTH.

The Evidence of Inherent Worth – PERSONAL ATONEMENT

Why do we need a Savior? In trying to keep things simple I will say the following – one of the great burdens of a prophet is to declare to the people the nature and character of God. One of the characteristics that has been highlighted by every prophet is that God is a very clean and a very pure Being, and no unclean thing can enter into His presence (1 Nephi 10:21; 3 Nephi 27:19; Moses 6:57). What makes us unclean? Many would answer and say "Sin." While that qualifies as an accurate response, I would like to break down the term in acknowledging that sin is to willfully disobey or violate the laws and commandments He has revealed to us. Laws are signposts that lead to progression if adhered to. There is multiplicity of blessings that accompany adherence to law. However, infractions or violations of law will always require some sort of payment to right the wrong. The following story will highlight this principle.

You and I are driving in my car up Saint George Blvd. I am driving you are my passenger. You are going to find out something about me and that is I lose my patience when I am driving behind an older driver who insists on going ten miles below the speed limit; and that is exactly who we find ourselves behind. Unfortunately in the very next lane is a person of the same mindset and so we are behind two people that are racing for last place and both are winning. In my increasing frustration, I look to the other side of the Boulevard and realize that I have enough space to cross over through one of the openings in the median and zoom past these two drivers and then get back over.

As I cross through one of the openings, I accelerate and I am now going 95 miles per hour on the wrong side of the street. In my attempt to get back over, I was not aware of a red light and I end up running it. Unfortunately an officer has witnessed all of these violations of law and when he is finished assessing all of the laws willfully ignored and broken he hands me a piece of paper informing me that it is going to cost me $2,000.00 dollars to right all of the wrongs. I have a problem. I only have $3.00 dollars in my account, far short of what is required. But that is OK because I am riding with you and I know something about you – you are a millionaire – so I look at you with these very sad and desperate eyes causing you to respond with, "Don't worry Larry, I will take care of it." Now here is the question we must honestly ask, do the courts even care where the money comes from? The answer is "NO." That is justice. Justice demands that wrongs be made right, but it doesn't care who pays for that wrong. Even though this is not the best analogy, Christ is my millionaire. He is the only one that has enough to pay for all that justice requires in order to have the wrong made right. He has paid for it all – he left nothing undone. Now that justice has been paid, it has no claim on me as long as I am willing to accept His invitation to come and follow Him. If I accept the terms of faithful discipleship, the Savior can turn to you and I and extend mercy and say, "I will make you clean based upon my merits" (2 Nephi 2:8; 2 Nephi 31:19; Alma 22:14, Alma 24:10;Helaman 14:13; Moroni 6:4; D&C 3:20). Again, what unlocks that blessing for you and I is accepting His invitation to repent and come and follow Him.

It sounds like then that violation of law is a pretty big deal. It sounds like something that we better pay attention to. I am now going to take you down a theological path that is unsound, as the scriptures testify, "For all have sinned and come short of the glory of God" (Romans 3:23). I do believe that, but in order to make my point, I would like you to consider the following. Currently we have approximately 7.8 billion people inhabiting this planet. Christian theology informs us that there have been t least six thousand years of existence before you and I ever showed up. Do you suppose that there have been tens of billions of people having occupied space here prior to our time? Christian theology also informs us of a coming Millennium, a thousand years where Christ will dwell personally upon this earth. The revelations to us indicate that children will continue to be brought forth in families during that time (D&C 101:30-31; See Also: Isaiah 11:8). Do you suppose that a few billion more will come and dwell here during that time period? Now comes the question – Out of all of the people that have dwelt, do now dwell or will ever dwell upon this earth, what if you were the only one that violated the law? Your answer to this question will largely be formed through your understanding of the character and nature of God. We may receive a hint in the following teaching of the Savior:

> How think ye? If a man have an hundred sheep and one of them be gone astray, doth he not leave the ninety and nine, and goeth into the mountains and seeketh that which is gone astray?
>
> And if it so be that he find it, verily I say unto you, he rejoiceth more of that sheep than of the ninety and nine which went not astray.
>
> Even so it is not the will of your Father which is in heaven, that one of these little ones should perish. (Matthew 18:12-14)

When we are willing to answer the question from revealed truth, perhaps we begin to see something and so we ask, would God, our Eternal Father still send His Beloved Son just for me?; and we can't ignore the second question, because it too has to be asked; would the Son be willing to come and suffer, bleed and die just for me? The answer is obvious.

So do you hear what you are saying? A God, enthroned in yonder heavens with all glory, majesty, and might, the Creator of all things, the Holy One, the meek and lowly Lamb would be willing to step down, for a moment, and take upon Himself the experiences of all mankind, "... he will take upon him their infirmities, that his bowels may be filled with mercy according to the flesh, that he may know according to the flesh how to succor his people according to their infirmities" (Alma 7:12). This Great God would be willing to come and die just for you? What does that begin to say about your worth?

This personal perspective is emphasized in one great Christian hymn, "I Stand All Amazed." This is the doctrinal song that begins to help us understand that everything He did was done for each of us personally. As we grow in this understanding it becomes both wonderful and amazing to us.

> I stand all amazed at the love Jesus offers ME; confused at the grace that so fully He proffers ME.
>
> I tremble to know that for ME He was crucified; that for ME a sinner He suffered, He bled and died.
>
> Oh it is wonderful that He should care for ME enough to die for ME. Oh it is wonderful, wonderful to ME.

So persuasively complete was His suffering that Paul declared:

> Thou hast put all things in subjection under his feet. For in that he put all in subjection under him, he left nothing that is not put under him....... (Hebrews 2:8)

The accumulative and multitudinous payment of generations, past, present and future to His day, was born meekly by the Savior. But this was no impersonal Atonement for Paul continued:

> But we see Jesus, who was made a little lower than the angels for the suffering of death, crowned with glory and honour; that he by the grace of God should taste death for *every* man. (Hebrews 2:9)

Every man, woman and child was personally thought of during this suffering so incomprehensible to any of us. Though the suffering unfathomable to our mortal mind, we get a sense of the immense weight He carried when we look at Luke's description of this moment:

> And being in agony he prayed more earnestly: and his sweat was as it were great drops of blood falling down to the ground. (Luke 22:44)

As I ponder this description, I place myself outside of the Garden of Gethsemane, picturing in my mind what Christ would have looked like as he exited the Garden. What I see is a man of determination, but one who was exhausted from the experience. I see His clothes soaked red because of the pressure he felt as he bore so much pain, so much sorrow; so much anguish associated with our experience here in mortality. Added to the suffering in the sacred garden is the physical punishment of lawless men; the scourging, the beatings, the penetration of thorns into his head; and then the cruel cross where he hung in agony for hours. I personally don't think we would have even recognized him, so great would have been the swelling his body would manifest from this treatment. We are fortunate to have modern revelation and actually hear from the Savior Himself relating to us what that experience was like for Him.

> Remember, the worth of souls is great in the sight of God. For, behold, the Lord your Redeemer suffered death in the flesh; wherefore he suffered the pain of all men, that all men might repent and come unto him.............. For behold, I, God have suffered these things for all, that they might not suffer if they would repent. But if they would not repent they must suffer even as I; Which suffering caused myself, even God, the greatest of all, to tremble because of pain, and to bleed at every pore, and to suffer both body and spirit – and would that I might not drink the bitter cup, and shrink – Nevertheless, glory be to the Father, and I partook and finished my preparations unto the children of men. (D&C 18:10-11; 19:16-19)

Some that are reading this may not be acquainted with the word Gethsemane. Gethsemane means "OIL PRESS." I do not think it was a coincidence that the very place He would suffer and bleed from every pore itself describes the intense pressure required to move internal fluid through skin. The stone press used in olive gardens required a very heavy stone to be let down on the olives that were piled upon in a concave shaped stone. As the weight of the upper stone was pressed onto the olives and then moved on top of them, the pressure of the weight caused the oils in the olive to press through their skins.

Yes, each of us, individually added to the suffering of the Son of God, and yet He bore that burden gladly because He could see our worth and because He loves each of us. Only the Savior can be our Savior, and that relationship is always personal. We go to him alone. He accepts us that way only.

I am not exactly sure why most of my home teaching career was spent working with less-active families. Maybe it was because of where I lived, I don't know – but I learned some things about those that would shrink from being active in the kingdom – surprisingly it rarely had to do with doctrinal or church historical issues. One of the main things I kept hearing over and over again was the idea that they had done too much and that God was no longer interested in them or seeing them as having worth enough to save. Such reasoning is counter to the doctrine of the Infinite Atonement. In essence, people are saying, "Yes, the Infinite Atonement is true for everyone else, but when it comes to me and my sins, it is finite. It will reach as far as it needs to help and heal others, but for me it loses power to heal me."

Hear the voice of one of the greatest Christian authors:

> He (Christ) has infinite attention to spare for each one of us. He does not have to deal with us in the mass. You are as much alone with Him as if you were the only being He had ever created. When Christ died, He died for you individually just as much as if you had been the only man in the world." (Lewis, Quotable Lewis, 248)

And from the voice of one of the Lord's anointed:

> "Not only did Jesus come as a universal gift. He came as an individual offering with a personal message to each one of us. For each one of us He died on Calvary and His blood will conditionally save us. Not as nations, communities or groups, but as individuals." (Grant, Marvelous Growth, 697)

What is the application of these penetrating truths? One of the fixed qualities of INHERENT WORTH is that there is nothing we will ever do that will add to or diminish that worth. Here is my invitation – please go out and become a highly charactered person. Have love in your heart for all men everywhere. Treat others with great respect. Influence others to be encouraged and to have hope. Go and make billions and billions of dollars and give that money away to bless all of mankind. Become so spiritually powerful that you have the Holy Ghost to be your constant companion, that you are worthy to entertain angels and that the Lord uses you in positions of incredible influence and leadership. None of that, not one bit will add to your worth.

Oh, go ahead and make lots and lots of mistakes, Stay stuck in your sins and negative patterns – and do so for years. Be filled with shame and self-absorption. View relationships from a standpoint of what you can get from others through manipulation. Be dishonest in your dealings with mankind. Hurt many along your path of self-absorption. Convince yourself you are beyond saving – none of that, not one bit of it will ever take an ounce away from your worth. None of it!

Why is an understanding of our WORTH being INHERENT so vital? In working with a host of people, whether that has been in church callings or even in my profession as a therapist, there is one prominent feature that keeps showing up in people that have ongoing struggles. That prominent feature is that many cannot see their worth. When our view of our worth is diminished or completely absent, we never produce enough energy to improve our circumstances. But once INHERENT WORTH is understood, feelings of hope, of interest and motivation increase within us and when this occurs, what do people do when it comes to taking better care of themselves? The answer is obvious they begin to use the power in them to improve each area of their life. Can you see why INHERENT WORTH has to be a foundation stone?

So what is self-esteem? Self-esteem is the measurement of the confidence we are experiencing in how well we are taking care of ourselves. We have the power, each one of us to improve in any of those areas listed on the right side of the triangle. So, even if we are a "two" in a given area, we recognize through planning, consistency and effort we can improve that number, thereby increasing our confidence.

Self-esteem is not Inherent Worth. They are two separate things, though they do interact with one another. That correct interaction should always be viewed from the foundation of INHERENT WORTH influencing our care for ourselves.

Here is the problem of mankind. Because so many have never distinguished what SELF-ESTEEM is and what INHERENT WORTH is, most humans when reflecting on their confidence levels in how well or not so well they are taking care of themselves, they confuse Self-Esteem with Inherent Worth. They believe those numbers are a reflection of their worth. In other words, they assign those numbers to their worth. When they view things incorrectly they operate from a completely different model than the one highlighted in the diagram.

If you will go back and review the diagram again, you will notice another model depicted at the bottom of the page. When people assign their self-esteem to their worth they build a completely different model. These folks take their life and place it down as their foundation. Since most have experienced a degree of SUFFICIENT LOVE, I will keep that also in the foundation. However, what should be the foundation such people place INHERENT WORTH on top of their life.

I ask, "Does that look very stable to you?" No, in fact, this unworkable model places one's worth in incredible jeopardy. One false move in the person's life and their worth shatters. Since their worth is affixed to the external things of life, they use their life to prove their worth. Do you know how exhausting it gets trying to prove something that is inherent? I bet you do! Chasing after jobs that promise untold wealth but end up putting money into the pockets of those who brought us in, wearing what is in style, spending beyond our means and living to the edge of credit so that we can buy that thing that will make us feel better, trying to become more knowledgeable than others, out arguing another to come off smarter, attaining to positions of honor, etc. will never provide an ongoing, stable sense of ourselves, because there will always be someone that knows more, has more influence, has more buying power and so on. If in our comparisons to others we ever find ourselves lacking, then we are robbed of empowering feelings and that is why until we understand and believe that our WORTH is INHERENT, our sense of our self will never stabilize.

Since Self-Esteem is not Inherent Worth and we no longer are focused on proving worth, why do we want to improve our confidence in taking care of ourselves? Here are some reasons. As we improve in taking care of ourselves, peace of mind increases, stress no longer has the same impact on us. Our relationships get healthier and happier. We become filled with greater hope and assurance. Hearing Heaven's guidance is improved. We are able to give back rather than being in a position of dependency and we become more refined, more Godlike as we take increasing responsibility for our life. Those are a few reasons why we want to improve our confidence levels.

Here comes the pop quiz to assess your understanding of INHERENT WORTH. Your answer will determine if you get this concept. Who is worth more, you or God? If you answered – "It is the same" – then you have understood INHERENT WORTH. This is in no way putting us on the same level of God, because God is completed. We are complete, we are just not yet completed. We have a long way to go to fulfill the measure of our creation. But our worth is identical and equal. But do you know why that would be? In the words of Joseph Smith, we are the same species as God. God and men are of the same divine, eternal species.

If you can imagine yourself at a zoo looking at an exhibit, we get so tickled when we see the babies of whatever species we are looking at. "Oh, baby elephants are so cute!" "Look at that baby chimp," we say with a smile on our face. Sometimes we look at the adults and go, "Look how tall he is!" or "Look at how strong he is!" You will notice in these expressions we are never questioning whether the worth of the adults is greater than the baby or visa versa. We are simply just appreciating the different levels of development. The worth of any species is the same within the species. Worth is inherited because of the relationship the babies have to the parents. And so it is with us. Our WORTH is INHERENT. We received it because of our relationship to our Father in Heaven (Hebrews 12:9; Romans 8:16; Acts 17:28-29). We are his children and our worth is exactly the same as His.

To get this into your mind, I would like you to picture us standing on a playground watching children play. We are simply observing and nothing else. Suddenly we hear one of the children declare, "My father is the Captain of the local police department. "Big deal," we hear another kid say, "My father is the Mayor." Another kid pipes in – "Oh, your dads work for city government? I'm sorry, my dad is a Neurosurgeon."

These outbursts are evidence that these children are trying to get a sense of their worth based upon what their fathers do. Ask me what my dad does. At this point I raise my arms upward and declare, "My Father made all of this, the universe, the very planet you and I are standing on. He created all of this."

INHERENT WORTH is a gift that is fixed. We have received it because of a relationship. INHERENT WORTH is not something that is earned or expanded upon. Our worth is the same as God's because we are His offspring.

Now that you can see things clearly, now that you have a very clear definition of what self-esteem is, and just as importantly, what it is not – how has what you learned going to help you go and live a happier life?

Some client's at this point have said, "Intellectually I get it, I see it, but I don't feel it." The explanation for that experience is because their old implicit memory has been formed by associating self-esteem as worth. I simply say to the client, "Do you believe it?" The response is always favorable. I then add, "You are on a journey unlearning the falsehood of what you currently believe and then replacing your implicit memory with a correct view of yourself. Today you have been given correct information. If you can only desire to believe what you have learned and been shown, let that desire work in you (Alma 32:27). That desire is demonstrated in doing the homework that will one day unveil all of the distortions held in unhealthy implicit belief. The homework also teaches us how to do things correctly when faced with challenges, difficulties and negative experiences. If we will do things correctly and if we do those correct things well enough and long enough, that repetition will now form a very healthy view or a very healthy implicit belief about ourselves, our true identity; and we will feel increasing power in our lives as a result. More importantly a healthy love of self will replace our fears and insecurities.

THE BASICS OF HUMAN WORTH

Unconditional human worth means that you are important and valuable as a person because your essential, core self is unique, precious, of infinite, eternal, unchanging value, and good. Unconditional human worth implies that you are as precious as any other person.

Unconditional human worth is beautifully described by five axioms, which I call Howard's Laws, based on the work of Claudia A. Howard.

1. All have infinite, eternal, and unconditional worth as persons.
2. All have equal worth as people. Worth is not comparative or competitive. Although you might be better at sports, academics or business, and I might be better in social skills, we both have equal worth as human beings.
3. Externals neither add to or diminish worth. Externals include things like money, looks, performance, and achievements. These only increase one's market or social value. Worth as a person, however, is infinite and unchanging.
4. Worth is stable and never in jeopardy (even if someone rejects you).
5. Worth doesn't have to be earned or proved. It already exists. Just recognize, accept, and appreciate it.

These axioms can be compared to a seed, as Alma does in his famous address to those that had been severed from the Zoramites, due to their poverty (Alma 32). The axioms are a message to each of us; the question is, do you believe it? I have had many clients, after having have clarified self-esteem and what it is, but more importantly, what it is not say to me, "I have never had anyone so clearly delineate the difference between self-esteem and individual or inherent worth. And then they add, "And intellectually I see it, but I don't feel it." The obvious reason why the feeling has not yet developed is due to the strong implicit belief of self that had been formed through incorrect perception of ongoing experience. The transformation of feelings will occur when someone has changed their personal belief about self. It is then I ask, "Do you have a desire that what you have been shown to be real?" The answer is always "Yes!" I then invite the client to let this desire work in them until it does become an established belief (Alma 32:27). The *working* is the key. In Alma's comparison the seed is understood to be a good seed but the work involved in getting it to develop into what it was created to be has everything with how we take care of the seed, not whether the seed is good or not. Interestingly, Alma invites his listeners to not cast out the seed because of their unbelief. I hope you can appreciate what it is I am asking of the reader. Feelings are an outgrowth of belief, whether that belief is accurate or not. Emotional experience is simply reflecting the energy of the belief.

With that understanding, don't ignore what you see to be intellectually true just because of your ongoing negative emotional experience that says otherwise (Alma 32:36). The intellectual awareness of the difference between self-esteem and inherent worth is a manifestation that the seed is a good seed (Alma 32:32). Its ongoing strengthening will only occur if we nourish it with great care, so that it might develop a root system. But if you neglect the seed and take no thought of its nourishment, it will not develop the root system that will establish it (Alma 32:36-38). Most of the work in nourishing a good seed is found in the soil that it grows in. If we are developing the soil to be rich with nutrients and moisten it from time-to time, then the seed has the environment it needs to flourish and provide fruit (Alma 32:39).

Alma's language reminds me of the Parable of the Sower (Matthew 13:1-9). Sometimes I refer to it as the Parable of the Soils, as it seems the focus is not on the seed being sown, but on the ground in which the seed falls. As in Alma's allegory, the seed represented in the parable is a good seed. Sometimes truths, like the one of inherent worth are impenetrable in the hearts of certain individual's. Their ground or heart is hardened so that when the seed is cast their way it remains on top (Matthew 13:4). Many have interpreted so much of their life experience in such a way that they create a soil filled with stones. These are the walls, the guards and the protective measures they implement in order to ward off further disappointment. They want something different, but in essence have covered the good earth with so many rocks that when the seed falls on their soil, the roots are not able to get a good bedding (Matthew 13:5-6). Some may have prepared their soils to be sufficient recipients, but they are not consistent in its need to be replenished and moistened. In time, the lackadaisical approach allows other things in life to consume the nutrients of the soil, for example when someone begins to place their hearts so much on the things of the world, trying to prove their worth through externals, which at times will include behaviors that break God's commandments (Matthew 13: 7). Those that understand their worth is inherent and who go through life operating from healthy-esteem are keeping their soils filled with the correct nutrients that allow the seed to establish an intricate root system that will bring forth an abundance of fruit (Matthew 13:8).

As you move forward through the book, whether you will prepare a soil, rich in nutrients or not will be directly related to your attitude in doing the assignments outlined herein. Doing the assignments from a place of discovery (Alma 32:27), and with sincerity, will lead to the seed of truth about who you really are to get an intricate root system.


THE CORE SELF

We are who we are. I have spoken quite a bit about DNA, or the human genome. The human genome informs us who we are at the core. Much like a newborn baby, the core is fundamentally right and whole – complete, but not completed. Completed means fully developed and finished. A person is complete in the sense that each has every attribute, in embryo, that everyone else has – every attribute that is needed. The core is beautiful, loveable, and full of potential. The inner quality of the core self is of a Divine inheritance. As Elder Neil L. Anderson taught:

> While a child's earthly situation may not be ideal, a child's spiritual DNA is perfect because one's true identity is as a son or daughter of God. (April 2016 General Conference)

The spiritual core self can be counted on, though over time and ongoing life experiences, we seem to forget our Divine inheritance. If we allow the core to be measured or defined by externals, then those externals have the tendency to hide the core. For example, mistakes or criticism may camouflage the core, making it difficult for one to see and experience one's worth. On the other hand, we may equally become confused when positive environmental signals are interpreted as worth, for example, when we wait for the love of others to help us feel our worth or when someone gives us positive feedback based upon a talent or accomplishment. These change the way worth is experienced, not the worth itself.

Some spend their lives trying to look good on the outside to cover up shame, or a feeling of worthlessness, on the inside. If, however, we use externals to fill the empty feeling at the core, we will remain unfulfilled, perhaps always seeking approval, perhaps becoming cynical or filled with doubt reaffirming our already core distortions. Psychiatrists tell us that their offices are filled with people who ask, "Doctor, I am successful. Why am I unhappy?" The answer is found when we finally come to recognize that happiness is an inside job.

It is impossible to earn core worth through personal performance or any other external. It already exists. The person with healthy self-esteem beholds and appreciates the core self. This person sees flaws as external to the core, which requires attention, developing, nurturing, and/or acceptance when change is not possible.

Scriptural References:

Worth of Souls – D&C 18:10; Moses 1:39; John 3:16; Jacob 2:21
Purpose of Life – Alma 34:32; Abraham 3:25-26; Moses 6:55
Personal Atonement – Hebrews 2:9; Isaiah 53:10; Mosiah 15:10-11; Moses 1:28; Ether 3:25

For those that don't believe, there is never enough proof, and for those who believe, no proof is necessary.

— Chinese Maxim

"It is extremely important for you to believe in yourselves not only for what you are now but for what you have the power to become. Trust in the Lord as He leads you along. He has things for you to do that you won't know about now but that will unfold later. If you stay close to Him, You will have some great adventures.......The Lord will unfold your future bit by bit."

— Elder Neal A. Maxwell


THE POWER OF BELIEF

As has been pointed out, each of us form or have shaped within us beliefs about our self. Depending on what a person has come to believe will continue to shape and influence ongoing experience. If that belief is realistic and healthy, then a person is empowered to develop confidence in them self and live in the manner of hope, happiness, and assurance. On the other hand, if one has formed an intrapersonal belief that is devalued in some way; such belief sends ongoing signals that elicit fear, doubt and other power-robbing emotions.

If you are not free of feelings of inadequacy, of unacceptability, of worthlessness, anxiety, depression or other negative emotions, then you have shaped within your implicit memory falsehoods or distortions about who you really are. The truth of who we really are begins to take hold when we realize that the molecule of DNA is the very blueprint that identifies us. We recognize that we are humans, but still, many will hold varying perspectives of their identity. Some see themselves in more positive reflections, while others struggle seeing themselves in any good way. Those perceptions are registered at the DNA level and influence ongoing experience.

What resources does mankind turn to in order to gain insight to this central and vital question, "Who am I?" How does someone begin to get a realistic sense of who they are? What are the fundamental explanations for our existence?

Here are some possibilities, at least as far as my limited mind can suggest:

1. Science/Evolution – Here we see an existence of no purpose. Science has never bothered to ascertain the purpose of life only that life exists as an extension of early events that brought our universe into existence and the ongoing evolutionary battle that has organisms stay in the chain or become eliminated due to inferior adaptations in evolution's march forward.
2. Philosophical – Again no purpose is exemplified except for debating what may or may not be. When we die, it may go out of existence, or it may not indicating that it is more important to debate all the possibilities rather than develop a course that assists mankind in answering the terrible questions of life, i.e., Who am I, and What is the purpose of my existence?

3. Religious/Man's Learning Mingled with Scripture – Varying opinions including never losing existence by being involved in a system of reincarnation that may have us spend eternity in various forms or perhaps being created by God and predestined to either spend eternity in His presence or being cast-off forever to spend eternity with the Adversary. Some religious instruction teaches that we were created by God so that He would not be lonely and so He could have people worship Him forever.
4. Unknown – There is an explanation of our identity and purpose, but we don't know what it is because we have never found the explanation or perhaps we are unable to comprehend life beyond the mortal time-frame.
5. Revelation/Revealed Truth – Here the God of the Universe announces His relationship to us; each of us being His child and the purpose of our existence; that is to overcome by faith through Christ's Atonement and go forward and fulfill the measure of our creation.

It becomes clear that only one of these approaches gives us the incentive to investigate as it provides an understanding of our identity and the purpose of our existence. Here it is belief begins to take shape as there is something tangible to believe in.

The simple truth of being a child of God is revealed knowledge (Genesis 1:27, See Also: Genesis 5:1-3); and yet all of creation supports the incredible truth that all living things have seed within itself to produce after its own kind. That seed contains the DNA Code. We are told that we are made in the likeness and image of God. That makes sense as we are His children. We have to ignore a lot of evidence to so easily dismiss this idea. In a world filled with disbelief comes the opportunity to examine a pearl of great price and weigh in the balance of all understanding and knowledge, how this singular idea compares in value. The only way we could be made in His image is to have received his DNA.

The world would have us easily dismiss this information by saying there is no way to know. The world props up and celebrates the approach of doubt, cynicism, and skepticism. It praises the absurdity of such approaches. It touts that believing is impossible until we can actually see the tangible evidence that supports our beliefs. It is not uncommon to hear from such, "A loving God would never have allowed me to suffer as I have," as a reason to dismiss the idea of even investigating.

Yet, many have discovered another way of knowing. This approach requires for us to believe first so that we can see things accurately. In this approach, wanting to believe is the first step. It is supported by our willingness to being open both in mind and heart. It is constantly empowered through humility; recognizing that we must trust in those that have obtained their understanding in the same way (2 Peter 1:19)

The power of belief exponentially grows when we put forth effort to believe. If we make no effort to believe then we cut-off the Source that leads to increasing light and knowledge. By taking out the effort to believe our only honest estimation is that we have learned nothing – not that there wasn't something to be learned.  Why do people short-change themselves by not putting forth the effort to believe? Perhaps it is the harder path because ultimately it requires personal responsibility. There are steeper grades and perhaps more distance to cover. At times the path may seem impossible to traverse. At times the path requires some of its distance to be covered in darkness. Stepping out into the darkness is the stretching we are required to experience if belief is going to get its results. Doubt, fear and cynicism are the easy path. Most of the world walks within her confines. Those that walk in faith, believing, will have their outcome. Those that approach life through fear and doubt will have an outcome as well, though very different from those that believe. Perhaps we can take counsel from the Master Teacher, when He invited the man who had just lost his daughter, "Be not afraid, only believe" (Mark 5:36).

If belief is a flame, then effort to believe is the fanning that will convert a small flicker into a bonfire of sure understanding. The revealed knowledge that we are the children of the Highest (Psalm 82:6) is perhaps a tiny flicker to you now, but one day may burn so brightly within you that doubt and fear will be burned out like dross. There is nothing wrong with a flicker of light though; because it still provides the ability to see better than if there was no candle lit at all.

If we believe, all things are possible! Sometimes the urgency to believe grows out of difficult moments. When we have exhausted all of our own reasoning and have tried everything we can think to do, there come those moments when we reach out for help. The scriptures provide an example of this process. A father, in desperation appeals to Jesus to assist his son:

> ..... but if thou canst do anything, have compassion on us, and help us. Jesus said unto him, if thou canst believe, all things are possible to him that believeth. And straightway the father of the child cried out, and said with tears, Lord, I believe; help thou my unbelief. (Mark 9:22-24)

It appeared that all resources had been exhausted for this son. The constant worry and fear imbedded in and experienced by this father had created emotional exhaustion as well as urgency. The appeal to the Savior for help is met by a tender, learning response – BELIEVE. Believing is the prerequisite to finding the assistance any of us seek. There was no requirement to have an understanding or a perfect knowledge of all things to have belief operate. The father's admission that his belief was limited; but then the further plea to have the Savior "help his unbelief," was a tender moment of submission. The father then witnessed a miracle, a miracle that he had part in because of his tiny flicker of belief (Luke 17:6). Obviously the miracle performed on behalf of his son would have fanned the father's flame of belief, creating greater faith within him.

To what end was this father able to grab hold of any belief in Jesus and His power to heal? One scripture provides some insight to this question. While placed before King Agrippa, Paul appeals to what would have been common knowledge concerning the acts of his friend, Jesus Christ. Paul declares to the King:

> For the king knoweth of these things, before whom also I speak freely, for I am persuaded that none of these things are hidden from him; for this thing was not done in a corner. King Agrippa, believest thou the prophets? I know that thou believest.
>
> Then Agrippa said unto Paul, Almost thou persuadest me to be a Christian. (Acts 26:26-28)

The ministry, the power and the miracles of Jesus were well known. None of it was done in a corner. The things He did were noised abroad. It is hard to conceive otherwise considering the many stories of the multitudes following Him and pressing on Him. Surely this father was acquainted with the stories of healings the Savior had performed prior to his own plea for help. It was the many witnesses of Jesus' merciful power to heal all forms of physical and mental issues, which allowed belief to rise enough to seek assistance for his own son. An important lesson here is to acknowledge what you do believe and don't let doubt or fear rob you of what you have come to know to be true. Show integrity to what you believe so that your belief can grow and develop. In fact, if you desire for that belief to grow then you must start with what you do believe, not from what you are not sure of.

In scientific research, theory is formed by what has been discovered. A good scientific inquiry never starts trying to prove a negative. Scientific theory always starts with what is known and then experimental design moves forward postulating that if such is true, a hypothesis is then formed as to what the outcome is expected to be based upon the former discovery.

This is the crux of effort to believe. It is experimenting. This is the fanning of the small flicker which helps the flame get strength providing even more light. It takes a willingness to no longer be satisfied with limited belief and understanding. It requires a new heart, a new determination to try God on whether He really does want us to know what He knows (Mark 4:22-25).

> For behold, if ye will awake and arouse your faculties, even to an experiment upon my words, and exercise a particle of faith, yea, even if ye can no more than desire to believe, let this desire work in you, even until ye believe in a manner that ye can give place for a portion of my words." (Alma 32:27)

Alma describes and compares belief to a seed. He starts out with the idea that the seed is a good seed. It is how the seed is attended to is what reveals to us its goodness. Because we believe it to be a good seed, we attend to its planting, to its watering, to its fertilizing, and to removing obstacles, like weeds so that it may gain strength. This purposeful attending precedes the miracle of emerging from the ground, where the seed was planted, a small stem of green. The seed is producing the truth it contains. It grows and becomes a healthy vibrant plant that provides many fruits and more seed to keep the process going. Our original small belief of it being a good seed led to the extended effort of good horticulture skills, resulting in the growing and productive plant. Doing nothing would have us question whether the seed was good. Many of us question our belief because we do nothing to strengthen the truth it contains (Alma 32:28-43).

One thing Alma points out about this process is the importance of the soil the seed is planted in. If the soil is barren, even if the seed is good, it will not have the nourishment needed in order to come forth in strength (Alma 32:39)

This is the same direction we get from the Parable of the Sower (Luke 8:5-15). The seeds that are being sown are good seeds. Whether they get root and become strong healthy plants depends upon the soil they fall in. Sometimes our "soil is barren" and so our small seed of belief has a hard time getting root and thriving. So, how does one prepare their soil? What exactly is the effort that fans the flame of belief?

We must begin with a good seed, which is the revealed truth of our identity, WHICH POINTS TOWARD OUR INCREDIBLE WORTH:

> The Spirit itself beareth witness with our spirit, that we are the children of God. And if children, then heirs of God, and joint-heirs with Christ; if so be that we suffer with him, that we may be also glorified together. (Romans 8:16-17; See Also: Hebrews 12:9; Acts 17:29)

Now that we have a truth or a seed, it is our responsibility to put forth the effort to allow that seed to get root and grow. Because God wants us to believe Him, He has provided an experiment for us to assure us that He never is dishonest with us. We begin to see the parameters of that experiment when we consider the words of Moroni:

> "And when ye shall receive these things, I would exhort you that ye would ask God, the Eternal Father, in the name of Christ, if these things are not true; and if ye will ask with a sincere heart, with real intent, having faith in Christ, he will manifest the truth of it unto you, by the power of the Holy Ghost. And by the power of the Holy Ghost ye may know the truth of all things." (Moroni 10:4-5)

God is our Father. He desires us to grow in faith and understanding. Because of this sacred relationship, He has invited us to come and learn from Him. One of the ways we make contact with Him is through prayer. In our prayers, we are invited to ask Him in faith, believing, whether the revelations through His servants the prophets are true. But you will notice the manner of that asking. First, we must be sincere in our request. We are seeking an answer with a clean motive, meaning we really desire to know the answer. Second, we must ask with real intent. What this means is that we really intend on doing something with the information we receive of Him. Without sincerity without real intention, we are not properly prepared to receive assurance. Sincerity and real intention prepare our soils to receive the seeds He wants to plant within us, which likewise provides the important nutrients so the seed may bud and grow. Here is the problem; somehow we think He will not discern our motive or intention. That is where we make the wrong assumption.

In The Adventures of Huckleberry Finn we find young Huckleberry at this very point of dilemma:

> And I about made up my mind to pray, and see if I couldn't try to quit being the kind of a boy I was and be better. So I kneeled down. But the words wouldn't come. Why wouldn't they? It warn't no use to try and hide it from Him. Nor from me neither. I knowed very well why they wouldn't come. It was because my heart warn't right; it was because I warn't square; it was because I was playing double...... Deep down in me I knowed it was a lie, and He knowed it. You can't pray a lie – I found that out. (Chapter 31, Pg 3)

God already knows if we are sincere. He already knows whether we really intend on doing something with what He would offer us. Part of preparing our soil is in the intention or motive for wanting to know. Likewise we must ask with faith in Christ. The only way faith in Christ can develop is when we begin to read about Him and begin trusting in His words and in His character. Our growing trust manifests in keeping His sayings.

The verse of scripture that opened the Restoration has similar language to that found in Moroni's promise:

> If any of you lack wisdom, let him ask of God, that giveth to all men liberally, and upbraideth not; and it shall be given him. But let him ask in faith, nothing wavering. For he that wavereth is like a wave of the sea driven with the wind and tossed. For let not that man think that he shall receive any thing of the Lord. (James 1:5-7)

Let me first point out, when Joseph Smith read this scripture, the reason it came with such power unto his heart was because he was sincere and really intended on following the answer he would receive (See: JSH 1:12-13). His relentless searching, seeking and asking questions were the evidence of his sincerity and intent. James' promise is available to all that seek to know the truth, but again, the requirement on our part is to exercise faith and not waver on whatever He may gives us. We should have no expectation that the Lord would take sacred things and give them to those that have no intention on being useful with the information (Matthew 7:6).

Be assured that we will not receive in one fell swoop all that the Father has to give us. Keeping our soils pliable and filled with the nutrients so that our seed gets root and strength to grow requires our ongoing effort to ask, seek and knock:

> Ask, and it shall be given you; seek and ye shall find; knock, and it shall be opened unto you. For everyone that asketh receiveth; and he that seeketh findeth; and to him that knocketh it shall be opened. (Matthew 7:7-8)

The Savior taught us the next part of the experiment. Said He:

> For there is nothing hid, which shall not be manifested; neither was any thing kept secret, but that it should come abroad. If any man have ears to hear, let him hear. And he said unto them, Take heed what ye hear; with what measure ye mete, it shall be measured to you: and unto you that hear shall more be given. For he that hath, to him will be given and he that hath not, from him shall be taken even that which he hath. (Mark 4:22-25)

All things that the Father knows, all things that the Father has He delights in giving to us His children. So there is nothing "hid" or kept "secret" that will not be manifested unto those who desire and want what He has. Christ is revealing the process by which our tiny flames of belief may grow into bonfires of understanding. He teaches us that we will receive in increments, knowledge and then be measured by what we receive. How and what we do with the new information is how He is discerning our growing belief. If we do not respond to His impressions or other gifts and blessings he bestows upon us, then "with what measure we mete, it shall be measured to us." What this means is if we respond favorably to His answers to our ongoing asking and seeking, He will give us more. But if we fail to act with real intent, the gates of ongoing revelation will be closed. In time, we may even lose the greater light of belief because we stopped putting forth the effort to believe.

Isaiah summarizes this experimental process:

> Whom shall he teach knowledge? And whom shall he make to understand doctrine? Them that are weaned from the milk, and drawn from the breasts. For precept must be upon precept, precept upon precept; line upon line; line upon line; here a little, and there a little. (Isaiah 28:9-10)

The reference of being weaned and drawn from the breasts is imagery. It is suggesting that much of our sustenance was dependent upon others. But the day comes when we must be able to obtain our own sustenance. Perhaps the early dependency for sustenance is suggesting on how we come to develop a flicker of belief. The consistent, early caring of our childhood develops within us belief; belief that we can trust; belief that we are safe; belief that we have capability; and belief that we matter. That is the flicker of belief, but in order for it to grow brighter within us we have to start doing something that will grow confidence in ourselves to become self-sustaining. Isaiah is suggesting that to increase our belief, our knowledge and understanding of truth (doctrine), we must be involved in a process where that belief grows brighter and brighter through receiving ongoing, incremental understanding, coupled by integrous living to our growing belief.

This is no different than the academic process we go through. What is being taught in first grade are lines or precepts that, if learned, will allow us to understand things in the more advanced or progressive grades. Knowledge is power. The more we obtain of it, the greater power we have in life; as well as the greater confidence we have within ourselves. Belief is the same way. The stronger our accurate belief about our self; the greater power we will experience in life, as well as greater confidence in ourselves. Each of us is His child. When we come to believe that revealed truth, if we will put forth the effort to fan that belief that understanding will act as a buffer when life's winds blow against us. The development of belief requires doing small and simple things consistently and for the right reason. In time, those well intended small and simple things will bring about great things (Alma 37: 6-7).

When I was a teenager, I approached my mom complaining about prayer. I told her that I found no joy in it. I said, "How many times can you say the same phrases over and over again." I told her that I did not look forward to prayer; that it seemed more of a chore than anything else.

My mother then asked me, "Larry, what do you think the purpose of prayer is?" I responded by saying, "Isn't it where you are supposed to thank God for everything you have and then ask for whatever you think you need?" My mom replied, "Well I suppose that is part of the reason for praying.... But Larry," she continued, "What if prayer was really about being able to feel your Heavenly Father's love for you so you would know He is aware of you and cares about you? What if that was the real purpose of prayer was to feel His love?"

I had never thought about prayer in these terms. My mother was giving me a seed. Was it a good seed? My mother then instructed me on how to prepare my soil, "Larry, tonight when it is time to say your prayers, I want you to prepare your heart to receive a gift. 'Prayer is the soul's sincere desire, uttered or unexpressed,'" she reminded me. My mother then taught me that "God already knows what we are going to say. He already knows what we need. One of our greatest yearnings is for us to feel like we matter, that we are known. That is always the soul's sincere desire. So Larry, when you kneel down tonight I want you to address your Father in Heaven the way you always do, but then I want you to be quiet, I want you to be still and I don't want you to get up from your knees until you feel His love" (D&C 101:16; Psalm 46:10;.D&C 52:17; 2 Nephi 4:21; Alma 5:26; Moroni 7:48)

My mother had given me a good seed. She also helped me prepare my ground. My approaching prayer in this manner was me putting forth the effort to believe. I did as she instructed and then it happened, I felt His love for me. I knew that the feeling I was having was not self-produced. I felt His Spirit speak to mine, to hug mine. Tears began to well up in my eyes. I had received what I had gone and asked for and because He knew that I would do something with that gift, He gave it to me. This pattern that I am describing really does work. It does so because of the laws God has instituted whereby we can progress. Coming to the knowledge that I am known to Him, improved my understanding of the doctrine and commandment to pray. There is much more to prayer than what I described above, but coming to know that God exists; that He has the power to manifest His love to each of us individually was an important part of increasing intelligence.

So belief, especially humble belief is fundamental if we are going to grow in confidence and in understanding of who we really are. Belief encourages and moderates our efforts. It informs the paths we will choose in life. The gift of belief is planted as desire within each of our hearts. If we put forth the effort to fan that flame of true belief, we then become more assured that the path we are on is the right path. Mere lip service of what we believe will never have us obtain the degree of confidence necessary to get through life in a good way. Belief must be coupled with effort to cultivate and strengthen belief.

Life has a way of manifesting what we truly believe, especially what we believe about our self. Life's ongoing experience will be shaped by our individual belief. If we believe we are the children of the Highest, such belief has us begin to organize our efforts to support that belief. Naturally growing out of that belief is that each of us is endowed with power to become like Him. It could not be otherwise. As previously stated, all of nature speaks to this fundamental truth. To somehow disavow that as His children we have no power to become as He is, defies all of the truth that stares at us every single day. All of nature is evidence that all things have the power to become as their progenitor. We are the sons and daughters of God. This basic tenet is fundamental; it is the very foundation if we are going to get our bearings straight. This is what the Apostle Paul was trying to settle in the minds of those philosophers, so common in his day:

> Then Paul stood in the midst of Mars Hill, and said, Ye men of Athens, I perceive that in all things ye are too superstitious. For as I passed by, and beheld your devotions, I found an altar with this inscription, TO THE UNKNOWN GOD. Whom therefore ye ignorantly worship, Him declare I unto you.

> God that made the world and all things therein, seeing that He is Lord of heaven and earth...... And hath made of one blood all nations of men for to dwell on all the face of the earth, and hath determined the times before appointed and the bounds of their habitations; That they should seek the Lord, if haply they might feel after Him, and find Him, though He be not far from every one of us.

For in Him we live and move, and have our being, as certain also of your own poets have said, For we are also His offspring. Forasmuch then as we are the offspring of God, we ought not think that the Godhead is like unto gold, or silver, or stone, graven by art and man's device. (Acts 17:22-29)

In other words, God is knowable and if we would use our experience and wisdom, we too ought not think that God is somehow different from us. We are His offspring. We are the same species. He is the epitome of our species, an example of what each of us are capable of becoming. The question is asked in Job, "Canst thou by searching find out God? Canst thou find out the Almighty unto perfection?" (Job 11:7). The answer is of course. When one looks at the bigger picture of the scriptures, it is plainly obvious that God desires us to seek Him and it is likewise obvious that He provided the very means whereby we can find Him. Finding God and coming to a full understanding of His perfections is a walk of faith. Without the walk of faith in discovering God and our relationship to Him, we tend to experience greater strife, more difficulties, darkness and ongoing contentions. We must fan the effort of belief by stretching ourselves. We may turn to others that have already found Him and learn from them. We may turn to others that have met Him and then in acts of goodness have spoken about His nature, His character and His attributes. As we learn of Him, faith has the foundation to be exercised. I do know this; all that humbly and sincerely seek after Him will discover that He is literally their Father. When that truth is engraven within us, and it will be by the Holy Ghost, we have begun the process of seeing ourselves for who we really are. Remember, how we see ourselves will shape all of our experiences.

I would like to conclude this chapter with the words of someone who has met Him:

> We believe in the divine origins of man. Our faith is founded on the fact that God is our Father and that we are His children. As members of His family, we dwelt with Him before the foundations of this earth were laid, and He ordained and established the plan of salvation, whereby we gained the privilege of advancing and progressing as we are endeavoring to do. The God we worship is a glorified being in whom all power and perfection dwell, and He has created man in His own image and likeness with those characteristics and attributes which He himself possesses. (Joseph Fielding Smith, April General Conference, 1970)

When we firmly establish the idea that we have a divine nature; that we are the literal off-spring of God, that correct understanding acts to motivate us to emerge from the metaphorical ground and establish a root system from which we derive strength, whereby one day we will grow to fill the measure of our creation. Such firmly grounded belief assists us in buffering the challenges of mortality and developing the wisdom to avoid deception and the strength to keep moving forward; organized around our true identity.

As we are willing to accept this foundational truth, our intelligence increases. This becomes a significant part in understanding how we live with healthy-esteem as opposed to unhealthy-esteem. Intelligence, as described by the scriptural authors is a characteristic of our species, each of us being a child of God. Of Him it has been revealed:

> The glory of God is intelligence, or, in other words, light and truth. (D&C 93:36)

The terms "light and truth" are here employed to give us an understanding of what intelligence is. They are different words designated to have us understand the same thing. Suppose you and I are in a large hotel conference room. This room has been set up for a presentation. Round tables and chairs take up the floor space, along with supporting buffet tables that will hold refreshments for the participants of this event. You and I are in this room. All of the doors are shut and the lights are turned off. There is no visible light at all, including any coming through the cracks of the room's doors. It is completely black. I then say, "Make your way across the room." You realize that you're in for it as there are many obstacles in your way and without any light to reveal the positions of these obstacles, your journey will be slow and likely you are going to run into several things, impeding your task. But what if I were to just give you enough light that you could see an eighth (1/8) of an inch in front of you? Would your attempt to cross the room be a little easier? What if we were just to turn the lights on, how will that assist in your task (John 11:9-10)?

The example given has us see something that is real and observable. First, light allows us to see things clearly enabling us to manage the obstacles that otherwise we would have stumbled into, that would have obstructed our progress. Second, under the first and second scenarios described, every one of us would desire to face the challenge under the auspices of having complete light. As we reflect on the benefit of having a fulness of light, we are now prepared to understand why both terms are used to describe intelligence. TRUTH IS LIGHT! Our journey through life is filled with less failings, less stumbling when we operate from truth. An intelligent being searches for truth and upon finding it adjusts their lives in accordance with it. In doing so they position themselves to advance and to gain greater light and truth until they become like their Father, the Supreme Intelligence (Abraham 3:19, 21, See Also: 1 John 1:5).

> God himself, finding he was in the midst of spirits and glory, because he was more intelligent, saw proper to institute laws whereby the rest could have a privilege to advance like himself. The relationship we have with God places us in a situation to advance in knowledge. He has power to institute laws to instruct the weaker intelligences, that they may be exalted with himself, so that they may have one glory upon another, and all that knowledge, power, glory, and intelligence, which is requisite in order to save them. (Joseph Smith, TPJS, p. 354).

One of the problems of mankind is that we often blur the line of belief and truth or we confuse fragments of truth with the whole truth. As has been pointed out, we can believe things that are true, but equally we can believe things that are not true. When we come to believe things that are not true, in our mind we make them true, thus blurring the line. Truth is independent of belief. Whether we are aware or unaware of a truth doesn't alter the truth. Whether we believe or disbelieve a truth does not alter the truth. Truth is unchangeable; it is eternal in nature. Truth is absolute and unassailable. Likewise, truth is discoverable and when discovered and implemented in ones way of being, that person is said to have faith. Faith is active! It is the way one does things as a result of discovering truth. So faith is the principle of action in all *intelligent beings*, and clearly more than the law of action, it is also a principle of power in all *intelligent beings*. A person's life increases in power by believing truth and living by it. Thus, faith in God and our relationship to Him has us use our moral agency to abide by and live in compliance to the laws He has instituted for our advancement.

But without faith it is impossible to please him: for he that cometh to God must believe that he is, and that he is a rewarder of them that diligently seek him. (Hebrews 11:6)

It makes our Father in Heaven proud when we use our power of intellect, our mental faculties of reasoning and logic to find truth. He enjoys our endeavors of scientific inquiry, experimental designs, our measurements and observations of our physical world and universe. But it pleases Him when we will listen to His inspiration as is at times obtained through the Light of Christ, through Heaven's public announcements recorded in scripture, through distinct and individual revelation given through the Spirit's power to teach, through His servants and friends the living prophets, through the symbols He has instituted before the world was, whereby we might understand, through wisdom of parent's and leaders that are placed in a position to guide us, and even through a seemingly chance encounter of another that crosses our path (Hebrews 13:2). In each of these ways we are being led to see truth. But the sure fire gift of discerning truth is found in the Gospel of God, now so named as the Gospel of Jesus Christ. Christ is the way, the truth and the life. He is the revealer of all truth because He is the embodiment of all truth; and He came to set an example for how we too can find all truth.

In contrast, Satan is a being filled with knowledge, but he is not an intelligent being. There is no light in him because he does not espouse the laws of truth instituted by the Supreme Intelligence that allows one to become. He rejected those laws. As such, he has become miserable and desires that all may become miserable as he is (2 Nephi 2:27). One of the most cunning ways he leads other to being miserable is by creating doubt about their true identity.

In a world filled with competing perspectives and an Adversary that wants to deceive came a heavenly gift that will illuminate our mind to understand all truth if we are willing to receive it. This is the gift of the Holy Ghost (John 14:17; 16:13). We are told how we might obtain this gift and I encourage any to claim it. Christ Himself showed us how to obtain the companionship of the Holy Ghost (Matthew 3:13-17; See Also 2 Nephi 31:6-13).

The purpose of this book is to understand the truth of our existence, the very nature and purpose of our being. It is to show how we can rid ourselves of distortions, of inaccuracies, and of falsehoods we have come to believe about ourselves. What one comes to believe about them self will shape their ongoing experience. The things we tell ourselves are intrinsically connected to the development of what we believe about ourselves. This book will reveal that so many things we tell ourselves are not true at all. The question is: Are you an intelligent being? Will you come to recognize truth when it stares at you so clearly that you will reject and let go of false belief? In doing so, will you exercise faith thus strengthening the truth of your eternal, unchangeable identity?

"The greatest thing in the world is to know how to belong to oneself."

— Michel de Montaigne

## A GROWING DISCUSSION OF SELF-ESTEEM

We have considered much up to this point. We have set forth what I call, correct information. When we begin operating from correct information, it is like walking a lighted path. We begin to have greater confidence in our journey. It is now time to expand our view of human experience. I want to say clearly that in our increasing view, the clarity is not intended to judge ourselves or others; it is simply an observation that may help us see our current Implicit Belief, allowing us to get honest with our self. It is intended to have us accept that we have a work to do within our self – and that is the focus of this entire book – is to direct our efforts from looking at external reasons for our ongoing struggles and begin to recognize that the real reason for our ongoing struggles is because of what is stored inside of us at the cellular level. Whatever is stored as learning and memory within our cells, a good portion of that has been contributed to by our own self. Our perception of ongoing experience and environment has programmed our cells to operate the way they do. Depending upon what has been learned will have us experience life from a more positive perspective or a more negative viewpoint. Cellularly stored learning is never dormant. Cellularly stored learning is consistently sending signals that influence how we see ourselves, because learning is organized matter and matter and energy are so highly entangled that wherever there is matter, there is energy. This energy is the basis of the signals we experience. That energy is highly influential on the view we have of our self.

In my experience in dealing with a host of issues and complaints, it has become very obvious that all of the issues related to fear of intimacy, depression, anxiety, mood dysregulation; ADHD, loneliness, isolation, anger, addiction, abuse, relationship struggles, etc. are all traceable to unhealthy-esteem. That is why we are having this discussion, and why the most important thing we can ever do, is develop a healthy, truthful personal belief system, as what we believe about ourselves has serious, ongoing ramifications. How we see ourselves tends to be our destiny.

Based upon the above referenced model of building Self-Esteem, Self-Esteem and Inherent-Worth are two different things; however interact with each other for the purpose of achieving a healthy sense of self. Self-esteem is a person's confidence level in being able to take care of them selves; the ability to cope with the basic challenges of life, and demonstrate an ongoing consistency of managing what life throws at them in each of the areas listed within the model.

Personal effectiveness, or the measurement of our confidence in the six areas we take care of ourselves, is detected and measured by ones ability to analyze, acquire and apply knowledge, and then demonstrating good judgment when making decisions in the face of life's challenges and constant change. But healthy self-esteem would still be found lacking if a person did not also believe that they were deserving of the positive outcomes associated with their personal effectiveness. As strange as it may seem, there are some who don't believe that they deserve happiness, and by extension the other outcomes that lead to feeling joy, including a sense of ability, feelings of hope or personal pride that are associated with achievement, trust in relationships, unconditional regard, being paid attention to, love and fulfillment, respect, forgiveness, and so forth. Without the belief that these outcomes are individually deserving such denial will interfere with experiencing healthy esteem. If this resonates with you, it is a very common response when we have formed some distortion in our self-belief. It is something that can be overcome as you do the homework assigned in this book.

Everyone self-evaluates. This is part and parcel with human experience; but depending upon how one sees them self will impact every other aspect of one's life, i.e. how we respond to stress, how we interact socially, our personal efforts, our goals and dreams, our view of the world, our belief about what others think of us, our relationship choices, our career path, how we take care of ourselves, etc. There is nothing more important than an understanding of how our self-perception shapes our ongoing experience.

Unfortunately, the vast majority of the human population is alienated from themselves. They go through life, day-after-day, in kind of a fog. They seem to experience the same routine, the same feelings; the same implicit beliefs, all of this being kind of programmatic rather than ever really being highly aware of what they are truly thinking, feeling, and believing about themselves. For so many, this programmatic living has them experiencing over-and-over again, a routine battle with self-esteem and feeling secure in them self. It is if the person is just surviving every day. The battle becomes self-absorbing, but without truth and proper resources, such individual's struggle getting out of the daily negative perception – they just remain stuck. Because they don't know who they are, because they become filled with so much self-doubt, other parts of their lives are negatively impacted.

One of the ways that negative impact shows up is in relationships. The inability to develop and maintain rewarding relationships makes sense if we are understanding that an incorrect view of our self is going to interfere with social awareness and attunement, because the more distant we are from ourselves, the more distant we are going to be from others. If we cannot comprehend ourselves and be attuned to our own real self, then we are going to find it difficult to relate to others. Instead of having the ability to attune to others, we may simply assure ourselves that others are appraising us and perhaps not finding us interesting or good enough to know or we may continue to find disappointment in relationships as we continue to believe that others are responsible for our, emotional regulation and growing healthy sense of our self. These types of ongoing self-appraisals are what develop a sense of shame in us.

Here is the first time I am introducing a concept that is largely misunderstood. Being ashamed and developing an identity organized around shame are two different things. Feeling ashamed or feeling guilty or bad about going against some moral principle is appropriate. Such feelings are designed in us so that we might stay on the strait and narrow path (Matthew 7:13-14; Helaman 3:29-30). Such feelings are beneficial if it causes us to repent or change. Taking such course-correcting feelings beyond their intent though, has no redeeming value. But that is what so many of us do. When we begin to feel consistently bad for having not measured up to the high standards of righteous living, which are intrinsically understood (Alma 32:35), we then take the bad feeling and convert it into an identity, i.e., "I feel BAD, therefore I am BAD." Another way that the identity of shame develops within us is when we define ourselves by comparing our self-esteem with others that are perhaps doing better than us and then converting that evaluation into a measurement of our worth. Hopefully our earlier conversation has provided course-correcting perspective in that regard. Simply put, shame based identities develop when someone has labeled themselves in a devalued or inferior manner.

Shame is multifaceted. Like the concept of love, it becomes a deeper matter of thought to truly understand all of its components. This paragraph is a weak attempt to have us begin looking at the various ways individuals experience shame, but it does begin to shed light on what people begin to take on as an identity.  For individuals that see themselves through the prism of personal shame; and here are some ideas, i.e., I am worthless, I don't matter, I am bad, I am not worth knowing, I am unacceptable, I am unlovable, I'm helpless, I am useless, end up contending with something that is not real, but don't trust others enough to ask for assistance, for the fear of being judged. The feeling attached to shame can be described as a sense of smallness, worthlessness, or powerlessness in a given situation. Its problem is compounded because the person that experiences shame also believes that others think and feel about them as they do about themselves. Shame has an amplifying effect, meaning that when a person feels poorly about them self; here are some further examples, i.e. I'm different, I'm ugly, I'm not normal, I'm helpless/powerless, I'm not important, I'm inadequate, I am not safe, I can't trust anyone, I'm not good enough to be loved, what I do is not really all that great – anyone can do that, etc., the negative feelings associated with such self-talk compounds the shame because the person frequently is ashamed of feeling shameful.

In our ongoing quest to provide a foundation of correct information, I would like to point something out. It is true that every human will experience a degree of shame during their lifetime. I am not denying that. What I want every reader to understand is that what drives shame are things that are *not real*. Your ongoing work outlined in this book will help you see the distortions that drive shame. Those are the distortions I mentioned earlier that get formed and stored in our implicit belief. I have learned something about human nature. Most humans, not all, but most when they realize that their personal belief is shaped by things that are not real, very easily let go of the distortion. The reason for this response is because we are intelligent beings. Intelligent beings, when seeing truth accept it and begin to conform their lives to it. Likewise they easily dismiss things and move away from things that are not true.

Realistically though, the identity of shame when formed, becomes a self-absorbed, self-centered, and isolating experience. While acutely feeling shame, an individual is not considering the implications of his or her behavior on or toward others, but is solely focused on the possible impact to one's self. This has a tendency, over and over again, to disrupt the process of creating and maintaining healthy relationships. As an example, some shame-filled individuals will turn to behaviors that further disrupt trust in relationships. The ill-advised behaviors become an immediate source of relief for the negative feelings being experienced by the shame-filled identity, but continue to keep in place the ongoing criticism of the person that experiences betrayal. This becomes an awful cycle that is difficult to get out of.

Let's talk about the formation of shame as an identity. If we have understood the message of Epigenetics then we begin to understand the importance of a good family life, as early-life experience and environment has the greatest impact on shaping identity. Typically, shame is bred in childhood. Sometimes the effects of an attachment break (an attachment break is when a child has lost one or both biological parents) can create a physiological reaction of identity crisis and safety, likewise trauma, whether a one-time event or chronic repeated stressful events may severely alter self-identity. Other factors may include when a parent does not spend much time with their child, or when a parent's interaction is perceived by the child to be hostile, or when a parent fails to recognize and speak well of a child's positive behavior, if discipline seems too harsh. Some of the harshness is reflected in parenting styles. Some parents manipulate outcomes by creating guilt in the child, in other words making the child believe that they are the reason for whatever has made others unhappy or why things did not work out, or their being rejected because of a poor choice. Some parents are very rigid, such as 'It's my way or the highway,' or demanding strict observance to family values or a religious mindset. Going outside of or bumping up against the rigidity many times is met with hostility or rejection. Some parents have very limited tools in dishing out consequences when a behavior does not conform to the parent's wishes. Isolating children, meaning too many time-outs, being grounded or sent to their room on a consistent basis can shape an identity of being undesirable, unwanted, or not acceptable. Another limiting parenting style is what I call deficit model consequences, which means utilizing forms of corporal punishment or taking things away from the child. It's not that these interactions by parents can't help teach a child, but when they are the parent's only go to, it develops or shapes negative, self-identities in the child. Another parenting style that negatively impacts a child's belief system are too over-protective parents, or parents who fail to take the responsibility of being a good parent, thus the child having to assume the parental role, if acceptance and love are perceived by the child as conditional, when parental emotions are utilized as weapons and tactical control, when discipline is associated with who the child is rather than the behavior the child exhibited, when the child is consistently humiliated in public,  when the child is told he or she is not deserving of good things, when a child estimates that another sibling is favored by the parents, or when parents create a feeling in the child that they have to choose which parent to love, as is the case in many broken homes,  these all have a tendency to shape an inner experience in the child of not being worthwhile, needed or wanted, and personally undesirable. This inner experience then develops into a template of shame, by which the child continues to perceive the world through, even carrying into adulthood.

While home-life is probably the most influential aspect in developing belief in children, there can be many more environmental experiences that shape belief. School experiences, exposure to media, religious affiliation or lack thereof, predators, significant life events, economic status, rural vs. large populated regions where one is being raised, quality of sibling relationships (Mosiah 4:14-15), peer or friend associations, and behavioral choices, such as reading, extensive gaming, hobbies, participation in activities such as dance, athletics, music training, etc.

One of the main reasons why the unhealthy template becomes established in childhood is because of the developmental limitations. There is no way for a child to cognitively navigate in the adult's perspective. A child has no capacity to think like an adult (1 Corinthians 13:11). As stated earlier in this book, the most critical years for setting in a healthy template in children is from in-utero up to age seven. Here is one of the main reasons why. The prominent brain waves of these years are delta and theta waves. Delta waves, when in dominant position, have us fall asleep. Think about how much younger children and babies sleep. Theta waves are just a bit faster than delta waves and they provide the gateway to learning, memory, and intuition. When theta is dominant we are more reflective, daydream, and can easily be influenced. In a simple term, when theta is the dominant brain wave, you can get that person to believe anything. There is no buffering. Things are easily downloaded into the person. This is what hypno-therapists do when working with clients. They get their client to go into a theta dominant wave state and then begin making suggestions to their client for which they are now more open to receive. Suggestibility is the very state our young children are in, so our interactions may suggest things about their own identity, which they learn and memorize and then form into implicit memory or a template of themselves. How easy is it to influence belief while in theta wave dominance? This is the reason why children believe that there is a fat man that lives in the North Pole, who makes toys, and then delivers these toys to all of the boys and girls in the world in one single night, by sleigh pulled by flying Reindeer. I hope that has you understand how susceptible little children are to their environment.

Here is an example of how my interaction with my five year old boy can influence an unhealthy template. Please pay attention to all of the verbal and non-verbal signals being absorbed by my child. I am a bit upset at how my five year old boy's room looks and so with a terse tone in my voice and an unhappy look on my face I say, "Son, your room looks like a pig-sty. You are to get in there and get it cleaned up before you can do anything else. I don't want you to get distracted, just get busy cleaning. If I come by and see that you are not working you are going to be in big trouble." Five minutes later I walk by my son's room and I see that he has become distracted and has made even a bigger mess. "Son, I am so sick and tired of having to tell you a hundred times to get things done. You are lazy. You are a bad boy." My son is in theta and what I am saying is being received as suggestions of how he should see himself. To reinforce this whole concept, later that day I am making chocolate chip cookies and the aroma is filling the house. My son comes running into the kitchen and I say, "You don't deserve any!" As a parent I am trying to teach about consequences, but my child may have just heard he doesn't deserve things. The scene I just described is what I thought would be a typical scene played out in many homes. It almost seems benign, but these repeated verbal and non-verbal cues are astoundingly influential in shaping belief in our children.

It is our responsibility as parents to shape a home-life that sends the correct messages to our children so that our children will develop a healthy, truthful template of themselves. Even well-intentioned, well-motivated parents many times send the wrong message. The correct messages are difficult to send when we ourselves as parents struggle with our own identity. Foremost, we must see our own self accurately; for it is only when we are able to see who we truly are that we become who we are truly meant to be. A correct self-view empowers us to steer the next generation in accepting their own true identity. My other book, "The Greatest in the Kingdom," helps parents develop the resources in sending the messages to their children that will result in children believing in themselves. Once children believe in themselves they tend to do pretty well in life. One of the natural outgrowths of children believing in themselves early in life is their increased capacity to believe in Christ (D&C 68:25). Have you ever wondered why the age of eight is being pointed to in this scripture?

Shame-based identities are more susceptible to their emotions and feelings. Due to the consistent, intrusive negative feelings associated with shame, individuals struggling with a secure sense of themselves put into operation protective devices that somewhat reduce or manage the negative feelings but do not actually lead to resolve of the real issue. The protective devices put into play by a person that experiences the template of shame, act instead in keeping the distorted (unreal) template in power. As I begin to describe these protective devices, please remember that this is not about judgment or criticism. It is about increasing our observation of human experience and behavior for the purpose of recognizing when someone is struggling, including our own selves. There are four main strategies observed in the human experience that act as tell-tale signs that someone is struggling with having a healthy or correct view of them self.

The first of these protective strategies are what I have called Pre-Emptive Strikes. Pre-Emptive Strikes are designed to divert attention away from being focused on. Here are some examples; i.e. blaming others, minimizing one's contribution to the problem or minimizing one's behavior, accusing others, being angry at, excuse making, rationalizations, justifications, interrupting others, changing the subject, providing deceptive or partial answers, making a joke about what is being addressed to avoid addressing the substance of it, deflecting praise, selectively answering questions, unwilling to recognize the good in others, denying and then attacking others trying to reverse the role of victim and offender, creating drama, gas-lighting, out arguing, etc. These are all strategies that create distance and avoidance in taking ownership of one's struggles. The psychological under-pinning that drives this behavior is the fear of being found unacceptable. The more distance the shame filled person believes they are creating, then the less chance that he or she will be discovered for who they really are, meaning who they believe they are; the fear being, " If someone knew who I really was they would not want to have anything to do with me!"

Another way to escape the pain of shame is to disconnect to some degree or even entirely from one's emotions. Here, the shame-filled individual insists on keeping control of the environment. He or she may share what they think about things, but will not allow feelings to be a big part of the conversation. Constriction of, and carefully guarded emotions are the hallmark of this approach. The purpose of keeping emotions in check is to provide a defense against the overwhelming and intrusive negative responses felt by shamed filled individuals. The act of denying and suppressing or not having to deal with these negative emotions is hard work. Such people appear perhaps more indifferent, apathetic, easily distracted, disassociated, and in more extreme forms of shame, past feeling. For most, this strategy is not very effective, because these negative feelings have a way of showing up, as an important part of our design, which therefore is hard to ignore or outright deny.

A third strategy incorporated by shame-filled individuals is to focus on the external. This becomes a blueprint for perfectionism. The goal is to "appear" by some sort of standard, (i.e., world standards, family standards, cultural standards, church standards) acceptable. However, the pursuit of superficial changes becomes an exhausting quest of trying to prove one's acceptance, never really creating the change that leads to peace and fulfillment. Based upon the diagram in the earlier chapter, those that place their lives down as their foundation and then place worth on top of their life are those that are focusing on the external.

Finally, many seek relief for their intrusive, uncomfortable feelings by engaging in behaviors that provide temporary relief or distraction. Going against personal values, being a bit rebellious at times, leading a double life, engaging in behaviors that may lead to various addictions is also a common response to issues of unhealthy esteem. I have yet to meet a person that struggles with addictive behavior that has healthy esteem.

If any of the four strategies relate to how you are handling life, then it is likely that there is something in your implicitly held belief that is distorted.

Shame is cognitively disorganizing. This observation of how confused the shame-filled individual experiences life is vital if we are going to understand how the "internal conversation" shapes the identity of shame within us.  It is very difficult for someone that is in the midst of a shaming episode to reflect on the thoughts associated with the experience that led to the negative emotions. The internal conversation, just like walking, has become so well-learned that it drives the distortions, which in turn keep the negative emotions in the place of master. It is because the internal conversation is an automatic response, a so well learned procedure that the individual is no longer attuned to the self-talk that drives the negative emotions. Shame filled individuals are simply highly attuned to the emotions of the memorized self, they are driven by their emotions, they make decisions based upon the emotions being felt; they are largely run through their emotions. It is difficult for them to see what is driving all of their uncomfortable feelings. They just know that they are experiencing difficult emotions and so their focus is on how to manage those emotions or to reduce their impact.

One thing is very clear in the research, but not in the shame-filled individual. As life comes at us, we are constantly evaluating life's experiences through our thoughts. When our thoughts are negatively attuned, especially toward ourselves, we form an internal conversation that grows these negative feelings. But the shame-filled individual is not aware of this. Living Consciously is not part of the shame-filled person's experience. This resource of Living Consciously is an attribute that leads to an increasing sense of healthy-esteem, but is typically found vacant in a shame-filled individual. In its place is found anxiety filled analyzing (what if…, if only…, I should, I ought, etc.), or even self-deprecating talk; therefore learning is impeded and shame simply reinforced. Typically the anxiety filled analyzing simply has the person reaffirm that the problem exists because the person's 'badness' created the problem in the first place and the self-deprecation creates a quickly evolving darkening and downward spiral. Just the other day I was sitting at the DMV waiting for my number to be called when I observed a teen walking away from the counter where he just found out that he did not pass his driving exam. As I watched his countenance it became obvious that his internal conversation had been quite negative and distorted for some time. His face became more hardened, angry and dark. He was obviously experiencing shame. This was not simply being upset about not passing his test; this was a full-on attack on his identity in relation to not passing the test. As I watched his father take up the rear, it was obvious that the father understood that now was not the time to engage with his son. Many of us experience dad's response in relation to our loved one's that go around with the template of shame. It is like walking on eggshells at times.

Shame based identities are all-encompassing and tend toward a person being negatively attuned (i.e. focuses on the negative, finds it difficult to see the good, to be thankful, etc.) to life and relationships in general. If paid a compliment, if praised, if given any positive reference, many times the individual will become confused and believe that the person is obviously not informed correctly.

So how does someone who has organized around the distortion of shame, create the scenario or environment that leads to a more realistic and positive template of oneself?

The answer to that question is to be found in understanding the effects of shame. Shame plays heavily on self-perception, which tends to a person struggling with a sense of healthy esteem. Therefore, creating experiences of learning, and of practicing those things that support healthy esteem, are what is needed to challenge the distortions created by the shame-filled template.

Obviously, the Model of Self-Esteem described earlier is part of the education and learning that provides the foothold to climb another path. When someone comes to understand that individual worth is inherent, it unlocks the door of self-beatings and allows the possibility that significant others, who were responsible for developing a healthy sense of self in me as the child, were themselves found lacking and therefore could not interact in such a way that would have led to a better outcome. Inevitably, the shame-filled individual must accept that environment plays a significant part in shaping personal belief. That is the great message and insight of Epigenetics. If parents are optimistic, if parents are able to model healthy esteem, if parents interact with a child in a way that allows the child to practice the aspects of healthy esteem, then the percentages really turn in favor of the child. With these attributes lacking in parents, the child will more likely develop an implicit belief filled with self-doubt and insecurity.

Truth be told, we cannot teach beyond what we are. Many, many parents struggle with their own self concept and so do the best they can without understanding that the ongoing false beliefs are what drive much of their ongoing, ineffective ways in being a parent. As we grow into adults ourselves, we begin to see that our parents may have struggled with unhealthy-esteem. However, this new and growing understanding is not intended in having anyone blame their parents. That is not the direction I am suggesting at all. In fact, if the reader really understands what has been taught up to this point should recognize that their parent's lacking was likely due to their own genetic inheritance and/or their incorrect perception of their own environment growing up. For many, the understanding of Epigenetics allows for greater compassion toward others. At the same time, having greater understanding on how unhealthy esteem is shaped does not necessarily alleviate the suffering of the past; it does not change what has happened, it simply begins to empower a person to take the path of personal responsibility in overcoming the devastating effects, and choose to live, to think, and to act in a way that naturally produces healthy esteem. This transformation's footing occurs by changing their internal environment, the one shaped and formed by a long-term, repetitive negative internal conversation.

The benefit of those who do exhibit a realistic confidence in their mind, who feel secure in themselves – tend to experience empowerment, energy, and motivation. Such individuals are inspired to achieve and also permits them to take pleasure and pride in their life experience and to feel satisfaction. Likewise, a person that has a realistic sense of their identity does not allow mistakes and failures to rob them of the power to improve. They likewise forgive themselves for mistakes and behaviors that elicit guilt.

Let's explore a cost/benefit analysis of healthy esteem to unhealthy esteem, of which the latter is experienced within shame-filled individuals:

| HEALTHY ESTEEM | UNHEALTHY ESTEEM |
| --- | --- |
| Psychological growth expands | Psychological growth is stunted |
| Attuned to feelings, utilized for improvement | Out of tune with feelings, seen as threat |
| Provides resilience to negative experiences | Crumbles under negative experiences |
| Can go deep into the experience of another person without fear of being unknown themselves | Is acutely attuned to only his or her internal state and fears being discovered as lacking or undesirable |
| Wants to experience joy | Works to avoid pain |

| | |
|---|---|
| Positive alignment – can find the good, can find the lesson in the experience and utilize it for better outcomes later, can be grateful for | Negative alignment – focuses on the bad of a situation, replaces victimization for learning, complains |
| More effective in most areas of life | Less effective in most areas of life |
| More creative | Doubts self |
| Appreciative for achievements | Nothing I do is good enough |
| Experiences the world as open | Experiences the world as a threat |
| Seeks the challenge and stimulation of worthwhile goals | Seeks the safety of the familiar and undemanding |
| Meets the demands of career improvement | The less one aspires to |
| More open, honest and appropriate communications | Muddy, evasive, and inappropriate conversations because of uncertainty about personal thoughts and feelings or fear of the listener's response. |
| Forms nourishing relationships | Avoids relationships or maintains toxic relationships |
| Vitality and expansiveness | Emptiness and dependency |
| Inclined to treat others with respect, fairness, benevolence and good will | Perceives others as a threat |
| Interprets relationships as mutually beneficial | Automatic expectation that relationships will bring rejection, humiliation, manipulation, and betrayal. |
| More kind, more cooperative, more socially adept | More anti-social tendencies |
| Experiences happiness | Believes unhappiness is normal |
| Believes in others and is accepting that others can and do make mistakes. Has faith that people desire healthy, happy relationships. | Believes that others are not to be trusted and operates from a position of control – highly alert to avoid being hurt. |

While many of you reading this may find yourself a little on both sides, the point is that when taking a look at the Cost/Benefit Analysis, you recognize that living with Healthy-Esteem is filled with benefit, while the Unhealthy-Esteem tends to cost us too much. However, the truth is either one is merely a choice. Whichever path one *chooses* though becomes self-perpetuating. The beliefs, emotions, interactions and behaviors of those that experience healthy esteem continue to enforce a positive self-concept, while those that operate under unhealthy-esteem tend to experience the misery connected with its traits.

Those that are reading this that operate under unhealthy-esteem, may be in the process of negative self-judgment, after having read the comparisons in the chart, associating the information of the Cost/Benefit Analysis as mere enforcement of their low-self-concept, rather than utilizing the information as a catalyst for change. That was not the purpose of the chart comparisons. The purpose was to activate one's observing of how they are going through life, with a realization that anyone can form healthy-esteem if they so desire.

Healthy-esteem cannot be worked on directly however, because healthy-esteem is a product of correct learning and then practicing consistently the attributes that lead to a positive self-concept. Part of that correct learning is seeing individual worth for what it really is – it is

INHERENT! If we remove any part of the foundation that sustains confident living the structure of our lives will crumble. We will only achieve a healthy sense of self when we operate from a correct view of ourselves and when we live in a manner that reflects our true self. Society is crumbling because so many in the populace are in a state of identity crisis. They either struggle with seeing themselves correctly or are found lacking of attributes and behavior that develop and sustain healthy-esteem. Confidence in our true identity is solidified not in just knowing who we are but also organizing around that true identity. If healthy-esteem is to be achieved, it requires practice. It is never enough just knowing who we are; it is also living in a way that supports our true identity. When correct learning and correct doing combine then the power to become emerges naturally within us. The volitional practices or 'doing' that lead to healthy-esteem are:

- The Practice of Living Consciously
- The Practice of Self-Acceptance
- The Practice of Personal Responsibility
- The Practice of Self-Assertiveness
- The Practice of Living Purposefully
- The Practice of Integrity

When these practices are an integral part of an individual's way of living, healthy-esteem is realized. In the absence of such practices, a low-self concept maintains it presence in the life of the individual. In comparison to this idea, one time while working with a client who was attending the L.D.S Addiction Recovery Program told me of an experience he had with one of the missionaries called to that Program. This missionary said to my client:

> "Bob, this is a program of action not one of going through the motions. The Atonement of Christ is a real power that requires more than just our intellectually understanding the Steps. It requires that we are incorporating and consistently practicing the action steps outlined in the program."

Such is the essence and truth of human experience. Happiness comes from the combination of doing correctly that which grows out of our correct learning (John 13:17). Let us now take a closer look at The Practices.


## THE PRACTICE OF LIVING CONSCIOUSLY

It is difficult to feel effective in our lives when we choose not to accept our current realities. One of those realities is how we are designed to absorb ongoing experience and environment and store our perception of those experiences as learning and memory. Perception becomes stored by the thoughts we tell ourselves, Repeated negative self-talk develops patternistic struggles, which lead to an unhealthy view of one's self. Most people, when struggling with issues associated with unhealthy esteem, incorporate ways in which those struggles disappear from awareness, either through forms of grandiosity or being a victim. Unfortunately, such strategies employed do not lead to resolve and more than likely lead to a deepening of the struggle. Individuals that operate from unhealthy-esteem have not learned that incorrect and negative thoughts directed toward one's self is actually the root cause of the ongoing shame they experience. They believe that their negative emotions cause the negative self-perception. This lack of understanding keeps individuals stuck.

The key to resolve of struggles associated with unhealthy esteem is to become hyper-aware of our processing – being able to look at our internal conversation - even if we don't like what we see. By looking at it long enough allows for growing options that can finally lead to resolve and dismissal of the penetrating "psychological thorn" (2 Corinthians 12:7). That is because our beliefs are stored as matter and Quantum Theory informs us that by observing matter we can change how it is organized.

When problems arise, every human goes through the same process, but because of the Law of Associative Memory, especially as it applies to Implicit Learning and Memory, that process becomes incredibly rapid and therefore we tend to react rather than respond. In other words, we are being driven by what is already formed and stored. Our approaches to the ongoing experiences of life become procedural and patternistic. There is no real high consciousness, we are simply reacting. The Practice of Living Consciously slows down the process, giving us the opportunity to examine each point carefully, which in turn empowers us with real choice. This power of choice then is responsive and not reactive. If you think about it, reactivity is a case against choice, as we are unaware of why we feel or do the things we do.

By practicing new choices, we literally create a work of regeneration physiologically, both in neural pathways and in DNA functioning – a work that because we were so involved in the process through our correct observing, automatically impacts our esteem positively. The only way to practice new choices is to learn how to do something new. People that are organized around a template of shame have not learned how to Live Consciously. This is something new for them, but is the basis of developing a realistic, truthful belief about one's self.

## THE PRACTICE OF SELF-ACCEPTANCE

Self-acceptance is the virtue of commitment to the value of one's own person. Self-acceptance must necessarily include those parts we don't like about ourselves. Those that struggle with issues related to unhealthy-esteem understand that the pain associated with thoughts, emotions and behaviors are undesirable. But rather than spend any time being realistic about their prevalence and presence, such individuals work very hard denying or disassociating from them, as if they were not a part of their reality. Disassociation, distraction, denying and diversion are the ingrained, learned behaviors of those that don't practice self-acceptance.

Rather than creating a disownment of these negative experiences, self-acceptance moves an individual to become a willing partner in them for the purpose of resolve. Self-acceptance is a willingness to experience rather than disown whatever may be present at any given moment. So rather than fight and quarrel with oneself, self-acceptance admits that "Though I may not admire or like what I am experiencing, nevertheless I am experiencing it and I want to learn from it and simultaneously discover how I can change it." Self-acceptance is the precondition of change and growth.

Those that have practiced non self-acceptance for the parts that they do not like, many times create sub-parts of the self. In the adult those separate parts are displayed in roles rather than in being the authentic person. Adults that walk around with the template of shame play out Grandiosity and Victim through the learned strategies of being abusive and controlling, being a victim, or being a rescuer. All those that are closely associated with someone thus organized are easily caught in the chaos of this way of living, assuming one of the other roles at any given time.

Years back, I worked with a pediatric neurosurgeon, a very nice and accomplished professional. Once he divulged to me that he looks for things to do at the hospital when it would come time to go home. He stated that his anxiety would overwhelm him with the prospect of going home and having to face his wife. He shared that it was a no-win situation for him. He explained:

> Upon entering my home I would be greeted by my wife who would ask, 'How was your day?' If he replied that he lost a young patient that day or one of his patients wasn't doing well, his wife would say, 'Well, it couldn't have been worse than my day'........ and then go on and complain about all of the reasons why she was unhappy and how he needed to fix it.

> On the other hand, if he were to reply that it was a pretty good day, she would respond, 'Well, at least someone had a good day'...... and then go on and complain how bad her day was and why it was his fault.

In both of these scenarios, his wife played out perfectly the strategies of being a victim and being abusive. This had a strong tendency to have my client see himself as not good enough. From time-to-time, being made to feel responsible for her misery he would become angry at her, he now being the abusive one. She then would act as a victim making sure her children knew how abusive their dad was, having the children adopt the strategy of being the rescuers of her. This type of environment breeds shame; especially in children as children have no cognitive capacity to understand what drives these strategies.

In children, the separate roles may be forming different personalities to deal with the stresses stemming from abuse or severe forms of neglect. Whether it is the strategies used by adults or the different personalities of children, the truth is that such is being produced to protect the shame-based identity. The work of self-acceptance is to integrate all of it back into one whole. By doing so, healthy-esteem begins to develop and grow. One feels stronger and more complete thereby strengthening self-concept.

THE PRACTICE OF PERSONAL RESPONSIBILITY

Brian Tracy offered this insight:

> "Peak performance begins with your taking complete responsibility for your life and everything that happens to you."

Many individuals that struggle with self-esteem issues find it difficult to take personal responsibility for their circumstances. By avoiding responsibility, such individuals continue to ignore the very means by which they can resolve the negative self-concept they experience (2 Nephi 2:16). To feel competent and provide the key for greater fulfillment and happiness, individuals need to experience a sense of control over their existence. This requires that individuals be willing to take responsibility for the actions and attainment of goals that lead to well-being. All growth depends upon activity. There is no development without effort, and effort means work.

The practice of self-responsibility entails these realizations:

> ➢ I am responsible for the achievement of my desires
> ➢ I am responsible for my thoughts
> ➢ I am responsible for my choices and actions
> ➢ I am responsible for the level of consciousness I bring to varying situations
> ➢ I am responsible for the level of attunement I bring to my relationships
> ➢ I am responsible for my behavior with other people, co-workers, associates, customers, spouse, children, church members, friends, etc.
> ➢ I am responsible for how I prioritize my time
> ➢ I am responsible for the care of my body
> ➢ I am responsible for the quality of my communications
> ➢ I am responsible for regulating my emotions
> ➢ I am responsible for my personal happiness
> ➢ I am responsible for the values by which I live
> ➢ I am responsible for becoming self-sufficient
> ➢ I am responsible for achieving healthy-esteem

When these are absent, healthy-esteem suffers. When these are an integral part of someone's life, healthy esteem is strengthened. One of the most important moments in an individual's life occurs when he or she realizes that no one is coming to save them, no one is coming to redeem their childhood, no one is coming to make them happy, no one is coming to do for them what they can only do for themselves. If someone wishes to eliminate the negative thoughts and feelings they experience on a consistent basis, they will have to take responsibility for doing something different than what they automatically and procedurally do, and do it over and over again, until it becomes the new nature of the person.

One of the common tragedies of those that struggle with unhealthy-esteem is that the adults in their lives, as they were growing up, limitedly modeled and limitedly taught healthy-esteem. Likely they simply passed on to their children the effects of their own low self-concept. The messages children receive from such parents is that they are lacking, or worthless and inadequate. These children suffer emotionally and carry with them into adulthood the ugliness of shame and doubt.

Coping with shame and self-doubt creates many survival strategies including making excuses, blaming others, and complaining. Until we get rid of the excuses, the blaming and the complaining, we will continue to empower others to rule over us, we will continue to stay stuck in our personal and emotional development, and we will continue to attract those that bring us down rather than lift us up. George Washington Carver said:

"Ninety-nine percent of all failures come from people who have a habit of making excuses."

Wayne Dyer taught:

"All blame is a waste of time. No matter how much fault you find with another, and regardless of how much you blame him, it will not change you."

Lou Holtz quipped:

" The one who complains about the way the ball bounces is likely the one who dropped it."

Blaming, complaining and making excuses keep us from achieving what we want in life and what we can ultimately become. To take back control or finally learn what it means to take control of our destiny is to assume 100% responsibility for everything we experience in our lives.

## THE PRACTICE OF ASSERTIVENESS

One of the common characteristics of those that suffer with unhealthy-esteem is the inability to express themselves in a way that has them feel like they are respected; that their thoughts, feelings and wants are important to others and will be valued by them.

So highly sensitive to the expectation that one's most inner desires, hopes, opinions, and emotions are going to be devalued, the individual makes it a habit to not be seen, not be heard, and not be noticed. In essence, they never develop the social prowess that provides the pathway to increasing self-confidence and positive feedback from others.

If one has difficulty honoring their own self-expression of needs, wants, values and convictions, that individual shouldn't expect that others will. If one wants to be known, counted, and made to feel included socially and relationally, then one needs to present themselves as one that should be known, counted, and included. The non-verbal communications of timidity, including poor eye-contact, an unenergetic voice, posture that says I don't want to be noticed or encroached upon, stuffing everything, shutting down or withdrawing are translated in a way that makes others uncomfortable and therefore are less likely to have the desire to connect. Likewise, negative attention seeking in our interactions interrupts productive outcomes. If we are condescending, telling other people how to solve their problems, impatient, sarcastic, passive aggressive or dismissive in our communications, those styles too will lead to conflict and difficulty in relationships. Each of the examples above are all reflections of unhealthy-esteem. Unfortunately, the individual that is sending the strong signal of unhealthy self-esteem ends up interpreting the resulting lack of connection as evidence that their unhealthy self-concept is correct – a maddening cycle of self-defeatism.

Healthy self-assertion is respectful and entails the willingness to confront rather than evade the challenges of life and to strive to become an effective communicator. Communications is how we as humans get things done (Isaiah 55:11; Remember, we are the species of God)! When someone expands their ability to communicate effectively, he or she expands self-efficacy and self-respect.


## THE PRACTICE OF LIVING PURPOSEFULLY

Why are we here? What is this mortal experience all about? What is it that I really enjoy doing? What do I want to become? What goals do I want to achieve? What do I really believe in? What really matters to me? What am I truly passionate about? What am I really good at? Any of these types of questions lead to the process of creating purpose in our life. It is through purpose that we organize our behavior, giving it focus and importance. Through purposeful living we create the sense of structure that allows us to experience control over our existence.

Those that struggle with issues of unhealthy-esteem can easily get caught in a trap when considering this practice. The trap of "what I do or what I accomplish or what I acquire" are evidence of my worth and standing. Those that have a healthy self-concept understand that accomplishments are not the underlying measure of self-esteem. The root of self-esteem is not tangible achievements. It develops from having an accurate view of one's self and those internally generated practices derived from that correct view. It is a correct belief of self that among other things make it possible to achieve, as truthful, healthy self-assessments are the basis of empowering emotions.

Purpose also reveals potential. When we recognize our divine inheritance, we correctly conclude that we are capable of great things, we see ourselves as acceptable and loveable and we esteem this body as an absolute miracle. When we think of ourselves in our current standing and compare it to what we believe we can become; it humbles us to recognize the vast, inherent ability to grow. It is all inside of us; we simply need to begin walking in the direction that allows our potential to be unlocked and realized. As we increase in wisdom, in stature, and in favor with God and our fellowmen through purposeful living, our self-concept takes on an increasing positive nature.

Living a purposeful life requires the principle of work. We work so that we can face the real world optimistically. Henry Ford once said:

"Nobody can think straight who does not work. Idleness warps the mind."

Henry Ford was right, absolutely right! Many people who try and avoid the hard path of personal effort end up looking at the real world through their own distortion. Examples of this distortion can be found around us everyday:

1. I would have received a better grade, but my teacher doesn't like me.
2. I deserved the promotion because I have been here longer.
3. We lost because the refs were against us.
4. I lost my job because of the economy and any job out there does not pay what I am worth.
5. The rich are getting richer, while the poor are getting poorer.
6. A loving God wouldn't have allowed me to suffer as I did.

Hopefully one recognizes the distortions in each of these few examples. It is apparent that any of these complaints do not accomplish what each of these individuals truly desired, i.e. a better grade, a promotion, a win, getting paid what one believes they're worth, having a fantastic lifestyle, and an easy life.

Is it possible however, that what is truly lacking in each example is the price one has to pay through consistent, extended effort to obtain what is really desired? Likewise, the achievement of healthy-esteem requires concerted effort. A half-hearted attempt to practice new things, the excuses we enlist to avoid the hard work, the expectation that someone else needs to extend the effort on our behalf will never create an increase in understanding, the light necessary to stay the darkness, or the hope of being valued. It will be by the consistent effort in the small and simple things that one day will result in our desired confident self.

It is the Adversary that keeps trumpeting instant results, instant success, instant gratification; instant solutions. In our journey to Godhood, we have already lived for eons of time in growing toward our divine potential. We have an average of seventy years of mortality to continue to grow unto Godhood. I suppose that death brings us to the next step of development. To become as our Heavenly Parents is not an instantaneous experience. Elder Jeffery R. Holland in speaking of our ongoing eternal experience perspectively added:

> I am convinced that [mortality] is not easy because salvation is not a cheap experience. Salvation never was easy........ how could we believe it would be easy for us when it was never, ever easy for Him. (Missionary Work and the Atonement; October General Conference, 2001)

When we decide to construct our character through excellent actions and determine to pay the price of a worthy goal, based upon our purpose, the trials and challenges we encounter along the way will introduce us to our strengths. If we remain steadfast, one day we will build something that endures; something worthy of our potential.

One aspect of being human is our ability to imagine. We all have had times where we imagine what it would be like if we had all the money in the world. We dream about homes, vacations, cars, boats, clothes and so on. Sometimes we look at other's success and think about how lucky they are. Thomas Jefferson had some interesting insight on the connection between hard work and good luck:

> "I am a great believer in luck, and I find the harder I work the more I have of it."

The great truth about our imagination is that if we have the ability to picture in our mind what we want, we also have the ability to make our imagination become reality. No one ever accomplished anything without first thinking about what they wanted to accomplish. Richard Bach put it this way:

> "You are never given a wish without also being given the power to make it come true. You may have to work for it, however."

The purposeful life requires effort. When purpose is missing, effort loses its value. However, when we have a purpose then effort expands into a symbiotic relationship in becoming and fulfilling our purpose. Work provides for so much of our human interest and needs. Work provides us with experience, an increasing skill base, and confidence that through our effort we can achieve. It certainly assists in providing for essentials like shelter, food and clothing. It allots for the reduction of depression and anxiety and replaces these with hope. Work teaches patience, charity, teamwork, economics and personal accomplishment that comes from consistent effort. All of these outcomes lead to a growing sense of self-confidence and as reinforcement that living purposefully is necessary in order to feel happy with one's self.

Too many of us are driven by the wrong purpose. Examples of these wrongly driven purposes are things like guilt, perfectionism, entitlement and fear. Others are driven by resentment, anger and revenge. Some are driven by materialism. Too many are driven by approval from others. Some wake up every day driven by their doubts. These examples lead to losing hope and keeping an unhealthy view of ourselves in place.

THE PRACTICE OF INTEGRITY

As one matures, one also develops a sense of principles and values and recognizes the importance and benefit of abiding by these truths they discover. Over time, these principles take on a greater importance, and in extension so does our integrity to live by what we believe and hold as valuable.

Integrity is the integration of true ideals, convictions, standards, beliefs, and behavior. When behavior is congruent with professed values, a person is said to have integrity. Those who behave in conflict with their own judgment of what is valuable are faced with an internal battle that leads to a decreasing sense of self-esteem. Or in other words, when someone goes against what is true, it robs them of power to live optimistically.

Whenever a breach of integrity occurs, the only way to heal the wound is with a return to integrity. A lapse of integrity impacts self-esteem because we are acting against our own accurate judgment, in essence we betray ourselves. Hypocrisy, by its very nature is self-invalidating. A default on integrity undermines us and contaminates our sense of self.

We do need principles to guide our lives, as the principles we accept are not just reasonable, they are true. If we betray them, our self-esteem will suffer. *Integrity is one of the guardians of good mental and emotional health.* As what this book is focused on, you will discover that part of the struggles you have experienced is due to the lack of integrity to who you really are. Russell M. Nelson put it this way:

> Our precious identity deserves our precious integrity. We must guard it as the priceless prize it is. (Integrity of Heart; Ensign, August 1995).

SPIRITUAL UNDERSTANDING – Do Not Skip This

Before we move on to the first practice of Living Consciously, I would like to direct your attention to a speech Elder Lynn G. Robbins delivered at the 2017 BYU Campus Education Week. You may find it by putting the following address in your URL:

Elder Robbins gets to the heart of what prevents us from living life more confidently and more abundantly. You will recognize that many things you have read to this point is communicating the "why's" and "how's" in the development of Unhealthy Esteem. Elder Robbins speaks of the cunning and effective ways the Adversary keeps us from progressing and becoming who we were designed to become by exposing the ineffective ways in which we approach life. Elder Robbins speaks to concepts that work hand-in-hand with each other. Each concept is incomplete without the other. When any of us attempt to accept only one concept and ignore its complimentary pair, we will begin to experience difficulty in our "journey here below." Elder Robbins refers to these complimentary concepts as "doctrinal pairs." This separating of doctrinal pairs is one of Satan's foremost tools in controlling and destroying lives, especially their healthy view of themselves. Elder Robbins' insight will add greatly to what I have offered in terms of growing in Healthy Esteem.

The reason why "The Practices" matter is because they operate within these doctrinal pairs. When we fail to incorporate these practices into our way of being, in essence we are attempting to separate at least one of the doctrinal pairs Elder Robbins highlights.

"Everyone thinks of changing the world, but no one thinks of changing himself."

— Leo Tolstoy

"But this much I can tell you, that if ye do not watch yourselves, and your thoughts..... even unto the end of your lives, ye must perish" (Mosiah 4:30)

— King Benjamin

## THE UNINSTALLING OF AN UNHEALTHY IMPLICIT MEMORY

To uninstall the distortions that can be formed within our Implicit Memory requires our ability to observe what it is we have come to believe. Belief of self may be influenced through genetic, parental inheritance, but it is also conditioned and shaped through the absorbing and storing of our environmental experience. While at times, it may be helpful to connect some past experiences that played a role with our developing personal belief; for the most part it is not. The most important work to do is to look at the *belief* itself. By looking at what we have come to believe about ourselves, we may recognize that some of the things we believe are not even real. Discovery of untruths, distortions, lies, and the like lead to us dismissing the falsehoods and replacing them with things that are real.

The First Practice of Living Consciously is the method whereby we can take a clear look at held beliefs about self and uninstall any parts of it that are unhealthy.

## THE PRACTICE OF LIVING CONSCIOUSLY

As I began to understand the research I was studying, it profoundly impacted my approach of how to help others overcome their patternistic struggles, their negative and intrusive emotions and especially their unhealthy esteem. I still remember that moment when this thought came clearly into my mind, "The key then is developing a system that allows people to *observe* their implicitly stored belief of self." Many aspects of my past training began to combine in a way, which had me realize that this would be possible.

Most of the work you will do in developing a healthy sense of yourself will come when you learn how to Live Consciously. As stated earlier, our thoughts are the most impactful environmental signal our cells absorb, which shapes our ongoing view of our self. The reason for the shaping is when you recall what the Epigeneticists are telling us. The DNA molecule has incredible capacity to be encoded upon and stored upon. Whatever is encoded upon that material transmits signals to the living organism, whether we are highly conscious of it or not. These signals influence how we see or experience ourselves. Living Consciously slows the whole internal conversation down so that we can see how we contribute to our own unhealthy esteem.

Quantum Theory states that all matter is influenced in how it organizes based upon energy acting upon it. Our beliefs are organized as matter. Our mind is part of the quantum field of energy of this universe, and its energy is being exerted by how it observes. This is the Creation or Organization Principle. We are made of matter, which includes our Implicit Memory where belief is stored. By carefully observing or looking at our internal conversation, we will begin to see distortions that have formed in our judgment of self. It is the correct observing of our personally held distortions that provides the power to let them go. Likewise, purposeful and sincere observations while Living Consciously teaches us how to evaluate life's ongoing experiences in a way that that shapes a very truthful and healthy self-perspective.

As my Program moves forward, I have broken Living Consciously into two parts:

1) Uninstalling Unhealthy Implicit Memory
2) Installing a Healthy Implicit Memory.

To conceptualize what it is we are doing, I give the following analogy.

On my computer I have installed Microsoft Office 2003. The latest version is Microsoft Office 2019. I can install the latest version, but if I attempt to do so without first removing the existing software, I will receive error prompts informing me that the install process cannot be completed until I first remove the existing program. That is very much like our Implicit Memory, where our belief about our self is stored. To try and teach someone how to do things correctly without first having the individual recognize what is interfering with the successful completion of the install process would prove ineffective. The distortions of the unhealthy implicit belief have to be made manifest in the observation of the individual trying to change their self-concept. To recognize and deal realistically with distortions is just as important as learning how to do things correctly. Without removing the distortions, they will interfere with the new program being installed fully and effectively. Cellular memory is both real and powerful. To program our cells correctly will require more than just a passing glance at incorrectly stored belief. It requires intentional observing, so that you, as an intelligent being can forever dismiss the incorrect information that your cells have held onto for such a long time.

I am going to now explain and describe for you how we begin Living Consciously. In Homework Assignment #1: Getting to Know Your Internal Conversation, there is a form that contains the information I am getting ready to describe. It may be helpful to locate that form and follow along as we begin this process. In this book it is found beginning on Page 104.

The way we start Living Consciously is by asking, "Share with me a time this past week where you recognized you were experiencing some negative emotions. What were the emotions you recognized? " The next question is, "What was the event or problem that was the context of these emotions?"

Here is an example to these foregoing questions. "This past Thursday, my husband knew I had to be to a meeting at church and he promised that he would not be late coming home from work. Well, he forgot and I had to call him. I was angry, disappointed and felt like I didn't matter."

Now that we can observe cells absorbing thoughts and how cells respond to our thoughts, it has become clear that the vast majority of negative emotions, like the ones pointed out in the example, are occurring due to the AUTOMATIC NEGATIVE THOUGHTS (ANT's) we tell ourselves. Thoughts are converted into protein messengers, which are amino acid chains.

These protein messengers dock to receptor sites on our cells. Information being absorbed into cells is eliciting tens of thousands of chemical reactions within a cell, some of which then promote the nervous system responses. Emotions are simply the result of neurochemicals being released from the end of axons. Electrical signals generate, due to our thoughts. Thoughts are the precursor or stimulating force in opening up sacs at the end of neurons, where neurotransmitters are stored. These neurotransmitters then have the capacity to affect central and periphery parts of the nervous system. Like wise, some neurotransmitters can act as hormones and break through the blood-brain barrier, which allows neurochemicals to be absorbed into cells. One area of the central nervous system that interprets these neurochemicals is the Limbic System, including the Amygdala. This area has been dubbed, "The Seat of Emotions," as a good amount of the translating of neurochemicals is occurring here. The entire nervous system however is complicated and making a simple statement that the Limbic System alone is interpreting neurochemicals doesn't do the complex system justice. There are constantly billions of neurochemicals flowing through neural pathways, in our bloodstream and being absorbed into cells. But in trying to keep it simple for the reader, just remember, every thought is carried as an electrical signal in the nervous system. It is these electrical signals that influence the release of a host of neurotransmitters. Negative or untruthful thoughts about our self are directly related to the release of neurochemicals that have us feel negative. Likewise, positive or truthful thoughts about our self initiate the release of chemicals that have us feel more positive.

The connection between thought and neurotransmitter release should begin to suggest that we have incredible control on how we feel, if we can get our thoughts to be more consistently realistic and truthful. But to get to that better place of control, it becomes necessary to look at our more negatively attuned thoughts and how such thoughts influence our overall view of how we see ourselves. The AUTOMATIC NEGATIVE THOUGHT is defined as follows. *It is the negative thing we are saying to ourselves about ourselves.* Since learning how to Live Consciously is your current focus, one of the best ways to find our Automatic Negative Thoughts is by starting with "I AM." This won't always be the case, but many; many times we can find the thought when we do.

In the example given above, what might this wife be saying to herself about herself that is negative? What is her Automatic Negative Thought (ANT)? Could it be, "I don't matter?" Could it be, "I am not in complete control?" If that resonates then let's move forward.

While Automatic Negative Thoughts are the precursor to most negative emotions we experience, there are two other things we will do in our processing before those negative emotions will materialize. I know that sounds a bit crazy, especially seeing how quickly negative emotions arise, but it is true. Remember, the Law of Entanglement, within Quantum Theory is the explanation for the rapidity of the response. The greater the association, the quicker the associations are triggered. Like walking as an example of implicitly stored learning, we have so integrated our negative thoughts about ourselves that these thoughts and emotions are wired in neural pathways that are easily set-off within us.

The next thing we do in our processing is attach MEANINGS to our Automatic Negative Thoughts. In the case of our example, perhaps the MEANING attached to "I don't matter" is "My husband is thoughtless." To the thought "I am not in complete control" may be "Others will be affected by my being late" I hope you are beginning to see the difference between an

Automatic Negative Thought in contrast to the MEANINGS we place on those thoughts. Again, the Automatic Negative Thought is the negative thought I am saying to myself about myself. The MEANING arises in our consciousness when we stop and reflect on what that thought meant to us. The MEANING is subjective and will emerge as you continue to reflect on the Automatic Negative Thought in context of the background problem or event. Just stick with it and it will come – I promise.  One way I promote my client in finding a MEANING is I will simply say, "Hey, speak to me as if I am a friend, what does that Automatic Negative Thought MEAN to you?"  In giving an example of this as it relates to the wife's AUTOMATIC NEGATIVE THOUGHT of 'I don't matter," I would ask her, "Hey, I just heard you say, 'I don't matter.' Tell me, what does that mean to you?"

   Now I am going to tell you a very little known truth. If you consider what I am getting ready to divulge, in a way, it is pretty good news. There are actually only three things that drive most of the negative emotions we experience. Yes, only three! If we are experiencing negative emotions then we will likely be tapping into at least one of the three things and sometimes two of the three and sometimes all three. The reason I want you to appreciate there being only three things, is that it should begin to suggest that the Uninstall Process may not be as difficult as you think. These three things I have named or titled NEGATIVE CORE BELIEFS. They are as follows:

1) Helplessness – If we ever sense we are helpless, to any degree, this state will drive negative emotions.
2) Unlovability – If we believe we are conditionally loved, or it seems no one takes the time to reach out, or if we believe that if someone got to know us they would not want to be our friend or be interested in us, being rejected, being betrayed, etc. these type of internal moorings will drive negative emotions
3) Negative Body Image – Learning is associative and since we learn through our physical body, sometimes people have experiences which begin to have them associate their body in a negative way. Some examples of how the negative body image may form are through comparison. When we get into the habit of comparing ourselves to others and then concluding that we are lacking in some way, i.e. 'I am not smart enough; I am not pretty enough, I am not successful enough, I am not thin enough,' etc. these devaluations can begin to shape a negative sense of our body. Likewise, if we have a physical characteristic that we are not fond of, something that we believe draws negative attention to ourselves, this can create a negative sense of our body. Mental processing would be associated with our body and for some who struggle with paying attention, or staying organized, or finishing something they start, or who struggle with memory and comprehension could begin to develop a sense that they are broken. If a person struggles with ongoing health issues that may influence the image of the body being negative. Finally, this body of ours is exactly that – it is ours; and when serious boundaries are crossed and someone does something to our body that we do not give them permission to do, that can create instantly an identity crisis and impact how we view our body. Forming a negative body image will drive negative emotions.

   When you have determined what NEGATIVE CORE BELIEFS you have tapped into, simply put in parenthesis the numbers reflecting those NEGATIVE CORE BELIEFS you believe you were tapping into next to the MEANINGS you described. Every MEANING should have parenthesis afterwards with at least one of these numbers in them. "1" is Helplessness; "2" is Unlovability; and "3" is Negative Body Image. See the example in the Uninstall Form below.

It is at this point that we begin to feel negative emotions, which surprises some people, seeing how quickly our emotions manifest. It is difficult for people to surmise that three distinct things occur prior to emotional recognition. Again, the explanation of the rapid recognition of negative emotions is clarified in the Law of Entanglement. The Law of Entanglement is stating that once things become associated, the almost immediate or simultaneous reaction in one association will trigger all of the other associations. As quickly as we incorporate Automatic Negative Thoughts in response to life's events, these thoughts have a long term association with the meanings we place on them, the negative core beliefs that have shaped within us and the emotional response tied to implicitly held processing. That is what is being "triggered" is the unhealthy, implicit belief we have formed and stored within our cells and formed in neural pathways.

No human likes or enjoys negative emotions and so we get busy trying to somehow manage these negative emotions to prevent them from consuming ourselves. The way we look to manage these emotions is through our behavior. In the example we have been using with regard to the husband forgetting to be home on time so that his wife could attend her plans that evening, we see that she "was short tempered with her husband and then gave him the cold shoulder." This passive-aggressive behavior certainly provided a release from some of the energy she was experiencing because of her emotions. Like I said, behaviors in reaction to negative emotions are designed to manage the negative emotion better. But I already know that. For example I can ask the man, "Hey did getting drunk help you deal with your negative emotions?" Getting drunk is the behavior. The answer I will receive will likely be, "Yes, getting drunk definitely helped me with my negative emotions. I didn't have to deal with them." That is why in my reviewing with clients in the reporting of their own internal conversation I never ask the question, "Did your behavior help manage the negative emotions you were experiencing?" I already know the answer to that question. Instead of that question, this is the question I do ask clients to answer; "Did your behavior in any way challenge, make less true or help you overcome the Automatic Negative Thought you said to yourself." This is important because the thought is the catalyst of the sequential responses we experience in the implicit, automatic and procedural self. Since the thought is the catalyst, then I want my client to *observe* how their behaviors associate with their thoughts. Associating behavior with thought is the initial intervention that begins to break-up the unhealthy implicit, automatic, procedural self.

Observing is the means or power that shapes matter stored at the cellular level. I am simply using this Quantum Law to get my client to become a better observer of their own internal conversation. It will be the improving observation that will set in motion the desired changes due to increasing clarity. All of us have the ability to observe our behaviors in terms of how it correlates to or impacts the original Automatic Negative Thought. To assist the client in this part of their homework, I ask the question, "Did your behavior in any way challenge, make less true or help you overcome the Automatic Negative Thought you said to yourself." The answer to that question can be answered in three ways:

1) YES it did
2) BETWEEN – it seemed to a little but not really completely or it kind of did but not all the way

3) NO it did not

In the example of our husband and wife, the wife concluded that NO – it did not. When you look at the Uninstall Form below, I have recorded this information on our imaginary husband and wife scenario in each of the boxes. The very last box in the column is what I call the RESULTS box. It is here the client is recording their own awareness in how their Behavioral Response (BR) interacted with the original AUTOMATIC NEGATIVE THOUGHT(S). The way to understand this last box is to view it in columns. The first column is assessing the BEHAVIORAL RESPONSE (BR) BOX. The top BR Box is the "Yes" my behavioral response did challenge, make less true or have me overcome my original Automatic Negative Thought. The BETWEEN box, if checked, means that my behavior seemed to work a little bit in challenging the original Automatic Negative Thought, but not really all the way, and the bottom BR Box is the "No" my behavioral response did not challenge, make less true or have me overcome my original Automatic Negative Thought.

You will notice that I have drawn an arrow from the bottom "NO"BR Box up to the PLANNED BEHAVIOR BOX or PBR BOX. That is what the PBR stands for in the RESULTS Box in that second column. The PBR Column only has two options however, "Yes" my PBR did help me challenge, make less true or overcome the original AUTOMATIC NEGATIVE THOUGHT or "No" my PBR did not help me challenge, make less true or overcome the original AUTOMATIC NEGATIVE THOUGHT.

The PLANNED BEHAVIOR BOX is *only* utilized when a client marks the Bottom "NO" BR Box found in the first column of the Results Box. That is why I drew an arrow from that box up to the Planned Behavior Box. The way we determine if another behavior needs to be considered is when the client determines that the original behavior they utilized did not in any way challenge, make less true or resolve the original Automatic Negative Thought. When a client marks the Bottom "NO" BR Box I simply ask; "Well if the behavior you chose did not in any way assist you in challenging, make less true or overcoming the original Automatic Negative Thought, what might you do next time that you believe may alter and help you overcome that original Automatic Negative Thought?" The client is then to reflect on what behavior might make that Automatic Negative Thought less realistic in their mind. So in the case of the scenario between the imaginary husband and wife, I would ask the wife, "If being short tempered and then giving your husband the cold shoulder in no way challenged, made less true, or helped you overcome the Automatic Negative Thought, what might you do next time, as a behavior that would?"

At this juncture, some clients may recognize that they are unable to identify a behavior that will lead to challenging or altering the original Automatic Negative Thought. In this case, I allow the client to record the word "STUCK" in the Planned Behavior Box. Now I want to say something here. I really want my client to take the time to identify a behavior that they believe will challenge, make less true or overcome the original Automatic Negative Thought. I don't want the option to write "Stuck" to be used as an easy out. I really want my client to work at finding a behavior that suits the purpose. However, I do recognize that there are times when clients become sincerely stuck in doing so. That is when I want the option to be utilized.

When we begin to see a lot of "Stuck's" piling up, it is likely that the client lacks the resources to handle a majority of perceived negative events. Usually the resources that are lacking are found in one of the Practices of Healthy Esteem covered previously. It is my experience that the one that is lacking in most individuals is the Practice of Self-Assertiveness. When this Practice is learned, many, many negative experiences are overcome.

Now let's take a closer look at the Uninstall Form. In the big box on the front page in Item 1 it talks about and describes what an AUTOMATIC NEGATIVE THOUGHT is, how it forms and the effect of their repeated use. Please read that now and acquaint yourself with what Item #1 says and then return here.

Item 2 provides an understanding of the Negative Core Beliefs that drive negative emotions, how they get shaped in us and the long-term effect they can have on how we see ourselves. Under Items 2A, 2B, and 2C are examples of Automatic Negative Thoughts that a person may be saying to them self, which shapes the Negative Core Beliefs. These are not exhaustive in nature; merely samples of the negative things individual's can be saying to themselves that would shape the Negative Core Beliefs. It is important that you remember where to find these, because in the process of Living Consciously I am asking my client to find the Automatic Negative Thoughts they are saying to them self. This is a new process for most and since these thoughts are well stored in our Implicit Memory I have provided these samples as a resource. If you can't seem to find the thought on your own I encourage you to look at the one's I have provided to see if any of them resonate. Likely one of them will or they will assist you in identifying your own.

If you ever record a thought that is *not* negatively directed toward your self, it is *not* an Automatic Negative Thought. I have seen examples where a client will record a negative thought that is directed externally. Externally directed negative thoughts are more likely an awareness of the MEANINGS we have placed on our Automatic Negative Thought. For example, "He is so manipulative" is a negative thought, but obviously directed externally, not internally toward one's self. An example of an Automatic Negative Thought in this example might be, "I am not important." Another example, "I am tired of her being irresponsible." While this thought starts with an "I am," it is not directed internally it is directed externally. An example of an Automatic Negative Thought in this example might be, "I am a failure as a parent." Please read Item #2 and familiarize your self with its information, especially what Automatic Negative Thoughts look like and then return here.

Item #3 is a place of evaluation through increasing awareness. In the Uninstall Process I am trying to take my client out of the self-defeating, patternistic implicit responses that continue to keep them stuck. By deepening or expanding their ability to observe their own process, unlocks the power to gain a sense of control and to create the changes in their Implicit Memory they are seeking. No one ever asks the question asked in Item # 3, but when they do, it alerts them to other possibilities. Even if they recognize that their original behavior did not help them challenge the original Automatic Negative Thought they are led to *continuing observing* when they are asked to consider what behavior might lead to challenging the original Automatic Negative Thought. After reading Item #3 return here.

Before I give you your first assignment, please make sure to review the Uninstall Form below (Pg. 104) and how the first column is filled out in relation to the husband – wife scenario we used as an example. Recall that the first question that is asked prior to doing a column is, "Was there a recent time when you recognized you were experiencing negative emotions?" Negative emotions are the cue to fill out a column. The fictional wife used in the scenario recognized that she felt anger, disappointment, being disrespected or unimportant (See the Emotional Box). The context of those emotions was her husband forgetting to get home on time so that she could attend to her responsibilities that night at church (See the My Problem Is Box). Her Automatic Negative Thought in her mind was, "I don't matter," and "I am not in complete control" (See the Automatic Negative Thought in My Mind Was Box). The two meanings to the Automatic Negative Thoughts she discovered were "My husband is thoughtless" followed by the #2 in parenthesis. Her recording of #2 has her recognize that she is tapping into a sense of Unlovability in her meaning. The second recorded meaning was, "Others will be impacted by my being late" followed by the numbers 1 and 3 in parenthesis. Her recording of numbers 1 and 3 has her recognize that she is tapping into a sense of being helpless and having a negative sense of her body in her meaning (See the What Did My Automatic Negative Thought Mean to Me Box). Her Behavioral Response to the Negative Emotions was "I was short tempered with my husband and then gave him the cold shoulder" (See the Behavioral Response Box).

After filling out the Behavioral Response, the wife evaluates in the last box whether her behavior in any way helped her challenge, make less true or overcome her original Automatic Negative Thought, She concludes it did not and so she marks the Bottom BR Box, this is the NO BR Box (See the Results of My Behavior Box). Because she marked the NO BR Box, she is asked, "Well if being short tempered with your husband and giving him the cold shoulder does not help challenge, make less true or overcome the original Automatic Negative Thought(s), what might you do next time, as a behavior, that would challenge, make less true or overcome the original Automatic Negative Thought?" At this point the wife decides that "Be forgiving, but still be assertive – inviting an emotional connection" would challenge the original Automatic Negative Thought (See the Planned Behavior Box).

Please notice that there is no discussion on the person's reporting. We are not trying to judge her awareness nor are we trying to provide her any solutions. This is a process that simply has her begin to observe her own Internal Conversation. This is a very different approach from traditional therapeutic models but remember, I am approaching the process of change from sound scientific concepts found in Quantum Theory. Quantum Theory explains how all of nature is influenced. Each of us is part of nature. Each of us is made of matter. Our belief about how we see ourselves is stored as matter, both in neural pathways as well as being encoded upon the molecule of DNA. Matter is influenced in how it organizes, how it is shaped and how it behaves based upon how it is observed. This then is the foundation of the homework that I assign. The homework is designed so that an individual can begin seeing what they have come to believe about them self. It will be the individual observing that will result in better outcomes, because the individual will begin to see for them self the distortions that have been shaped within them due to their ongoing, negative internal conversation.

Because I believe in and trust Quantum Theory, I want you to know that I have no agenda for you or for any of my clients. I am in no way trying to create a cookie cutter outcome for everyone that comes and seeks my assistance. While each of us shares a true identity, agency, or the power to choose our life is something that is sacred and should never be tampered with. As I have done this program for over six years with a few hundred clients, it has become apparent to me that as individuals come to see themselves accurately, they almost instinctively (INTELLIGENTLY) make the changes that allow them to live life with more confidence and happiness. That is why I do not have any agenda for any person completing my program.

The INTERNAL CONVERSATION associated with Unhealthy Esteem is filled with distortions. In fact, each piece of that negative internal conversation has distortions within it. The homework is designed to have you recognize the distortions that are stored in your Implicit Memory that are driving the struggle of not seeing yourself in a more positive light.

As the Program unfolds, we will first focus on the Behavioral aspect of the Internal Conversation. What we are trying to discover is the principle behind why some Behaviors do challenge Automatic Negative Thoughts and others do not. There is a KEY that when finally in your possession will never have you question how to select behaviors that will improve your self-identity. When you prove through your homework that the KEY is real and that you have control of it, we will move onto the emotional aspect of the internal conversation.

Most people that have been operating from unhealthy esteem have become highly acquainted with the constant companionship of Negative Emotions. Their hyper focus on these emotions has trapped them into a pattern of working hard to avoid the pain of them. It is this incorrect focus that has them remain stuck in the unhealthy view of their identity. A correct view of emotions, including Negative Emotions alters perspective and has us begin interacting with these Negative Emotions correctly. When we do so, their power and unhealthy influence wanes and we now grow in appreciation of our design.

Once we have accepted *why* Negative Emotions are designed in us, we tackle the Negative Core Beliefs that are associated with unhealthy esteem. These Negative Core Beliefs drive shame and all of the Negative Emotions associated thereto. Through a process of collecting information from your family, friends, and others, including children, you will easily dismiss the distortions inherent in the Negative Core Beliefs. This is where I have heard many clients exclaim, "That's not even real!"

The last piece of the Internal Conversation is the Thoughts we incorporate that are so negatively turned toward ourselves. You will learn why Thoughts have so much power and influence in how we end up seeing ourselves. You will also clearly see why AUTOMATIC NEGATIVE THOUGHTS are so distorted.

HOMEWORK ASSIGNMENT #1 – Getting To Know Your Internal Conversation

So here is your homework. In the coming week, I want you to complete ten of the columns found in the Uninstall Form. Part of the requirement in completing the ten columns is to do a minimum of one a day. There is a reason for this requirement. I have discovered that one's ability to increase awareness of their implicitly held patterns and belief increase exponentially when they are trying to pay attention to it on a daily basis. Without even understanding the path I am leading you down, your willingness to follow my advice will naturally improve how you handle the stresses and disappointments of life.

What gets you to write a column? Whenever you recognize that you are having a negative emotion. That is the cue that your internal conversation is active and contributing to your emotional reaction. The better you pay attention to any and all of your negative emotions being experienced, the quicker the learning curve. Recording all of the emotions experienced in the moment is what I am inviting you to do. Listing one emotion, like "frustration," is usually an indicator that your best effort is not being put forth.

Another way minimum effort is recognized is when a client will return with only two or three of these columns filled out that first week. They will say something like, "I know I had a negative emotion, but by the time I got around to writing a column I had forgotten about it." To these people I say, "I know it is difficult to carry around these columns in order to record that moment. Some people will buy a small spiral pocket notebook to quickly jot down enough information that will have them remember what to write in the column, maybe later that evening."

Other clients will report that it was a pretty good week and that they didn't really experience many negative emotions. It's like a disconnect; the individual that comes to my office or even the person that picks up this book does so because they have grown tired of the persistent negative emotions and when asked to go and record their internal conversation related thereto, suddenly they have stopped having persistent negative emotions. More than likely, such individuals do not want to look because they don't like what they see. Self-Denial rather than Self-Acceptance has contributed to their remaining stuck. For these people I have got some information, even healthy-esteemed people experience negative emotions daily. Healthy esteemed people though understand the Practice of Living Consciously and therefore regulate that emotion quickly, but still there was a negative internal conversation that led to that moment.

It may also be that the client may not recognize that their reactive behavior to disassociate quickly from the negative emotion is what has them deny that they experienced a negative emotion. Emotional limiting, disassociation or stuffing does not mean that the negative emotion did not occur. Some clients will conclude that though the negative emotion did occur, they quickly judge it as something that is not that big of deal, so they don't write about it. That is where I tell the client, "The assignment is not asking us to be selective in what negative emotions we will write a column about or not. The assignment is simply to write a column when a negative emotion is experienced; no mater how insignificant the event is judged to be." We are not looking for anything. We are only having you come to realize that you do have an internal conversation going on and what that internal conversation looks like. The internal conversation is filled with energy that is impacting the wave energy of our cells. Wave energy influences chemical reactions within the cell, meaning what proteins and enzymatic responses are occurring within the cell. It is the chemical reactions that are shaping or reinforcing matter's organization.

The final group of "emotional deniers" are those that are grandiose. Grandiosity is such a well-learned strategy in some individuals that they can not bring themselves to admit that there is anything wrong, except with others. I stated earlier that Grandiosity and being a Victim can so distort reality, but the individuals that have adopted these strategies may not be able to even recognize things as they really are (Jacob 4:13), meaning they cannot see their own negative moorings. Remember, Grandiosity says, "There is nothing wrong with me" and being a Victim says, "It is not my fault."

Since the Uninstall Form is what keeps your homework organized, you may copy the form from your book or you can go to my website: dixiefamilyskillscenter.com and download the form there. It is found under the tab; HELPFUL FORMS

# UNINSTALLING UNHEALTHY IMPLICIT MEMORY

1. *Automatic Negative Thoughts* arise in the mind, are quick and are words that are negatively pointed toward our self. They are associated with distress. These thoughts originate with self-defeating, negative processing, that become established Core Beliefs.

2. *Negative Core Beliefs* deal with helplessness, un-lovability and/or a negative image of our body; and can be painful. These Negative Core Beliefs are rigid, over-generalized and are believed to be true. They have developed by repeated messages we tell ourselves.

   A. Helpless core beliefs: I am inadequate, I am a failure, I am powerless, I am vulnerable, I feel out of control, I am incapable, I am dumb
   B. Unlovable core beliefs: I am unlikable, I am unwanted, I am bad, I am defective, I am only acceptable when I do something correct, I am unattractive
   C. Negative body image: I am ugly, I am disgusting, No one would ever want me. I'm gross, I'm broken

3. *Results:* Does my behavior in any way challenge, make less true or help me overcome the **ANT**?

## EXERCISES

| Date: | Date: | Date: |
|---|---|---|
| My Problem Is?<br><br>My husband forgot that I had a meeting at church. | My Problem Is? | My Problem Is? |
| My Automatic Negative Thought (ANT) in My Mind Was?<br><br>I don't matter<br>I am not in complete control | My Automatic Negative Thought (ANT) in My Mind Was? | My Automatic Negative Thought (ANT) in My Mind Was? |
| What Did My Automatic Thought Mean to Me?<br><br>Core Belief Option –<br>1. Helpless<br>2. Unlovable<br>3. Negative Body Image<br><br>My husband is thoughtless (2)<br><br>Others will be affected by my being late (1,3) | What Did My Automatic Thought Mean to Me?<br><br>Core Belief Option –<br>1. Helpless<br>2. Unlovable<br>3. Negative Body Image | What Did My Automatic Thought Mean to Me?<br><br>Core Belief Option –<br>1. Helpless<br>2. Unlovable<br>**3.** Negative Body Image |

| My Emotional Reaction to the Thought | My Emotional Reaction to the Thought | My Emotional Reaction to the Thought |
|---|---|---|
| Anger, disappointed, disrespected or unimportant | | |
| My Behavioral Response | My Behavioral Response | My Behavioral Response |
| I was short tempered with my husband and then gave him the cold shoulder<br><br>P | | |
| Planned Behavioral Response | Planned Behavioral Response | Planned Behavioral Response |
| Be forgiving but still be assertive – inviting an emotional connection | | |
| Results of My Behavior<br><br>Yes: Helped Solve My ANT<br>  BR ☐ PBR ☐<br>  Between ☐<br>No: Reinforced My Negative<br>ANT        BR ☒ PBR ☐ | Results of My Behavior<br><br>Yes: Helped Solve My ANT<br>  BR ☐ PBR ☐<br>  Between ☐<br>No: Reinforced My Negative<br>ANT        BR ☐ PBR ☐ | Results of My Behavior<br><br>Yes: Helped Solve My ANT<br>  BR ☐ PBR ☐<br>  Between ☐<br>No: Reinforced My Negative<br>ANT        BR ☐ PBR ☐ |

NOTE: The Automatic Negative Thought (ANT) is what I am saying to myself about myself that is negative. You can find many examples of these in the big box on the front page under 2a, 2b, and 2c.

REVIEWING HOMEWORK ASSIGNMENT #1

If you were sitting in my office, getting ready to report on your homework, you would hear me say, "My Problem Is?" Starting with the first column you wrote you simply read what you recorded in that box.

I then ask, "The Automatic Negative Thought in My Mind Was?" You simply read what you recorded in that box.

I then say, "What Did My Thought Mean to Me?" You simply read what you wrote in that box and then state the numbers you recorded in the parenthesis at the end of each meaning.

I then ask, "What Were the Emotions You Felt?" You then read the emotions you recorded in that box.

I then ask, "What Did You Do as A Behavior?" You then read what you wrote in that box.

I then ask, "Did This Behavior In Any Way Challenge, Make Less True, Or Help You Overcome The Original Automatic Negative Thought?" You then tell me which box you checked in the Results Box, i.e., Yes BR Box, Between Box, or No BR Box.

If you marked the Bottom BR Box or the NO BR Box, I then ask, "Well if Your Behavior Did not Help You Overcome, Challenge Or Make Less True The Original Automatic Negative Thought, What Might You Do As A Behavior Next Time That You Believe Would Lead To Challenging, Making Less True or Overcoming the Original Automatic Negative Thought? You then tell me what you recorded in the Planned Behavior Box. Again, there is no judgment on my part if whether the Planned Behavior would work or not. This is just simply a recognition that there are choices available to us that may indeed lead to challenging the original Automatic Negative Thought.

At times a client may honestly be unable to find a Planned Behavioral Response. If that is the case then simply write the word "STUCK" in the Planned Behavioral Response Box. I want to caution the reader here. Please do not use the word "STUCK" as a means to be lazy. I am training your awareness and I am asking you to stick with observing or finding a behavior that may alter in some way the original Automatic Negative Thought. However, there are times when an individual cannot seem to come up with a behavior in relation to altering the original Automatic Negative Thought and if that is the case with you then go ahead and put the word "Stuck" in the Planned Behavioral Box. If quite a few "Stuck's" show up here, then likely the client is lacking resources or is not being as sincere in their efforts as I am inviting them to be.

We simply repeat this process for all ten completed columns. The first time in reporting on your homework, I would like you to observe and acknowledge any patterns you see in your internal conversation. Patterns can be detected in any of the areas of our internal conversation. For example, you may find that you have a tendency toward certain Automatic Negative Thoughts or that you are more prone to one of the Negative Core Beliefs. Perhaps you discover that you experience one or two emotions more often than others, like anger, or you may recognize strong patterns in the behaviors you choose. Perhaps you find that you withdraw a lot or you confront a lot. Just simply pay attention to the patterns. Ask yourself the question. Are these patterns more recent in my life or do they appear to be a long-time pattern, perhaps reaching back to my childhood? Another question to ask yourself is whether you recognize these patterns in your parents as well or even siblings?

**NOTE:** DO NOT THROW OUT ANY OF THE COLUMNS YOU HAVE WRITTEN. YOU WILL NEED THEM FOR FUTURE ASSIGNMENTS

HOMEWORK ASSIGNMENT #2 – Oh That Pesky Internal Conversation

Go and complete ten more columns just as you did in the first homework assignment.

REVIEWING HOMEWORK ASSIGNMENT #2

Many clients report that the second week was a better week; better in terms that their increasing awareness of their internal conversation allowed them to catch the negative process and reason through what they were experiencing to the extent that they, themselves challenged the Automatic Negative Thoughts in the moment. These outcomes are evidence of Quantum Theory and the power that comes with observing.

At this point we simply review the columns in the same manner as we did when we were reviewing the first week's homework columns.

"My Problem Is?" You simply read what you recorded in that box.

I then ask, "The Automatic Negative Thought in My Mind Was?" You simply read what you recorded in that box.

I then say, "What Did My Thought Mean to Me?" You simply read what you wrote in that box and then state the numbers you recorded in the parenthesis at the end of each meaning.

I then ask, "What Were the Emotions You Felt?" You then read the emotions you recorded in that box.

I then ask, "What Did You Do as A Behavior?" You then read what you wrote in that box.

I then ask, "Did This Behavior In Any Way Challenge, Make Less True, Or Help you Overcome the Original Automatic Negative Thought?" You then tell me which box you checked, i.e., Yes BR Box, Between Box, or No BR Box.

If you marked the Bottom BR Box or the NO BR Box, I then ask, "Well if Your Behavior Did Not Help You Overcome, Challenge Or Make Less True The Original Automatic Negative Thought, What Might You Do As A Behavior Next Time That You Believe Would Lead To Challenging, Making Less True Or Overcoming The Original Automatic Negative Thought? You then tell me what you recorded in the Planned Behavior Box. We complete this process for all ten columns.

We repeat this for all ten columns, because doing so helps you become highly aware of the internal conversation itself, which in turn empowers you to gain control of it. Knowing it exists has you avoid denial and encourages you to take responsibility for overcoming what has been present in your memorized, procedural self that you have not admired or enjoyed.

Our main focus currently in the internal conversation is the Behavioral Response. As you have reviewed your columns you have been asked to assess whether the Behavioral Responses you are displaying in any way challenge, make less true or help you overcome the Automatic Negative Thought. From my experience, most clients predominately have recorded behaviors that more likely just keep the Automatic Negative Thought in place. Yet, typically, there have been some Behavioral Responses that have led to the client checking either the BETWEEN BOX or even the YES BOX. Hopefully you are inquisitive enough to be asking the question, "Why do some behaviors keep the Automatic Negative Thought in place while others tend to challenge them completely or at least to some degree? The KEY of why some behaviors challenge Automatic Negative Thoughts and others do not is understood in the research of Eric Berne.

Eric Berne is noted as being an incredible researcher. He is best known in the field of psychology and his research has helped clinicians to become better practitioners. One of his most insightful research projects was titled, "Transactional Analysis." Transactional Analysis focuses on social interactions. Eric Berne simply stated that when we are interacting socially we are *transacting* in the process. Our transactions are being driven or supported by one of three Ego States. The Ego State is reflective of different types of energy; whichever one we are in is predictive of the outcome of the transaction.

I have adapted Eric Berne's research in a way that keeps things simple. The three Ego States with their associated energy are as follows:

1) The Parent Ego State – Insecure Energy
2) The Child Ego State – Insecure Energy
3) The Adult Ego State – Secure Energy

The Parent Ego State (I'm OK You're Not) – operates from a one-up position. This is the controlling, micro-managing parent. While in the Parent Ego State we find ourselves in a position to be telling others what to do, or lecturing, or interrogating for the purpose of proving our superiority. We are operating from a self-imposed higher position. Sometimes we may find ourselves going in and saving others or doing too much for others; or manipulating others through guilt tripping. We do these types of things because we don't believe in others and so we feel like we have to take control of everything. Those that struggle with issues related to control will likely find themselves in the Parent Ego State often when dealing with or transacting with others.

The Child Ego State (You're OK I'm Not) – operates from the opposite vantage point; that of the one-down position. Think about how children negotiate in getting what they want. Sometimes children will try and manipulate others if they believe they may have an upper hand, i.e., "It's my ball and if you don't play the way I want to then I will take my ball and go home." Sometimes children will become angry and fight back if they don't get their way. Children can be persistent if they believe through their persistence they can eventually obtain what they want. You see this persistence in children when they have been told "No" by a parent. They will meet the resistance with persistent questions of "Why?" or "Why Not?" They are trying to obtain the background or decision making in the unwanted answer so that they can persist in overcoming the objection. However, if the child does not believe they have enough power, then children have very little stamina and you will find that the child has a strong tendency to give-up, withdraw or disassociate from their problems. Impulsivity is the hallmark of a child's response to stress.

The Adult Ego State (I'm OK You're OK) – operates from a place of value and consideration. The Adult Ego State individual recognizes their own worth and cares for them self. This healthy perspective however is not lost just on the individual. The person operating from the Adult Ego State recognizes that whomever they are interacting (transacting) with likewise has the same value or worth and therefore naturally demonstrates incredible consideration and care for others. They choose words and tones and facial expressions that consistently send the message of care and worth, both for self and for the other person.

In helping clients understand whether they are in the Adult Ego State or not, I have come up with a little saying. I have every client verbally repeat this saying. I have discovered when a client has this little saying within them it helps increase their awareness in difficult or negative moments to be more responsive in their behavior. This is the saying:

I Care <u>Very Much</u> For Myself, But I Also Care <u>Very Much</u> For You.

· I don't want you to lightly pass on this statement. Though the saying is simple, I have underlined the words "Very Much" to have you consider the true level of care that is represented in the Adult Ego State. When we begin to reflect on the quality of this self and other caring, we begin to consider how we interact or transact, both with our self and others.

So, let's see if Eric Berne knew what he was talking about. At this point I want you to go to the Behavioral Response Box in the columns. Read your Behavioral Response and then ask yourself what Ego State you believe you were transacting from. Write that Ego State in the smaller box contained in the Behavioral Response Box. The smaller box should be filled in with:

P: If you assessed you were operating from the controlling Parent Ego State
C: If you assessed you were operating from the Child Ego State
A: If you assessed you were operating from the Adult Ego State

After you enter one of the above letters, then review whether that behavior helped you in any way overcome, make less true or challenge the Automatic Negative Thought. That is done by going to the Results Box at the bottom in the same column. Keep track of the Ego States and see if you can begin to see a pattern in how Ego States are predictive in either maintaining or overcoming the Automatic Negative Thought. In the case of the example provided about the fictionary husband and wife, she placed a 'P' in that box, meaning she assessed that her behavior was growing out of transacting from the controlling Parent Ego State.

Since I am not sitting with you in my office I want to share with you my experience in doing this program for the past six years or so. There has never been, not one time, a client that has reported while being in the Child Ego State or the controlling Parent Ego State has chosen a behavior that in any way helped them alter the original Automatic Negative Thought.....not once. At times, if the Parent Ego State has seemed to assist in altering or challenging the original Automatic Negative Thought, it does so because the Parent Ego State was somewhat reflective of a nurturing parent, not the controlling parent. That makes sense as the Adult Ego State is the state of caring or nurturing for one's self or others.

Many of you reading this book will have recorded some behaviors that are reflective of the Adult Ego State. In doing so you will recognize that every time the behaviors growing out of the Adult Ego State in some way challenge; make less true or help you entirely overcome the original Automatic Negative Thought. For those of you that did not find much success in transacting from the Adult Ego State, I would now have you turn to the Planned Behavioral Response Box. As you consider the behaviors recorded in those boxes, see if you can determine the Ego State those planned behaviors reflect. My experience shows that most of the Planned Behaviors are reflective of the Adult Ego State. As you assess your Planned Behaviors and can see that I am correct then you have learned something about yourself. The Adult Ego State does exist inside of you it just has a harder time showing up when it needs to. Don't despair you will demonstrate to yourself that you have the power to get it to do so.

Let me be clear about one thing. You do not have to be completely in the Adult Ego State just simply moving toward it in order to influence the altering of the Automatic Negative Thought. If your behaviors or planned behaviors in any way are reflective of showing care for your self or care for someone else, you are moving toward the Adult Ego State. Behaviors performed from the Adult Ego State will always get you at least a "Between" in the Results Box. If you are fully in the Adult Ego State when choosing a behavior you will always get a "Yes" in the Results Box.

With this being the case, let me go ahead and challenge the reader a bit. If the original Automatic Negative Thought we said to our self is somehow challenged, made to be less true or even completely overcome by an Adult Ego State behavior, what does that say about the thought we said to our self? If somehow this original Automatic Negative Thought was so true, could a behavior make it become not so? That is a great question to be considering. Remember, truth is independent of belief and truth is unchangeable, unalterable, and unassailable. It is eternal in nature. Truth never changes. Intelligent beings recognize truth, accept it and live according to it. Are you an intelligent being?

**NOTE:** DO NOT THROW OUT ANY OF THE COLUMNS YOU HAVE WRITTEN. YOU WILL NEED THEM FOR FUTURE ASSIGNMENTS

HOMEWORK ASSIGNMENT #3 – Gaining Control of the Internal Conversation

The purpose of the diagram below is to have us become highly focused on what we have learned up to this point. The line/arrow represents time. The hash mark in the line simply represents negative emotions. If reading this diagram correctly then it is safe to say that each of us, in time, will experience negative emotions. However, these negative emotions are not showing up out of nowhere. The Uninstall Sheets are assisting you in understanding why these negative emotions appear. There are three things we are doing that are contributing to the negative emotions arising in us. The first thing we do is talk negatively to ourselves about ourselves i.e., the AUTOMATIC NEGATIVE THOUGHT; we then attach NEGATIVE MEANINGS to these original Automatic Negative Thoughts. The Meanings we place on our thoughts then begin to shape NEGATIVE CORE BELIEFS within us and then we experience the NEGATIVE EMOTIONS. On the diagram, the bumps represent these three things. After the NEGATIVE EMOTIONS, represented by the hash mark, is still an ongoing line, which represents the time after the NEGATIVE EMOTION. The question is, what will you do in that time? Will you continue to allow your old memorized, procedural self to react with Controlling Parent or Child Ego States? If you can now see that you are contributing to your ongoing negative view of yourself, do you believe that you have the power, in the moment of experiencing NEGATIVE EMOTIONS, to place yourself in the ADULT EGO STATE and choose a behavior that reflects and honors that ego state?

Time

| ANT | NEGATIVE MEANING | NEGATIVE CORE BELIEF | NEG EMOTION | ADULT EGO STATE BEHAVIOR |

It is obvious that the Adult Ego State is inside of you as sometimes your Behavioral Response or Planned Behavioral Response reflected the Adult Ego State. The question is, "Can you get it to show up when you are experiencing a Negative Emotion?" Can you slow everything down when feeling negative emotions, adjust your attitude and energy to the Adult Ego State and choose a behavior that demonstrates that you care *very much* for yourself and that you care *very much* for others? If you believe that you have the power to do so then your assignment is to write another 5 columns, but 4 out of the 5 columns have to demonstrate in the Behavioral Response Box that you did place yourself in the Adult Ego State in the moment. 4 out of 5 is 80%. I think 80% is a good passing grade in showing that you have learned something.

With this in mind your columns are going to look very similar because the thing that gets you to write a column is when you are experiencing a negative emotion. If you are experiencing a negative emotion then you have already had a negative Internal Conversation, including the Automatic Negative Thought, the Negative Meaning you placed on that Automatic Negative Thought and the tapping into or shaping of a Negative Core Belief, i.e., helplessness, unlovability, and/or a negative body image. The only thing that should become apparent is that you are no longer being reactive in your behaviors, but that you are using the KEY of the Adult Ego State to begin to take control of your implicit memory. There is no faking it here. This assignment will demonstrate whether you were able to catch yourself right in the midst of a negative emotion and alter the long-held patterns of operating from the Child Ego State or an unhealthy Parent Ego State.

REVIEWING HOMEWORK ASSIGNMENT #3

As we did in the previous two homework assignments we simply review the columns.

I ask, "My Problem Is?" You simply read what you recorded in that box.

I then ask, "The Automatic Negative Thought in My Mind Was?" You simply read what you recorded in that box.

I then say, "What Did My Thought Mean to Me?" You simply read what you wrote in that box and then state the numbers you recorded in the parenthesis at the end of each meaning.

I then ask, "What Were the Emotions You Felt?" You then read the emotions you recorded in that box.

I then ask, "What Did You Do as A Behavior?" You then read what you wrote in that box.

I then ask, "Did This Behavior In Any Way Challenge, Make Less True, Or Help You Overcome the Original Automatic Negative Thought?" You then tell me which box you checked, i.e., Yes BR Box, Between Box, or No BR Box. If you had actually chosen a behavior honoring or reflecting the Adult Ego State, then you should have marked either the Between Box or the Yes BR Box.

Please go through each column to determine that you met the criteria for passing, meaning 4 out of the five columns did demonstrate that the Adult Ego State was being utilized in the Behavioral Response Box.

It is important for me as the clinician to reinforce the power of the Adult Ego State and so I ask, "What was it about this behavior that allowed you to actually challenge the original Automatic Negative Thought?" I want to hear my client respond with understanding by pointing out that they stopped and considered their own value as a person, as well as the value of whomever they were interacting (TRANSACTING) with and that they intentionally honored the intrinsic value by choosing a behavior that showed caring toward self and the other person. When a client is able to be that clear in understanding the Adult Ego State, that client is now empowered to change the negative patterns that have been going on for years.

We go through all five columns determining if the client was able to achieve an 80% success rate. If not, we review what it would look like to be in the Adult Ego State, in other words, I usually take the role of my client and role play or model what the Adult Ego State would have looked like based upon their presenting issue. Obviously if you are trying to do this Program by simply reading the book and you find yourself not experiencing the Adult Ego State, and not able to come up with an 80% success rate, my invitation is for you to contact me directly and perhaps through a Skype session we can get you in a better place. Once the modeling or role playing has helped the client see how to engage the Adult Ego State, I simply challenge them to go and try again.

However, the vast majority of my clients find that once they understand the Adult Ego State that they are able to complete the assignment, demonstrating to themselves some power and control when experiencing negative emotions. The question I keep asking in the review of these five columns is, "Did that behavior, performed from the Adult Ego State, help you challenge, make less true or overcome the Original Automatic Negative Thought?" By demonstrating 4 out of 5 successful outcomes, I then provide a visual for my client tying what they are doing to the regenerative process of dismantling old neural pathways. The brain has the ability to reorganize itself by dismantling old neural connections and forming whole new neural networks. Neuroplasticity allows neurons to adjust their activities in response to new information, new situations or to change in the environment. The increasing awareness of one's Internal Conversation and the KEY of the Adult Ego State provides the brain with new information, it is a change in the environment, because as Epigenetics has proven, even our own thoughts are part of our environment. If our new awareness of the Adult Ego State is understood, then thinking of this State would provide the Automatic Internal Conversation with a change in one's environment.

Let us here do some review.

VISUAL RENDERING

IMPLICIT - LEARNING/MEMORY

Formed Through Repetition    When At Least Two Brain Cells Connect
(The Law of Associative Memory)

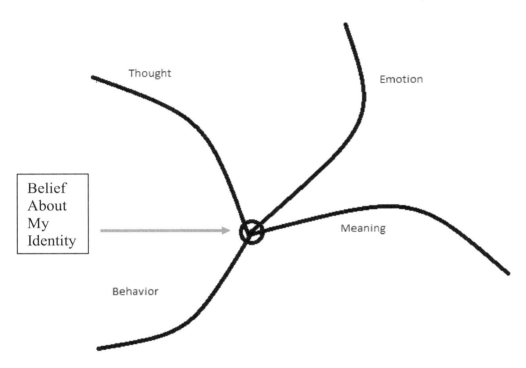

The four curvy lines that connect with one another is a simplistic drawing of neurons. If you have been paying attention to your homework, you will recognize in the drawing the same elements of the Internal Conversation, i.e., the thoughts we say to ourselves, the meanings we attach to those thoughts, the emotions we experience because of the thought and meaning, and then the behavior we utilize in direct relation to the emotion.

Thoughts are carried as an electrical impulse through neurons. This electrical impulse is energy, but likewise it is obvious that the meanings we place on our thoughts, the emotions growing out of the thought and meaning and the reactive behavior are all energy! Energy associates with other forms of energy and in doing so wires neurons together in unique ways. In observing the relationship each of these elements (or neurons) have with each other, and now that you know that learning is when at least two brain cells connect with one another, then the circle in the middle where the connection has occurred is where some of your learning is stored. What is in that area of storage is your belief about how you see your self. This is the formed identity based upon the Internal Conversation. Anyone that struggles with issues related to Unhealthy Esteem, their Internal Conversation has contributed to their distorted belief about them self. The problem is that their Internal Conversation has been repeated so many times that it has formed and stored within their Implicit Memory and they no longer are aware of their own contributions because the self-perception is an automatic response within their cells.

The purpose of Living Consciously is to get the client back in touch with their Internal Conversation so that they can both see how their distorted belief about self was shaped and how to take back control of the thing that has now become so automatic within them.

The control begins when we examine each piece of the Internal Conversation. Currently the piece we are more highly focused on is the behavior. There is a reason why I start with this part of the Internal Conversation. Behavior is the one part that is easiest to get control of, as it is both the last part of the Internal Conversation, but likewise the slowest part as well.

The diagram below is representing the accuracy of the Laws of Quantum Theory. If you will recall The Law of Entanglement states that as energy becomes highly associated, change in one association will directly influence all of the other associations. As we begin to observe our Internal Conversation our awareness increases of how we contribute to our self-perspective; how our core belief of how we see our self was shaped. Our thoughts are carried in neural pathways. The meanings we attach to our thoughts are likewise carried in neural pathways, but so are our emotions and behaviors. When these become highly associated it begins to shape within us our view of our self. As I introduced to you the Adult Ego State and asked you to choose a behavior honoring that Ego State when experiencing negative emotions, you proved that you were able to do so. In looking at the behavior chosen from the Adult Ego State we assessed that behavior's impact on the original Automatic Negative Thought. I would ask, "Did that behavior in any way challenge, make less true, or help you overcome the Automatic Negative Thought?"

The "Green" color is representing a new behavior and its ongoing impact on the original Automatic Negative Thought. If the Automatic Negative Thought has now been challenged, made less true or overcome, then the Meaning would likewise be altered as well as the Emotional response. Now that all four of these associations are being transformed, then the Core Belief stored at the junction of the associations is likewise being altered.

I ask all my clients, "How quickly did you begin to "feel" better?" Every client says that it was an immediate response. That rapidly altered experience of going from negative emotions to positive and welcomed emotions is a manifestation of the Law of Entanglement. When any new information or energy is put into one of the associated areas of energy, every other association will immediately experience a change.

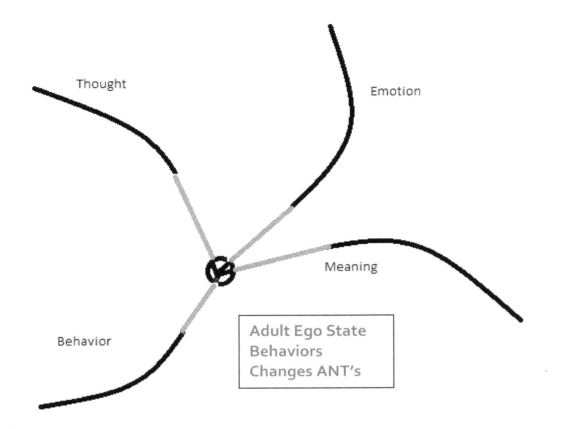

Thought

Emotion

Meaning

Behavior

Adult Ego State
Behaviors
Changes ANT's

 Hopefully the exercises have assisted you in realizing where once you felt out of control or to a degree powerless to your ongoing shame that you actually have control by implementing more and more of the Adult Ego State when experiencing negative emotions. As you do so, such consistency will continue to diminish the power of the Automatic Negative Thoughts, thus having you stay in touch with a more realistic sense of your self.

The intuitive question here is simply this; "If the original Automatic Negative Thought we say to our self is so real, so absolutely true, could a behavior have any power to change it?" The answer is obvious that it could not. Therefore, what are you perhaps recognizing about that type of thought?

The Adult Ego State allows us to have better outcomes, because it speaks to our true nature. Each of us are individuals of incomparable worth and value. When we choose to honor that value in ourselves and others our shame begins to be challenged and we begin moving toward healthy esteem.

**NOTE:** DO NOT THROW OUT ANY OF THE COLUMNS YOU HAVE WRITTEN. YOU WILL NEED THEM FOR FUTURE ASSIGNMENTS

FINAL THOUGHT – THE DISTORTION OF THE BEHAVIORAL RESPONSE IS THE CHILD AND CONTROLLING PARENT EGO STATES. THE REASON WE KNOW THESE ARE DISTORTED IS BECAUSE THEY DO NOT LEAD TO THE OUTCOMES WE ARE SEEKING.

TRUTH – The Adult Ego State speaks to our true nature. Each of us are beings of incredible value and as we care for our self in this manner, and others, we see the truth of who we really are. Are you an intelligent being?

If your emotional abilities aren't in hand, if you don't have self-awareness, if you are not able to manage your distressing emotions, if you can't have empathy and have effective relationships, then no matter how smart you are, you are not going to get very far.

— Daniel Goleman

If you can't think beyond your negative emotions you will remain stuck

— Joe Dispenza

EMOTIONS

Congratulations! You have graduated from the Behavior portion of the Negative Internal Conversation and have moved up to the Emotional Reaction portion of that conversation. What is an emotion? An emotion is the release of a neurochemical. How simple is that? Here are some examples:

1. Sad – low levels of serotonin
2. Anger – adrenaline
3. Happiness – endorphins, dopamine, serotonin, oxytocin
4. Motivation – dopamine
5. Confidence – testosterone, dopamine
6. Sexual Arousal – testosterone, estrogen, DHEA, oxytocin

All of the communication occurring in and between cells is largely chemical and electrical. What neurochemicals are being released influence and regulate so many aspects of our experience. But as it relates to the formation of our self view, the neurochemicals that are released are directly associated with our thoughts about self, even if those thoughts are implicit and automatic. The electrical charge elicited because of a thought is the catalyst in opening up the sacs or vesicles that store neurochemicals. In laymen's terms, our negative thoughts about our self releases neurochemicals that have us feel in correspondence to those thoughts. Likewise, positive thoughts directed toward our self release the chemicals that have us feel positive. This is why it is important to discover the truth of who we are, because if we don't, life has a way of convincing us that we are lacking on so many levels.

Most people that seek counseling experience ongoing negative emotions. Their assessment of those emotions has many believe that others or external events are the cause. The classic example is that of the husband/wife relationship or the parent/child relationship. This external perspective as the cause of persistent negative emotions has many engage in behaviors that exacerbate the negative emotional fall-out. Issues of control, jealousy, passive-aggressiveness, blaming, accusing others, getting angry and withdrawal are very typical behaviors people enlist in trying to mitigate negative emotions.

A typical response by many that struggle with ongoing negative emotions is that they will say, "Don't tell me how to feel. They are my feelings. Feelings are neither right nor wrong, they are just feelings." While such an approach is enlisted to drop the fear response to negative emotions, such conclusions will only have the person continue to struggle with these unwanted emotions. I can say one thing very clearly, is that there is a recent phenomenon in paying the wrong attention to emotions. Books like, "The Emotion Code," techniques like Mindfulness and Energy Healing and the ever increasing usage of anxiety and depression drugs all speak to us becoming hyper-focused on our emotions. Doing so however will only make the problem worse.

Other people have adopted the idea that the negative emotions exist as evidence that somehow they are broken or devalued in some way. This belief results in anxiety-filled analyzing or increasing self-deprecation. Learning is impeded when these are the go-to and if not corrected, panic attacks, immune system malfunctions, adrenal exhaustion, hyper or hypo thyroidism, pituitary issues, or other physical ailments will appear. Increasing levels of self-medicating is also a very likely response in trying to manage the negative internal experience, but self-medicating simply adds to the oncoming physical and mental health issues that are certain to rear their head.

Based upon the research associated with Epigenetics and Neuroplasticity, it has become very clear that the source of most struggles is the formation of an untruthful personal identity over a life-time of experience that gets stored at the cellular level. This core belief about oneself is never fully accessed consciously until shown how to do so. In its state of being below the threshold of awareness, or implicit, it continues to impact how one views all aspects of their life; many times creating patterns that lead to consistent, amplified negative feelings. Because the research is becoming so clear, I realized that in order to assist clients permanently, I had to develop a Program, a process that would allow someone to get rid of unhealthy parts of that stored learning and then provide a path of how to form a healthy, truthful identity, creating a whole new implicit memory. After approaching therapy from this vantage point for over six years, it has become clear that the research is very accurate in explaining the real source of problems in our life. I want to add here, my Program is not replacing the need for understanding what the revelations say about who we are and all that implies, it is simply providing a strategic approach to gain control of how we have formed belief that is contrary to our revealed identity.

As people evaluate those aspects of their lives they believe are causing unhappiness, stress, and intrusive, sometimes overwhelming negative feelings, many evaluate through a process of what is external to them. "My husband's infidelity is what has made me so angry," or "I am unhappy because nobody accepts me," or "Her addiction is tearing our family apart," or "My teacher is harder on me than the other students." While other people's behaviors can reasonably create difficulty, if we have a healthy view of our self and are highly aware of this view, then such external events begin to have less negative impact on how we experience ourselves and life in general. The real issue is what is going on internally. For example, "My husband's infidelity is usually processed through the template of.... "I am obviously not good enough (pretty enough, exciting enough, skinny enough, interesting enough, sexy enough, etc.) for my husband." That personal assessment now creates a sequential cascade of processes that becomes absorbed and is stored in neural networks and encoded upon our DNA. That learning and storing is never dormant, it is always in operation and continually broadcasts signals that has us view life from an unhealthy core belief or template.

If I were to shorten the explanation, I might simply say, if we view ourselves as victims to ongoing life experience, then practicing being a victim only allows us to see things in terms of suffering and no choice. Practicing not being a victim would allow us to see things differently. How we evaluate our external circumstances will create a reality, which will have us see things as they really are, or have us see things through a lot of distortion. *The evidence of distorted realities is ongoing negative feelings!*

As stated earlier, hyper-focus on our emotions is just going to have us stay stuck. Here is my analogy to help you understand. If I open the cabinet doors under my kitchen sink and suddenly I smell mold, I can get really busy focusing on the mold. I can pull everything out, wipe everything down and then finish by applying a bleach solution. I then put everything thing back, thinking the mold is taken care of. Three days later I open the cabinet doors again and find that mold has begun to grow. As before, I get busy pulling everything out, wiping it down, applying a bleach solution; followed by putting everything back. My point is that we can spend a lot of time, energy and resources in cleaning the mold, but if we would just fix the source of the mold, meaning the leaky pipe, the mold will take care of itself. Negative emotions are mold! The source of ongoing negative emotions that so many humans experience are the distorted beliefs they hold about themselves, which have become stored as matter and energy at the cellular level. Their unhealthy belief about them self is the leaky pipe.

To assist us in overcoming these distortions, it is time to spend some time with our emotions instead of always trying to clean them up as quickly as we possibly can. Have you ever noticed how quickly we get involved in trying to manage our negative emotions so that we won't be bothered by them? Have you also noticed that in your years of handling your emotions the way you have has never led to a resolve of the negative emotions? They just seem to keep coming back, just like the mold does under the sink. I have grown to have an incredible appreciation for the laws associated with Quantum Theory. Quantum Law has us understand that it is in the observing of the matter or energy that influences how matter and energy organize, shape or behave in any way that they do. Running away from the energy of negative emotions is not observing. It is time to spend some time observing our negative emotions.

HOMEWORK ASSIGNMENT #4 – Spending Time With Your Emotions

In having you begin the process of observing your emotions, I want you to find a half-hour to do this assignment. I do not want you to be interrupted or disturbed at all during this half hour. The good news is that you do not have to write any new columns this week, but I do want you to go back and look at the Emotional Reaction Box of the columns you have written to this point. Please do not try and break-up this assignment over several days. Do the assignment in the time-frame I am giving you. Find a half-hour, where no interruptions will take place and sit and complete the assignment.

The way I have you begin to observe your emotions is by looking at the first column you wrote, meaning the Emotional Reaction Box of that column and view that first emotion you recorded. I want you to continue to look at that emotion until you can begin to remember what it felt like. One of the ways to drum up that emotional memory is to look at the context of the column, meaning what it is you wrote in the "My Problem Is" Box. I am not asking you to create a full-blown emotional memory, for example, if "Anger" is the emotion you are looking at, I am not asking you to go into the full-blown experience of that emotion as it likely occurred originally. What I am asking is that you stick with that emotion you recorded until you can begin to remember what it felt like. After you have achieved that emotional memory, then continue to the rest of the emotions recorded in that box and pay attention to each one individually until you have achieved the emotional memory of each one. After having re-felt or re-experienced the emotions you recorded, I want you to ask yourself whether you like those feelings or you don't like those feelings. After you decide, then in an open space, either in that box or adjacent to that box I want you to put one of the following statements:

1) I LIKE THESE FEELING(S)
2) I DON'T LIKE THESE FEELING(S)

Continue to the next column and do the same for those emotions you recorded in the Emotional Reaction Box. Continue from column to column until every single box has one of the above statements written in or near the box. Here are the rules; you are to completely write out fully one of the statements above. "Ditto Marks" and the word "Same" are not allowed. I want you to fully write out the statement that aligns with your choice.

As you proceed from column to column you will recognize that you may have recorded the same emotion in different columns. If you run across the same emotion, I do not want you to skip it, by saying, "I have already dealt with this emotion." I want you to spend time with every single emotion no matter how many times you recorded it. So if you recorded feeling angry 17 times, then I want you to feel that emotion 17 times and decide, in writing, whether you like that feeling or you don't like that feeling.

That is the first part of the assignment. The second part of the assignment is to pay attention to what you are experiencing while doing this assignment. If you follow my instructions you will experience something. I want you to pay attention to it as it will prepare you when we review this homework assignment. Every client experiences the same thing, though maybe to different degrees. The important thing is to recognize what your cells are speaking back to you.


REVIEWING HOMEWORK ASSIGNMENT #4

In my experience, clients preponderantly choose "I don't like these feelings" as they review the recording of their negative emotions. I am sure that was your experience as well. It appears across the board, humans do not like experiencing negative emotions. As we review this assignment it is my objective to present enough information to perhaps have you begin to observe these negative emotions in a vastly different perspective than how you likely have viewed them previously. Too many, when experiencing negative emotions, conclude that the negative emotions are evidence that somehow they are broken or devalued in some way. When such a view is taken, the negative emotions intensify and the individual becomes busy in eliminating, managing or disassociating from them. The hyper focus on the emotions creates a roadblock, because in the running away, nothing ever gets resolved. It is only a matter of time before those same ugly, unwanted emotions appear again and again. Another typical way that individuals react to negative emotions is to increase their negative thoughts directed toward them self, resulting in a very dark, downward spiral. Finally, because some people incorrectly perceive their negative emotions being directly related to externals, they will turn to becoming more controlling of their environment. Whichever strategy you recognize as your pattern, please be an honest observer and ask, "Has either method ever resulted in resolving the ongoing pattern?" Perhaps it is time to take another viewpoint and in doing so begin to be thankful when experiencing negative emotions.

The other part of your assignment was to "pay attention to what you were experiencing" while doing the assignment. Some people report that by sticking with the emotions they began to notice that they became less problematic. Some report that their willingness to experience, the emotions over and over again in a short amount of time drastically reduced their fear response to them. However, most clients report that it was ridiculous to be going through life in this manner and that they wanted it to end. Some even become angry that they have wasted so much of their life in being overwhelmed by negative emotions. These latter conclusions, I have found are the sentiments and experience of every client that completes this assignment. If you can relate to what I have just said, congratulations, that experience is pivotal in overcoming the undesirable patternistic encounters of negative emotions and shame.

Earlier we talked about "building" self-esteem. In doing so we pointed out that sound structures require a very good foundation. Since this whole book is related to *building* healthy-esteem, which can only occur through a correct view of who we are, let me turn to the design or planning phase of construction. When building structures there are significant tools that are utilized in making sure the structure is built to specifications that will provide for long term viability. The COMPASS is such a tool. The Compass allows the architect to draw design specifications that keep structural dynamics within bounds or parameters that strengthen the building. The COMPASS accomplishes this by looking at and measuring angles. That is exactly what the Compass is utilized for; it is to circumscribe elements of the architect's design that will impose limits of weight and structural integrity so as to avoid collapse in the building. I would like to approach our discussion of emotions from this perspective of keeping things within the limits of what our negative emotions are informing us of. I would like to view as a whole, what we know about our design so that we might be able to keep negative emotions within the true limits they were designed for. If we take negative emotions beyond their intent is when we, like a building, begin to collapse under faulty design.

To provide a more correct view of these negative emotions, we will begin to dissect different angles or aspects of the emotional experience. As we look at each aspect, it should have you form a much better view or understanding of what these negative emotions are really trying to help us know and remember. In order to keep these features organized, I do so by providing a pie-chart, wherein we can look at the whole truth of what our negative emotions are communicating. As we view each angle of the pie-chart, hopefully when completely filled in it will create a whole understanding of what negative emotions are trying to have us understand and in the future we will no longer take our negative emotions beyond what they were circumscribed for.

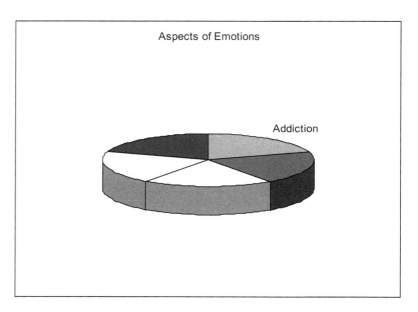

Aspects of Emotions

Addiction

If someone were to come to you and ask you to help them understand how to discern addiction, what would you say to that person that would provide clarity in knowing how to discern when someone is truly struggling with the addictive process? Some have suggested that the individual has been disconnected from their own will to the extent that they no longer have the power within them self to avoid the substance or behavior of addiction. Many have reported that the person struggles with healthy emotional connection, perhaps becoming desensitized, self-absorbed and withdrawn. Others have recognized that there appears to be a preoccupation with the issue, spending greater amounts of resources and time in pursuit of or surrounding the addiction. However, my experience in working with addiction I have recognized a prominent feature of the addictive process. This prominent feature has helped me to clearly discern whether a person is addicted or not. I have noticed that in spite of all of the negative consequences that result from the addiction, the person struggling with addiction just keeps doing the very same thing that keeps bringing the same negative consequences. This strong pattern illuminates the addictive process.

Let me highlight these revealing features of addiction:

1. The individual has become disconnected from their own will to the degree that the addiction itself has exerted greater power in the person's life.
2. The individual struggles with healthy emotional connecting; perhaps the person is desensitized from being able to attune to other's emotional expressions and caring about them. Perhaps the unhealthy emotional response leads to the individual being more withdrawn, self-absorbed, aloof or isolated.

3. There appears to be a greater preoccupation with; a greater amount of time and resources spent in pursuit of or surrounding the addiction.
4. In spite of all of the negative consequences the person experiences as a result of the addiction, the individual just keeps doing the very same thing that keeps bringing the same negative consequences.

As we review what has been highlighted, I ask, is it possible then that we can become addicted to the process that leads to ongoing negative emotions? Can we become addicted to our negative self and the emotions that accompany it? Without fail, clients pause and then answer affirmatively. Let's explore the backdrop to why this is likely part of the reader's emotional experience.

Neurochemicals have an astonishing influence on perception and experience. In the section, "A Growing Discussion of Self-Esteem," you will recall the Cost/Benefit Analysis of Healthy Esteem vs. Unhealthy Esteem. The second to last comparison in that chart points out that those that operate from Unhealthy Esteem believe that unhappiness is normal. It is reasonable that such oriented individuals would come to believe that, as the negative emotions associated with that perception have become such a constant companion to their daily experience. In other words, the abundant release of neurochemicals resulting from a negative perception flood their cells and thus he or she comes to believe the emotions are evidence that they are worthless, incapable or unacceptable. Bottom line, neurochemicals released through a repetitive negative internal conversation have an overwhelming influence on perception and therefore those that are so disposed to being negatively attuned become clouded in their self-perception. And without understanding what implicit memory is, how it forms and most importantly how influential it is, people that have become convinced that unhappiness is normal lose greater control in managing their negative emotions; they struggle in developing or maintaining healthy emotional connections with others, they appear to be more self-absorbed and withdrawn, they spend more time and energy in managing their negative feelings; and they do the very same thing that keeps bringing the same negative emotional response. That in large measure can explain the addictive process related to unhealthy-esteemed individuals.

The prophet Joseph Smith countered the false belief that unhappiness is normal when he taught, "Happiness is the *object and design* of our existence and will be the end thereof if we pursue the path that leads to it." The prophet then continued talking about how a portion of that path requires righteous living, the importance of keeping commandments and adopting the characteristics that lead to becoming holy. However I don't want to spend time with the latter things he spoke of, I want to focus on the first part of what he said; "Happiness is the object and design of our existence...." Now I know what "object" means; that is the goal. But what did he mean when he said it was our "design" as well? In my experience in listening to prophets, I have come to the conclusion that there are many things these holy men hint at but never fully divulge what their true level of understanding is. It appears in time we finally catch up with their inspired wisdom and intelligence and then are struck with a moment of reflection when we become aware of their advanced understanding. I believe this is true of Joseph's use of the word "design." As we continue our discussion of the different aspects of emotions, this will become much more visible to the reader.

The first basis of evidence that we are designed to be happy is your own assessment while doing this homework assignment. You were asked to make a conscious declaration of whether you liked or disliked the negative emotions you recorded in your columns. Additionally, if I asked you if you could replace those recorded negative feelings with any other feelings, what feelings would you choose? Inevitably, every reader will include the feeling of happiness. Other responses may include peace of mind, assurance, hope and confidence, but happiness appears to be the most common confession.

Years ago I was the Executive Director for a youth residential program in Lund, Nevada. Lund is out in the middle of nowhere. Our program resided on a working cattle ranch, which we incorporated as part of the program in helping youth, mostly youth from cities, in developing a healthier view of themselves. One day we received a new student, Elizabeth, seventeen years of age. Elizabeth, being made of a hundred trillion cells that were constantly absorbing her experience and environment; and a large part of her environment was that of an alcoholic father. He was not a very nice alcoholic. Elizabeth's father was not just critical of his daughter, but contemptuous as well when in his drunken states. Elizabeth heard many, many times of how she would never amount to anything, that no one would ever want her. He criticized her weight constantly and repeatedly called her things such as being a slut or whore. By the time Elizabeth arrived on our front porch, because she had been observed this way, she believed it herself. She was miserable.

After being with us for a couple of months, right after an evening meal, Elizabeth approached me and asked if we could talk. We went into my office, Elizabeth sitting on the couch and I at my desk chair. Elizabeth, with a look of great concern said, "Larry, the reason why I am here is because I think I am starting to feel happy." I responded by saying, "Well Elizabeth, I hear your words but your facial expression has me think that you are unsure about feeling happy?" She replied, "I am, I don't know what to do with it."

I hope, that though this was an incredibly sad reply, that you recognize it was also very insightful. Elizabeth's experience speaks to much of the human condition. So many become so used to feeling a certain way that they no longer consider that other options exist or for that matter, even knowing how to manage life from more positive emotions.

Elizabeth continued, "The reason I am here is because I have been thinking about doing something that will bring me back to the way I am used to feeling." I believe Elizabeth was showing our program respect because she was a self-harmer and wanted us to be aware of her current mindset. I spoke with Elizabeth about some of the seemingly harmful behaviors people utilize when experiencing stress, shame, anxiety, depression and other negative feelings and I told her that I have learned to view them in a way that demonstrates that the person actually cares about them self. Even though the harmful behavior in the long run does not do anything to resolve the patternistic struggle with such emotions, in fact, such behaviors can exacerbate them, yet the immediate effect of many destructive behaviors does provide immediate relief from the negative emotional experience. And it is that veritable experience that speaks to the motivation of self-care. The individual is so sick and tired of feeling the negative emotions they just simply want relief from them.

Elizabeth had said that she had never thought of it that way before, but that she could see how that would be. I then told Elizabeth that she could go do whatever she thought would help her manage her current stress. I reminded her that was one of the reasons why she was with us, was so that she could learn more about herself. I told her that I understood that she had grown so accustomed to managing life from the uncomfortable feelings that she was simply doing what had become programmed in her to do. I then added, "Before you go and do whatever you think you need to do, understand that whatever you do will not change one bit of how I think or feel about you." Elizabeth replied, "I am beginning to believe that, but please understand that has not been my experience." Another poignant confession of her life experience now stored at the cellular level, that her acceptance was conditional.

"Before you leave," I said, "Elizabeth you came in here and reported that you were beginning to experience happiness and then have been very forthcoming about the feelings you are used to experiencing. Tell me, between happiness and those other feelings you are so accustomed to, which do you like better?" Elizabeth replied, "Oh, I like happiness!" I suggested that like the other feelings she may grow accustomed to happiness if she began to experience it enough. "Just a suggestion," I said.

Elizabeth's story is an example of addictive emotions and the influence they have on ongoing experiences. Addictive emotions are evidence of a time we began to define our self due to the strength of the emotional response experienced. Elizabeth's environment provided the perfect backdrop to initiate a negative internal conversation, one that was repeated hundreds of thousands of times, resulting in the bombardment of negative neurochemicals in her cells.

In reviewing your homework, there was a reason why I asked you whether you liked the feelings you were reporting. I wanted you to begin breaking free of the addiction by acknowledging at a high conscious level whether you even liked those feelings. Again, if you could replace those persistent negative feelings with any other feelings, what feelings would you choose? Your honest response is evidence that all of us are designed to be happy.

Instilled in the DNA Code is the information on what frequencies of energy our cells should operate within. The marching orders for what cells should be doing is contained in the DNA. When they do adhere to that information we experience those welcomed feelings of happiness, peace of mind, hope, assurance, motivation and confidence. Our cells are made of atoms and water, which are in a constant state of wave motion. Having grown up by the ocean it was observed that waves would vary in energy as they approached the shore, depending on weather or lunar patterns. Just the energy in the water itself could be experienced as more calm and relaxing or having you exert more energy to navigate its sometimes raging strength. Visually anyone could observe this, but when you spend as much time in the ocean as I have, the differences in wave energy was noticeably diverse. If there was a storm off-shore the strength of the energy in the ocean was at times incredibly catching of my attention as at times such energy would elicit more caution. When our thoughts about our self align with what our DNA Code says who and what we are, it is then we experience the more positive, calm and relaxing emotions. When our thoughts go against our true self is when the wave energy in our cells increases; and at times rages. Outside of the range the DNA Code sets as desired wave motion is when we experience negative emotional states. The DNA Code is evidence alone that we are designed to be happy.

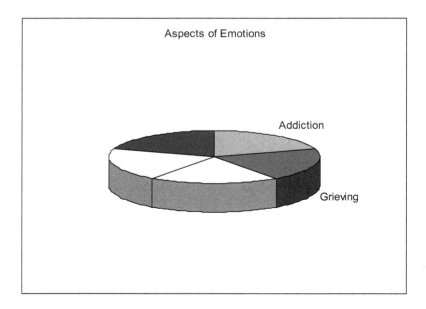

Aspects of Emotions

Addiction

Grieving

GRIEVING – LOSS OF AN IMPORTANT RELATIONSHIP

After having met with hundreds of clients over the past six years or so, it became obvious that part of the roller coaster emotional experience they were reporting was due to their grieving. If you will pay attention, you will likely conclude the same of your own reporting.

Grieving is designed in every human. There is that word again – design. If we are all designed to grieve, is there something that grieving is trying to have us understand?

Grieving is initiated whenever there has been a loss of an important relationship to us. The process of grieving has been so well researched that we can easily discern its effects. There are very specific experiences coupled with very specific emotions and when you begin to see these things show up together consistently, you begin to lean toward grieving as part of the overall struggle.

Denial

The first specific experience reported in the grieving process is that of denial. Denial can show up in many forms, such as, "Why does he/she do this to me," or "When will this ever stop," or "I can't believe this happening;" or "This will never end," or "I'm fine," when someone asks how we are doing, or putting on a brave face so no one else will know that we are struggling, etc., but denial is especially prominent when we fail to recognize our own contributions to the ongoing problem. Can you see in your reporting of the columns any denial? If you continue to see all of the external events in your life as the reason for your ongoing struggles, and if you consistently take those external events personally, you are in denial.

## Bartering

Bartering is another prominent feature of the grieving process. Bartering is a form of negotiating. People that are grieving go through several forms of negotiating trying to stop the rollercoaster of intrusive, overwhelming negative emotions and experiences. These negotiations may be a slew of forgiveness provided toward others no matter how many times betrayal is experienced. It may be found in the form of taking responsibility for someone else's poor behavior or obligations. It may be recognized in the ultimatums we give to others. It may be present when someone is constantly venting, complaining and getting anyone - that will - to listen. It may just show up when we drop to our knees and plead with the Almighty to simply take away the pain. It rears its head when we have said to ourselves a thousand times, "I'll never do this again!" It is present in the behaviors we choose to mitigate negative emotions, such as addictive behaviors. You may be in the act of bartering by simply reading this book! Can you see how many different ways you have attempted to get things to change?

## Depression

Feelings of sadness, lack of motivation, not having energy, wanting to sleep or veg-out, tears that seem to happen without a cue, gaming, excessive internet use, social media and other prolonged use of technology; procrastination, not keeping your living situation clean and tidy, starting things but not completing them, self-medicating, as well as emotional eating are all expressions of depression. How many times did you report depression or sadness in your columns?

## Anger**

Frustration, being easily agitated, taking out some of that internal feeling on others, impatience, fighting and raising our voice; trying to control everything, cutting people out of our life, wanting to hurt others, self-harming, resistance, rebellion, despising authority, passive-aggressiveness, sarcasm are all expressions of anger.. How many times did you report anger or frustration in your columns? As a side-note, some experts have expressed that depression is anger turned inwards!

## Acceptance

The final phase or stage of grieving is categorized as acceptance. I do not have a big definition for this stage except that the person is beginning to come to better terms with the loss. This appears to be a process. While still painful, the individual doesn't become as incapacitated as before. They are able to compartmentalize the loss, by having a correct or better perspective and continue to function with life's demands. The improved perspective buffers the pain of the loss. Perhaps they continue the memory of the person by living in a way that would make that person proud. Maybe they come to know that we are eternal beings and therefore relationships have the capacity to be renewed and restored. Maybe they take comfort in knowing that loss of relationships through death may still be intact as "the spirits of the just.....are not far from us, and know and understand our thoughts, feelings and motions, and are often pained therewith." (Teachings of the Prophet Joseph Smith, Deseret Book Company, Salt Lake City; 1959, Pg 326). In the losses of relationships we experience where death is not involved, perhaps acceptance is achieved through receiving new information that brings greater clarity. Perhaps the acceptance comes through repentance and forgiveness or by believing correctly, or taking ownership and personal responsibility for improving the relationship.

You will notice that I placed asterisks next to the phase of Anger. I did so because I want to discuss this very important aspect of the grieving process. Anger is a necessary part of the grieving process and there is a specific type of anger that must emerge if an individual is going to begin to experience or move into the stage of acceptance.

To introduce this type of anger, I turn to an example from the scriptures:

> And the Jews Passover was at hand, and Jesus went up to Jerusalem, and found in the temple those that sold oxen and sheep and doves, and the changers of money sitting. And when he had made a scourge of small cords, he drove them all out of the temple, and the sheep and the oxen, and poured out the changers money, and overthrew the tables. And said unto them that sold doves, Take these things hence, make not my father's house an house of merchandise. (John 2:13-16)

The next verse provides us a glimpse of the inner turmoil that led to the events just described:

> And his disciples remembered that it was written, The zeal of thine house hath eaten me up. (John 2:17)

The Savior's love and zeal for His Father kindled a fire in his soul that now on display was a tempest of emotion. To provide perspective and to give us a glimpse of what was eating Him up, remember, the temple was not an ordinary house. It was the House of God, erected by those that sought Him. It was a place of solace, a reverent house where upon entering the faithful could find peace and be reminded of eternal perspective. The House of God is a sacred holy edifice where the truly penitent may gather their bearings, offer prayers and receive wisdom that satisfies their soul. It is a place where God's spirit is felt in greater degree and where assurance of His love for us is magnified. This was always the spirit of this holy house (D&C 109:8, 13).

About 150 years before Christ was born, the Roman Empire had defeated the Greeks and took possession of the territory where the Jewish nation resided. But many people do not understand that not only did they take over the territory, the Romans also took over the temple. For example, the position of High Priest was hereditary. To be considered as a High Priest in the ancient order, you had to be a literal descendant of Aaron. But the Roman officials began to sell this position off to the highest bidder. You could now purchase the priesthood. This is an important backdrop to the two high priests mentioned in the New Testament, Annas and Caiaphas, father and son-in-law. Neither was a descendant of Aaron. These two were recipients of the office due to their wealth. This knowledge gives us perspective when we hear Caiaphas declare, "that one man should die for the people, so that the whole nation perish not"

(John 11:50). This he spoke in response to a discussion the chief priests and Pharisees were having after the miracle of Lazarus being raised from the tomb.

> If we let him thus alone, all men will believe on him: and the Romans shall come and take away…. our place. (John 11:48)

It appears that Caiaphas recognized that his place was in jeopardy being a false high priest and that he was up against the true High Priest (Hebrews 7: 17).

In 1947, a library was discovered named the Dead Sea Scrolls. In the documents we learn of this take-over in great detail. The Essenes, the owners of the library, left the Jerusalem area for this very reason. In great apocalyptic description, the Essenes anticipated a Messiah whom would arrive shortly and undo what the Romans had instituted. I might add here that the Maccabean's under Greek rule tell a very similar story. The Maccabean revolt was largely a result of the temple being desecrated by the ruling empire.

One of the outcomes of this purchased priesthood was a change in the way things were done (Isaiah 24:5). In the earliest revelations to Moses, when the annual sacrifice was to be performed, God knowing of the economic disparity that would exist, allowed his people to raise and bring their own animals. For those that had limited means, a dove was permitted to be offered. Raising a dove would not have created a hardship on the family budget. As long as the dove qualified by being a male, the first born, without spot or blemish, etc.; the dove was as wholly acceptable as a sacrifice as was any other animal such as a lamb or oxen. However, when the priesthood had been usurped, the wealthy pretenders no longer permitted the practice of raising and bringing your own animal, you now were required to purchase the sacrificial animal at the temple. Here a profit was exacted and the sacrificial animal was now being marketed as merchandise – taking away both the spirit of the temple and the means for all worthy individuals to participate in its ordinances.

With this insight we can better understand what was eating the Savior up. These changes were taking away from the spirit of temple worship and preventing all that were worthy to do so in participating, because of cost prohibitions, especially those that were instituted to get personal gain. In essence, the Savior's emotional response to the marketing occurring at his Father's House was 'ENOUGH IS ENOUGH,' we are not doing this anymore. His anger was kindled in the distraction and obstruction of what the temple was established for. He, being the Son of the Highest, took his zeal for his Father and in anger began to restore things to normalcy. This is the specific type of anger that is required in the grieving process if we are ever to begin to experience the acceptance phase. If we are ever going to return to a place of normalcy in our life, we must become upset at the way we have been living. We must decide "enough is enough" in allowing our negative emotions to reign supreme. This is why I had you pay attention to what you were experiencing when you were doing this assignment.

Are you tired of the constant intrusion of negative emotions? Are you tired of being a prisoner to your fears, your doubts and your assumptions? Has your incorrect belief prevented you from living life the way you really want to live it? Is enough, enough? Are you eaten up? Are you ready to find peace and confidence in who you are? On a scale of 1 to 10, how sick and tired are you of grieving? A 10 is, "I am so sick and tired of living in this roller coaster of emotional turmoil that I want it to change right now;" and a 1 is, "Whatever, I don't think it can ever change." Where do you see yourself on that scale? If you see yourself toward the upper numbers then you are experiencing the type of anger necessary to live life as it was intended to be lived. You are in a place where acceptance of the lost relationship can occur.

The next obvious question I want to ask you then is, "What relationship(s) have you lost?" Some of you may respond with various, traumatic losses of intimate and important relationships. Some of you may recognize that it may have only been one, maybe a parent at an early age, the loss of a boy or girlfriend, the breakup of a family due to divorce. Sometimes we can grieve the ideal relationship when we can't seem to get it to happen with our spouse or children. Perhaps you don't feel of God's warmth and wonder if your relationship with Him is in jeopardy. However, I would like you to consider one other loss you have experienced, and that is the relationship with yourself. Maybe that loss has come through doing too much, too often for others. Maybe that loss has come because of being in a controlling relationship. Maybe your lost relationship with yourself started early in life as you have experienced over and over again a routine battle with feeling insecure in yourself or feeling like you didn't matter to others. Maybe you lost your relationship with yourself because you believed acceptance was conditional. Regardless of the etiology, it is interesting to note that grieving is still the response even when that loss of a relationship is with our self. Is this response of grieving that is designed in every human trying to get us to understand something? It likely is and as we continue our uncovering of our true nature, perhaps you can better understand grieving's design.

Please just understand that part of your emotional experience has been partly seated in the grieving process. It is designed in every one of us. The overall grieving process is like being in a wilderness, alone, alienated yet desiring to be connected again in a good way. It does have a purpose as it is intended to remind us of the importance and eternal nature of relationships. Grieving encourages us to do all we can to make the relationships we want to become everlasting in nature, including the relationship with our self!

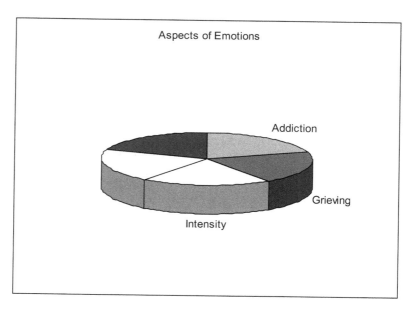

Have you ever noticed that emotions of the same kind may have varying intensities associated with them? For example, when someone is describing sadness, "sadness" may be experienced more lightly as disappointment or more heavily as severe, debilitating depression.

Since we are speaking of "loss" in association with grieving, then loss itself can be an emotion that may exhibit levels of intensity. Let me tell you about two losses I experienced and contrast the emotional intensity response to help you understand what I am saying. Several years ago, I was a contractor. At the time of moving to Saint George from California, my company was owed about $200,000.00. This wasn't in anticipation of work I was hoping to be awarded, this was work where labor, material and overhead had already been provided and it was time to get paid for the work. Now I know that $200,000.00 is not the all-in-all. In comparison to millions it seems kind of paltry. But I ask the question, "Is $200,000.00 dollars really a small loss?" I always ask my clients what they would do with $200,000.00. Their replies speak to the idea that $200,000.00 could make significant changes in their lives. So, it is not a small loss. I want you to know that we never received any of that money. This was the time of economic decline; the construction industry being one of the industries hardest hit. I also want you to know that I never felt any real intense, negative emotions about that loss. I never became overwhelmed with discouragement. I never became angry about being taken advantage of. I certainly didn't like what was going on, but again, I never felt any real intense emotional response to the difficulties then present.

Now let me tell you about another loss that I had. I have six children; the oldest being a girl and then five boys. When my daughter was about 10 or 11 months old, I lost her at Disneyland. She was already walking and when her mother and I were discussing what we wanted to do for the next few hours, Lauren walked away and neither one of us noticed. When I discovered she was gone and that I could not locate her, let me tell you about the intensity of that emotion! Many of you reading this story I know can relate to what I am describing. The feeling of loss was so intensified that it became coupled with several other emotions, i.e., panic, fear, worry, self degradation, guilt, you name it.

The question I have for my readers is can you explain why the intensity of the two losses was so different? The common answers I receive to this question are things like, "Your daughter has more value than money," or "You can always replace money, but you can't replace your daughter," or "You place greater value on your daughter than you do money." I appreciate each of those answers. I believe they are reasonable but I don't think they fully explain the response. If you will allow me, I would like to share my own impression of why feelings can become so intense; and in doing so expand your view. If I was Heavenly Father and I was trying to impress upon the minds of my mortal children the things that matter the most, I might create very intense feelings around those things that matter the most!

When we begin to observe intense emotions, it becomes clear that the most intense emotions we ever experience are in connection with relationships, including the relationship we have with our self. Grieving is intense!

PAIN

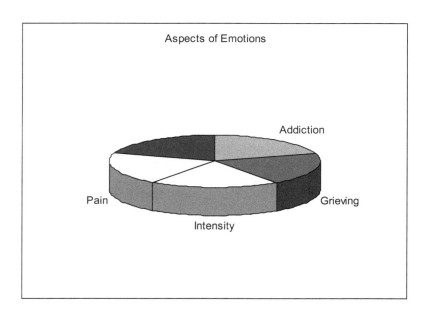

Now I would like to have us observe emotions from the angle of pain. Let me first state, that when it comes to physical pain, we humans are pretty brilliant. For the most part, when any of us feel physical pain, it catches our attention to the degree that we stop doing the very thing that led to the pain. We almost immediately begin to attend the area from which the pain derives; especially if the pain is significant and prolonged enough. We do so because we seem

132

to have established the understanding that attending to the reason for the pain will lead to resolve of the pain.

An example of this comes from my 4th child. One evening I received a text from my son Jacob, telling me to hurry down to the church. His older brother Carey had injured himself playing basketball. When I arrived, sure enough there was Carey lying on the wood floor in incredible pain. Now please understand that the following conversation was trying to create some lightness and reinforcement, because everything I am trying to teach you in relation to pain, I had already taught my children.

Dad: Carey, what happened?
Carey: I think I broke my ankle
Dad: How do you know you broke your ankle?
Carey: Because it really hurts!
Dad: Why aren't you still playing basketball?
Carey: Dad, not now. I am not in the mood

For those other leaders and friends that heard this conversation probably thought I was being insensitive, though I was just awkwardly reinforcing previous learning. At the point my son said, "Dad, not now," I actually became very attentive to his situation.

Many times I will ask my clients if they have ever broken a bone. Interestingly enough, many of my clients have. Whether you have or not is not important, but I would like to use the scenario of a broken bone to make a point. The first question I ask such clients is, "How do you know you broke your bone?" Somewhere in each of their replies is the following acknowledgement, "It hurt. The pain was telling me my bone was broken." I then ask this follow-up question, "What went wrong?" This kind of stumps my clients and they become confused. Usually they just tend to repeat that their bone was broken. This becomes the moment that I redirect them to the physiology of cells, because my whole program has grown out of an understanding from the field of Epigenetics. I say to them, "Your cells broke." I ask them what is bone made of and clients acknowledge that bone is made of cells. I then add, "When cells break they emit pain."

Pain is an indicator that something has gone wrong and in the realm of physical pain, what went wrong was that cells broke. I ask clients to describe for me what they began to do to address the pain. Inevitably, each tells about how they made their way to the hospital. They speak of X-rays, setting of the bone, usually some restrictive device like a cast and perhaps a device to prevent further stress, like a sling or crutches. I then ask, "Did the ride to the hospital heal the bone?" "Did the X-ray heal the bone?" "How about the setting of the bone?" "The cast or crutches?" Each time the reply is "No" because in fact none of those things actually heal the bone. They are the supportive acts we do to make sure that the healing goes as best as it can, but none of it actually heals the bone. What heals the bone? Our cells do! The properties of healing are found in every cell. Cells know how to heal.

So what are these things called negative emotions? They are pain! They are emotional pain. Pain is an indicator that something is going wrong. What is going wrong? Your cells are breaking! Why are they breaking? Because the information you are providing in the form of Automatic Negative Thoughts, the Negative Meanings you are associating with those thoughts and the Negative Core Beliefs that are shaping within you is breaking your cells. Here is why, your cells already know who they are. They know the source from which they sprang. Contained within their memory is a sacred consciousness. They know that they are the children of God and all that denotes. When we go about telling our cells things they are not they speak back to us in the form of pain or negative emotions. It is His design within each of us so that we might remember that the object of our existence is happiness. We can't be truly happy if we are going against ourselves. When we become accepting of our real self emotional pain dissipates.

One of the perspectives I share with some of my clients is that I firmly believe that the research is catching up with the revelations. So let me speak about the secular side of this concept I am touching on. Most of the research field is coming to understand that every cell is intelligent. Nels Quevli in the year 1916 in his book entitled "*Cell intelligence: The cause of growth, heredity and instinctive actions, illustrating that the cell is a conscious, intelligent being, and, by reason thereof, plans and builds all plants and animals in the same manner that man constructs houses, railroads and other structures.*" (The Colwell Press, Minneapolis, MN). I know, pretty long title for a book, but this is perhaps the beginning of looking at the characteristics of cells. The basic tenet of the book is that the actions and properties of cells are too amazing to be explained by anything but their intelligence.

Guenter Albrecht-Bueler at Northwestern University Medical School stated:

> Cells, not doctors heal patients. Our guess of the next stage may begin with the recognition that no physician in the history of humanity has ever healed a patient. Only the cells of the patient can heal the patient. Only cells know how to close wounds, understand what to do with insulin and how to destroy pathogens. The best a physician can do, is to move obstacles out of the way of cells (e.g. by surgery), supply materials and weapons to the cells (e.g. drugs and building blocks of life) and leave the fight against disease to the cells.

Epigenetics is a revolution that is going to transform medicine where the prevention and treatment of disease will be based upon your genome and epigenome and the intelligence of cells.

Sondra Barrett, PhD. adds her insight:

> The truth is cells are intelligent and wise – They carry the wisdom of the ages, the operating instructions of life. So clearly is this understanding now that the future of medicine will be built in the growing understanding of our cell's intelligence.

The first time I heard this concept of cells being intelligent, I had a few scriptures come rushing into my mind. One of those scriptures refers to our individuality as intelligence. In a vision given to Abraham, the ancient friend of God said:

> Now the Lord had shown unto me. Abraham, the intelligences that were organized before the world was; and among all these there were many of the noble and great ones. And God saw these souls that they were good, and he stood in the midst of them, and he said: These I will make my rulers; for he

stood among those that were spirits. And he saw that they were good......
(Abraham 3:22-23)

Without question we are organized as cells; intelligence being incorporated within each one. We are intelligent beings. As an example of cellular intelligence let us consider the following. Cell division is a process, but as we look at the intricacies of this process the evidence becomes overwhelming as to the purposeful, intentional and consciousness of the cell in accomplishing this formidable task. In order for cell division to be successful, DNA needs to be copied. The copying or replication takes place without incident. It is a highly organized, detailed and disciplined process that allows us to observe intelligence at a very high level.

The DNA molecule is comprised of a data storage bank containing 3.2 billion letters that are the sequencing in every genome. The structure and sequencing of these letters gives the DNA an appearance of a ladder that is twisted around itself; forming a helix. The process of replication is sequential. To copy the DNA requires the appearance of an enzyme called helicase which begins the process of unwinding and separating the "sides of the twisted ladder" in a zipper-like fashion. The enzymatic helicase never falters in its timing nor in its assignment of preparing the DNA to be copied.

Waiting in the wings, knowing exactly when to begin its function is another enzyme called polymerase. Polymerase creates an exact duplicate of each unwound strand of DNA, but in order to accomplish this step we must consider the very nature of an enzyme. An enzyme is made up of atoms and molecules, which from all appearances would not appear to have any specific knowledge, awareness, consciousness or intelligence. Yet Polymerase identifies the type of information needed to complete the replication of each strand of DNA and then locates the necessary components, wherever they may be in the cell and transports them to where they are needed. In human DNA copying, the process can replicate 50 nucleotides every second. In accomplishing this assembly the polymerase enzyme does not make even the slightest mistake. It identifies, sequentially the 3.2 billion letters or nucleotides and duplicates with exactness two completely new strands. The helicase enzyme works in cooperation with the polymerase enzyme as it maintains the separation of the two strands while polymerase completes its function.

If you were given a book with 3.2 billion letters and were asked to type a replica, you couldn't possibly do so without making a mistake. You would leave out a letter or perhaps become blurry-eyed and transpose some of those letters, perhaps even missing a line here or there. Are you beginning to appreciate the capacity for intentional and purposeful workings of just these two enzymes, not to mention many more that are involved in this incredibly detailed process? And they repeat this process trillions and trillions of times without fault, error or in anyway damaging the DNA. Each daughter cell that results from this process is carrying the same information as its parent cell.

The theory of evolution states that all of these enzymes; the information contained within the sequencing of the 3.2 billion nucleic acids (the letters), the process of genetic copying and this error-free organization I just described came about as the result of a string of coincidences. Evolutionary processes as an explanation of this process is highly improbable, in fact, the impossible assumption is a significant mistake that needs serious consideration. To be blind to the obvious workings of an intelligently driven process is like saying there is no light at midday.

Remember, the DNA Code is a message. It is comprised of four simple letters or nucleotides that are intelligently positioned. The DNA sequencing is the message of life. Its mathematical formula is the instructions for manufacturing proteins. Proteins are life and you and I are comprised of about 250,000 of them. There is nothing else, but DNA, that manufacturers proteins. Dr. Francis Collins, an atheist prior to his accepting the assignment to head up the Mapping of the Human Genome Project, converted to Christianity because of the intelligence he observed in the DNA Code. His comment was simply this, "Whoever wrote the DNA Code is the greatest mathematician in the Universe." He later went on to say, "I am assured that as we continue to decode the message, one day we will find written in the DNA molecule our very purpose in the Universe!" I imagine if we could map God's DNA, it would become abundantly clear what that purpose is!

So every cell is intelligent; every cell has consciousness and awareness. This consciousness and awareness is evidenced by the exact, error free division processes found in every cell. Likewise, every cell knows that it is working in cooperation with every other cell. Multi-cellular organisms serve as the ultimate example of cooperation on a cellular level, with millions, billions, or even trillions of cells working together to form the tissues and organs of a complex individual. Such organisms cannot exist without cooperation among their cells, and the cells cannot exist outside of the cooperative system. The surprising ease with which these systems arose may be attributed to the fact that all the cells of a multi-cellular individual carry an identical genome.

What is it that our cells are so aware of because of the DNA Code? How to maintain biological life is an obvious answer, by the information just presented, but there is another biological response for life manifesting itself within our cells. This is the secular observation, which supports the idea that our cells already know who they are.

I want to remind you that we live in a time where technology allows us to see our thoughts. Our thoughts are transformed into protein messengers called neuro or polypeptides. A single Automatic Negative Thought will be converted into billions of these long amino acid chains, which then get shot out into the bloodstream and influence various chemicals and hormones to also be released within the body. These protein messengers are now looking for cells to dock to in order to release the information they carry into our cells. As we release negative thoughts directed toward our self, cells immediately react by sending out chemical messengers that signal the release of adrenaline, cortisol and neuroepinephrine into the blood stream. If you are not familiar with these chemicals, when we see the combination of these three, then we know our "fight and flight" system, or sympathetic nervous system has been activated. The "fight and flight" system is *designed* in every one of us. What activates the survival mechanism is when there is a perception of harm or threat. Our Automatic Negative Thoughts are interpreted at the cellular level as a perceived threat or harm, but the only explanation for Automatic Negative Thoughts activating the threat modulating system is that our cells must already possess a knowledge of who they really are, otherwise the "fight or flight" system would have no reason to turn on. That true identity can be written in only one thing – our DNA!

The chemical composition of adrenaline, cortisol and neuroepinephrine are designed in us for preservation measures. This self-preservation mechanism is vital, signifying the preciousness of life. Automatic Negative Thoughts are manifestations of facing ongoing experience from a place of fear and doubt, which the Epigeneticists pointed out, would cut us off from our deep, positive emotions; and now we can see why. Adrenaline is the chemical that has us feel angry and with cortisol - stress. Neuroepinephrine increases the ability to speed up cognitive processes; in other words to find solutions, which is exactly what is required when we are under the perception of harm or threat; however it's problem is that when being produced under such conditions, can greatly enhance the negative emotional response thus creating distortions of self-perception. These chemicals and hormones, when experienced on such a consistent basis, due to a negative mindset, act powerfully in having us believe things about our self that are not accurate.

While the sympathetic nervous response serves a very important function, consistent elevated levels of these chemicals in the blood stream is the precursor to inflammation and inflammation is the leading cause to so many health problems. The reason for this physical response is that the immune system is turned way down when these chemicals are at elevated levels within the blood stream. Now you can see why negative mindsets lead to health issues. And so I ask again, why would this fight and flight system be activated by negative thoughts directed toward ourselves if the cells did not already know who they are? It appears that they do and when we provide them with information that goes contrary to their real identity, they respond as if they are being threatened.

I believe it is time that we begin to see negative emotions for what they really are – they are pain. Pain is always an indicator that something is going wrong and what is going wrong is that cells are breaking. Our cells can break and emit physical pain or our cells can break and emit emotional pain. Either way, it is time to begin to appreciate our incredible design that keeps us from harm. Unfortunately, without a background in physiology, too many of us interpret negative emotions incorrectly. Too many use negative emotions as evidence that somehow we are devalued in some way. But that is not accurate as negative emotions are part of our design to keep us on the path of happiness. Happiness cannot be achieved when we are going against our true selves. Let's begin to have appreciation for negative emotions as our belief about who we really are appears to matter if we are going to live in a manner of happiness.

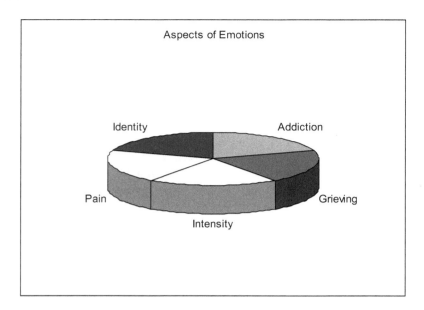

Based upon the foregoing discussion of the different aspects of our emotions, it is apparent that a correct view of our self, an understanding of our true identity is necessary if we are to live with peace of mind, with assurance, hope and happiness.

Obviously, I have worked with many clients who do not belong to the Church of Jesus Christ of Latter-Day Saints and therefore I have to appeal to their own experience to assist them in seeing their identity. One time I asked a client to tell me about his children. He began to smile and started talking about the different ways his children would do things. He spoke of them being clever, how they learned, their fun personalities, their instinctive love and affection for him as a dad, etc. Here this father was admiring all that his children were. I then asked him, "What will your children grow up to be?" He replied, "They will grow up and become what they want to become?" I asked him why he knew so much about his children's potential. He asked me what I meant. I said, "Well it seems like you know who your children really are." You seem to understand that they have the potential to become what their DNA says they can become." What is a human capable of? What are your children capable of? He began to reflect on what he did know his children could be because of what their DNA Code tells them they are…. And then I added, "You seem to understand what your children are designed to become and yet you are here in therapy because of your anxiety. Do you think if you become everything your children can become that you would ever experience anxiety?" He replied, "Wow! It's funny how I can easily see what my children can become and yet I forget I am capable of the very same thing. If I became everything that I see my children can become, then no, I would not struggle with anxiety." I thanked him for reinforcing the concept of what the research says drives ongoing negative emotions – it is when we lose track of our true identity.

We know more than we can tell. Sometimes the things we know take the form of knowledge about what is happening to us in life in which we sense our true design and its accompanying purpose. In our increasing reflections of life experience we sense there is a divine essence from which we are made, but which we have difficulty trying to express in words. As this client's experience suggests, there are simply moments of mute comprehension and of mute certitude. It is important to pay attention to these moments, because our Father in Heaven often gives us moments of assurance of our real identity, but not necessarily with the capacity to articulate these assurances to others.

For those that have an association with the church or even Christianity in general, I would like to discuss some elements of a Disney movie, Princess Diaries I and Princess Diaries II, starring Anne Hathaway and Julie Andrews to draw a better idea of personal identity. In the first movie we are introduced to a young adolescent girl, Mia, played by Anne Hathaway. If we were to attach some labels to Mia, we might say she is a bit insecure, clumsy, uncoordinated and a bit geeky. If you will recall, Mia's hair is frizzed and voluminous; she wears a beanie cap to keep it in place. Her eyebrows are thick and connected; whenever she pushes her glasses back up her nose bridge she snorts a little. Mia also has a good friend, Lily. Lily too would qualify under the same labels as Mia, but we also discover that Lily is a very loyal, strong minded friend.

The opening scene of the first movie we see Mia and Lily at the high school campus and like on every high school campus these two teen girls are trying to determine who they are, how they fit in and what group will accept them. The movie depicts a few interactions Mia and Lily have with different cliques or groups of students and let's just say it doesn't go very well for these two girls. In fact, there is a moment where Mia takes one of the interactions very personally and we see Mia standing there, silent but obviously upset. Lily comes to Mia and says, "Oh, don't you listen to them!"

Mia goes home after school that day and meets someone for the very first time; it is her grandmother on her father's side. Mia has been living with her single mother and doesn't know much about her father. Grandmother, played by Julie Andrews, is sensitive to the situation seeing there has been no relationship between her and her granddaughter previously, but grandmother has a purpose. Grandmother explains the reason for her visit and asks Mia if she would like to learn about her father's side of the family? Grandmother then explains to Mia that she herself is a queen of a little country called Genovia and then informs Mia that she is the next person in line to inherit the throne. Grandmother's inquiry to Mia's interest is not to compel her to the throne, but merely an invitation to learn what it means to be Royal whereby she can have the basis to make a fully informed decision. Grandmother does not want Mia to feel any pressure in her decision and explains to Mia that whatever she decides that it will not create any disappointment as grandmother respects Mia's agency.

Mia immediately goes to her mother and asks, "Why didn't you tell me about this? You have been lying to me for sixteen years! You never told me I was a princess!" Mia's mother replies, "I didn't want you to have any extra pressure in your life." Mia returns to grandmother and informs her that she would like to learn what it means to be Royal. So grandmother opens up, for lack of a better expression, Princess School. Everyday after Mia gets out of high school, she is to meet with her grandmother to become educated in the graces, manners and diplomacy of royalty. At first, it does not appear that Mia takes princess school very seriously. She is constantly late. Sweet, patient grandmother simply reminds Mia, "A princess is never late."

One day when Mia arrived for her tutelage, there was a dining room table arranged with all of the formal settings. Mia was to learn about dining etiquette since she would host many foreign dignitaries. We observe Mia, in her discomfort, pick up some of the silverware and tap the various dishes and glasses present, as if she was playing a xylophone. Mia breaks one of the crystal charges, bringing looks of "Will she ever get this" from those that were trying to bring royal understanding and refinement to her. There is this one scene where Mia begins to cross her legs immediately drawing the attention of her grandmother who instructs, "Mia, a princess never crosses her legs. She crosses her ankles."

Again, Mia is not taking any of this early training very seriously until an event occurred in the Princess school. Though this event was portrayed in a humorous way, still this appears to be the turning point in Mia's attitude of learning of what it means to be Royal. The event was a makeover. If I could give an academy award for just a single look, I would have given it to Anne Hathaway when she looked into the mirror when this makeover was completed. Mia's expression was one of astonishment and awe. Mia could not believe this was her looking back at herself. She could not believe that she could ever look this way. Her hair no longer frizzed out but straightened and shiny, her eyebrows shaped, contacts instead of the thick-rimmed glasses; make-up applied, Mia's true physical beauty emerged. Yet, still insecure, Mia gets ready for school on Monday in the same manner, school uniform, beanie cap on head, glasses, etc. However, there is still enough visible difference that it catches the attention of one of her school peers. In her closer examination and attempt of discovery, this classmate approaches Mia and pulls her beanie cap off revealing her beautifully straightened hair. Mia then removes her glasses and in this moment, many were taking notice of her beauty. You could hear the "awes" coming from her peers, the smiles; and the extended looking. Mia was experiencing something new from her classmates. They were noticing her and in a positive manner. Mia's confidence begins to grow and from this point forward, Mia begins to take Princess school much more seriously. That is enough of the first movie.

In the second movie, Mia has completed all of her training. She is fully prepared to inherit and rule from the throne with confidence and dignity. Mia approaches grandmother and asks, "Grandma, just because you are born royal, do you have to inherit your throne?" Grandma replies, "Oh no Mia. Just because you are born royal you may abdicate your throne at any time." For those of us that live in the western hemisphere may not understand accurately words that are associated with cultures that operate under kings and queens. The word abdicate has a very specific meaning, it means to give up that which you were *born* to receive, though we may use it in other various ways.

As promised from the beginning, grandmother is allowing Mia to make her own decision. Now fully informed, grandmother is applying no pressure one way or the other. Grandmother believes in Mia. Grandmother's confidence in Mia's correct decision is based in the training she has just received. Grandmother is relaxed and is now honoring the great gift of Agency with which Mia is endowed. She also has confidence in Mia's correct decision because Mia had fundamentally changed her perspective of self.

Mia decides to inherit the throne. As soon as she does the movie fasts forward to the coronation ceremony. I ask every client at this point, "Do you know what a coronation is?" Have you ever seen a coronation?" Most have an idea that it is a ceremony where the new king or queen is formally crowned and recognized.  Interestingly, it is dual in its nature as it is also seen as an accession to the highest office. The ceremony is born of spiritual roots and is actually a formal representation to God's service. It includes being washed and anointed, prior to being dressed in formal ceremonial robes and receiving implements as tokens by oath. Symbolism is present in each stage of the ceremony, pointing to the minds of those that are present the very nature and purpose of eternal precepts and identity. Though we find the coronation rites in every culture, it is obvious that some alterations in the ceremony, which have taken place over time, indicates that the real meaning was lost to mankind in general.

When you consider the high office being assumed, meaning that of a queen, you might think that the coronation would take place in the castle. But coronations never take place in castles. In every culture and in every age, coronations take place in sacred, holy edifices. Likewise, since grandmother is the reigning queen, you might think that grandmother would be the one to invest in her granddaughter all of the rights, privileges and responsibilities of that office, but grandmother has nothing to do with the coronation.

As the coronation unfolds, after Mia has been washed and anointed, we see Mia come to the entryway of a cathedral, a sacred holy place. She is dressed in a tunic like garment with a girdle about her waist. As we peer into the cathedral there are others that have likewise prepared themselves to be there, already seated, to act as witnesses to the sacred event. Mia, having come to the entryway is greeted by the high priest of this religious organization. In the movie he is fashioned to look like the Anglican Bishop. The first thing the high priest does is to dress Mia in the robes pertaining to this holy order. He then escorts her to her throne. As Mia is seated, she brings forth one hand in cupping shape and in this hand the high priest places a ball of curious workmanship. I use that language purposefully as that is the description of the Liahona. The Liahona was much more than a compass, it was an instrument, whereupon faithful response provided the travelers with messages that provided perspective and understanding (See: 1 Nephi 16:29). It allowed them to know things that were previously unavailable to their understanding.

The scriptures indicate that for those that overcome will be given a stone (Revelation 2:17), which in the revelations given to us will become a Urim and Thummim to each individual who receives one, whereby things pertaining to a higher order of kingdoms will be made known (D&C 130:10). It is an instrument in obtaining revelation and knowing all things that God knows. In other words, those that possess a Urim and Thummim have all things present before them (See: D&C 130:7), which is a description of the state of God. The Liahona and the Urim and Thummim appear to suggest the same thing and here is Mia, receiving an instrument symbolizing that she has prepared herself to continue to rule and reign with enlightenment and access to God's knowledge. I might suggest that the ball placed in her hand represents OMNISCIENCE. In his painting, Salvator Mundi, Leonardo da Vinci shows Christ with a glass orb in his hand. When I saw that the orb was made of crystal glass, my mind caught hold of the following scriptures, wherein the Apostle John is given a vision of the throne of God:

> And before the throne there was a sea of glass like unto crystal..... (Revelation 4:6)

> And I saw as it were a sea of glass mingled with fire and them that had the victory over the beast, and over his image, and over his mark, and over the number of his name, stand on the sea of glass.... (Revelation 15:2)

Modern revelation has provided more understanding of what the Beloved John was observing:

> Q. What is the sea of glass spoken of by John, 4th chapter, and 6th verse of the Revelation? A. It is the earth in its sanctified, immortal, and eternal state. (D&C 77:1)

Speaking of the nature, mission and environment of God's ministering angels we have further been informed that:

> ..... there are no angels who minister to this earth but those who do belong or have belonged to it. The angels do not reside on a planet like this earth; but they reside in the presence of God on a globe like a sea of glass and fire, where all things for their glory are manifest, past, present, and future, and are continually before the Lord. The place where God resides is a great Urim and Thummim. The earth in its sanctified and immortal state will be made like unto crystal and will be a Urim and Thummim to the inhabitants who dwell thereon...... Then the white stone mentioned in Revelation 2:17, will become an Urim and Thummim to each individual who receives one, whereby things pertaining to a higher order of kingdoms will be made known. (D&C 130:5-10)

I have the sense that Leonardo da Vinci's painting was derived by ancient knowledge, knowledge that was lost in time, but has now been restored. Of all orbs the famous artist could have chosen, he chose an orb made of crystal glass. I sense it was a purposeful choice. In the symbolism is a constant reminder that those that overcome and are redeemed are made to be kings (and queens), priests (and priestesses) unto God and will be appointed unto offices of dominion (Revelations 5:9-10; D&C 76:50-70).

Omniscience is to know all things and thereby discerning the truth that frees us from every false principle. That is the very definition of overcoming is when through truth we reject false principles and live by the truth thus obtaining or inheriting all that God has (Romans 8:16-17). We become liberated from the confusion falsehoods create, the cloud of darkness is taken from us, and the light of eternal truth shines upon our minds.

> And if your eye be single to my glory your whole bodies shall be filled with light, and there shall be no darkness in you; and that body which is filled with light comprehendeth all things. (D&C 88:67)

As we learn of and adhere to the laws that lead to the greatest light, we will be raised to receive that glory forever and ever (D&C 88:29). God lives with eternal life. That description has less to do with longevity and more to do with quality. God is a Creator. He has created a Universe and worlds upon which, the children He has given organized identity to, may dwell. He has created the laws upon which they could advance and become as He is, or in other words live with eternal life as He does (D&C 132:20, 24). Eternal life consists in living and being as He is. In other words, eternal life is to gain the power of God, which power is faith, and thus be able to do what He does and to live as He lives. The power of faith will dwell independently in every person that gains eternal life, as it does in God Himself. Truth is light! Faith is the child of truthful knowledge.

Salvator Mundi, c. 1500
Leonardo da Vinci

Stained Glass Panel in the Transept of Saint John's Anglican Church
Ashfield, New South Wales

After being given the Orb, Mia then brings forth her other hand with the palm down and the thumb extended. In this hand the high priest places a scepter. The scepter represents that dominion has been given to the recipient. Other symbolism suggested by the scepter is that the recipient has attained to a station of purity, virtue and righteousness that allows the Holy Ghost to be a constant companion (See: D&C 121:46), and upon which the power of God operates (D&C 121:36). I might suggest that the scepter also represents OMNIPOTENCE. To be given dominion suggests that we have been appointed to govern. We, like those that have before attained to this higher office, are trusted to govern by the laws that lead to fulfilling the measure of our creation. Omnipotence is the state whereby there is nothing more powerful outside of us than what is inside of us. Omnipotence is to have all power, yet to administer such power to protect (1 Samuel 17:37; Malachi 3:11), to produce faith in the minds of others (1 Nephi 1:14), and to help bring others to a state of exaltation (D&C 11:30). God's power is named faith. By it, the worlds were and are made. By it all things exist and are upheld, By it all things are possible. Faith is power and the very power of God Himself. We exercise and grow our faith

143

because of who God is and the attributes of holiness which are perfected in Him (D&C 121:41-44). His power grows in our lives when we develop and perfect these same attributes.

It is difficult to produce faith in a being that is not Omnipotent or Omniscient. Faith would always be found diminished or lacking in us if such perfections were limited in Him to any degree. So let me get a bit serious here and apply this to my reader. You were born to become a king or queen. But who would ever have confidence in a being that sees them self in terms of worthlessness, of inadequacy, of not being important, of being helpless, or lacking power? Who would ever want to follow a being that sees them self that way? Exactly, no one! No one will ever attain to the higher office believing those kinds of things about themselves. When we understand the character and power of God, we then can understand who we really are; and while not fully developed in our current state, yet we recognize these are the very things that improve our state of being even here in mortality. The more we know and adhere to correct information, the more control we gain over our existence.

After the scepter is placed in the initiate's hand, the high priest then moves behind Mia and places a crown on her head, signifying to all present that she has fully qualified herself to rule and to reign forever. The crown may also suggest glory (D&C109:76) because she has become all knowing (Omniscient) and placed in a position of power (Omnipotent). In some cultures, the glory is represented by a sun appearing above the Initiate's head. The symbol of the crown also suggests trust to follow she who has learned how to live. Righteous kings and queens are to their people servants, teachers and examples of righteousness (Mosiah 2:9-17; 2 Nephi 31:16). Their years of preparation are a token to the people that there is safety and peace in following their example.

The crown has embedded in its gold - gems, jewels and precious stones. When counted the appropriate number is twelve, representing the Twelve Tribes of Israel. The symbolism is the same as the twelve gems, jewels and precious stones that existed on the high priest breastplate in ancient times. Twelve also represents priesthood authority and power.

Yet in further display, these jewels are also representative of our importance to our Heavenly Father and of the blessings foreshadowed to those who will accept their true identity and press forward in the paths that lead to exaltation:

> Your words have been stout against me, saith the Lord. Yet ye say, What have we spoken so much against thee?
>
> Ye have said it is vain to serve God: and what profit is it that we have kept his ordinance, and that we have walked mournfully before the Lord of hosts?
>
> And now we call the proud happy; yea, they that work wickedness are set; yea, they that tempt God are even delivered.
>
> Then they that feared the Lord spake often one to another: and the Lord hearkened and heard it, and a book of remembrance was written before him for them that feared the Lord, and that thought upon his name. (Malachi 3:13-16)

Of them found written in that book, the Lord continues:

> And they shall be mine, saith the Lord of hosts, *in that day when I make up my jewels*; and I will spare them, as a man spareth his own son that serveth him.
>
> Then shall ye return and discern between the righteous and the wicked, between him that serveth God and him that serveth him not. (Malachi 3:17-19)

The scripture in Malachi reminds us that the Lord our High Priest is discerning those that have prepared themselves through their faithfulness to His law and ordinances and who will be written in His book of remembrance. In the movie, likewise notice that the person that is officiating, overseeing and performing the rites of royal leadership is the high priest. He is the one that is the rightful judge of preparation. It is not therefore a surprise that for those that overcome will hear from the true High Priest,

> Well done thou good and faithful servant. Thou has been faithful over a few things, I will now make thee ruler over many things, enter thou into the joy of thy lord. (Matthew 25:21, 23; See Also: 2 Timothy 4:7-8)

Not demonstrated in the Disney movie is more symbolism in the coronation ceremony. Recently, the British Empire celebrated Queen Elizabeth's 65th year of reign. I was looking at a picture of her on her day of coronation. There she is seated on her throne, wearing a tunic style dress with a girdle there about. She is likewise dressed in the robes of that holy order. One hand is in cupping shape wherein a ball of curious workmanship rests and in her other hand a scepter. Upon her head is a crown with the embedded gems, jewels and precious stones. However in this picture her feet are visible. Do you have any idea what her feet are shod in? There are no dress shoes or any fancy wear at all present. Her feet are shod in humble slippers. Perhaps our first awareness of this symbol comes when Moses, upon the holy mount, converses with the Lord. The words of Jehovah, the eternal high priest are as follows,

> Draw not nigh hither: put off thy shoes from off thy feet, for the place whereon thou standest is holy ground. (Exodus 3:5)

I think there is more to the ground being called holy ground other than the fact that the Holy One is present. I think it is also the information being received; that if kept, will lead a person to becoming holy as Jehovah is holy (Leviticus 11:45). The wearing of slippers is emblematic of humility, a willingness to be taught and to follow what is learned. Places that are set apart where sacred knowledge is revealed are not common, they are sanctified, holy places (See: Ezekiel 42:20; 44:23; Isaiah 6:1-7;and D&C 115:7-8 as examples of special places being set apart to receive special information). Covenants made in these sacred, holy places, if kept will lead us to becoming holy. Since God proposes to make us holy as He is, He must reveal the laws that pertain to His dwelling. He has us receive these laws by covenant. If we will keep the associated covenants that are delivered through ordinances, the sacred priesthood ordinances will change us, sanctify us, and prepare us to enter His dwelling place, even the Celestial Kingdom (D&C 88:17-20; 28-29). Returning to the picture of Queen Elizabeth; interestingly is that her feet are resting upon a stone. One of the names it bears is the Stone of Scone as Scone is the district in which this sacred object is stored. To give us an idea of what this stone represents I turn to a description the apostle Paul gave concerning the wandering Israelites, said he:

> Moreover, brethren, I would not that ye should be ignorant, how that all our fathers were under the cloud, and all passed through the sea; and were all baptized unto Moses in the cloud and in the sea; and did all eat the same spiritual meat; and did all drink the same spiritual drink: for they drank of that spiritual Rock that followed them: and that Rock was Christ. (1 Corinthians 10:1-4)

Christ Himself announced, "Wherefore, I am in your midst, and I am the good shepherd, and *the stone of Israel*. He that buildeth upon this rock shall never fall" (D&C 50:44; Italics added for emphasis).

The primary hymn, "And the wise man built his house upon the rock".... likewise reflects the same understanding. With her feet upon the Stone of Scone, Queen Elizabeth is making an oath and covenant that she will rule based upon the Law of Christ.

This stone has been present at every coronation in the British Isles, including England, Scotland, France, Scandinavia and Ireland. By tradition it is known as the Stone of Jacob, referring to the ancient patriarch, the grandson of Abraham. In Genesis 28 we find a story that indicates that Jacob, while traveling from Beer-sheba, where he had just received the birthright is headed toward Haran. In his travels he had an experience, that of a vision that took up the space of a night. When one pays attention to the details of this event, it becomes obvious that Jacob is given certain promises that are associated with the rites of coronation. It is therefore no coincidence that Jacob names this place Beth-el, meaning House of God, a sacred holy place (Genesis 28:16-19).

If you will recall when Joseph's visit from the Father and Son left him lying on his back with no strength (JSH-1:20), or when Moses had spoken to God face-to-face and had been shown the workmanship of God's creative powers and when the presence of God withdrew from Moses, Moses fell to the earth and it was for the space of many hours before Moses did receive his natural strength back (Moses 1:9-10); so it appears with Jacob in the vision he had. His natural strength was likewise drawn from him and he had to rest. The scriptures indicate in doing so, he had laid his head on some stones (Genesis 28:11).

It was from this place that Jacob took a stone that he had laid his head on the night before in memoriam of this event (Genesis 28:18). It is this stone that Jeremiah the prophet carried with him to Ireland. This is, by tradition, the very stone still used in the ongoing coronations of those northern countries (Jeremiah 31:8). This tradition may have merit as the Saxons that poured into this area is the name given by those who were already present, Saxon meaning Isaac's sons! They brought with them the rites of coronation or in other words, the temple rituals. It is no coincidence that we see in these northern kingdoms these rites being a natural part of their society.

For those that have been endowed may be recognizing elements of that ceremony. Endowment is a gift of oaths and covenants that allow us to progress and assume a high position. After being washed and anointed, we are presented with instruction whereupon we are reminded that the washing and anointing was in preparation to become hereafter, kings and queens, priests and priestesses unto the Most High God. We are told that through our faithfulness we will be crowned to rule and to reign forever in the House of Israel. We then proceed through the endowment making every sign and token pertaining to our true identity in relationship to our Eternal Father. We do so symbolically dressed in the manner pertaining to this holy order, including the tunic-style dress with its girdle and the robes of the holy priesthood.

That holy order, which administers the ordinances of Salvation, is called Melchizedek. The ordinances are put in a sequential manner that godliness may be manifest (D&C 84:19-21). When godliness is manifest completely then we have become like God; to be like God is to assume a high office, wherein we are entrusted to be a ruler over many things. The miter cap worn by the men of this order is present to act as protection when the crown is placed upon the head of the faithful high priests. The soft edges of the miter cap will fold down when the crown is placed, providing protection to the skin, from becoming abraded by the metal of the crown (See: Exodus 28). The very name of the priesthood which administers in these saving ordinances means 'righteous king,' a constant reminder of our true identity, a reminder that we belong to the order of righteous kings.

Now let's turn to a scene in the Savior's life to further support our true identity as children of the Highest. The Jewish leaders were growing more and more uncomfortable with the rising popularity of Jesus, as he went about doing good. As previously mentioned the crowning miracle that created urgency in these men was the raising of Lazarus from the dead. In response to this event it is recorded:

> Then gathered the chief priests and the Pharisees a council, and said, What do we? For this man doeth many miracles. If we let him thus alone, all men will believe on him; and the Romans shall come and take away both our place and nation. And one of them, named Caiaphas, being the high priest that same year, said unto them, Ye know nothing at all, nor consider it expedient for us, that one man should die for the people, and that the whole nation perish not. (John 11:47-50)

These verses reveal the conspiracy to have Jesus put to death. Since the Jews had no authority to put any man to death, as that was held by the State, Caiaphas and others approached the Roman officials and laid false charges against Jesus. In paraphrase, one of those false charges was that Jesus was going about declaring himself 'King of the Jews,' meaning the Messiah, The Promised One, and that everyone was to worship him. Now this would have held some weight under Roman law, seeing that Caesar was touted as a king-god and that worship was reserved for him alone. I don't think this law was highly enforced, yet it still would have held weight in its strictest sense.

Due to the charge laid at the Savior, we can further appreciate one of the interrogations held by the Roman official, Pontius Pilate. Pilate asks Jesus, "Art thou a king then?" Jesus answered, "…. To this end was I born, and for this cause came I into the world…." (John 18:37). In appreciation of our earlier definition of the word 'abdicate,' I hope that you find the Savior's reply striking. Jesus knew who He was. He knew who is Father was and therefore He knew that

He was born to become a king. To some degree, I believe He is also manifesting the truth that mortal experience was part of the necessary occurence to prepare Him for what He was born to become (Mosiah 3:7; Alma 7:11-12).

But what about you? What if you were standing before Pilate and he asked you, "Art thou a King then? Art thou a Queen then?" What would be your reply? If you have been paying attention to the revelations, then it would be completely appropriate to answer in the same way..... "To this end was I born, and for this cause came I into the world." Each of us are children of the King and Queen of the Universe. We each possess the power to progress to become like Them, because we carry Their spiritual DNA. The chosen path for our development is to experience mortality, wherein a veil is drawn over our previous experience in the pre-mortal realm. It is in this condition that our belief is being measured in what has been revealed about our true identity. Do you know what this earth-life experience is? It is Prince and Princess School. It is here that we are learning how to overcome all false principles; all of our enemies, so that one day we may be entrusted to rule over many things. As it relates to our true identity I believe it would be impossible to advance and receive that which we were born to receive if we continue telling ourselves things that are contrary to who and what we really are. Holding false ideas about our true self is one way that abdication takes place.

We approached the subject of emotions by looking at it from different aspects. Each aspect provided perspective, culminating in seeing emotions from a complete whole. These negative emotions are designed in us to keep us on the path of happiness. Happiness starts with a correct understanding of who we really are and building that healthy relationship with ourselves. As we do so, we will find it easier to keep our sacred covenants, and adhere to laws that will make us holy. From our correct perspective, we will also be able to relate better with others; to better attune to others and become their friends. In doing so, we become their environment, and the correct views we hold of our self will assist them in a way that supports their true identity.

As Melchizedek Priesthood holders it is obvious the invitation to magnify our callings is preparing us to do just that. Each of us is given the responsibility for the welfare, and encouragement, and the development of others. Largely this authority is used within the walls of our own home, paying special attention to our wives and children. The husband who is devotedly true to his companion, the father who raises children to believe in goodness and in themselves, the patriarch that reigns with love and affection, such men magnify their true calling to become kings unto the Most High God. Being a husband and a father is an apprenticeship to godhood. There is great reason for the perfect educational system we live here in mortality and for being organized as families. It is what prepares gods to become Gods!

This is what we see in Mia. At first she is seeking her identity through acceptance of her peers. She never realizes who she really is until it is revealed to her. It takes time for Mia to grasp an understanding of her true self, but she fans the flame of belief by attending princess school and doing all things her grandmother is asking her to do. As her belief in herself increases, her confidence grows, until one day we view a young woman filled with confidence, grace and charity for others. This is one of the amazing outcomes of coming to a belief about your true identity – it allows you to go from a place of being more invested in your own insecurities and begin to become highly attuned to others. When we first meet Mia, her energy is more directed inward, worrying about what others think of her, worrying about will anyone ever find her acceptable, worrying about her performance, whether academically or socially; worrying about her appearance. But at the end of the second movie we see a young woman who is no longer concerned about such things. You can see that her energy is now invested toward others, especially those that she will serve. She is encouraging; she pauses and takes time to notice others, to listen to others and to deeply care for others. She has confidence in her ability to lead, to set a proper example of living with faith and assurance of the future of her country. She loves her people. She is now able to better love because she has come to love herself – therefore she does what she does for the right reason. I cannot help but to think of King Benjamin when I watch Mia transform. Every time I read King Benjamin's discourse I am uplifted, not just because of his message but perhaps even more so because of who he is, because of his great character. What an incredible ruler and example of what it means to "become." Who wouldn't want to follow a king like him?

Let me share with you a few insights about this true identity as has been repeatedly revealed to us. It seems like so many of us still forget or doubt what has been revealed:

> Have you forgotten who you are, and what your object is? Have you forgotten that you profess to be Saints of the Most High God, clothed upon with the holy priesthood? Have you forgotten that you are aiming to become kings and priests to the Lord, and queens and priestesses to him? (John Taylor – The Gospel Kingdom, 1987 p.229-230)

> Holders of the Melchizedek Priesthood have power to press forward in righteousness, living by every word that proceedeth forth from the mouth of God, magnifying their callings, going from grace to grace, until through the fullness of the ordinances of the temple they receive the fullness of the priesthood and are ordained kings and priests. Those so attaining shall have exaltation and be kings, priests, rulers, and lords in their respective spheres in the eternal kingdoms of the Great King who is God our Father. (Bruce. R. McConkie – Mormon Doctrine, 1966 p. 425)

> Whatever disappointments may come, still be true to him and I promise you, in the name of the Lord, that if not in time, in eternity, you shall have like honors and glory and privilege. If you are faithful over a few things here, you shall be ruler over many things there, and become kings and priests unto God. And you sisters who have dwelt in reflected glory will shine in your own light, queens and priestesses unto the Lord forever and ever. (Melvin J. Ballard – Conference Report, 1934)

The coronation ceremony is both ancient and pervasive. It is found in every culture and in every age. Its prominence speaks to the idea that it has a Source of its beginnings. Our awareness of its rites being centered in Europe is because that it is where we find it most apparent in recent history. Its European origin though appears to be traced to a group of people that immigrated to this region during a major shift or movement in world populations. It is very likely that the Northern Ten Tribes of Israel are a significant part of those that entered into the northern regions of Europe as Esdras, an apocryphal writer records the escape of the Kingdom of Israel from Assyria and then their travels through the Caucasian Range, by the Black Sea and up into Euro-Asia lands (Apocrypha, 2 Esdras 13:40-47). It was about this same time that other records indicate a large group of immigrants from Media did settle many areas of Eastern and Western Europe. The Saxons were one group that filled territories in Germany (Saxony) and Denmark. Likewise, the Celts of Ireland and the Britons of England share similar timelines.

It is not my purpose here to develop an entire narrative of the connection of the tribes of Europe with the Northern Tribes of Israel, as many have already done that research. My purpose is to have us recognize that the coronation was sacred information held by the House of Israel and an explanation of why kings and queens play such an important aspect of the more recent European history. Here are a few examples of interest:

1.  Saxon – Means Isaac's Sons
2.  Briton – Means The People of the Covenant
3.  Celts or Celtics – A tribe associated with Northern Ireland. Its flag consists of a hand, palm forward with the fingers pointed upwards and the thumb extended, as is common when making an oath. The backdrop of the hand is the Star of David (Sacred Geometry), with a crown positioned above the Star. The Druids were the priesthood of the Celts, and there are many, many similarities of their organization and practices as it relates to the organization and practices of the priesthood recorded in the Old Testament.
4.  Franks – In Obadiah 1:20 it states, "And the captivity of this host of the children of Israel shall possess that of the Canaanites, even unto *Zarapeth [Tserafati]*..... (The Hebrew word for France or Frenchman).

The fact that the rites associated with enthronement were brought by these immigrants is well attested. As stated earlier, the rituals associated with receiving the high office of king and queen are nearly universal, yet not everyone in a tribe, or people in the community were necessarily acquainted with these rites. They were shrouded in secrecy, yet there appears to be an agreement among scholars that being appointed to these higher offices was a Divine appointment, a gift given by the God of the Universe, and that all called to be a king could trace their kingship to the First King, a Cosmic Deity who founded the kingship rites. Many of these ritualistic and symbolic practices are associated with the Creation Drama. The ritualistic displays took place in temples or other sacred places. The initiate in receiving the symbols, signs and tokens was endowed with power and authority by which alone the Sovereign's rule was possible. The coronation rites are inextricably associated with the priesthood. Those who officiate in the giving of these rites are always of sacerdotal rank and even the king himself is of priestly grade or endowed with priesthood power. It appears that the coronation rites are a display of our true identity (Psalm 82:6; John 10:34-36).

As we have spoken about the intelligence of cells, let us not forget the other aspect to INTELLIGENCE as is explained in the scriptures, which also ties into cellular knowledge. Our spirits were organized to receive knowledge and intelligence; other terms used to describe this aspect of intelligence is "light and truth" (D&C 93:36-37). As previously explained glory is increased when we understand truth and abide by it. We are children of God. Receiving light (truth), continuing in God's revelations and receiving more light (truth) are what we are created to do. From our pre-mortal experience of being a part of His family, we followed the light. We followed our Heavenly Father and His plan. Seeking the light (truth) is in our spiritual DNA.

That which is of God is light; and he that receiveth light, and continueth in God, receiveth more light; and that light groweth brighter and brighter until the perfect day. (D&C 50:24)

To assist us in our ongoing pursuit of truth in our mortal experience and as evidence of God's love for each of us, we were given the Light of Christ (D&C 84:46). It influences us to seek truth, to discern truth and strengthens us to abide by it (Moroni 7:16).

Negative thoughts directed toward one's self is not intelligent because the thoughts are not true; therefore there is no light and we see things dimly when involved in an ongoing pattern of self deprecation. Every person that goes around with a negative internal conversation feels gloomy, depressed; having a sense of darkness shrouding them. Please understand and remember that knowledge is truth of things as they really are. Your cells already know who they really are. If you have doubt about your true identity it is because you have not yet obtained the knowledge of who you are, or you have not come to take it seriously yet, just like Mia when princess school was first opened for her. The evidence of not having a correct view of our self or that we have lost that relationship with our self is ongoing negative emotions.

When our focus is on *who we are not*, darkness, confusion, emptiness, fear, and doubt become our companion. But when our focus is on our true identity, we experience love and joy, no matter what is or is not happening in our lives. The Light of Christ has us likewise focus on Him and in doing so witness a marvelous example. Christ knew who He was, so come what may, His focus was constantly on that truth and all that it implied. It is what allowed Him to finish His preparations unto the children of men. His focus was on the joy of what could everlastingly be ours and so He lived up to His true identity. Focusing on the truth of who we are, focusing on the plan of Happiness, focusing on Him who showed us how to live, focusing on our blessings, and as we focus on going to the Source of all good, our joy will increase. Men are that they might have joy (2 Nephi 2:25). We are literally designed to be happy and in that design we were blessed with having negative emotions. These unwanted, undesirable emotions arise within us when we go against our true self. What an incredible design!

NOTE: For a more detailed understanding of our being born to become Kings and Queens, please turn to APPENDIX B: A VIEW FROM ABOVE. This was a speech given by President Spencer W. Kimball on the subject. In my opinion, it will open your eyes and understanding. It is a powerful speech!

FINAL THOUGHT – THE DISTORTION OF NEGATIVE EMOTIONS IS WHEN WE USE THEM AS EVIDENCE THAT WE ARE DEVALUED IN SOME WAY

Reminder: TRUTH – Every cell already has incorporated within its consciousness an understanding of their true identity. When our perceptions align with our real self our emotional states resonate with peace of mind, hope, assurance, happiness, motivation and empowerment. When our perceptions of self go against our true identity our cells activate the sympathetic nervous system; evidence that such unhealthy perceptions are perceived as harm or threat. Are you an intelligent being?

Our enemy within are our Core Negative Beliefs. Negative beliefs hide from the consciousness and they get exposed by the magic of mindfulness and awareness. Explore your core beliefs and challenge existing unhealthy beliefs.

— Natasa Pantovic Nuit

"As you recover, you will find yourself letting go of many of your negative beliefs........ you will come to see, for example, that the names you were called as a child are simply not true. You are not 'stupid,' 'lazy,' 'ugly,' or a 'liar'. You can discover just who you really are. You can let go of your pretenses and masks and discover who the real person is underneath."

— Beverly Engel

## NEGATIVE CORE BELIEFS

Since negative emotions are a physiological response to having lost a relationship with ourselves, it is now time to see how it is that you began to lose that relationship. We are now in the "MEANING" box of the Uninstall Sheets. The MEANING box is where you began to realize that the MEANINGS you were associating with your AUTOMATIC NEGATIVE THOUGHTS had you tap into NEGATIVE CORE BELIEFS. As a reminder, there are only three things in all of our human experience that drive most of these negative emotions. If we ever are tapping into a sense of HELPLESSNESS, UNLOVABILITY, or a NEGATIVE IMAGE OF OUR BODY, we will experience negative feelings. Since negative emotions are an indication that we have lost, at least partially, the relationship with our true self, the next couple of assignments are designed to show you how that occurred.

HOMEWORK ASSIGNMENT #5 – Are You Helpless Or Are You Capable

**How Would Someone Know They Are Capable?** Your assignment is to go and collect 25 responses to this question. A few rules:

1) Please do not alter the words – keep the question just as it is presented.
2) You may answer the question yourself twice, which means the 23 other responses must come from others.
3) Do yourself a favor and ask people of different ages – you might be surprised what children might say
4) When someone asks you, 'Capable of what?" just simply reply, "I cannot further define it. Just how would someone know they are capable?"
5) You may use any means to gather these responses, including social media.
6) Write out on a piece of paper all of the responses.

REVIEWING HOMEWORK ASSIGNMENT #5

You are probably wondering about why I wanted you to gather information from others and now what to even do with the information you collected. The first thing I check with my clients when they return is how many responses they did get. If they only came back with 12 or less, I simply kick them out and tell them it is not enough. Most clients that are struggling with a healthy perspective about their true self are not reliable to turn to as the source in answering the question, "How would someone know they are capable?," hence our need to rely on a greater population size in providing information to this important question. If your own effort to collect the information was less than stellar, I recommend that you stick with it until you gather the 25 responses.

In my office, I have my client read each response, one-by-one. As the client reads the response, we process it to determine if the client believes that the response would lead to an idea that someone is capable. If so, then I have the client put a STAR next to the response. We continue in this manner until every response has been processed. Many times we will have multiple STARS to one response, as the response provides more than one idea that would lead to a person sensing they are capable. When we are done, I ask the client to count how many STARS we came up with. If it is 17 or above then I think that provides a pretty good basis to determine capability. I then invite the client to read the very first response that had been STARRED and then I ask, "Have you experienced that to any degree?" If the client has, then I ask them to place a CHECKMARK next to the STAR. We then go to the next STAR and again ascertain whether the client had ever experienced that to any degree. If yes, then we place a CHECKMARK next to the STAR. I then ask my client to proceed through the rest of the STARRED responses, placing CHECKMARKS next to those STARRED items in which they have experienced to any degree what is being recognized as evidence for capability.

When the client has completed their assessment, I then ask, "Are there any STARS that were left UNCHECKED. Usually the answer is "No," however for any that are left UNCHECKED, with a little input from me, most often clients find that they have experienced every single STARRED item. It is not imperative that every one is CHECKED, but only having one or two UNCHECKED still leaves ample evidence to the idea of personal capability.

Since you are not personally with me at this moment, I can't go through your list with you, but what I can do is provide a list coming from a few hundred clients that have gone out and done this homework and then have you assess whether first, the information being provided would lead a person to sense they are capable and second, whether you have experienced, to any degree, those things that would give us that sense. I would however recommend that you don't just simply use the provided list. I strongly urge your own efforts in obtaining answers to this vital question. I think by doing so will heighten your observation of your true self, because when we are personally involved in our own discovery, the learning is more indelible.

DIRECTIONS: In the following list, please place a STAR in the first box if you believe the information being provided would lead to a sense of a person being capable. Once you have gone through the list then return to all of the items STARRED and in the second column place a CHECKMARK next to those items that you have experienced to any degree. Below the list I have provided a KEY to the listed items. If you have any question about any specific item, I suggest that you turn to the KEY, locate the item you are not sure about and then after reading what is presented there, return to the checklist and provide a STAR if you agree with what is said in the KEY.

Example:
★ ☑ If you can teach it.

If you believe that if a person can teach something would lead to a sense of capability then put a STAR in the first column. If then you yourself have ever been able to teach anything then put a checkmark in the box of the second column.

HOW WOULD SOMEONE KNOW THEY ARE CAPABLE?
- ☐ ☐ 1) If you can teach it
- ☐ ☐ 2) If a person is goal oriented
- ☐ ☐ 3) If a person is willing to try
- ☐ ☐ 4) If a person receives recognition
- ☐ ☐ 5) If a person removes fear and doubt
- ☐ ☐ 6) If a person is resilient
- ☐ ☐ 7) If a person would learn how to ask for help
- ☐ ☐ 8) If a person knew he or she was a child of God
- ☐ ☐ 9) If a person was determined
- ☐ ☐ 10) If a person put forth their best effort
- ☐ ☐ 11) If a person would increase their knowledge
- ☐ ☐ 12) By acquiring skills
- ☐ ☐ 13) If you have ever been successful
- ☐ ☐ 14) By observing others and doing the same thing
- ☐ ☐ 15) Being an honest human observer
- ☐ ☐ 16) By having a testimony of Christ and His Atonement
- ☐ ☐ 17) By having a growth mindset
- ☐ ☐ 18) By believing in him or her self
- ☐ ☐ 19) By approaching tasks with faith
- ☐ ☐ 20) Helping others
- ☐ ☐ 21) If a person sensed they were
- ☐ ☐ 22) Through work
- ☐ ☐ 23) Starting something and finishing it/accomplishing something
- ☐ ☐ 24) Learning from past mistakes
- ☐ ☐ 25) Passing a class
- ☐ ☐ 26) Being able to read
- ☐ ☐ 27) Through trial and error
- ☐ ☐ 28) Through critical thinking, reasoning
- ☐ ☐ 29) By listening (following) to spiritual impressions or intuition
- ☐ ☐ 30) By doing something new or outside of comfort zone
- ☐ ☐ 31) By being responsive and not reactive to negative experiences
- ☐ ☐ 32) By imagining something and then creating it
- ☐ ☐ 33) Through personal responsibility
- ☐ ☐ 34) By past experiences
- ☐ ☐ 35) By earning money/Being able to provide for self
- ☐ ☐ 36) A realistic sense of personal strengths and limitations
- ☐ ☐ 37) If a person believes in me
- ☐ ☐ 38) If a person becomes autonomous

KEY to above responses:

1) If a person could teach someone else anything, wouldn't that lead to a sense of capability?
2) Goal oriented contains three elements. Any one of the elements would lead to a sense of capability – a. setting a goal, b. working towards a goal, c. accomplishing a goal. If a person can even set a goal then it is obvious the person has recognized something that leads to improvement and further development. If a person is working toward a goal, the small accomplishments along the way are evidence of capability. Of course accomplishing a goal would necessarily have someone see themselves as capable
3) If a person is not willing to try would they ever get a sense of their capability? Of course not. If a person was willing to try might that lead to a sense of capability?
4) If a person receives recognition of any kind, that could be a diploma, a certificate or just a slap on the back and someone saying, "Good job! You really did that well." Would that lead to a sense of capability?
5) If a person would stop worrying and quit approaching life through fear and doubt, wouldn't that lead to a sense of capability? Fear and doubt rob of us power to do.
6) Resiliency is the ability to learn from past mistakes, pick ourselves up and keep moving forward. Would a person sense they were capable through resiliency?
7) I am not very mechanically inclined, but my brother is. Whenever something would go wrong with one of my vehicles, my brother would lovingly come over and work with me in fixing whatever the problem was. One day I went into the garage and saw a puddle of water coming out from underneath my van. I called my brother and asked him if he could come over to fix it. He replied, "Oh Larry, I'm sorry but I am going to a wedding today." He then added, "But I don't like weddings, so you call me and I will walk you through it." Without my brother even being there, my willingness to ask him for help, I changed a water pump that day. If a person would learn how to ask for help, wouldn't that still give them a sense of their capability?
8) If a person really knew they were God's child, wouldn't that give them a sense of how capable they really are?
9) If a person was determined, meaning that have that tenacity of not giving up, wouldn't determination lead to a sense of capability?
10) If a person really put forth their very best effort, wouldn't that lead to a sense of capability?
11) By increasing our knowledge, wouldn't that increase our sense of capability?
12) If we kept acquiring skills, wouldn't that lead to an increasing sense of our capability?
13) If you have ever experienced any success wouldn't that lead to a sense of capability?
14) Do we as humans learn by observing others? If so, wouldn't that lead to a sense of capability?
15) Does anyone have to teach a baby how to crawl? Nope, it seems to be built in. How about walk? I know we stick our fingers out to have the small child hold on to while they are moving their legs and feet, but wouldn't the baby walk anyway even without that help? What about language acquisition? Don't babies brains just naturally pick up on the patterns of language and they begin to communicate and understand as a result? What about the apparent design in each of us to learn? If we are being an honest observer of the human experience, wouldn't that lead to an idea that we are capable? It appears that capability is built in each of us.

16) Here is a scripture from Philippians – "I can do all things through Christ, which strengtheneth me" (Philippians 4:13). How many things can we do through Him? If I have a testimony of Christ and His Atonement would I get a sense of how capable I am?

17) Stanford University did a research project on "Mindsets." The term "growth mindset" comes from the groundbreaking work of Carol Dweck. She identified everyone holds ideas about their own potential. Some believe that their intelligence is more or less fixed, for example in math, someone with a fixed mindset would conclude that you can do math or you can't. About 40% of students have these damaging "fixed mindset" ideas. Another 40% have a "growth mindset." – they believe that they can learn anything and that their intelligence can increase. The other 20% waver between the two mindsets. Students with a fixed mindset are those who are more likely to give up easily, whereas students with a growth mindset are those who keep going even when work is hard, and who are persistent. If a person has a growth mindset, wouldn't that lead to a sense of capability?

18) People that believe in themselves; that have confidence in themselves, wouldn't that lead to an increasing sense of capability?

19) To get an idea if faith would lead to a sense of capability we must have an operating definition of faith. The apostle Paul taught that "Now faith is the substance of things hoped for, the evidence of things not seen" (Hebrews 11:1). Also, "And now as I said concerning faith, faith is to not have a perfect knowledge of things; therefore if ye have faith ye hope for things which are not seen, which are true" (Alma 32:21). I always kid with my clients that I am a fan of Taco Bell. From my office, you cannot see Taco Bell, but then I ask my clients, "What is the moving force that would have me leave my office to go to Taco Bell? That is when we bring in the elements these scriptures are describing. Even though I can't see Taco Bell at the time of my departure, I have hope that when I arrive it will be there. But that hope is not coming from a place of no substance, in fact there is something in my experience that has me realize that I can have warranted expectation that when I arrive Taco Bell will be there and that they will have food. The reason why I sense the substantive feeling is because of the evidence that suggests to my mind that I can believe, which gives place for hope, which is the moving cause of my action to go there. What is my evidence? I have driven by Taco Bell numerous times and it has always been there. Every time I go there to eat, they have always had food. I have seen others eating there. I have heard many commercials that they will feed me if I come, etc.

So, if a person is operating from faith, might that give them a sense of capability? I think so! With that, let's go down a theological path to ensure understanding, Can a person exercise faith in something that is not true? Most of my clients answer 'Yes' to this question, but actually they cannot, because the very definition of faith is that the belief is centered in things that are true. A person can sincerely believe in things that are not true, but they will never be able to exercise faith in falsehoods. So, through faith would a person gain a sense of their capability?

20) If I were to help others, wouldn't that give me a sense of my capability?

21) If I just had an internal sense that I was capable, wouldn't that lead to a sense of being capable?

22) If a person were to develop a work ethic, wouldn't they get a sense of being capable?

23) If a person not only starts a project but also completes it, meaning they accomplish something, wouldn't that give them a sense that they are capable?

24) If a person actually learns from their mistakes, wouldn't that create a sense of capability?
25) If a person is able to master the curriculum or material of a given class, wouldn't a person get a sense of their capability?
26) If a person learns how to read and comprehend what they are reading, wouldn't that create a sense of capability?
27) Thomas Edison finally found a filament that would create light when electricity was applied to it. Someone asked him, "How did it feel to fail a thousand times?" Thomas Edison replied, "I didn't fail a thousand times. The light bulb was an invention of a thousand steps." Through trial and error, might we see get a sense that we are capable?
28) Does the ability to reason; problem solve; make observations and engage critical thinking develop a sense of being capable?
29) Following intuition or obeying the Spirit's voice, wouldn't both of those lead to a sense of capability?
30) If someone challenged them self, went outside of their comfort zone or just did something they had never done before, wouldn't that lead to a sense of being capable?
31) If a person would put themselves in the Adult Ego State when feeling a negative emotion, wouldn't being responsive, rather than reactive lead to a greater sense of being capable?
32) If a person came up with an idea and followed through and developed it, or let's say an artist could picture something in their mind and then create it wouldn't that provide a sense of capability?
33) If a person continues to take more and more responsibility for their own life, in all of its facets, wouldn't that create a greater sense of capability?
34) Can our past experiences shape a sense of being capable within us?
35) If a person can provide for all of the necessities of life for them self and perhaps a family, wouldn't a person's sense of capability rise?
36) Sometimes I will say to a client, "You are never going to be a NFL Linebacker, but couldn't you run up and down a field and blow a whistle and throw a penalty flag? So even though we know we have some limitations, wouldn't that still lead to a sense of what we are capable of?
37) Can a person begin to sense they are capable because someone else believes in them? Children are constantly demonstrating increasing capability when a parent says, "You can do this."
38) Autonomy – autonomous individuals have achieved the recognition that they are separate from others and in doing so have learned how to master their environment to the extent that they take good care of themselves.

I imagine that you likely have experienced most of the items you ended up STARRING. The reason we are doing this assignment is to reinforce the understanding of how powerful Implicit Learning and Memory is. The ongoing, repetitive INTERNAL CONVERSATION we have with our self becomes stored at the Implicit Level. Once stored, we no longer pay high attention to the individual aspects of that conversation and begin to see ourselves from the framework of our INTERNAL CONVERSATION.

If you can picture the Uninstall Sheets in your mind, you will recall that the first box says, "My Problem Is," the box below that asks, "What Was the Automatic Negative Thought In My Mind," and then below that the "Meaning" box. The Meaning box always asks, "What did my

Automatic Negative Thought mean to me?" Here the client is instructed to write out a sentence that provides insight as to what the Automatic Negative Thought actually meant to the client. After the client provides a Meaning, the client is asked to put parenthesis after the Meaning and in the parenthesis to place the number(s) associated with the Negative Core Belief(s) they sense they are tapping into, based upon the Meaning provided. If you recall, #1 was associated with the Negative Core Belief of Helplessness; #2 Unlovability, and #3, a Negative Image of the Body.

I invite you to return to your Uninstall Sheets, go to the Meaning Box and see how many times you recorded the #1.for Helplessness. Likely you recognize that you did so over and over again. In other words, at the Implicit Level you sense or believe that you are Helpless, because of the repetitive Internal Conversation. However, Quantum Theory invites us to become Observers and that perhaps through increasing awareness that comes from our Observation, we can begin to change how that belief or sense, which is stored as energy/matter can be altered into a belief or sense that is more realistic or true about our identity.

We just completed an assignment wherein you were asked to make some inferences from the answers provided to the question, "How would someone know they are capable?" Those inferences were directed toward evidence of capability. You recognized that if someone had experienced to any degree those items then likely someone would have a clear sense of capability. After Observing through the assignment you just completed, I have a question for you, "Are you Helpless or are you Capable?" Every client at this point answers, "Capable." I then add, "How much evidence must you continue to ignore in order to stay so helpless?" Every client recognizes quite a bit of evidence. The framework of your ongoing NEGATIVE INTERNAL CONVERSATION is what shaped a sense of helplessness in you, which has been stored IMPLICITELY. That is the only reason why helplessness had formed as part of your belief, not because it is real, but because of the information your cells were encoded with through your mindset. Yet when we became honest observers we took a good look at helplessness and what is that we discovered about helplessness? It is only one thing – it is a huge distortion; it is not even real. The following diagram illustrates what you have just learned. The line represents Awareness. Above the line, Helplessness is discovered to be a distortion, ascertained through correct observing. Below the line is a false sense or belief held within our Implicit Memory, which was shaped in us because of our ongoing, NEGATIVE INTERNAL CONVERSATION.

HELPLESSNESS IS A DISTORTION.          DISCOVERED THROUGH OBSERVATION

---

HELPLESSNESS IS BELIEVED TO BE REAL       PROGRAMMED IMPLICIT MEMORY

The purpose of the Uninstall Process is to find and free ourselves of those things within our Implicit Memory that are keeping our negative patterns, including any negative view of our self in place and that is preventing us from living within the truth of who we really are.

Now that we know Helplessness is not real, I would like to talk to you about one type or sense of helplessness we all experience, but when we are experiencing this sense of helplessness, we are likely in very good company. I am going to ask you a question. Your answer will come from your understanding about God. Do you believe that God would really want all of us, His children, to return to Him and live the way He lives? Do you believe that is what He would want? The answer is obvious, like any loving parent, He too desires that all of His children are happy. In measuring this want, I ask, "How is He doing?" Does it appear that all of His children will return to His presence and live the way He lives? Recognizing that such will not be the case, I may incorrectly conclude that the most capable Being in the universe isn't so capable after all. In fact, I might conclude that God is helpless. When I present this line of questioning, every client speaks to a gift that each of us have been given, which is the gift of agency, in dispelling the idea that God is helpless. It becomes obvious that we too must desire and live in a way that allows the blessing of Eternal Life to be realized. Elder John A Widstoe offered some insight to our responsibility in gaining the type of life God enjoys:

> The plan of salvation, conceived and proposed by our Heavenly Father, is for all of his children. Our Father will never cease to labor with our stubborn wills, until the last of his children has accepted the requirements of the gospel and has conformed to the plan of salvation. That may lead us far into the eternities, for though every knee will bow and every tongue confess that Jesus is the Christ, yet many will refuse to bend their wills to the requirements of the gospel of Jesus Christ. Such persons must wait for the full blessings of the Lord, until their stubborn wills have learned obedience..... During this endless journey, man may rest secure in the eternal love of God. Our Father will help us forever. Never will he forsake us. He will ever seek to convert the sinner to better ways. (Joseph Smith – Seeker After Truth, Prophet of God; Bookcraft, 1981. Pg 168)

So, next to life itself, the greatest gift we were given was the gift to choose that life. Do you have any understanding why we were given the gift to choose? The first answer is likely the most obvious. Without the gift of choice, we would never be able to learn, to grow and develop. When used righteously, agency allows light to dispel darkness, especially the darkness that invades us concerning things that are not true about who we are. When we understand who we really are, we experience hope, and we are enabled to live with purpose and joy.

But I think it is important that we speak about the second reason we were given the gift of agency. We were given this gift so that in the end the record might be very clear who it was we chose, did we choose Him or did we choose some other way? The only way that record can be clear is with and through the gift of choice. Let me side-step and draw upon a character that most of us are familiar with to reinforce this second reason agency was given.

In his story, "A Christmas Carol," Charles Dickens introduces us to a character named Ebenezer Scrooge. The beginning of this story opens up on Christmas Eve and we find two gentlemen who are going around to the business owners seeking donations for those that are less fortunate this time of the year. When coming upon Mr. Scrooge they inquire, "What may we put you down for?" Scrooge replies, "Nothing," "Oh, you wish to remain anonymous?" they question. "I wish to be left alone," Scrooge retorts. But then Scrooge continues, "Are there no prisons?" The reply, "Plenty of prisons." "And the union workhouses," demanded Scrooge, "Are they still in operation?" "They are. Still," returned the gentlemen, "I wish we could say they were not." Scrooge then responds to their answers, "The Treadmill and the Poor Law are in full vigor then?" "Both very busy, sir" replied the gentlemen. Scrooge then reminds these men that through the process of taxes, "I help to support the establishments I have mentioned – they cost enough; and those who are badly off must go there."

The problem with Scrooge's reply is that though filled with accuracy there is no clarity. It is true that his resources are going to support the workhouses and debtor's prison, but those expenditures are coming through his taxes. While taxes are voluntary, they are kind of a forced voluntary. I have to ask myself this honest question, already getting a sense of Scrooge's character. Would I with any confidence really believe that if left just to his own that Scrooge would willingly give of his resources to support these two institutions? The answer is obvious and so there is no clarity. But now, let's go to the end of the story. Scrooge has had all three spirits visit him and it is now Christmas morning. What do we see Scrooge doing with his resources? We observe that he is taking of his resources and using them to bless and lift other's lives. Is there any doubt he is doing so willingly? No doubt at all! Now the record is very clear regarding Scrooge's agency and so it is with each of us; each of us having been given the gift to choose our lives will one day create a record of clarity (2 Nephi 10:23; 2 Nephi 2:27)

What is the application of all of this? Agency is given to all mankind as a gift and you will notice sometimes others use their agency in a way that may negatively impact our life. Sometimes that may be as simple as a person being rude and selfish in their interaction with us; it may show up in some form of betrayal from a spouse; it may arise in the form of disobedience in one of our children, etc. It may appear as undesired changes in social standards and mores. The question is, when other's agency does negatively impact our own life, how is it that we display capability?

Joseph Smith taught, "If men do not comprehend the character of God, they do not comprehend themselves." From this principle Joseph also taught, and this is a paraphrase, "If we are going to be like our Father in Heaven we have got to learn how to be like Him." Please take notice on how our Father in Heaven interacts with our agency. He never interacts with our gift to choose from a place of control. While it is true that we will be held accountable to Him for how we exercised the divine endowment of choice, He does not try and control us..... as the scripture indicates, ..."thou mayest choose for thyself, for it is given unto thee;... (Moses 3:17). In contrast, the Adversary presented the idea that he would operate from a place of control. From what camp do we find ourselves interacting with other's agency?

For example, some parents micromanage every aspect of their children's lives. Some use manipulation to get the child to conform to the parent's wishes. I have met many parents who too quickly involve themselves in their children's choices, not allowing their children the opportunity to learn from those choices. This does not represent capability, because such approaches stem from a parent not believing in their children or that their children can learn through their choices. The reason why God does not try and control is because He believes we can actually learn from our choices and grow the power of faith within us. He has devised the greatest educational system and He believes in it and He believes in each of us. He is willing to allow us to experience the consequences of our choices for the purpose of learning, of growing, and becoming. Sometimes our choices are incredibly wonderful and we recognize the blessings that flow from such choices. Likewise, we can make some incredibly poor choices and learn from them as well (Deuteronomy 30:15, 19).

In learning how to become like Him it is imperative that we begin to see how He does interact with other's agency; and if you will, since we are His children; how He interacts with our choices. Heavenly Father operates from a place of influence, not control. What does influence look like?

1. He informs us
2. He invites us
3. He encourages us

Can you see how each of those terms is supporting influence and staying away from control? God influences through persuasion, through being long-suffering, by gentleness and meekness and by love unfeigned. He is kind and provides us the things He knows. The gift of agency is directly connected to the light of Christ and so we will feel reproved at times when we go against that light, but that is not a rejection of us, it is still coming as a way to influence us. In our appropriate choices we will feel a greater manifestation of that Light. When we feel that we have pulled away from that light, it is His hope that we so enjoy living within light and truth that we will do everything in our power to stay connected to it.

As evidence of His belief in us, He continually sends us His love. His love is stronger than any other power to influence us to do good. He does not exercise control or dominion or compulsion upon the souls of the children of men in any degree of unrighteousness to get us to do good. Here is the application, we too can show incredible capability even when others use their agency in a way that disappoints us, that strains relationships, and that creates suffering. Forgiveness is one of the noblest forms of influence; hence the reason He is so inclined to do so (Ephesians 4:32). If we too would operate from a place of influence in those moments when other's agency negatively impacts us then we are showing incredible capability in upholding and sustaining one of the most vital parts of our progression.

> Agency has always been the heritage of man under the rule and government of God. He possessed it in the heaven of heavens before the world was, and the Lord maintained and defended it there against the aggression of Lucifer and those that took sides with him.... By virtue of this agency you and I and all mankind are made responsible beings, responsible for the course we pursue, the lives we live, and the deeds we do. (Discourses of Wilford Woodruff)

Each of us, every person we come into contact with, every relationship we form, every person we have been given authority over to teach and direct, every colleague, every peer, in essence every human being has been granted this privilege to choose. Agency is an endowment of every intelligent being and we ought to do all in our power to continue to understand its significance and learn how to interact with it from a Godly perspective.

The very power of God is called FAITH. By faith all things are created and exist. As with any power, there are fundamental principles that govern the power of faith. J. Reuben Clark provided a more in depth look at this power, said he:

> As I think about faith, this principle of power, I am obliged to believe it is an intelligent force. Of what kind I do not know. But it is superior to and overrules all other forces of which we know. It is the principle, the force, by which the dead are restored to life. (Conference Report, 1960)

> Faith is not belief; it is more than that. It is not a confidence that something can be done; it is more than that. Faith is an active principle which we must consciously exercise; consciously bring to bear, in order that our purposes may

be accomplished. Our scriptures tell us that the worlds were framed by faith, and that was not merely a thought, unconscious thought of what might be done or what should be done, it was an exercise of a force and a power what we little understand and yet which most of us have experienced and perhaps all of us have seen. When we administer to the sick, it is not an expression merely of confidence. It is not merely a prayer alone, but behind the prayer there must be a knowledge and there must be an active principle of faith. (Selected Papers on Religion, Education and Youth. Brigham Young University Press, 1984, p. 173)

The fundamental principles upon which the very power of God operates are enumerated in Section 121 of the Doctrine and Covenants. Collectively these are called the principles of righteousness (D&C 121:36). These principles form the Constitution of operating from a place of Godly power. There are several things that will diminish that power in our lives, but the one we are focused on here is when we begin exercising control, or dominion or compulsion upon the souls of the children of men, in any degree of unrighteousness (D&C 121:37).

We simply cannot force others to do the right thing. The revelations make it clear that this is not God's way. Elder Larry Y. Wilson reported on the negative effects resulting from being in an environment of control:

> Compulsion builds resentment. It conveys mistrust, and it makes people feel incompetent. Learning opportunities are lost when controlling persons pridefully assume they have all the right answers for others........Unrighteous dominion is often accompanied by constant criticism and the withholding of [material blessings], approval or love. Those on the receiving end feel they can never please {such friends, such spouses}, such leaders and or parents [that incorporate these tactics. Such recipients begin to believe that they will never be good enough]..... if parents hold on to *all* decision-making power and see it as their "right," they severely limit the growth and development of their children...... Such children often either rebel against this compulsion or are crippled by an inability to make any decisions on their own.... An additional and tragic side-effect of unrighteous dominion can be a loss of trust in God's love. I have known some people who were subject to demanding and controlling {spouses}, leaders or parents, and they have found it hard to feel the very love from their Heavenly Father that would sustain them and motivate them along the path of righteousness. (Only Upon the Principles of Righteousness, General Conference, 2012).

The influence we wish to have upon those that we love will emerge when we have developed a wonderful relationship with them. Naturally, instinctively man resists control. That is because it goes fundamentally against our true nature. We lose influence in the lives of others when we try and control them in any degree of unrighteousness. If we are going to develop a true sense of our own capability, as well as have others we love see that they are likewise created capable, we must understand the Constitution of Heaven to bring bear upon our understanding and increasing power of faith.

There are three areas of righteous control we have been granted to take. These are found in the Title of Liberty (Alma 46:12-13). One area we have been told it is okay to exercise control over someone else is when our life or the life of another is being threatened. We are given permission to use physical control to protect the sanctity of life. Likewise, we have been granted permission to use physical force when others are trying to take our homes and lands forcibly. Finally, we have been given consent to use control when our liberties are being threatened. My purpose here is not to go into deep doctrinal explanations of justification of using righteous control, but just to point out that the Lord has spoken to both righteous and unrighteous use of it. My purpose has been for us to focus on how we demonstrate our capability in light of the gift of agency that every being possesses.

Since one aspect of agency is to provide clarity, one of the things we will give a certain accounting for is our responsibility to learn, through meekness, what it means to act from a place of influence. The Controlling Parent Ego State and the Child Ego State are both operating from places of pride, not meekness. The former demands respect, while the latter demands that other's be responsible for our lack thereof. The Adult Ego State avoids these prideful approaches. The responsibilities of Godhood require spiritually adept adults. Our willingness to love others that act against our good intentions and desires, our excellent teachings, our vast experience, our wisdom and our sincere interest in their happiness is what is required of us. It is being meek enough to recognize the vital role agency plays in the large picture, knowing that it will be misused, resulting in many that we love and care about experiencing heartache, missed opportunities and even falling short of one's true potential. The Controlling Ego State manifests in parents that don't believe in their children, who don't believe that their children can learn from their experience. The Controlling Parent Ego State is motivated by subordinating other's self-will for their own easiness or to protect their own unhealthy-esteem. This style of overseeing only leads to developing false beliefs in those that are recipients of this approach. A sense of inadequacy and limited and conditional acceptability are the beliefs that begin to develop in those that are being raised through the Controlling Parent Ego State. The hallmark of such developed beliefs is resentment and resistance.

I hope now that we see that we are capable; that helplessness is a huge distortion. This is an important concept if we are going to experience our self correctly. Being capable is part of our design. So what are you going to do with helplessness?

In support of this concept that we are capable, I share the following story with permission to do so. Paula was a client of mine, oh probably about five years ago. Paula was married to a man that operated from very unhealthy-esteem. Her husband interacted with her not only in a critical fashion, but also in a very contemptuous way. Over the years of marriage these critical and contemptuous interactions had Paula come to believe that she was a person of no worth, no importance and that in every aspect she was so flawed that she should be thankful that at least one man was willing to tolerate her. As Paula progressed to this point in the program and after having processed the evidence she collected from others determining capability, I asked the question, "So, are you helpless or are you capable?" Paula's facial expression and pause indicated that something was beginning to work in her. At first her reply was soft, like a new bud piercing out of the ground; when the first evidence of life emerges, "I am capable," she said in a whisper. As I watched her, it was obvious that light and strength were building as she declared again a little bit firmer, "I am capable." Paula then began to weep as this truth began to gain its footing. After taking time to gain greater composure, in a voice of great confidence, Paula the third time stated, "I AM CAPABLE!" It was apparent that her experience was beyond just an intellectual understanding.

Many times when a client returns for their next session, I will ask, "Is there anything that you have learned in this program that has shown up when it needed to and helped you in a difficult situation?" I asked Paula this very question when she returned. She replied, "Yes, as a matter of fact it did so this past week." Paula then explained that her husband had become highly critical and contemptuous with her this past week and she said, "I did the very thing I always do when that happens. I went to my room, pulled the covers over my head, began to cry and feel like the worst person that has ever walked the planet." She told me that normally she may find herself in bed for two to three days after such an interaction, but then she added, "Suddenly the thought came into my mind – 'I am capable.' With that I suddenly felt strength grow inside of me. I pulled the covers off of me, went and found my husband saying, 'You are never to talk to me that way again. None of it is true.'" She then went and continued doing what she was doing for the family.

At the end of the program, Paula had another experience that demonstrated the power of her accepting the truth of her identity. It was Paula's time to come in and so I stepped into the hallway outside of my office. At the end of the hallway was a glass door that allowed me to see out into the waiting area. As I did so, there was Paula standing and talking to her husband. I had never met with her husband so I wasn't sure if he had been invited by Paula to attend the session. I caught Paula's attention signaling to her to come back when she was ready.

A little background is needed here. When I first started working with Paula, her husband had been disciplined by their church for moral violations dealing with marital infidelity. At some point, her husband had some of those restriction removed as he sought repentance during the time I was seeing Paula.

Paula entered my office without her husband and did not even sit down. As she stood there in front of the couch, she said, "Well that was really different." She then went on to explain that her husband had come seeking her to inform her that he had been having another affair, and that the reason it was urgent to let her know was because the affair was going to be made public the next day in the city's newspaper. She then said, "What was different was that I took none of it personally. It was as if the love for self did not allow such tragic information to in any way change how I now saw myself. Don't get me wrong," she continued, "the information is still disappointing and hurtful, but I found myself saying in my head, 'Oh Kim, you don't have to live this way.' I felt great compassion for what he was experiencing and was no longer self-absorbed with worries about my worth or importance as a person."

Changing how we see our self, becoming accepting of our true identity has us handle life's difficult moments in a way that never alters that true identity.

One last way capability is realized is when we become willing to submit our will to truths that are found either lacking or not fully developed in us. Many struggles we experience are in direct relation to vital data not yet discovered or implemented. If we are found lacking then improving capacity is experienced when we begin to rely on the wisdom of those who have found what we have not as yet acquired. As an example, for those that struggle with severe depression and anxiety likewise have severe doubts and fears. Such debilitating attributes influence deepening struggles because they have programmed their cells to operate from a perspective of worst-case scenarios. This shrinking perspective programs the individual belief as being incapable as ongoing experiences will dictate ongoing *reactivity* rather than being settled in one's true identity and measuring experiences through the lens of being capable. Humans are more dependent on learning for survival than other species. Our perspective is always limited by how much we know. Expanding our knowledge will transform our mind and ongoing experience. It is important to trust others that are living with greater confidence and happiness. It is obvious they know something that allows them to live the way they do.

Meekness is the attribute that provides the insight to blessings unmeasured, as meekness allows us the wisdom and strength to become submissive. Such submissiveness leads to far better learning, which in turn directs our having much better outcomes. The meek become better hearers, better learners and better doers. When the mind is filled with meekness, then an individual can be shown things that were previously missing in their perception. Such learning likewise stretches the individual in discovering that capability is in direct relation to accepting and living by truth. Too many think there is nothing more to do as they settle incorrectly on misperceptions of their true identity. Such individuals lack meekness of the mind.

I had a client that was referred to me by her physician. She had serious metabolic issues, which were attributed to mental stress. As we were processing one of her homework assignments she disclosed that she had come to believe that everything she needed to heal was already inside her. Though her understanding of God was fluid, her belief in God allowed me the opportunity to challenge her understanding. Her fluid view of God was everything from a creator to an energy source. She did believe she was created, but her assumption was that she had been created with everything she needed to heal herself.

I shared my belief that while we are incredibly made, we did not create ourselves. Someone with far greater understanding, intelligence, wisdom and power created us and that we ought to be meek enough to consider that truth and all that it implies. I turned to the story of the woman that struggled with an issue of blood for twelve years:

> And a woman having an issue of blood twelve years, which had spent all her living upon physicians, neither could be healed by any, came behind him, and touched the border of his garment: and immediately her issue of blood stanched. And Jesus said, Who touched me? When all denied, Peter and they that were with him said, Master, the multitude throng thee and press thee, and sayest thou, Who touched me?

> And Jesus said, Somebody hath touched me: for I perceive that virtue is gone out of me. And when the woman saw that she was not hid, she came trembling, and falling down before him, she declared unto him before all the people for what cause she had touched him, and how she was healed immediately. And he said unto her, Daughter, be of good comfort: thy faith hath made thee whole; go in peace. (Luke 8:43-48)

Her faith was based not in that she already had everything she needed to be healed, but it was in Him, because of who He was! Faith in God is essential for healing:

> If there be no faith among the children of men God can do no miracle among them....(Ether 12:12)

There was an immediate change in my client's countenance as we considered the New Testament story. She became accepting of what I was suggesting, thereby strengthening her capability. Submissiveness is not easy, but it is the one sure-fire way to develop power, control, and capability in our lives. Why? Because when we submit our will to those who have already attained wisdom, power and happiness, we can be assured that we will be led aright, even though the journey may be difficult. Being led by more intelligent beings is evidence that there is still much development required (Abraham 3:19). It is an intellectual honesty that has us own up to our misperception of self formed through a negative internal conversation and begin to accept the truth of who each of us really are as it is announced by those who already know.

My client began to understand as she quietly quoted the relationship between the Potter and the Potter's clay:

> Surely your turning of things upside down shall be esteemed as the potter's clay: for shall the work say of him that made it, He made me not? Or shall the thing framed say of him that framed it, He had no understanding? (Isaiah 29:16)

We are the clay. Our Father in Heaven is the Potter. If we will meekly submit to His Omniscience, we will become as He is because we are created in His very image. It is only by yielding to God that we can become what we were created to become. If we truly trust God, why not yield to His Omniscience? After all, having made us, He knows us and our possibilities much better than we do.

While I speak of this truth, yet it is seemingly difficult for many to do. Perhaps meekness of mind is necessary as such prevailing approaches allow us first to recognize God's perfect love for each of us. When we become acquainted with God's love, the process of submission becomes easier and fuller. Full submission will be required if we expect full development. Becoming aware of His pure love for us shifts our perception of His interest in us. His counsel is no longer filtered incorrectly as we come to know that He is tutoring us to likewise fully develop the attributes of godliness, one of which is omnipotence. Until fully developed we may rest assured that He will continue to abundantly give:

> Fear not I am with thee; oh, be not dismayed, For I am thy God and will still give thee aid. I'll strengthen thee, help thee, and cause thee to stand, Upheld by my righteous, omnipotent hand. ("How Firm a Foundation," Hymns, No. 85)

HOMEWORK ASSIGNMENT #6 – Are You Unlovable Or Are You Lovable

**How Would Someone Know They Are Lovable?** Your assignment is to go and collect 25 responses to this question. A few rules:

1) Please do not alter the words – keep the question just as it is presented.
2) You may answer the question yourself twice, which means the 23 other responses must come from others.
3) Do yourself a favor and ask people of different ages – you might be surprised what children might say

4) A forewarning – this question is of a much more sensitive nature than the previous question of capability. I am saying this because you may wonder why your close friends and family did not respond to this question, when they did to the question of capability. It is likely they did not because they are wondering the same thing in relation to their own experience.
5) You may use any means to gather these responses, including social media.
6) Write out on a piece of paper all of the responses.

I will share with you a poignant response that came from a third grade, nine year old boy:

They don't. Technology has made it that no one knows they are loveable!

As I heard this reply, I could picture this boy's home environment. Family members living under the same roof but so disconnected from one another because of the various electronic devices that occupy their attention; a profoundly sad; yet growing reality in so many homes. One of the cutest answers came from a three year old girl, "Because mommy kisses my cheeks!"

REVIEWING HOMEWORK ASSIGNMENT #6

Just as the previous assignment, it is now time to select those responses that would give someone the sense that they are lovable and then measure our own experience against those accepted suggestions that provide evidence of being lovable.

The first thing I check with my clients when they return is how many responses they did get. If they only came back with 12 or less, I simply kick them out and tell them it is not enough. Most clients that are struggling with a healthy perspective about their true self are not reliable to turn to as the source in answering the question, "How would someone know they are lovable?," hence our need to rely on a greater population size in providing information to this important question. If your efforts fell well short of the number of responses suggested, I recommend that you stick with it until you gather the 25 responses.

In my office, I have my client read each response, one-by-one. As the client reads the response, we process it to determine if the client believes that the response would lead to an idea that someone is lovable. If so, then I have the client put a STAR next to the response. We continue in this manner until every response has been processed. Many times we will have multiple STARS to one response, as the response provides more than one idea that would lead to a person sensing they are lovable. When we are done, I ask the client to count how many STARS we came up with. If it is 17 or above then I think that provides a pretty good basis to determine lovability. I then invite the client to read the very first response that had been STARRED and then I ask, "Have you experienced that to any degree?" If the client has, then I ask them to place a CHECKMARK next to the STAR. We then go to the next STAR and again ascertain whether the client had ever experienced that to any degree. If yes, then we place a CHECKMARK next to the STAR. I then ask my client to proceed through the rest of the STARRED responses, placing CHECKMARKS next to those STARRED items in which they have experienced to a degree what is being used as evidence.

When the client has completed their assessment, I then ask, "Are there any STARS that were left UNCHECKED?" Usually the answer is "No," however for any that are left UNCHECKED, with a little input from me, most often clients find that they have experienced every single STARRED item. It is not imperative that every one is CHECKED, but only having one or two UNCHECKED still leaves ample evidence to the idea of personal lovability.

Since you are not personally with me at this moment, I can't go through your list with you, but what I can do is provide a list coming from a few hundred clients that have gone out and done this homework and then have you assess whether first, the information being provided would lead a person to sense they are lovable and second, whether you have experienced, to any degree, those things that would give us that sense. I would however recommend that you don't just simply use the provided list. I strongly urge your own efforts in obtaining answers to this vital question. I know by doing so will heighten your observation of your true self.

DIRECTIONS: In the following list, please place a STAR in the first box if you believe the information being provided would lead to a sense of a person being lovable. Once you have gone through the list, return to all of the items STARRED and in the second column place a CHECKMARK next to those items that you have experienced to any degree. Below the list I have provided a KEY to the listed items. If you have any question about any specific item, I suggest that you turn to the KEY, locate the item you are not sure about and then after reading what is presented there, return to the checklist and provide a STAR if you agree with what is said in the KEY.

Example:

★ ☑ If a person is remembered on special occasions.

If you believe that if a person is remembered on special occasions would lead to a sense of lovability, then put a STAR in the first column. If then you yourself have ever been remembered on special occasions, then put a checkmark in the box of the second column.

HOW WOULD SOMEONE KNOW THEY ARE LOVABLE?
☐ ☐ 1) If a person is remembered on special occasions
☐ ☐ 2) If a person is thought of
☐ ☐ 3) If a person receives acts of service
☐ ☐ 4) If a person is shown affection
☐ ☐ 5) If a person is told they are loved
☐ ☐ 6) If a person is sacrificed for
☐ ☐ 7) If a person is invited to do things with others
☐ ☐ 8) If a person knew he or she was a child of God
☐ ☐ 9) If a person has a testimony of the Savior and of His Atonement
☐ ☐ 10) If others want to spend time with that person
☐ ☐ 11) If someone is listened to
☐ ☐ 12) If someone's thoughts, feelings and opinions are welcomed and respected by others
☐ ☐ 13) If someone is understood
☐ ☐ 14) When a person comes to appreciate and love them self
☐ ☐ 15) Being an honest human observer
☐ ☐ 16) Through being loving toward others (reciprocity)
☐ ☐ 17) Through "love maps"

- ☐ ☐ 18) When others are happy to see that person
- ☐ ☐ 19) When someone is treated fairly and nicely
- ☐ ☐ 20) When a person is helped
- ☐ ☐ 21) When someone's needs are important to others
- ☐ ☐ 22) When someone receives forgiveness
- ☐ ☐ 23) By receiving gifts
- ☐ ☐ 24) By being thrown a party
- ☐ ☐ 25) When a child receives correction
- ☐ ☐ 26) When a person is chastened
- ☐ ☐ 27) When a person is shown commitment
- ☐ ☐ 28) Through small thoughtful gestures
- ☐ ☐ 29) By receiving spiritual impressions
- ☐ ☐ 30) When acting unlovable others still treat them with patience and kindness
- ☐ ☐ 31) When others put their electronic devices away while visiting
- ☐ ☐ 32) By considering the Creation
- ☐ ☐ 33) When others in the family do their responsibilities without being asked and reminded all the time
- ☐ ☐ 34) By receiving compliments and positive feedback
- ☐ ☐ 35) When someone wants to be with them no matter what they are doing
- ☐ ☐ 36) When someone is thanked
- ☐ ☐ 37) When others come to them seeking advice

KEY to above responses:

1) If a person is remembered on special occasions, such as birthdays; anniversary's, etc. would that person get a sense that they are lovable?
2) An example of being thought of could be as simple as receiving a text that says, "Hey, what are you doing later," or "I can't wait to see you tonight." If a person knows that they are being thought of, might that give them a sense that they are lovable?
3) If a person is a recipient of acts of service, whether those are the quiet acts, or even more obvious examples of service like in times of great need, wouldn't a person get a sense that they are lovable?
4) If a person receives hugs and kisses, or somebody wants to snuggle up with them, or a person enjoys holding their hand, wouldn't a person being shown affection realize that they are lovable?
5) If a person hears, "I love you," especially if that phrase was a consistent part of their experience, wouldn't they get a sense that they are lovable?
6) Every parent has experienced the scenario where the family budget has its limits and both the children as well as the parent has needs or wants at the same time. When faced with this dilemma, parents tend to forego their current need or want in favor of their children's. This is an example of a sacrifice. So, if a person was sacrificed for, would that person get a sense that they are lovable?
7) If a person is reached out to and is invited to go do things with others, wouldn't that person get a sense that they are lovable?
8) "For God so loved the world…….." (John 3:16), if a person had the knowledge that they are God's child, wouldn't that increase the truth of being a lovable person?
9) As evidence of that love for each of us, God sent His Son to minister to us and offer Himself as a ransom so that through Grace, we might be reconciled to our Father

through repentance and that we might also be sanctified enabling us to live with Him eternally. If a person truly understood the Savior and His role in our lives, wouldn't a person feel assured about their being lovable?

10) When others seek our company; want to be together to make memories with us, wouldn't a person sense that they are lovable?

11) When others take time to listen to us; want to be there for us and cares about our experience, wouldn't that lead to a sense of being lovable?

12) When other's invite our input and respect our thoughts, opinions and feelings, wouldn't being invited to share our perspective and then have positive feedback in doing so give a person a sense of being lovable?

13) One of the great human needs is to be understood. If a person responded accurately in acknowledging another's perspective and seeing that the person's shared experience is reasonable, or that a person hears support from another individual, wouldn't being validated and supported and understood have someone sense they are lovable?

14) When a person is able to see them self in a healthy perspective and can be accepting of them self, even with weaknesses and limitations (Healthy Esteem), wouldn't self-acceptance alone have them recognize that they are lovable?

15) We used this same language in the "Capable" assignment, but in this perspective, while all humans can have incredibly difficult experiences in relation to others, yet isn't it true that everyone has had someone that has loved them? If everyone has had someone that has loved them, then if I were being honest wouldn't that also include me? If I am being an honest human observer, wouldn't that allow me to see that I am lovable?

16) If I interact with others in a consistent, caring manner, wouldn't I likely receive feedback that would also support the idea that I am lovable? How would someone who chooses to show others love be responded to? More likely in a loving manner. If people are acting loving toward me in response to my first loving them, wouldn't I still experience the idea that I too am lovable?

17) When someone has gotten to know your "inner world" so well and has been a part of building that world, in other words, someone knows so many of your life stories and experiences, your likes and dislikes, your favorite food, your favorite flower, your favorite color, your hopes and dreams, the way you fold towels, your greatest triumphs, your most embarrassing moment, how you perceive the world, your favorite snack, someone who has shared memories with you, etc. When someone has taken the time to be involved with you that your life is embedded in their own self that they have formed love maps in their mind concerning you, wouldn't you get a sense that you are lovable?

18) When other's verbal and non-verbal communications display happiness when they see someone, wouldn't that display of happiness give a person an idea that they are lovable?

19) If someone was treated fairly and with kindness, wouldn't that person believe that they are lovable?

20) If a person receives help from others, wouldn't that person get an inkling that they are lovable?

21) If someone's needs appear to be a high priority to others, wouldn't the person who has their needs consistently taken care of by someone else get a sense that they matter and are lovable?

22) When someone receives the gesture of forgiveness from others that they have harmed, wouldn't that person receiving forgiveness get a sense that they are lovable?

23) If a person receives gifts from time-to-time, wouldn't that person feel like they are lovable?

24) If a person is thought of and made to be the focus through being thrown a party, even if that is a small family party, wouldn't that person recognize that they are lovable?

25) When a parent provides correction for their child, doesn't the correction actually demonstrate concern for the child that they will make better choices and doesn't that demonstrate that the child is lovable?

26) "For whom the Lord loveth he chasteneth......." Hebrews 12:7-10. If a person is chastened by the Lord, is it not evidence of being lovable?

27) When a person experiences commitment from someone else, wouldn't that person recognize that they are lovable?

28) If a person is the recipient of small gestures, are not small gestures a token of being lovable?

29) If someone recognizes spiritual impressions, would they not recognize that God's ongoing interest in them by providing the means for direction, growth and happiness is evidence of their being lovable?

30) If a person is in a foul mood, is displaying a poor attitude and is acting in a way that does not necessarily engender good feelings in others, yet others still are patient and reciprocate with kindness, wouldn't that patience and kindness help the person so embittered recognize that they are lovable?

31) In a time when so many can't seem to put down their electronic devices, if a person recognizes that others will put away their devices to be with them and give them their full attention, wouldn't that send a signal that someone is lovable?

32) D&C 59:18-20 – God's love is written symbolically in creation. The zodiac, when understood as it was revealed to Enoch, has us see the Plan of Happiness set in the heavens as a constant reminder of our worth to God. When one stops and considers all of creation, might they get a strong impression of their lovability?

33) Though it may seem rare at times, still, when members of a family pull together and accept and complete their responsibilities without having to be reminded and with a good attitude wouldn't members of that family sense they are lovable?

34) When sincere compliments are given or when someone is the recipient of positive feedback from others, wouldn't that lead to an idea that someone is lovable?

35) When it is not conditioned on what someone is doing, it is simply understood that a person just wants to be with someone no matter what they are doing, wouldn't that heighten a sense of being lovable?

36) When someone receives expressions of thankfulness and gratitude, wouldn't that help someone know they are lovable?

37) If a person is sought out as one that is trusted to provide good insight, sound advice and reasonable suggestions, wouldn't that person get a sense that they are lovable?

Just as in the previous assignment, I imagine that you likely have experienced most of the items you ended up STARRING. Remember, the reason we are doing this assignment is to reinforce the power Implicit Learning and Memory plays upon our self-perception. The ongoing, repetitive INTERNAL CONVERSATION we have with our self becomes stored at the Implicit Level. Once stored, we no longer pay high attention to the individual aspects of that conversation, but begin to see ourselves from the framework of our INTERNAL CONVERSATION.

Your Uninstall Sheets, revealed how your INTERNAL CONVERSATION had you many times questioning whether you were lovable. However, through the power of observing, you are able to take a realistic look of how someone would know they are lovable. Correct and realistic viewing easily challenges the distortion of the Negative Core Belief of UNLOVABILITY. In seeing things correctly, we are able to maintain an identity that we were created to be lovable.

In completing this assignment wherein you were asked to make some inferences from the answers provided to the question, "How would someone know they are lovable?" those inferences were directed toward evidence of lovability. You recognized that if someone had experienced to any degree those items then likely someone would have a clear sense of their lovability. After Observing through the assignment you just completed, I have a question for you, "Are you Unlovable or are you Lovable?" Every client at this point answers, "Lovable." I then add, "How much evidence must you continue to ignore in order to stay fixed to the sense that you are unlovable?" Every client recognizes quite a bit of evidence. The framework of your ongoing NEGATIVE INTERNAL CONVERSATION is what shaped a sense of unlovability in you, which has been stored IMPLICITELY. Yet when we became honest observers we took a good look at unlovability and what is that we discovered about unlovability? It is only one thing – it is a huge distortion; it is not even real. The following diagram illustrates what you have just learned. The line represents Awareness. Above the line, Unlovability is discovered to be a distortion, ascertained through correct observing. Below the line is a false sense or belief held within our Implicit Memory, which was shaped in us because of our ongoing, Negative Internal Conversation.

UNLOVABILITY IS A DISTORTION.          DISCOVERED THROUGH OBSERVATION

**————————————————————————————————————**

UNLOVABILITY IS BELIEVED TO BE REAL       PROGRAMMED IMPLICIT MEMORY

The purpose of the Uninstall Process is to find and free ourselves of those things within our Implicit Memory that are keeping our negative patterns, including any negative view of our self in place and that is preventing us from living within the truth of who we really are.

Now that we know Unlovability is not real, I would like to talk to you about why it is others will interact with us in a less than loving way. If we are so lovable then how do we explain such negative behavior directed toward us? My first insight into explaining this phenomenon has been shared throughout this book.

UNHEALTHY IMPLICIT MEMORY IN OTHERS

Many times the reactive, negative behavior we witness in others is due to their own unhealthy implicit memory. As that implicit memory gets triggered, the reactive behavior displayed in others is just part of their own patterns and evidence of the distorted identity they carry. In other words, every person has formed within them an implicit memory housing their own belief about them self. False beliefs are easily triggered and most of what we experience from others is a projection of that triggered false belief.

## LACK OF SOCIAL GRACES AND MANNERS

I was privileged to be raised with Southern Graces and Manners. Social graces and manners is something that has to be learned and many have not been taught these things and therefore that might also explain some of these behaviors we experience. When we are taught to say 'please' and 'thank you,' when we are taught to listen rather than interrupt others, when we are taught to consider others and not just our self, when we are taught how to look someone in the eye and smile, when we are taught to say 'excuse me' or 'forgive me' when we may do something that raises uncomfortable feelings in others; when we are taught to not talk when our mouth is full of food, when we are taught good hygiene, when we are taught to respect the dignity of women, such social regulations help us to interact with others that would display their lovability. When such learning is absent, many times our crudeness interferes with sending the right message.

## UNDERDEVELOPED ATTRIBUTES OF CHARACTER

As humans, each of us have attributes that are in different stages of development. Patience, as an example, is an attribute that can be highly developed. Have you ever known someone that has learned how to be incredibly patient? Have you also not known individuals that have not developed this attribute? Which one do you enjoy interacting with better? These attributes are the very attributes of God. Within Him, these attributes are perfected, however with us they are found to be in different stages of development. Underdeveloped human attributes suggest more of the "natural man" we have in us rather than conforming to the refining process of becoming like God. The natural man also provides some support of these types of unwelcomed behaviors. The less charactered we are the more rough we are around the edges, and that roughness may cause difficult feelings in others.

## REACTION TO OUR OWN WAY OF BEING

Finally, if we are operating from a place of unhealthy-esteem, then likely our interactions will manifest in many negative ways. If we are always having to be right, if we are telling others what they should do, if we are forever complaining to others and sucking the life energy out of them, if we are flaky, if we won't take personal accountability, if we gossip or undermine others, if we are the loudest person in the room, if we try and gain attention in negative ways, if we are short-tempered, impatient, unkind and unable to attune and be sensitive to others' emotional cueing; if we are controlling, negative, argumentative, rigid, cut-people off, try and make others feel guilty and responsible for our own emotions, and a host of other poor behaviors, these all will all have a tendency to have others interact with us in obvious, limited ways.

In our viewing of the four things that contribute to difficult behaviors that we may experience from another person, and in spite of the length of time or environment we have found ourselves in, where such poor behavior has been displayed, I need to ask you the question again so that you can declare it from a place of awareness – "Are you unlovable or lovable?" The answer is obvious. You are lovable!

There have been some occasions with clients who have struggled to feel like they are lovable, even after concluding that they are lovable. This can be a normal response as the Old Implicit Memory still has a strong hold of that person. Yet the beginning of changing that feeling is by seeing things clearly. This is the good seed that just got planted in their soil, yet still needs attention to nurture its growth and increasing strength.

In one such case, I spent a session with a client listening to her life experience and how that experience had her come to believe that she was unlovable. However, because we had built a strong foundation of Epigenetic Influence in shaping belief, rather than just acknowledge and validate her experience we also provided the opportunity of reinforcement by having her see how environment played such a significant role in shaping that belief. Her recognition of what Epigenetic Science is demonstrating allowed her to make a break from simply seeing herself as unlovable and could accept that perhaps it was just her evaluation of life experience and environment that was the real reason for the ongoing difficult identity. With this idea firmly planted in her understanding, this woman recognized that she had the power of changing her distorted learning by changing her internal environment of negative self-talk, which had contributed to her false perception.

Epigenetic research proves that we are free to make decisions that impact our lives and those of others. *Our beliefs about ourselves influence heavily ongoing experience.* My clients come to know assuredly that they have power to change their belief and that they have the power to heal themselves, increasing their feelings of self-worth and improving their emotional state. This was her new awareness.

I shared with her how up to my teen years I had struggled with the same negative core belief. I then shared with her the story of when my mother directed me to stay on my knees until I felt my Father in Heaven's love for me. If you recall this story, when I was *still* (Psalm 46:10), His love came and engulfed me, which was an experience that began to shake loose in me the idea that I didn't matter to others. She took notice of my story and without me knowing it decided to do the same. She settled on the idea that if she could feel that heavenly hug as I had that she would be accepting of the idea that she is lovable.

As she came back and reported her experience, she told me a story that is not too uncommon in many other clients' experience who sincerely seeks to know of God's love for each of us. I could see a change in her emotional state and in her countenance. She announced that she knew Heavenly Father did love her and she felt clearly His love for her. Interestingly though, as she reported that she followed my mother's advice and tried to duplicate my experience, she stated that no such feeling or heavenly hug came. She said she was discouraged by not having the anticipated experience. She told me that she asked, "Heavenly Father, do you love me?" She said that she repeated the question in prayer several times with no response.

Not too long after her attempt, a feed came across her Facebook Page. It was a video of a woman sharing her experience. The woman in the video explains that on a Sunday afternoon, suddenly she blurted out, "I don't want to be married anymore; I don't want to be a mom, I don't know who I am and I am miserable." With that, this wife and mother left her house and went on a walk, a walk where she kept asking her Father in Heaven, "Do you love me?" Notice that this is the very same question my client had asked Father in Heaven. The woman described that after asking this question several times, that she did not receive any assurance. At that time, a couple of women, a bit older than her approached while roller-blading. They recognized that this woman was struggling with something so they paused and asked her if there was anything they could do? The woman simply stated that she was alright and kept walking down the path she had been on. The two older women skated on.

The woman of focus persisted in her pleas to Father in Heaven, again with no recognized response. While she continued to walk, the two other women had returned to her, stopped and said, "Please don't think we are stalking you. But we would like to tell you something. While we skated away, we stopped for a moment and asked Heavenly Father if there was anything we could do for you. Both of us clearly felt an impression, which was that Heavenly Father wants you to know that He loves you."

With this, the woman began to weep and feel relief. She knew that this was not a coincidence, but a tender mercy. My client recognized that this video coming across her Facebook Page was likewise a tender mercy as she began to feel of her Father in Heaven's love for her.

In my experience with helping clients understand these truthful ideas about their identity, this story was far from the first time such experiences have been reported. These almost miraculously timed experiences have reconfirmed in my mind that each of us are known and thought of (Psalm 8:4; Job 7:17). It is in the experiences that reason and emotion combine in a way that strengthens the truth we are observing about our real self. I have watched many clients become very emotional as they experience the freedom from past pain as their mind observes correctly their true self.

As a therapist, there are times where I recognize that even though the intellectual understanding is present that the emotional tethering is not fully aligned yet. For those clients that I can still sense an ongoing internal struggle, it has become a habit of mine to trust the Lord in these matters. There are times I will pray for my client, expressing to Father in Heaven what I sense may be in need of influencing. I then leave it to Him and time and time again, He has proved to be faithful.

Our Father in Heaven wants us to know the truth about ourselves. He wants us to know that the gift of agency allows us to improve in taking responsibility for the outcomes we are seeking and that we are capable of achieving the desires of our heart. We indeed are made capable, but He also wants each of us to know that being His sons and daughters that each of us are loved, not only by Him, but being made in His very image, we are made lovable to every one else.

A couple of thoughts concerning the love of God and our capacity to develop this holy characteristic, enabling us to get beyond the false idea that we are unlovable. In wanting us to comprehend the nature and being of God, the Apostle John simply declared, "God is love" (1 John 4:8, 16). Why is this important for us to consider? The Prophet of the Restoration gave some insight when he taught:

> God is love. That is to say, this characteristic or attribute of love shapes, mediates, and influences all of God's other attributes. With all the other excellencies of our Heavenly Father's character, without love to influence them, they could not have such powerful dominion over the minds of men. (Lectures on Faith, 3:24).

Each of us is on a journey of development. The same holy characteristics and attributes of God dwell in us, though not yet in their perfected state. Please consider a significant promise for those of us that will begin taking seriously our design and very purpose of our existence:

> And we have known and believed the love that God hath to us...... Herein is our love made perfect, that we may have boldness in the day of judgment: because as He is, so are we in this world. (1 John 4:16-17).

This is what Moroni was trying to help us understand. Without love, it really would not matter how well we do in developing the other attributes (1 Corinthians 13:1-3, here the Apostle Paul reinforces this concept). In straight-forward language, without love we are nothing (Moroni 7:46), because of what love produces within our mind and character (Moroni 7:45). And so like the Apostle John, Moroni concludes his thoughts on the importance of being filled with love, said he:

> But charity is the pure love of Christ, and it endureth forever; and whoso is found possessed of it at the last day, it shall be well with him. (Moroni 7:47).

Why will it be well with those that are possessed of this quality of love? Because we will be like Him and that is why we will experience *boldness* in the Day of Judgment. Elder Uchtdorf reinforces this truth:

> We are created in the image of our heavenly parents; we are God's spirit children. Therefore, we have a vast capacity for love—it is part of our spiritual heritage. (Ensign, Nov. 2009, Dieter F. Uchtdorf, Second Counselor in the First Presidency p. 21)

If you cannot see yourself as being lovable, then you are denying your true nature and will become blocked from progression. No one will enter Celestial Glory with the idea in their mind that they are not lovable. False beliefs imprison us, and rob us of the power to become what we are designed to become. Too many of us rely on other's interactions with us to provide a view of what we should believe about our self. I have exploited this ridiculous approach to life in dealing with young women, who many times are on top of the world because a boy they are attracted to smiles at them, but then the very next day the boy does not and the young woman begins to doubt herself being lovable. How exhausting does it become to approach life from that manner? Terribly exhausting! Here is the grand secret, when we begin to appreciate our design and see ourselves as already lovable, the confidence of that self view reflects in our countenance and in our behaviors, which radiate to others having them take greater notice and interest in us. God is able to love us because He loves who He is. He does not spend His time in eternity worrying about whether He is lovable or not.

Intelligence is the capacity to see truth, accept it and live by its precepts. You have taken a good look at the truth that we are all lovable. What will you do with it? True love requires personal action! Again, it is not just knowing something, it is also doing something that has us fulfill the measure of our creation. Charity, or the pure love of Christ, grows as we do those things that develop it.

In developing greater love for our self Father in Heaven wants us to gain a greater appreciation for and to accept that our body is part of our identity. In spite of the things we don't like about it, it is still an absolute miracle and gift. This last comment now leads us into the final assignment related to the three Negative Core Beliefs that can be shaped in us.

HOMEWORK ASSIGNMENT #7 – You Are An Absolute Miracle

The Prophet Joseph Smith taught that "....we came to this earth that we might have a body and present it pure before God in the celestial kingdom." However, too many of us, through faulty perception, have formed incorrect beliefs about the tremendous gift this body is. I remind you, my whole program is directed toward having a correct view of ourselves as the research of Epigenetics states that our ongoing experience is being shaped by what we have come to believe about our identity. Our body is part of our identity and therefore it is vital that we have a correct understanding of its workings and with that knowledge it is equally important that we prepare it for what it was destined to become. If we are going to experience something new we must do something new in accordance to what we are learning. It is my hope that the following information will fundamentally change any incorrect views you may have formed about your body and have you begin to observe the magnificence of its design. In reverence of its design, you will likely begin taking better care of it.

I have witnessed many clients shed pounds after they have learned to observe themselves correctly. In every instance the better care was driven by the love they were developing for themselves. I had one client state, "Before this Program I would go to the gym because I hated myself. I now go to the gym because I love myself." Likewise, I have witnessed many clients come off of medications, including the self-medications; reverse metabolic issues, reverse heart disease, improve their memory and a host of other ailments their bodies were manifesting.

From the very beginning of this book I have stayed true to keeping the reader focused on how our body plays a vital role in how we continue to experience life, due to its design in absorbing and storing environment and experience. When I began teaching the process of Living Consciously, I had stated that there are only three things in all of our human experience that really drive ongoing negative emotions. We have hopefully settled in your mind that the first two of the three things are hugely distorted and that you are now empowered to confront the distortions when they raise their ugly, untruthful head.

The third Negative Core Belief held by so many in their Implicit Memory is that of a Negative Image of their Body. A Negative Body Image is formed when through our experiences we begin to associate our body in a negative way. Because learning is associative I had stated that people that go around comparing themselves to others and in that comparison consistently seeing them self as 'less than' such as, "Not skinny enough," "Not pretty enough," "Not smart enough," "Not toned enough," etc., that negative evaluation would shape a negative association with their body. Likewise, if a person has a physical characteristic that they are not fond of and that physical characteristic draws too much negative attention; that may shape an ongoing negative view of their body. When people struggle with focusing, memory, comprehension, etc. these mental deficits may lead to a person creating a negative image of their body. When a person struggles with ongoing health issues may create within the individual a negative sense of their body. When a person has been violated, meaning when someone does something to their body that they do not give permission to do, that violation may lead immediately to viewing their body in a negative way. For any that are reading this book who has struggled with a Negative Body Image, it is time to take a critical look at our body and begin to see what an absolute miracle each of us are. To assist us in becoming accepting of a correct view of our body, let us here observe some information about our bodies that few even know about and certainly would never even consider or find themselves thinking about.

Each eye has an auto-focusing lens. Nerves and muscles control two eyes to make one three-dimensional image. The eyes are connected to the brain, which records the sights seen The human eye can distinguish about 10 million different colors. Your nose can remember about 50 thousand different scents. What I have just stated is absolutely true and it is going on all of the time, but the question I have is, "Are you doing it?" I love seeing the reaction on client's faces when I ask this question. The looks of perplexity or perhaps they are wondering if I asked the right question, because honestly, none of us ever spend time thinking about how all of these magnificent truths about our body are upheld.

If you were to lay out all of the alveoli of the lungs, it would take up almost an entire tennis court. I play tennis, and likely if I were to just take you and lay you in the corner of the court, you would hardly get in the way. You might get hit by a couple of balls, but relative to the size of the court, you are not that big. However, the body is highly enfolded on itself. Those two little lungs, if we were to unfold them and then lay the alveoli side by side would indeed take up almost an entire tennis court. If you are wondering what alveoli is, those are the thin membranes in our lungs that allow the gasses to pass through, oxygen in and carbon dioxide out. All of the surface area of the collective alveoli is indeed large enough to take the up the square footage of a tennis court approximately 2800 square feet. If that is not impressive enough then consider that the lungs contain approximately 1500 miles of airway passages! Usually I hear a "WOW!" from my client who is hearing this for the first time. It is a "WOW!" That is a highly impressive design, a design you probably never even thought about or less even considered the mechanism that upholds the breathing process.

As another impressive example of this enfolding are the intestines. The intestines measure about 25 feet in length, however the entire surface area of the intestines would take up two tennis courts! They do a pretty good job in distinguishing what the body needs in form of nutrients, though it is not clear to researchers how they learn to discriminate in what they absorb. I am sure in the future, as we learn more about cell intelligence, we will understand how the cells of the intestines distinguish nutritional needs.

On average there is a minimum of 100 trillion neural connections in your brain. That is about 1000 times the number of stars in our galaxy. About seven percent of the human genome is dedicated to the working of synapses or electrical communication in the nervous system. A single human brain generates more electrical impulses in a day than all of the telephones of the world combined. Again, this is constantly going on, but are you doing it?

Your heart is an incredible pump. It has four delicate valves that control the direction of blood flow. That alone is a significant fact to consider. How blood flows is critical. These valves open and close more than 100,000 times a day – 36 million times a year. Unless disease enters, these valves will last forever. I want you to consider that number 100,000 as it relates to other mechanical objects. A car when it begins to approach 100,000 miles, we know that we are going to be putting money into the vehicle to keep it running. I have owned several sump pumps, and usually within 50 hours of running they begin to exhibit deterioration. Our heart is a pump and I hope you are beginning to see an incredible design – valves that will not fail, only unless disease enters. By the way, the blood pressure in a human can actually pump blood up four stories high.

The heart pumps two gallons of blood per minute, well over 100 gallons per hour. The vascular system is about 60,000 miles in length – twice the circumference of the earth; yet the circulatory system makes up less than 3% of our body mass. Betcha didn't know that! By the way, where does the energy come from that uphold the workings of the circulatory system?

Every 20-60 seconds each blood cell makes a complete circuit through the body. In the second it takes you to inhale, you lose three million red blood cells and in the next second the same number will be replaced. At that ongoing rate, if all of the red blood cells manufactured by your body throughout an average lifetime were lined up it would reach 31,000 miles into the sky. Satellites hover between 250 and 400 miles above the earth. The red blood cells we will manufacture during a life time would take us a third of the way to the sun. That is a lot of activity. Here is some more activity to consider, in one second, 100,000 chemical reactions occur in every cell of your body. That is 100,000 chemical reactions per cell. Since there are 70 to 100 trillion cells that make up our body, you are beginning to see the level of activity that is constantly going on. I ask the question again, I know it is happening, but are you doing it? Are you the one responsible for upholding all of the activity that keeps us living?

Just now, overall, 10 million of your cells just died; and now 10 million more were just born. The single-layer lining of the intestinal wall regenerates itself about every seven days. The pancreas regenerates almost all of its cells in one day. The stomach wall is renewed every four days, which is very important because the gastric juices incorporated within the digestive system will dissolve a razor blade. The constant creation of new stomach cells allows protection against those destructive enzymes. The skin will replace itself about every four weeks, the liver about every six months, and the entire skeletal system about every eight years. While there are many areas of the brain that will have the same cells from birth to death, yet there are many areas of the brain that do become renewed through cell division. It is estimated that we manufacture 40,000 new neuron cells everyday. The hippocampus we know has the capacity to renew itself. Ongoing stress directly impacts the hippocampus, but if the stress is removed, the hippocampus springs back. There are varying opinions on cellular communication between cells, yet it goes without saying that communication between cells is incredibly rapid.

Something other than your conscious mind causes the secretion of enzymes in exact amounts in correspondence to the food you consumed so that it can be broken into its component nutrients. This is a very interesting phenomenon. As soon as food is placed in your mouth, the cells of the mouth begin to communicate with the rest of the digestive system. The cells of the mouth correctly identify what food you have eaten; and the amount and then sends signals to other cells responsible for digestion so that the correct enzymes can be present to break down the food you ate into its component nutrients. Digestion is individualized every time we eat. This is likewise evidence that every cell knows it is working in cooperation with every other cell as previously stated.

Some mechanism of a higher order is filtering liters of blood through your kidneys every hour to make urine and eliminate waste. This higher intelligence maintains the 66 functions of the liver, although most of us would have never guessed the liver does so many functions.

A mother's breast has the capacity to recognize whether a boy or a girl is latched to it, creating changes in nutritional differences the breast supplies. There are subtle differences nutritionally needed depending upon gender and the cells of the mother's breast naturally respond to these differences. Likewise, the female breast also detects illnesses within the baby and produces immunological nutrients based upon the needs to fight-off whatever illness is being detected.

Every cell contains your DNA. Stretching out the DNA in just one cell would create a 6 foot high tower of material. If we were to stretch out all of the DNA incorporated in every cell within our body, that material would reach to the sun and back 150 times. Remember, DNA is the material in the universe that has the greatest capacity for storage and retrieval. DNA can be encoded upon and whatever gets encoded has the potential to send ongoing signals that impact how we continue to experience mortality, especially how we experience ourselves. This Greater Intelligence which acts in us and through us orchestrates tiny protein enzymes that constantly zip through the 3.2 billion nucleic acid sequences that are the genes in every cell, checking for mutations. As an example, through a process of "proofreading" the polymerase enzyme makes sure that any wrong pairings or mis-paired pairings of the base are repaired. If they cannot be repaired apoptosis is one of the back-up mechanisms to avoid faulty or mutated genes getting passed down. As stated before, it is obvious that there is an intelligence incorporated within every cell.

The body's defense system is a wonder. To protect it from harm, it perceives pain. In response to infection, it generates anti-bodies. Our own inner version of Homeland Security knows how to fight off thousands of bacteria and viruses without our ever needing to realize that we are under attack. There are about 40,000 bacteria in our mouth and about 32 million on our skin. That is just a couple of examples of the amount of bacteria present both in and outside of our body. While much of this bacteria is beneficial, the bacteria that is not is detected and dealt with, without our ever even knowing it. We must acknowledge that while most of this protective mechanism goes on without thought, yet we clearly understand that nutrition, exercise and thoughts all impact the body's defense system

The skin provides protection. It warns against injury that excessive heat or cold might cause It is completely replaced about 1,000 times during a person's life-span. The scaffolding of the human body called bones in some of its capacity can be as strong as steel. One cubic inch of bone can support 19,000 pounds.

As already discussed, the body renews its own outdated cells and regulates the levels of its own vital ingredients. The body heals its cuts, bruises, and broken bones. While the mechanism for healing is programmed in the cells, yet we know the impact of our thoughts on physiological functioning. For example, with correct thinking, the brain can be renewed. What that means is that if earlier established neural pathways are filled with toxicity (untruthful beliefs about self) those neural pathways can be disintegrated and replaced with very healthy neural pathways. If we view things correctly, then the brain wires for that reality. When we perceive things as they really are, then we literally are involved in a work of regeneration. Our correct perceptions act to heal any of our past incorrect wiring.

As we have provided a few incredible facts about our bodies, simultaneously we have been emphasizing the upholding power that supports the number of these processes. That upholding power is evident from the moment of conception as this life force manifests itself as soon as an egg and sperm join together. When a sperm and an egg come together there will be a manifestation of energy that is visible through electron microscopes. From conception, this energy or life force is involved in the creation of our almost 100 trillion specialized cells. Its intelligence is supporting the compositional mediums that allows for differentiation of cells. Having given us life, it then continually regenerates that life and regulates an incredible number of processes.

The power that made the body is the power that maintains and heals the body. This power of intelligence animates our trillions of daily chemical reactions within the body, without thought. This light, which lighteth every man... (John 1:9; D&C 93:9), is expressing itself through us, it orders all things, and directs all things, and governs all things, and regenerates all things. Each descriptive word just used identifies the processes of biological survival we experience every second of our life.

This now becomes a very important consideration as we keep enforcing the idea that there is a power that sustains biological activity that has us live, move and breathe (Mosiah 2:21), because as you are sitting there reading this book, you are blowing about 30 to 40 watts out of your head. A watt is a measurement of power. But to keep things in perspective, surrounding all of us are many items that are incredibly designed. Our 4K television sets, our computers, our smart phones, our kitchen gadgets, our power tools, etc. But no matter how well designed any of these gadgets are, without a source of power to run that design it just wouldn't matter. Now here is the problematic consideration. Each of us have measurable power within this physical body, yet none of us have an extension cord that comes out of us that is plugged into a recognizable source of power. The question is then, this measurable power within each of us, are we producing it ourselves or are we simply connected to it? The correct answer will likely provide a view of our body that will support it being an absolute miracle and incredibly important as to our true identity.

Quantum science with all of its related technology and research has opened up a vista in understanding our bodies, that just a few years ago would have never been possible. While we look very "physical" if we were to utilize current technology on your body you would finally become convinced that the matter from which you are made is energy. This is what Albert Einstein was trying to get us to understand, when he taught that, matter and energy are different sides of the same coin. Matter can become energy and energy can become matter. The point is each one of us is literally an energy field connected to a Universal Energy that is found everywhere. And while all of us are connected to the Universal Energy, some of us are more in-tune with its uplifting frequencies than others. Those that are living happier lives are intentional in having a mind that produces frequencies which align with the Universal Energy that each of us are connected to. Einstein's theory of relativity reinforces this understanding. We do not live in a universe with discrete, physical objects separated by empty or dead space. The Universe is one indivisible dynamic whole in which energy and matter are so deeply entangled it is impossible to consider them as independent elements. Matter/Energy is found everywhere. We are connected to all of it – it is all entangled.

Please understand something about this body of yours. It is made up of approximately 100 trillion cells. The DNA is the same in each cell, yet we recognize that cells differ from one another. Muscle cells are distinctly different than neuron cells, bone cells or cartilage cells, to name a few. The differentiation of cells is due to the culture medium in which they are formed. Bone cells are formed by a compositional difference to that of muscle cells or neurons, and yet they all have identical genetic blue prints. Understanding that cells take on different natures by the compositional differences in the mediums from which they form is but a "type and shadow" of how cells can take on the perfected nature of their Progenitor as the Universal Energy emanates from His presence (D&C 88:12). Likewise, we may respond to some other lesser form of energy based upon our incorrect perception (1 Corinthians 15:40-41). The frequency of energy we choose to align with will one day be manifest in our bodies.

With this in mind, the blueprint, no matter how perfect or how flawed can be altered by the energy of the mind. Our thoughts, our perceptions of self, our understanding of the Universal and Supreme Energy will all affect the blueprint. In having worked in construction and trying to follow the architect's blueprints, truth be told, many times what the architect had drawn would not work. That is usually when a meeting was held to discuss alternatives that would work. Many, many times, through the power of the mind, we were able to conceive how to alter the architect's blueprints and have a better outcome. So it is with each of us, our mind has the capacity to get better outcomes in spite of what the blueprint is suggesting. If the blueprint is suggesting addiction or depression; I don't deserve a happy life, or a host of other deficit leading outcomes, the power of the mind has the ability to introduce a compositional medium that can alter cell functioning and rewrite the blueprint. The mind is part of the quantum energy that is found everywhere. We are simply connected to it. Because we are entangled with the Universe, our energy impacts the energy that comes from this living planet. As our energy distances itself from the Universal Energy the earth responds with negative environmental patterns (Moses 7:48-49). I agree that men do contribute to issues of global environmental catastrophe, but do so more from a place of living contrary to the laws the Universal Energy suggests we live in order to fulfill the measure of our creation. Likewise, our energy impacts our relationships, both here and in eternity. Generations may be blessed or cursed based upon the frequency of our own energy.

Modern research recognizes there is a Universal Energy. They speak of it in terms of it being found throughout the entire universe; that it is responsible for taking matter from its unorganized, chaotic state and organizing it into worlds, solar systems and galaxies The various manifestations of this Universal Energy then upholds these systems and pushes out the Universe in degrees, creating greater space that we have no mathematical formulas to even comprehend it. And then the researchers acknowledge that each of us is connected to it and it is the very life-giving energy that upholds us and sustains our incredible design.

As I have read about their description of this Universal Energy, I have come to believe that the research is catching up with the revelations. From the scriptures we hear about a force or energy that is called the Light of Christ. When we think of "light" we can think of it in terms of enlightenment, increasing knowledge and understanding. When these are enjoyed, we experience an uplifting, ennobling, preserving influence. But the Light of Christ we are told is the true light that lighteth every man that cometh into the world (D&C 93:2; John 1:9). I find this expression interesting in connection with what modern scientific research is telling us. Matter can be found in an unorganized, chaotic state, but what activates it into becoming organized is when energy acts upon it. Light is a form of energy and matter does absorb light. What we visibly see in the universe is light infused matter (Moses 1:36-38). Further we are told that the light of Christ fills the immensity of space and is the means by which Christ is able to be in all things, and is through all things, and is round about all things. It giveth life to all things and is the law by which all things are governed (D&C 88:6-13, 41). The description found from the revealed word and the language of modern astronomers and researches bear such an uncanny resemblance, I conclude it is the same.

If therefore Christ is the true light that lighteth every man (D&C 93:2), then it begins to have us ask, why does Christ spend so much energy upholding this body of ours? The second question may be more grabbing of our attention – would Christ expend so much energy in upholding this body were it not important? Contrary to the early creeds of Christendom, and the falsehoods found in Immaterialism or Existentialism, the opening of heavenly communication has informed us that glory, eternal life; and salvation requires that we become like our Progenitor. He has a body of flesh and bones as tangible as man's (D&C 130:22), therefore the body is a vital part of our ongoing progress and development. In fact, knowledge of our identity as both body and spirit is crucial to our eternal progression. As I began to lay hold upon the importance of having a body, I began to put into perspective how many bodies appear to have significant deficits.

Because we live in the mortal condition, imperfections are part of this experience. Sometimes a sperm and egg come together and things don't go as hoped for. For example sometimes genetic mutations occur. Down Syndrome is a genetic mutation. But as I view someone with Down Syndrome would I ever safely conclude that the light of Christ was not upholding the trillions of daily chemical reactions occurring in their cells? Or maybe a woman is pregnant and does not realize it and maybe she is on a strong antibiotic at the time. That strong antibiotic may lead to interfering with the proper development of the child's limbs. Deformations can occur, but when I see someone that has a deformity would I ever conclude that the light of Christ is not upholding their daily trillions of chemical reactions occurring in their cells? As I contemplated these mortal realities, I began to see that maybe it doesn't matter what we may encounter as deficits in this mortal body, but just that we obtain a body; for as the scriptures help us understand is that the Hope of Israel assures us that one day we will come triumphantly from the grave to be given a body that will have a perfect frame (Alma 40:23; 11:45; D&C 138:17; Ezekiel 37:1-6). Going from a state of corruption, being raised in incorruption (1 Corinthians 15:42-44).

REVIEWING HOMEWORK ASSIGNMENT #7

For those that struggle with a negative image of their body, I hope the foregoing has left a lasting impression of what absolute miracles each of us are and the investment of energy being expended in upholding the biological process necessary for us to move, live and breath (Mosiah 2:21). Every one that knows me knows that I have a paunch, meaning a little bit bigger tummy than desired. When I look into the mirror I say in my mind, that is not attractive, yet I know I have the power to shape my body. Though I do not necessarily like what I see, I still recognize what an absolute miracle I am. How could I not considering all of the ongoing level of activity required for me to exist (Acts 17:28; Galatians 2:20). It is through a correct observing of our body that we begin to experience the sacredness of this tabernacle. The ancient Tabernacle, if you will recall was a portable Temple. Perhaps that is why the scriptural authors referred to this body as a Temple; a place where the Divine can enter and change our very nature (1 Corinthians 6:19; D&C 93:35).

Capacity for spiritual communication from the Divine is directly linked to the care we provide for our physical body. Spiritual enhancement is likewise in direct proportion to how we treat our bodies. Our bodies, no matter what condition we may find them in are of such proportions and fitness to enable the expression of our spirits to grow and become as our Heavenly Parents. Our bodies are sacred and we should do all in our power to avoid taking in environmental signals that will harm them. This is not just the substances we ingest, but also the thoughts we think. We should become highly aware of all things that influence our thoughts and avoid those things that have us produce thoughts that lead to destruction, both physically and spiritually.  The body is the instrument of our minds and the means by which our character is developed and manifest. To attain to the fullness of our creation will require that we follow the commandments, including the ones related to our physical bodies. As we follow the commandments directly related to the care of our physical body we are promised that we will receive great treasures of knowledge, even hidden treasures (D&C 89:19).

Sister Barbara Lockhart gave us the following to consider:

> When we accept our Heavenly Father's unconditional love for our soul (D&C 88:15), - SPIRIT AND BODY – we too can love our total selves, body and spirit, and feel grateful for the opportunity of progressing to become like Him. When we see our bodies as a blessing and not a burden, we will rid ourselves of excuses, complaining, and procrastination. We will want to live the commandments, magnify our talents, and do all that we can to know and overcome our weaknesses. We will learn how to live with an eye single to the glory of God, that we may be among those "made perfect through Jesus the mediator of the new covenant,... whose bodies are celestial, whose glory is that of the sun, even the glory of God" (D&C 76:69-70). (The Body: A Burden or a Blessing. Ensign; February 1985, p.57)

We were born as spirit children of Heavenly Parents in the premortal experience. We were born to earthly parents in this life. The great doctrine of who we are requires an understanding that we are both body and spirit. Both are part of our identity. A fulness of joy, which each of us were designed to receive (2 Nephi 2:25), can only be accomplished when the spirit and body are eternally combined (D&C 93:33-34). Even the righteous dead are pained by being separated from their body. They view it as a sense of bondage (D&C 138:50).

For the most part there are many things about our body that we do not have to give any attention to because the Light of Christ appears to be upholding the trillions of chemical reactions we experience everyday of our lives. Yet in the midst of all of this life giving power is one thing we are given to think about as it relates to how we are experiencing ourselves. This thing is a real power, this power is the gift of agency – the gift to believe or disbelieve what has been revealed about us.

How important it is that we view ourselves correctly? Without an honest assessment of our true self come the falsehoods to fill the voids produced by an unwillingness to explore and accept the truth of who each of us are. In the very beginning of teaching the Practice of Living Consciously, I spoke about the three, generalized Negative Core Beliefs that come and occupy the spaces where healthy belief should reside. So many clients become surprised that indeed these are the three areas that are tapped into consistently when our mindset insists on being negatively attuned. We become deeply impacted by the experiences that have us doubt our capability, whether we are seen as acceptable to others, and the myriad of struggles that arise due to the appearance, health and natural desires and urges the physical body produces within us.

Prior to Jesus' ministry He was led by the Spirit into the wilderness to be with God. For forty days he did eat nothing and then when this appointed prepatory meeting was completed, Jesus was afterward hungered. In this state of great physical need and want, the adversary appeals to this most pressing awareness and invites the Lord to use His power to transform mere stones into bread. The adversary then tempts Jesus by having Him view the vastness, power and glory of the kingdoms of the earth, with the promise that it all could be had by the Lord if He would choose to serve him, the evil one. Finally came the challenge of performing a feat that would draw incredible attention of the population if He would follow through.

"There is, of course, running through all of these temptations, Satan's insidious suggestion that Jesus was not the Son of God, the doubt implied in the tempter's repeated use of the word 'if.' "If thou be the Son of God...." (Howard W. Hunter; The Temptations of Christ. October General Conference, 1976). Elder David A Bednar commenting on this episode of the Savior's experience said:

> "It is interesting to note that the overarching and fundamental challenge to the Savior in each of these three temptations is contained in the taunting statement "If thou be the Son of God." Satan's strategy, in essence, was to dare the Son of God to improperly demonstrate His God-given powers, to sacrifice meekness and modesty, and, thereby, betray who He was. *Thus, Satan attempted to attack Jesus' understanding of who He was and His relationship with His Father.* (The Character of Christ; BYU Idaho Religion Symposium. January 25, 2003; Italics added for emphasis.)

In walking down this path of application to the 'Temptations of Christ,' then please also notice the three fundamental areas of exposure within the adversary's approach – the Lord's body (stone to bread), the Lord's capability (the kingdoms of the world), and the Lord's lovability (casting Himself down from the pinnacle of the temple). The adversary's approach is to have us doubt the fundamental aspects of our identity. Our identity includes our physical body right along with our design as being capable and lovable beings. The Savior withstood the temptations of Satan, in part, because He remembered His identity and the purpose of His existence.

We all have basic physical, spiritual and emotional needs. When these needs are not met by others, we can feel as if the reason for their absence has something to fundamentally do with our own lacking. It is time to stop ignoring the vast evidence of these three fundamental areas of our true self and get on with living life with purpose. The message of who we are, if we are hearing, is a voice of gladness! We are beings of light with the potential to become as the Father of lights (D&C 67:9). Should we not go forth then and fulfill our ministry; our purpose as Christ did His? The entire Universe is rooting for us! It was all created to help us fulfill the measure of our creation. Salvation, glory, immortality and eternal life is what were born to receive and there is nothing that the Lord did not create that was not brought into existence for that glorious purpose (Moses 1:39).

> Let the mountains shout for joy, and all ye valleys cry aloud; and ye seas and dry lands tell the wonders of your Eternal King! And ye rivers, and brooks and rills, flow down with gladness! Let the woods and all the trees of the field praise the Lord; and ye solid rocks weep for joy! And let the sun, moon, and the morning stars sing together, and let all the sons of God shout for joy! And let the eternal creations declare his name forever and ever! And again I say, how glorious is the voice we hear from heaven. Proclaiming in our ears, glory, and salvation, and honor, and immortality, and eternal life, kingdoms, principalities, and powers! (D&C 128:23).

Beings that are destined for such greatness were not created as helpless, unlovable or with bodies that could not become glorious and perfected. Each of us were born with the capacities, intelligence, attributes and bodies that can receive glory, salvation, honor, immortality and eternal life, whereupon in such states will receive kingdoms, principalities and powers! In essence, we have received the DNA of an exalted, glorified, immortal Being thus enabling our ability to become such. The message of who we are is indeed a message of gladness!

FINAL THOUGHT – THE DISTORTION OF THE MEANINGS WE PLACE ON OUR AUTOMATIC NEGATIVE THOUGHTS ARE THE NEGATIVE CORE BELIEFS THAT GET SHAPED IN US. ALL THREE OF THE NEGATIVE CORE BELIEFS ARE DISTORTED.

Reminder: TRUTH – We are made as capable, lovable beings; and there is nothing in the universe that is so incredibly designed. Are you an intelligent being?

"If you realized how powerful your thoughts are, you would never think a negative thought."

— Peace Pilgrim

"As a single footstep will not make a path on the earth, so a single thought will not make a pathway in the mind. To make a deep physical path, we walk again and again. To make a deep mental path, we must think over and over the kind of thoughts we wish to dominate our lives."

— Wilfred Arlan Peterson

## AUTOMATIC NEGATIVE THOUGHTS – I AM - Are You?

### HOMEWORK ASSIGNMENT #8

Congratulations, you have discovered many distortions that have been stored within your Implicit Memory, distortions that have been the source of so many ongoing negative patterns you have experienced. Let me review some of those with you. The distortion we find that drives behavior that keeps us stuck is the controlling PARENT EGO STATE or the CHILD EGO STATE. The evidence of these being distorted is that we don't get the outcomes we are looking for while in these ego states. The reason these are distorted is because each of us have the capacity to see our value and to care greatly for our self. Likewise, once our own value is recognized we correctly determine that each person we interact with has the same value and is deserving of being shown incredible care. As we operate from the ADULT EGO STATE everything begins to get better, largely because we are creating an environment that has us stay connected to our true identity.

The distortion of negative emotions is WHEN WE BEGIN TO USE THE NEGATIVE EMOTIONS AS EVIDENCE THAT WE ARE BROKEN OR DEVALUED IN SOME WAY. That is not why we experience these negative sensations. Negative emotions are designed in us to keep us in touch with who we really are. When we go outside of the limits of what negative feelings circumscribe, we become stuck. For example, negative emotions are pain and pain is always an indicator that something is going wrong. Pain emerges when cells begin to break and emotional pain is evidence that our cells perceive they are under threat when we keep providing them information that goes contrary to who they know they are. They begin to break because we are trying to convince them that they are something they are not.

The three NEGATIVE CORE BELIEFS are filled with distortion as is evidenced by your own assignment to collect information of how CAPABILITY and LOVABILITY are detected. The evidence is pretty clear that each of us is designed as capable and lovable beings. This is so because of our inheritance from Heavenly Parents who are Love (1 John 4:8) and who are completely Capable (Revelation 19:6; Mosiah3:5; Omnipotence means having unlimited power; able to do anything). Their capability is manifest in their overcoming all things; and reigning as the Supreme King and Queen of the Universe. In looking at our inheritance of a nature that is so incredibly complex, we in awe consider all that the Lord's hands have made. Not only are we created in the image of God, His power upholds us and sustains our trillions of daily chemical reactions in the body. We are incredibly designed and it is His power that we are connected to that allows this design to fulfill its measure of creation.

We are now faced with the task of coming to understand the distortion found in the Automatic Negative Thoughts we tell ourselves. In order to accomplish this task I would like you to return to your Uninstall Sheets and the only box I want you to pay attention to is the Automatic Negative Thought Box. I want you to get a separate piece of paper and begin to record all of the Automatic Negative thoughts you said to yourself. Here is an example:

1) I am worthless
2) I am inadequate
3) I am not good enough
4) I am a failure
5) I am inadequate
6) I am only acceptable if I do things the right way
7) I am worthless.
8) I am worthless
9) I am a failure
10) I am inadequate
11) I am inadequate

You will notice that in the sample list that some of the Automatic Negative Thoughts are the same, e.g, I am worthless; I am a failure and I am inadequate. When you come across the same thought you do not have to write it out again just simply tally the thoughts. Here is what it would like based upon the foregoing list:

1) I am worthless III
2) I am inadequate IIII
3) I am not good enough
4) I am a failure II
5) I am only acceptable if I do things the right way

In the list above I recognize that I said to myself four times, "I am inadequate," three times "I am worthless," twice "I am a failure, etc.

Your assignment is to go and tally your Automatic Negative Thoughts and record in the following spaces what you observe to be your top three, meaning what are the top three Automatic Negative Thoughts you say to yourself. In the example given above it would look like this:

1) I am inadequate
2) I am worthless
3) I am a failure

RECORD YOUR TOP THREE AUTOMATIC NEGATIVE THOUGHTS HERE:

1) _____

2) _____

3) _____

Now that you have recorded your top three Automatic Negative Thoughts you say to yourself, I would like to shift your attention to our Savior. I ask you, was Jesus a fairly controversial figure back during His mortal sojourn? Most that know the scriptures conclude that He was. How could He be otherwise considering the many wonderful things He was doing? When you hear that the multitudes pressed on Him, or you consider how many kept trying to undermine Him; or those that sought after Him for blessings, it is obvious that the question present in every one's minds was, "Who is this man?" Jesus, himself was aware of the varying opinions. He even comes directly to His closest associates and asks, "Whom do men say that I .......AM?" To those he put forth the question answered by saying that some thought he may be one of the past prophets having come forth again. Jesus continued His line of questioning, "But whom say ye that I AM?" To this came the declaration, "Thou art the Christ, the Son of the Living God" (Matthew 16:13-16). Just in those two responses it is apparent that there were varying opinions of who Jesus was. To the man that was born blind come various representations of who Jesus is based upon his growing understanding. When first asked about the miracle of eyesight; "How were thine eyes opened?" this man replied, "A man that is called Jesus made clay, and anointed mine eyes......" When confronted again by the agitated religious leaders the man strengthened in his own conviction stated, "If this man were not of God, he could do nothing." The man's confession that Jesus was of God, caused him to be cast out of the synagogue. Shortly thereafter, this man comes upon Jesus, whereupon Jesus asks, "Dost thou believe on the Son of God?" He answered and said, "Who is he, Lord, that I might believe on him?" Jesus answered and said, ".... It is he that talketh with thee." In response to this declaration, the man that had been healed from a lifetime of blindness acknowledged Jesus as the Son of God (John 9:10-38).

One of the things that I find fascinating about those that were so vehemently opposed to the Savior was the fact that not once did they ever deny the miracles He performed, they simply declared that He did such marvelous things through the power of Beelzebub, the prince of the devils (Luke 11:15). Therefore in their assessment, Jesus was an ambassador of the evil one. The question asked to some of the religious rulers of the Savior's day, "What think ye of Christ?" was one way the Savior was demonstrating His desire that all may come to view Him correctly.

With that said, let us get a perspective that likely too many of us overlook. The Savior, as a tender mercy, wanted everyone to know who He was and more importantly to believe in Him. As a demonstration of this truth, Jesus would provide information about Himself that would enlighten their understanding and encourage those who were willing to accept Him for who He was. When he would provide this information, many times He would do so by starting with....... I AM. Following are a few examples. Are you aware of any of these?

I am the light of the world (John 8:12)
I am the resurrection and the life (John 11:25)
I am the law (3 Nephi 15:9)
I am your lawgiver (D&C 38:22; 3 Nephi 15:5)
I am the bright and morning star (Revelation 22:16)
I am the bread of life (John 6:35)
The Lord is the living waters (Jeremiah 2:13; John 4:10)
Jesus the author and finisher of your faith (Hebrews 12:2)

I am your advocate with the Father (D&C 110:4)
I am the vine (John 15:5)
I am the door (John 10:9)
I am the good shepherd (John 10:14)
He is the Lamb of God (John 1:29; Revelation 5:6, 8, 12-13)
I am the God of thy father (Exodus 3:6)
I AM THAT I AM (Exodus 3:14)
I am Alpha and Omega (Revelation1:11)
I am the true light (D&C 93:2)
I am meek and lowly (Matthew 11:29)
I am the Son of God (John 10:36; D&C 45:52)
I am the way, the truth and the life (John 14:6)
I am the Master and Lord (John 13:13)
I am the first and last (Revelation 1: 17)
I am he that liveth (Revelation 1:18)
I am the root and descendant of David (Revelation 22:16; 5:5)
I, the Lord, am your Savior and Redeemer (Isaiah 60:16)

I would like you to now look at your top three Automatic Negative Thoughts and the thoughts the Savior shared about Himself and begin to reflect on what you are noticing. There is no right or wrong answer, just simply observe the way Christ speaks of Himself in contrast to the way you have consistently identified yourself. What are you beginning to notice?

One of the most common answers I receive to this question is, "Well, it seems like Christ is a lot more positive than I am." I appreciate that answer because it allows me to ask a more searching question, a question that allows my client to observe even deeper; I ask, "Is Jesus merely being positive, are these just self-affirmations or is He just being truthful?" That becomes the moment when we recognize that Christ is not involved in a bunch of self-affirmations and just trying to be positive and have a good attitude, it appears that Christ knows who He is and acknowledges His true self!

As I began to reflect on these true confessions, I asked myself the following question, "I wonder what it was like to be a 12 year old Jesus." The reason I ask this is because we have a story where Jesus travels down to Jerusalem with his family to celebrate the feast of the Passover. But when the celebration is completed and the families return to their villages, the young Jesus stays behind:

> And when they had fulfilled the days, as they returned, the child Jesus tarried behind in Jerusalem; and Joseph and his mother knew not of it. But they, supposing him to have been in the company, went a day's journey; and they sought him among their kinsfolk and acquaintance. And when they found him not, they turned back to Jerusalem, seeking him. (Luke 2:43-45)

After three days, they found their son in the Temple. What was Jesus doing here? The scriptures indicate that he was sitting with the most learned men having a discussion about the scriptures, the law, the prophets and even the hymns. These are those that were considered the best of the best in understanding the writings of the prophets, the history of Israel; and the line of prophecies concerning the Promised One. Please notice, these great and learned men were not dismissing this 12 year old Jesus, in fact it is recorded that Jesus' contribution to the conversation is so impressive that "all that heard him were astonished as his understanding and answers" (Luke 2:47). The Joseph Smith Translation gives us an insight of this young 12 year old boy:

> And it came to pass that Jesus grew up with his brethren, and waxed strong, and waited upon the Lord for the time of his ministry to come. And he served under his father, and he spake not as other men, neither could he be taught; for he needed not that any man should teach him. And after many years, the hour of his ministry drew near. (JST Matthew 3:24-26)

As would occur many times in His teaching in the future, this moment of a 12 year old boy held the attention of those that were fiercely acquainted with the writings of the prophets. They were astonished at His doctrine, for He taught them as one having authority, and not as the scribes (Mark 1:22). What this meant is that what this young Jesus was teaching was carried with power to the hearts and minds of those listening. Truth is always conveyed with power, meaning that the Holy Ghost ratified the Lord's instruction so that those that heard also felt the witness from the Holy Ghost that what Jesus was teaching was true (Moroni 10:5; John 14:26).

12 year old Jesus' understanding then would have had Him not miss what the Apostle Peter announced, that "To him give all the prophets witness......" (Acts 10:43), meaning that every author of the books contained in the Old Testament, each of these holy men were granted the privilege to look down the corridors of time and witness the ministry of God's Son and then were permitted to provide some sort of detail about His life, about His ministry, about His mission. They recorded this detail for the purpose of being able to identify and recognize Him when He did appear (Moroni 7:23); and here was 12 year old Jesus, a master of the holy writings; He would not have missed this point.

If you will recall the wise men that came from the East searching for the Babe; when they arrive in Jerusalem they report to King Herod. I always say, of course they reported to the king. If anyone would know where this special baby was, certainly it would be the king of the land! Yet when they had audience they inquired, "Where is he that is born king of the Jews, for we have seen his star in the east, and are come to worship him " (Matthew 2:2), King Herod was troubled by their announcement and inquiry and it comes to light that King Herod knows nothing of this prophesied event. He calls a meeting where the chief priests and scribes are pooled and he demands of them where Christ should be born (Matthew 2:4)? One of them references the prophet Micah, what we call today Micah 5:2 and declares that the birth place of the Promised One was revealed 700 years before the occurrence and that the birthplace was to be Bethlehem.

Do you know the story of when Jesus enters into Jerusalem on the back of a foal of a colt amidst the shouts of Hosanna (Matthew 21:5-9)? Zechariah the prophet gave us the details of that event some 500 years prior to it ever occurring, "Rejoice greatly, O daughter of Zion; shout, O daughter of Jerusalem: behold, thy King cometh unto thee: he is just and having salvation; lowly, and riding upon an ass, and upon a colt the foal of an ass" (Zechariah 9:9).

When we attend our Sunday meetings, we sing hymns as part of our worship. Well we have a good portion of the ancient hymnbook. It is called the Book of Psalms. Jesus would have been familiar with and sang many of these hymns. So I wonder what it was like for 12 year old Jesus to sing what we call Psalm 22, wherein King David, some 1000 years before Jesus was even born revealed the opposition and oppression the Lord would encounter in His day, wherein they would end His life by crucifixion. In this Psalm we hear so many elements of that impending moment, a description of the agony He would feel while hanging on that cruel cross; and even some of the very words He would utter while hanging as He is being mocked and laughed at. I wonder what it was like for 12 year old Jesus when he sang this hymn?

If there was any prophet that was given a view of the totality of the pain Jesus would suffer in offering Himself as an Atonement, it was the prophet Isaiah. I wonder what it was like for 12 year old Jesus to read, what we call today Isaiah 53, the suffering Messiah verses? He would be despised and rejected, He would bear our griefs and sorrows, He would be wounded for our transgressions and bruised for our iniquities, the chastisement of our peace was upon Him and with His stripes we are healed. He would be oppressed and afflicted and like a lamb be brought to be slaughtered. Some 700 years before the Atonement would ever occur a prophet's witness would have been familiar to the young Jesus.

I have only listed four examples of these ancient seers and yet there are nearly 300 such prophesies concerning just the Savior's first coming, not to mention about double that concerning His second coming. This young Jesus, who taught from the scriptures with authority, would certainly have gotten some idea about who He was from what had been revealed about Him. I am not saying fully, but to some degree He would have begun to understand who He was. The reason I say not fully is because as is true of each of us, Christ too had a veil placed over His mind, wherein the pre-existent Jehovah would have been erased from His mortal memory. Sometimes I look to the example of Joseph Smith in helping understand this concept. Though Joseph was foreordained to be the Prophet of the Restoration, with the veil appointed in mortality would have covered his memory of that calling. It is apparent that Joseph never could have pulled off the Restoration by simply appealing to the scriptures. We are informed that heavenly messengers were sent to give understanding, keys and power to the young Joseph (D&C 128:20-21; Moroni 7:23-25); likely it was the same for Jesus. Yet clearly, Jesus would have begun to understand something about His identity by what had been written about Him.

Interesting enough, John the Baptist recognized that some prophets looking down the corridors of time also gave witness of him. When the religious leaders come to John the Baptist and ask him to tell them who he is, he references a passage of scripture written by Isaiah to help them understand, "For this is he that was spoken of by the prophet Isaiah, saying, The voice of one crying in the wilderness, Prepare ye the way of the Lord, make his paths straight (John 1:22-23; Isaiah 40:3). Joseph Smith likewise came across scriptures written anciently identifying him as the prophet of the Restoration (D&C 113:3-5). Can you begin to imagine what it would be like to read from these ancient witnesses and recognize that they were talking about you? Would that in any way help you see yourself better, knowing that the Lord knew you and gave some sort of information about who you are and what you would do, long before those events ever occurred?

Well if it is from the writings of recorded verse that Jesus would have in some degree began understanding who He was, let us turn to Him and pay attention to some of what He revealed.

Do you see in the list above where He said, I am the light of the world? In another place He said these following words, speaking to those that would follow Him:

> Ye are the light of the world. A city that is set on an hill cannot be hid. Neither do men light a candle and put it under a bushel, but on a candlestick; and it giveth light unto all that are in the house. Let your light so shine before men..... (Matthew 5:14-16)

Is this perhaps some revelation about you? I so enjoy the hymn, "Brightly Beams Our Father's Mercy." Here we are informed that the Lighthouse on the shore radiates Heavenly Father's mercy to those that are lost at sea. It is the Lighthouse that brings them toward shore, but then we are informed that to us He gives the keeping of the lights along the shore. The lower lights represent those lights that would bring someone safely into the harbor. These lights were important to the sailor as they assisted him in navigating the waterfront. And so we with humility sing:

> Let the lower lights be burning;
> Send a gleam across the wave.
> Some poor fainting, struggling seaman,
> You may rescue; you may save.

Do you see in the list above where Christ says, I am the Son of God? Again coming from His lips, recorded in the New Testament is perhaps some more revelation about our identity. To those that were so opposed to his teaching that He was the Son of God, Jesus countered with the following reasoning:

> Is it not written in your law, I said, Ye are gods? If he called them gods unto whom the word of God came, *and the scripture cannot be broken*, Say ye of him, whom the Father hath sanctified, and sent into the world, Thou blaphemest; because I said, I am the Son of God? (John 10:34-36; Italics added for emphasis)

The law from which Christ references is Psalm 82:6 identifying the true nature of each of us that we are gods because He is God, and children of the most High because He is our Father. Is this perhaps some portion of information recorded by the ancients that is helping us see who we really are?

Have you ever got to the point in trying to help another person that the only resource left was to draw upon the blessings of Heaven; to go and plead with the Father to help someone you cared for that you knew God was the only one left that could intervene and turn things around? In doing so, did you realize that you were acting as an advocate with the Father in behalf of that person? How many of us advocate for our own children (Mosiah 27:14)? I hope you are beginning to recognize something.

Do you see where Jesus said, I am the good shepherd? Is there anything in the scriptural record that points to the idea that we too are good shepherds? As a background to this suggestion I would like us to pay attention to the confusion of Jesus' closest associates in who they were and what their purpose was after Jesus had been put to death. To appreciate this confusion we have to span out and remember the bigger picture of their experience. Part of that bigger picture was developed several centuries earlier when the remaining Israelites were conquered by the Babylonians in about 597 B.C. From that moment all the way until 1947, Israel never stood as an independent nation. She always found herself governed by some larger country or empire, except for a few brief moments during the Maccabean Revolt; this was a very short lived autonomy.

Yet, if you and I would have grown up in the area of Jerusalem as did Peter, Andrew, John and the other close Disciples of Christ, the culture would have heavily influenced our belief. Part of their culture was attending synagogue and hearing the Rabbi's or Teachers rehearse the many prophesies of the 'Conquering Messiah,' the one that upon His appearance would destroy the wicked, eliminate Israel's enemies and restore the kingdom to Israel. This was a very strong theme that ran through the Jewish culture. With that as a backdrop, if you and I would have followed Jesus closely for those three years of His mortal ministry I think we would have been impressed to the point that we would have given Jesus serious consideration as to being the Promised One.

Who else but the Messiah could with but a few words calm the raging elements – "Master, carest thou not that we perish?" came the words from the Savior's friends?

> And he arose, and rebuked the wind, and said unto the sea, Peace be still. And the wind ceased, and there was a great calm. (Mark 4:39)

Who else but the Lord's Annointed could reverse blindness; cause the lame to walk, the deaf to hear and the living death of those afflicted with leprosy to receive new, healthy skin? Who else but the Son of David could take but a few morsels of bread and a couple of fish and multiply these to feed over ten thousand people and afterwards take up a collection of what remained? Who else but the Son of God could take a corpse, lying for four days and restore the spirit to that man raising him from the dead? Yes, I think you and I would have been impressed by what we would have witnessed, Certainly Jesus would have been a good candidate for the One we were seeking. But then He died and His body was placed in a tomb. By all of the prophecies so strongly taught in their culture, this death would have created some serious doubt as to Jesus being the Promised One. The Conquering Messiah would not die!

Here then we pick up on this confusion as we read about the two disciples on the road to Emmaus. The scriptures indicate that while these two were walking they were likewise talking about the events surrounding the death of their friend. At this moment, the resurrected Savior appears and joins these two disciples, but the scripture indicates that "their eyes were holden that they should not know him" (Luke 24:16). I don't have any explanation for this phenomenon, yet it appears to be an important aspect as to what Jesus is getting ready to teach them.

Jesus asks the reason for their sadness, whereupon one of them replies, "Art thou a stranger in Jerusalem, and hast not known the things which are come to pass there in these days?" (Luke 24:18). Jesus continues, "What things?" Now listen to their reply:

> Concerning Jesus of Nazareth, which was a prophet mighty in deed and word before God and all the people. And how the chief priests and our rulers delivered him to be condemned to death, and have crucified him. *But we*

*trusted that it had been he which should have redeemed Israel....(Luke 24:19-21;*
*Italics added for emphasis)*

"But we trusted it had been he which should have redeemed Israel" can you hear their doubt and confusion? Jesus answered their doubt by saying,

> O fools, and slow of heart to believe *all* that the prophets have spoken....... And beginning at Moses and all the prophets, he expounded unto them in all the scriptures the things concerning himself. (Luke 24:25, 27; Italics added for emphasis)

These disciple's cultural pinnings were interfering with their understanding. So great was the usage of scriptural prophecy concerning the Second Coming that the only Messiah they were looking for was One that would come and conquer, that would put all wickedness under His feet, defeat Israel's enemies, and then restore the kingdom to Israel. Interestingly enough, so persuasive is the cultural teaching that after His 40 day ministry; when Jesus is getting ready to be taken up, the apostles ask him, "Lord, wilt thou at this time restore again the kingdom to Israel" (Acts 1:6)? In response the Lord answers, "It is not for you to know the times or the seasons, which the Father has put into His own power" (Acts 1:7). In essence, they were not living in the time or season for this promised event. To overcome their cultural pinnings, Jesus opens the scriptures and begins to rehearse ALL that the prophets had written about Him:

> Then opened he their understanding that they might understand the scriptures...... these are the words which I spake unto you, while I was yet with you, that all things must be fulfilled, which were written in the law of Moses, and in the prophets, and in the Psalms concerning me. Thus it is written, and thus it behoved Christ to suffer, and to rise from the dead the third day. (Luke 24:45, 44, 46)

Now the disciples understood. In having Jesus open and rehearse *all* that the prophets had written concerning the Messiah; they now understood that the Messiah had to come first to conquer sin and death before He could be given keys to accomplish the things concerning His Second Coming. Now they understood that the Messiah brings salvation twice. He ministered unto men and wrought the Perfect and Infinite Atonement. He shall return to slay the wicked, cleanse His vineyard from corruption and ransom those that have faithfully lived as He has instructed. So moved are these disciples by this experience that when they arrive in Emmaus, Jesus acts if He will continue on, but they do not want Him to leave. This is where we get the hymn, "Abide With Me," as the disciples constrained Him saying, "Abide with us, for it is toward evening, and the day is far spent" (Luke 24:29); so they invite Him to stay and have a meal with them.

> And it came to pass, as he sat at meat with them, he took the bread, and blessed it, and brake, and gave to them. And their eyes were opened, and they knew him; and he vanished out of their sight. (Luke 24:30-31)

Sometimes in my pondering of this verse I wonder what that means "and he vanished out of their sight;" was this a Star Trek moment or did He just simply get up and leave? I don't know, but what impresses me the most is what these two disciples say after the Savior does leave them. This is a paraphrase, and I mean no disrespect to the written word as I do paraphrase, but in essence these two disciples say, "Of course it was Him! We should've known it was Him, because did not our hearts burn within us, while he talked with us by the way, and while he opened to us the scriptures" (Luke 24:32)? Do you know how many times they had become acquainted with that experience of being taught with such clarity that their hearts burned within them? They walked with the Master Teacher for three years. They would have experienced many, many times their hearts burning within them, because the Savior taught as one having authority and not as the scribes. As mentioned earlier, this phrase points our understanding that when truth is being taught by authorized servants, that the message is conveyed with power to the hearts and minds of those that are being taught. The burning in the bosom is a dedicated sign provided to all those who sincerely desire truth (D&C 9:8: 8:2).

Now that we are considering the reasonable confusion these disciples experienced upon the death of their friend Jesus, it perhaps provides more meaning to another experience the resurrected Lord has with others of His disciples. It is in the morning and the resurrected Savior is walking on the shores of Galilee. Three years prior He had been in this same place when He met two men, brothers and fishermen by trade:

> And Jesus walking by the Sea of Galilee, saw two brethren.... Peter and Andrew his brother, casting a net into the sea: for they were fishers. And he saith unto them, Follow me...... and they straightway left their nets and followed him. (Matthew 4:18-20)

And follow Him they did. For three years they were mentored, schooled and partakers of events that completely transformed their understanding. And now here it is three years later and the very same location whereupon the beginning of this relationship occurred. Again I paraphrase, it is the morning and the resurrected Savior is standing on the shores of Galilee watching a vessel make its way to shore. When the small fishing boat is close enough we hear Jesus speak out, "Have you any meat," meaning, did they have any fish that they might share with him. They reply that they have not anything. Just as it had been three years earlier, when these men replied to a similar question, wherein they informed Jesus that they had toiled all night and had not caught one fish, Jesus then invited them to push back from the shore and let their nets down, and in doing so these fishermen "enclosed a great multitude of fishes," so much so that their nets began to break (Luke 5:3-8).

It was here that Peter first became acquainted with the power of the Savior. As it was then, so it is now and Jesus says to them, "Cast the net on the right side of the ship, and ye shall find" (John 21:6). As they followed the Lord's invitation, just as it had been before, the draw is so great that it was a great struggle to bring them in. But John and Peter, two of the Lord's valiant apostles are not missing the point. They know that the only one who could produce such a miracle was their friend. John yells out, "It's the Lord" (John 21:7). As they work to bring their bounty to shore, here the Savior has a tender conversation with His chief apostle and asks, "Peter, lovest thou me more than these?" speaking of the fish. Peter, in meekness and sincerity replies, "Yea Lord, thou knowest that I love thee." Jesus then pointedly says to Peter, "Feed my lambs," an invitation for Peter to become a good shepherd (John 21:15). So important is this development, that the Savior emphasizes the request three times.

Peter, being a holder of the Melchizedek Priesthood, is invited to fulfill the great responsibility of all those that are made benefactors of the Lord's authority to become good shepherds. The great brotherhood of this holy order is charged with the task of gathering the children of Israel back into the true fold and to go after even the one lamb that strays. It is apparent that herein the Lord is helping us understand something about our identity.

We have asked the question, "I wonder what it was like to be a 12 year old Jesus?" and then pointed our attention to the prophets, of whom each gave some witness of Him (Acts 10:43; 26:22). If we begin to understand the common theme of witness each prophet was charged with and are accepting that every one of them provided some sort of detail concerning the Promised One, so that when He did come we would recognize Him, then it is equally important to understand the other main theme of which they likewise equally spoke of. As these holy men (2 Peter1:21) looked down the corridors of time the other thing they gave the greatest witness of was the family line of Israel and mostly the descendants of Israel belonging to our generation.

We read in Deuteronomy that the family line of Israel was established pre-earthly, or as it is recorded,

> Remember the days of old.....when the most High divided to the nations their inheritance, when he separated the sons of Adam, he set the bounds of the people according to the number of the children of Israel. For the Lord's portion is his people; Jacob (Israel) is the lot of his inheritance..... he led him about, he instructed him, he kept him as the apple of his eye. (Deuteronomy 32:7-10).

Who is Israel?

> Israel, the Lord's chosen people, were a congregation set apart in pre-earthly existence. In large measure, the spirit children of the Father who acquired a talent for spirituality, who chose to heed the divine word then given, and who sought, above their fellows, to do good and work righteousness – all these were foreordained to be born in the house of Israel. They were chosen before they were born....... They were true and faithful in the pre-mortal life, and they earned the right to be born as the Lord's people and have the privilege, on a preferential basis, of believing and obeying the word of truth. (McConkie, The Millennial Messiah, pp 182-183)

The one thing those that were born through the lineage of Israel, the one thing they did better than their fellow, pre-existent brothers and sisters was to develop the talent of spirituality. This talent was such that they had become so acquainted with the Master's voice, had become so sensitive to truth and righteousness, and had become so faithful in adhering to those principles that lift and exalt, that when they did come forth in mortality they would recognize that voice as it came to them from authorized servants and from the whisperings of the Holy Ghost. This is why the Savior was able to say:

> My sheep hear my voice, and I know them, and they follow me: And I give unto them eternal life; and they shall never perish, neither shall any man pluck them out of my hand. (John 10:27-28)

His sheep have detected His voice in all generations. His voice is the same; it is unchanging. Having become so familiar with its light and the feeling of hope and peace that accompanied its truths, the saints in all ages are drawn to it as if it is home. It is seared in their spiritual DNA and when the message of truth and salvation are heard in mortality, it resonates because of their pre-mortal experience. This is the reason why the lineage of Jacob is referred to as "chosen." Having demonstrated such excellent faith in the pre-mortal realms, these are the one's that were chosen to continue their faithful ministry here in mortality (Isaiah 44:1; 45:4). It is not by chance or randomness that you were born in the family line you were born in, nor the nation, nor the dispensation. Your birth is a designation of reward for the kind of life you lived before you came here to have your mortal probation. You knew His voice then and loved it. You showed that love by keeping His commandments in the pre-mortal realm. Such faithfulness prepared you perfectly for the times and dispensation you came forth in.

For most of earth's history, His voice is transmitted by men He calls and appoints to reveal His mind and will (2 Peter 1:20-21). Jesus confirmed this pattern in His day when He said concerning the twelve apostles he chose, "He that receiveth you receiveth me, and he that receiveth me receiveth him that sent me" (Matthew 10:40), or to be even more clear, "Verily, verily I say unto you, He that receiveth *whomsoever* I send, receiveth me, and he that receiveth me receiveth him that sent me" (John 13:20). In our day the Lord reiterated this eternal pattern:

> What I the Lord have spoken, I have spoken, and I excuse not myself; and though the heavens and the earth pass away, my word shall not pass away, but shall all be fulfilled, *whether by mine own voice or by the voice of my servants, it is the same.* (D&C 1:38; Italics added for emphasis; See Also: D&C 132:7; 21:4-6)

In having us understand the eternal pattern clearly, President Ezra Taft Benson stated:

> Beware of those that would set up the dead prophets against the living prophets, for the living prophets always take precedence. *(Fourteen Fundamentals in Following the Prophet*; Ensign Magazine, June 1981)

Likewise, President Kimball gave attention to this problem when he stated:

> Even in the Church many are prone to garnish the sepulchers of yesterday's prophets and mentally stone the living ones. (The Instructor; 95:527. See Also: John 8:31-33, 42, 59; Acts 7:35-39, 2 Nephi 9:28-29, 42)

The eternal pattern is that He reveals His word through His servants the living prophets; such is the divine pattern (Amos 3:7) Elder McConkie gave us, the Lord's latter-day people; His sheep in this day something to consider, he asked:

> If you had lived in Jerusalem in the days of Jesus, would you have accepted him as the Son of God as did Peter and the Apostles? Or would you have said he had a devil and wrought miracles by the power of Beelzebub, as Annas and Caiaphas claimed? If you had lived in Nazareth or Cana or Capernaum, would you have believed the new religion preached by a few simple fishermen? Or would you have followed the traditions of your fathers in which there was no salvation? If you had lived in Corinth or Ephesus or Rome, would you have

believed the strange new gospel preached by Paul? Or would you have put your trust in the vagaries and traditions and forms of worship that then prevailed? (McConkie, Who Hath Believed Our Report, GC October 1981)

And then came the most obvious answer:

If you accept the prophets whom the Lord sends in your day, you also accept that Lord who sent them. If you reject the restored gospel and find fault with the plan of salvation taught by those whom God hath sent in these last days, you would have rejected those same teachings as they fell from the lips of the prophets and Apostles of old. (McConkie, Who Hath Believed Our Report, GC October 1981)

Israel, believing Israel developed the talent of knowing the Good Shepherd's voice, to desire it and to listen and obey its direction. But, it is one thing to be born into the House of Israel and quite another to be born into the lineage of Joseph. There are many shadows, imagery, types, and symbolism found in the son of Jacob that was separated from his brethren, but who became the means of their salvation many years later. That imagery pointed toward a future day, when Israel would be dispersed but gathered in again in the last days. When one follows the historical acts of birthright blessings, it is obvious that those that would come from Joseph's seed would be responsible for the salvation of their fellow Israelite brothers and sisters in the last days (Deuteronomy 33:17).

In the naming of Ephraim and Manasseh as his own, Israel gave them a blessing. While from our viewpoint Manasseh should have received the birthright blessing, he being the firstborn son, without explanation the ancient patriarch and prophet gave the birthright blessing to Ephraim. Even Joseph, while watching this event became concerned and displeased and tried to correct his father, But Israel was settled on the matter and said to Joseph:

I know it my son, I know it: he also shall become a people; and he also shall be great: but truly his younger brother shall be greater than he, and his seed shall become a multitude of nations. And he blessed them that day saying, In thee shall Israel bless, saying, God make thee as Ephraim and as Manasseh: and he set Ephraim before Manasseh. (Genesis 48:19-20)

That this action performed by their grandfather Jacob was ratified by the Lord, we hear another prophet declare the mind and will of the Lord when he said, "I am a father to Israel and Ephraim is my firstborn" (Jeremiah 31:9).

President Joseph Fielding Smith and others have made it abundantly clear that the descendants of Ephraim hold the presiding keys to carry forth the work of the Restoration and of the gathering of Israel in the last days. He taught:

"The members of the Church, most of us of the tribe of Ephraim, are of the remnant of Jacob. We know it to be the fact that the Lord called upon the descendants of Ephraim to commence his work in the earth in these last days. We know further that he has said that he set Ephraim, according to the promises of his birthright, at the head. Ephraim receives the 'richer blessings,' these blessings being those of presidency or direction. The keys are with Ephraim. It is Ephraim who is to be endowed with power to bless and give to the other tribes, including the Lamanites, their blessings. All the other tribes of Jacob, including the Lamanites, are to be crowned with glory in Zion by the hands of Ephraim. ... "That the remnants of Joseph, found among the descendants of Lehi, will have part in this great work is certainly consistent, and the great work of this restoration, the building of the temple and the City of Zion, or New Jerusalem, will fall to the lot of the descendants of Joseph, but it is Ephraim who will stand at the head and direct the work." (Doctrines of Salvation, 2:250–51; italics in original removed.)

President Gordon B. Hinckley reminded us:

This is the time when the God of Heaven has moved in fulfillment of His ancient promises that He would usher in the fullness of the gospel in the Dispensation of the Fulness of Times...... You're not here by chance. You are here under the design of God. (Teachings of Gordon B. Hinckley; 1997, p720)

So who are you that you should be born of the birthright line, to come forth in the Dispensation of the Fullness of Times (Ephesians 1:10), whose main charge and assignment is to prepare the earth for the coming of its King? Who are you? Understanding the nature of being a covenant people is essential in your growing sense of your true self. If you have a lack of covenant consciousness I invite you to study the subject, thus strengthening your identity.

What did these ancients see as they looked down the corridors of time and saw our day? As we read of their visions, many times they describe our day as a time of gladness and rejoicing (Psalm 14:7; 53:6; Isaiah 35:1; Zephaniah 3:13-14; Zechariah 10:7). But what is it that they saw that would have them describe our time as such? I think the most obvious answer is that our day is the great winding up scene, therefore all that was looked forward to was about to occur, The prophet of the restoration would be unveiled (2 Nephi 3:7,18), Ephraim would come forth out of obscurity and be given the keys of priesthood so that the gathering could commence (Jeremiah 31:6), and the faithful members of that tribe would begin in earnest preparing the earth for its rightful Ruler (Jeremiah 16:16-21). This tribe, as prophesied, would bring forth scriptural record that would herald in the great promised gathering (Isaiah 29:11-14, 18-19; Ezekiel 37:15-21).This was a day of great anticipation by those that were so favored to see it. But I also think there was another reason for their rejoicing. It wasn't until Joseph Smith that we were given an accurate view of past history. Joseph taught that the gospel had been delivered in its fullness to people in times past, but it appeared that they had a hard time holding on to it in a large sense. Joseph introduced us to the idea of there being large scale apostasies in the past, requiring the need to call up new prophets to head up new dispensations.

Yet, when Daniel the prophet looked down the corridors of time and saw our day, he declared that when the kingdom should come forth in our day, it:

....... Shall never be destroyed: and the kingdom shall not be left to other people... (Daniel 2:44)

This would be the first time in earth's history, where when the gospel is restored it would be held onto. There would be no large scale apostasy and the rightful heirs would not allow the truth to be usurped by anyone else. Who are we that would not let go that which others in the past had? Who are we that would protect the principles of truth to the degree that social pressures would not be the means for ongoing revelation? Who are we that though the inhabitants of the great and spacious building will point their finger to mock and scorn that we would be found still clinging to the iron rod (1 Nephi 8:26-30, 33)? One of the signs of the true kingdom would be that she alone will maintain the voice of truth.

Alma gave us some insight to who we are when he taught about those that would hold Melchizedek Priesthood:

> And this is the manner after which they were ordained – being called and prepared from the foundation of the world (pre-existence) according to the foreknowledge of God, on account of their exceeding faith and good works..... therefore they having chosen good, and exercising exceedingly great faith are called with a holy calling, yea, with that holy calling which was prepared with, and according to, a prepatory redemption for such. (Alma 13:3)

I might suggest here that foreordination means that because of our exceedingly great faith, not just here in mortality, but also in pre-earth life, that we were promised to be given the privilege of ministry through this holy calling when we did enter our earthly experience. We are living in a time in history where there are more Melchizedek Priesthood holders on the earth at one time then there ever has been in earth's history. That alone begins to suggest something special about who we are. The final battle is already raging and the Lord's army is assembled (D&C 88:112-115; Daniel 12:1)

Joseph F. Smith was given a vision of the spirit sons and daughters of God laboring in the Spirit World, said he:

> I observed that they were also among the noble and great ones who were chosen in the beginning to be rulers in the Church of God. Even before they were born, they with many others, received their first lessons in the world of spirits and were prepared to come forth in the due time of the Lord to labor in his vineyard for the salvation of the souls of men. (D&C 138:55-56)

From Abraham we receive a very good description of who we are:

> Now the Lord had shown unto me the, Abraham, the intelligences that were organized before the world was; and among all these were the noble and great ones; And God saw these souls that they were good, and he stood in the midst of them, and he said: These I will make my rulers; for he stood among those that were spirits, and he said unto me: Abraham, thou art one of them, thou wast chosen before thou wast born. (Abraham 3:22-23; See Also: Jeremiah 1:5)

President Harold B. Lee, commenting on this revelation asked:

"Who are you?" You are all the sons and daughters of God. Your spirits were created and lived as organized intelligences before the world was. You have been blessed to have a physical body because of your obedience to certain commandments in that pre-mortal state. You are now born into a family to which you have come, into the nations through which you have come, as a reward for the kind of lives you lived before you came here and at a time in the world's history..... determined by the faithfulness of each of those who lived before this world was created (Harold B. Lee, Understanding Who We Are Brings Self Respect, October GC, 1973)

And so we return to the truth that the Savior, becoming acquainted with the scriptures would have certainly gotten, to a degree, an idea of who He was. It was the multitude of details, these Messianic prophecies provided by the ancients that had me first gain my testimony of the Savior and the great gift of His Atonement. As I prepared my mind and began to delve into the written word, it became clear to me that what I was reading was significant. Each Messianic prophecy was like a puzzle piece and when fully assembled, the only picture that emerged was Jesus Christ. I marveled at how much had been revealed about Him. Men who lived hundreds, even thousands of years apart each gave some sort of detail about Him. The probability of someone coming forth in space and time and fulfilling just twenty of the prophecies would have been miraculous, and yet this Jesus came forth and fulfilled all of the prophecies concerning His first coming and He has already fulfilled some concerning the preparation of His second coming. My testimony gained footing because of this great fact.

And as these ancient holy men looked down the corridors of time, they also spoke about us and likewise provided some great detail concerning this generation. If Christ would have come to some understanding of who He was based upon what had been revealed about Him, might we also become more firm in our understanding of who we are based upon the same criteria?

Most of my clients take interest in what is being pointed out with this line of reasoning, yet one client in particular, who had struggled with a negative internal conversation her entire life, was faced with a decision because of her valiant testimony. What she was hearing was as if her soul was being penetrated and cleansed because His words were in her heart as a burning fire, engraven within her very bones (Jeremiah 20:9). The light of truth was shining with brightness and she realized she was faced with a decision. With tears in her eyes she said, "I think I can let go of my negative self-perception. I had never considered what has been brought to my awareness today."

Now let me add a couple of things before we wrap up this assignment. Melchizedek means "righteous king." In the very name of the priesthood many of us hold or have the privilege to hold through our faithfulness is the constant reminder of who we are. We literally belong to the order of righteous kings, foreshadowing the day of our calling and election being made sure, "Well done, thou good and faithful servant: thou hast been faithful over a few things, I will make thee ruler of many things: enter thou into the joy of thy lord" (Matthew 25:23). I believe these are likely the words of an ordinance wherein we are made kings and queens as the scriptures attest we were born to become.

Our Patriarchal Blessings also reveal much about our true nature. In paraphrasing one of my son's, he was told, "Be assured that you did not come forth from the pre-existence one moment sooner than you were fully prepared to fulfill the assignment of the dispensation of the fullness of times." To me it was announced, "Brother Bradley, thou art a stalwart. The Lord knew you were one he could depend upon to bring about His righteous purposes in these latter days." I don't think my son's or my Patriarchal Blessing are the only ones that contain language of this sort. I encourage you to read your blessing, or if you have not received one yet, to obtain the knowledge of who you really are by receiving your blessing of personal revelation.

In returning to the "I AM" of our Savior and the one's we recognized we have been saying to ourselves, I would like to point your mind to the very meaning of "I AM." "I AM" comes from the Hebrew and it means, "how one exists." It is obvious from the list we recorded concerning our Lord that He exists in the truthfulness of His identity. As you look back at the one's you recorded about yourself, at this point you already know that none of them are true, but your brain wiring and your DNA are designed to be influenced by your thoughts. Through repetitive incorrect messages we tell ourselves, we begin to exist in a manner that is contrary to our true identity.

If there is one area that the Adversary attacks us, it is our identity. He does not want us to know who we really are. Even to the Holy One came the attempts of creating doubt, "If thou be the Son of God." Three times did Satan use this strategy in trying to trip up the physically weakened Savior shortly after He had fasted for forty days. At the conclusion of His earthly ministry, this same strategy was employed again. As Christ was hanging in agony beyond compare, evil men reviling Him did so by using the language of their master Lucifer, ".....save thyself, *if* thou be the Son of God, come down from the cross" (Matthew 27:40).

One thing that becomes obvious is that Adam and Eve did not have the fullness of the gospel when they were exited from the Garden. We know this because ".....after many days an angel of the Lord appeared unto Adam saying: Why dost thou offer sacrifices unto the Lord? And Adam said unto him: I know not, save the Lord commanded me" (Moses 5:6). As the angel brought forth information, Adam began to have a full understanding, not only of a Savior, but that he and his wife and all of their posterity were the literal children of God. As Adam and Eve "made all things known unto their sons and their daughters" (Moses 5:12), Satan makes a quick appearance and says to the family members, "Believe it not" (Moses 5:13). Satan does not want us to know the truth of who we really are. When we come to a correct understanding of who we really are, then the knowledge of the course of our life unfolds. With certainty of our course we will not grow weary in our minds and faint.

So let me conclude by saying, there is a reason why I tell people about Princess Mia. When we are first introduced to Mia, she is insecure, worried constantly about what others think of her, and even has doubts about who she is and what her life course is meant to be. Then it is revealed to her, her true identity. Her life takes on a new direction. She is schooled in what it means to be Royal. She begins to organize around her true identity and begins to increase in wisdom and stature; and in favor with God and man. When her schooling is complete we see a young woman of confidence and grace who is no longer worried about herself. In her true nature, in her true identity she is now highly attuned to those she is called to serve. So it will be with all who will come to believe what has been revealed about them and as they then begin to organize around that true identity.

You are getting ready to conclude the Uninstall Process of the Program. In doing so, it is important to impose first a challenge and then secondly a question. The challenge is for you to open the scriptures and find anywhere in them where the Lord has ever revealed that you are any of those negative things you have been saying about yourself. As you are already realizing the challenge places a level of ridiculousness around even attempting to do so because you know that is not what He has revealed about you. The scriptures simply reveal that we are the children of God. Our true identity is revealed knowledge. That is how any of us have gotten a sense of who we really are, is because it has been revealed. This doctrinal truth, when understood, highlight's our very purpose in the universe. Our identity determines in large measure our destiny. Elder Tad. R. Callister queried:

> 'Why is it so critical to have a correct vision of this divine destiny of godliness of which the scriptures and other witnesses clearly testify?' He answered, 'Because with increased vision comes increased motivation.' (Our Identity and Our Destiny, BYU Devotional, April 2012)

Elder Bruce R. McConkie wrote:

> No doctrine is more basic, no doctrine embraces a greater incentive to personal righteousness... as does the wondrous concept that man can be as his Maker.

And why not possible for us to become like our Father in Heaven? Elder Callister continues:

> Do not all Christian churches advocate Christlike behavior? Is not that what the Sermon on the Mount is all about? If it is blasphemous to think we can become like our Father in Heaven, then at what point is it not blasphemous to become like Him – 90 percent, 50 percent, 1 percent? Is it more Christian to seek partial godhood than total godhood? Are we invited to walk the path of godhood – to "be ye therefore perfect, even as your Father in Heaven is perfect" – with no possibility of ever reaching the destination?

Intelligent beings see truth, become accepting of it and begin to live in accordance with it. Like the Savior, we must remember who we are and our mission in mortality. Just as He came and completed His preparations unto the children of men (D&C 19:19), we too were given an assignment to come and continue our faithful ministry. Elder Neal A. Maxwell, in speaking to my generation when we were youth said:

> I want you to know that I regard you highly ..... and have great expectations for you. The highest compliment I can pay you is that God has placed you here and now at this time to serve in His kingdom; so much is about to happen in which you will be involved and concerning which you will have some great influence...... and this will require us to accept with all our hearts – particularly your generation – the truth that there is a divine design in each of our lives and that you have a rendezvous to keep, individually and collectively. (But For A Small Moment; September 1, 1974, Devotional)

The adversary's strategy is to hide our true identity; yet we are who we are. Whether we are willing to make an honest investigation about the revelations concerning our identity is a matter of choice. Whether we do or we do not, will not change who we really are, what will change is whether we will become or not become what we were designed to be.

With the foregoing look at just a few of the prophecies concerning you and I; I think it would be very appropriate to acknowledge the truth of who each of us are:

1) I am a child of God
2) I am a noble and great one
3) I am chosen
4) I am of the birthright
5) I am a prince or princess in my Father's house

The apostle Peter put it this way:

> But ye are a chosen generation, a royal priesthood, an holy nation, a peculiar people; that ye should shew forth the praises of Him who hath called you out of darkness into His marvelous light. (1 Peter 2:9)

When the Savior told others who He was by starting with I Am (John 8:58), every pronouncement was intended for those who were acquainted with the scriptures, laws, traditions, prophets and hymns to recognize that He was the Promised One. What may seem to the scriptural illiterate as vague personal references, to the scripturally informed would have been bold announcements.

There is no reason for us to be ashamed of who we are. We are the very fulfillment of much prophecy. For those that are scripturally literate, would not have a problem with our pronouncements (Romans 1:16). I recall such an occasion. Years ago I was invited to a job walk in downtown Los Angeles. At that time, many of the old buildings in Los Angeles were being gutted and then turned into multi-use buildings, but mostly lofts. The building I was looking at had recently been sold by the University of Southern California (USC) to a very prominent Rabbi in Israel. This was the old theater building that USC used for their theater department.

I was joined that day by many other contractors, some who I had formed some good relationships with throughout my years doing construction. These other contractors knew of my affiliation with the Church of Jesus Christ of Latter-Day Saints, and from time-to time during the job walk teased me a bit about being a "Mormon." The person that was conducting the job walk's name was David. David was one of the Rabbi's sons. When the job walk was completed, David thanked everyone for coming and then to my surprise said, "Larry, would you mind coming to my office?" I received a few looks from my other contractor friends, if you can imagine.

When we sat down at David's desk he asked me, "Larry, who are you?" As I looked a little perplexed at the question, he continued, "Yesterday I received a call from my brother. He is in Salt Lake City. He asked me, 'David, have you ever been to Salt Lake City?' I told him I had not. He said, 'David, you have to come. You know that Spirit we feel in Israel? That same Spirit is here.'" I now understood his question. I opened some scriptures and said to him, "I am Ephraim." David did not even blink at that announcement, because faithful members of Judah and Benjamin absolutely understand that the first tribe to gather in the last days is Ephraim and that Ephraim would then gather in the rest of the tribes.

So as I previously stated that I was going to also ask you a question; the question I am getting ready to ask is reasonable as it pertains to the great gift of Agency each of us has been given. Many times we get confused about the power of Agency. Most of the time when we consider this gift we do so in relation to behavior and moral conduct, but I think agency has its greatest impact upon our thoughts and what we believe about our self, because it is from our thoughts about self that we assume an identity, even if that identity is contrary to our true nature. From identity comes purpose and destiny! With that said, here is my question, what do you want to believe about yourself, do you want to believe what has been revealed about you or would you like to continue to believe the Automatic Negative Thoughts you have been saying to yourself?

Either one will have its outcome!

In response to a summary of the revelations concerning our true identity, I had a client say, "I have been focused incorrectly my whole life on my identity. I so easily accept what has been revealed about Him and then shut my understanding of what has been revealed about me. I think I better start believing and stop doubting."

Scriptures to consider in relation to what our thoughts can lead to: Matthew 5:21-22; 27-28; Alma 12:14; Mosiah 4:30

FINAL THOUGHT – THE DISTORTION OF ANY AUTOMATIC NEGATIVE THOUGHT IS IT GOES AGAINST REVEALED TRUTH ABOUT OUR IDENTITY.

Reminder: TRUTH – Our true identity that we are the children of God is revealed knowledge. Are you an intelligent being?

> An intelligent person is never afraid or ashamed to find errors in their understanding of things.
>
> — Bryant McGill

> If you don't like something, change it. If you can't change it, change the way you think about it.
>
> — Mary Engelbreit

### INSTALLING A HEALTHY IMPICIT MEMORY

If you will become accepting of your design, I will simply remind you that you were designed as 100 trillion cells, each one being intelligent with the capacity to absorb your environment and your experience. What is absorbed into cells has not a small chance of impacting DNA activity and expression, but acts as an incredible influence in altering signals and performance. For example, a person who becomes a smoker can alter gene activity, which has the capacity to leave a marker on their DNA for up to 30 years. There are visible alterations in gene sequencing, or better said, mutations in the cells of the lungs, larynx and oral cavity; nearly 200 mutations after just one year of smoking. What that means is that the person's children conceived with the altered DNA will have a greater possibility of not just smoking, but the potential to have their DNA signal many of the diseases common to smoking, such as emphysema, COPD, asthma, high blood pressure, arteriole disease, etc., even if they themselves have never smoked.

A mental disorder classified as Anti –Social Personality Disorder is found in about 3% of the general population here in America, yet among the prison population that disorder accounts for over 60% of the inmates. An international team of researchers have conducted a genome-wide study in hopes of identifying the genes involved with this disorder. What causes this disorder is unknown; however it is believed that a person's environment, such as being abused as a child, neglect, instability, etc., could be a major contributor to the development of the condition. Having alcoholic parents was also seen as a high correlate in many of these inmates background.

The research did uncover a broad association between altered genes, known as nucleotide polymorphisms on very specific areas of a gene, which was the same in all of the participants (Genome-Wide Association Study of Ant-Social Personality Disorder; Translational Psychiatry; September 2016). Single nucleotide polymorphisms are called SNP's (pronounced 'snip;' plural, 'snips'). SNP's underline differences in our susceptibility to a wide range of both physical and mental health issues. If we are understanding the message of Epigenetics then it should not be difficult to connect some dots here. The challenging, inconsistent, neglectful and abusive relationships of these inmates early environment likely led to incorrect perceptions of self which influenced cellular activity as is manifested in the SNP's discovered. Likewise, some of these may have simply been genetic inheritances. Regardless of nature or nurture, the nucleotide polymorphisms are influencing the mental disorder.

A person that has experienced significant trauma may pass down the epigenetic fingerprints for that trauma for several generations. Scientists have observed these epigenetic memories in an experiment with mice. Mice, upon smelling fruit would simultaneously receive an electrical shock. This conditioned response not only had the mice avoid fruit, but that conditioning altered their DNA and that epigenetic fingerprint, or SNP was passed down two successive generations. What that means is that even though the offspring in the next two generations had never been shocked with electricity themselves, they likewise avoided fruit. This may be one layer of fulfillment when the scripture says, ".... Visiting the iniquity of the fathers upon the children, and upon the children's children, unto the third and to the fourth generation" (Exodus 34:7). It appears that previous generation's experience, beliefs, behavior, negative emotions and the like can be passed down as epigenetic fingerprints.

As was stated early on in this book, I am not approaching life experience from a nature vs. nurture perspective. I am revealing how both nature and nurture combine in a way that plays it roles out on physiology and how our physiology is highly involved in our ongoing experience. Experience and genetic endowment govern the development of the brain and both are directly involved in emotional and behavioral experience. We know now that our genes provide the foundation and overall structure of our brain, but that its myriad of connections are sculpted and molded by experience. Likewise gene activation or deactivation is also influenced through heredity and environment. Our brains are sculpted more so by our early experiences, therefore maltreatment of children heavily influences both form and function of neural activity, which will continue to play out even reaching well into adulthood. Negative childhood experience can rob someone of the sense of their true identity. When children learn early on that they don't matter and that they are not safe; that implicit, conditioned belief is not something that is overcome just because a person reaches a certain age.

I have cited these examples of research as a reminder that what is going on at the DNA level is highly influential in how we are experiencing life, including ourselves, others and how we will view the world. We can no longer ignore how environmental signals (the absorbing of our environment and experience), shapes so many aspects of being human, including emotional states, behavior, mental and physical health issues and of course how we end up viewing ourselves. Belief of all types is encoded upon DNA including the belief of personal identity. What it is we end up believing about our self will have ongoing ramifications. How we perceive ourselves heavily influences our ongoing experience. DNA is a material that has the capacity for memory storage. Remember, one gram of DNA is equivalent to a billion terabytes of storage capacity. What gets encoded upon DNA influences, alters, and impacts human perception, emotions, behavior and a whole host of other things. Yet, we have the power to filter what environmental signals we will allow our cells to receive, and that filter is the mind and its capacity to choose. Also vital in our understanding is that the mind has the capacity to observe correctly; i.e., meaning intelligently, and as it does, we can alter the blueprint of our DNA, even if incorrect information had become encoded or stored.

All learning is associative. Learning is understood in the context of "What fires together wires together." This concept is what I had taught early on. Learning is when at least two neurons connect. Of course the more neural connections we make and the number of times we reinforce and reintegrate that wiring has to do with how things become "STORED" within us. If through repetition we reinforce and reintegrate the same neural associations, then that repetition will develop and be stored as part of our IMPLICIT MEMORY. Once implicit, it will continue to operate within us but at a level of decreased awareness. With all the work you have done up to this point in the Uninstalling Process should act as a strong reinforcement of what I am repeating here.

By understanding and accepting how IMPLICT MEMORY is formed then hope should increase that each of us have the power to shape our implicitly held beliefs. If those beliefs are healthy and truthful about our self, then that implicit belief will be driving so much of what we do, which will lead to living life much more abundantly than when our implicit personal belief was filled with so much distortion.

Now that the UNINSTALL Process is complete and we have identified, and hopefully empowered you to remove the incorrect information, it is now time to learn how to do things correctly. Life is still going to happen, you are still living in an imperfect environment, so it is vital that you learn how to do things correctly so as to maintain your true self and continue to grow in confidence of your real identity.

To accomplish the INSTALL Process, there are three assignments. Each assignment builds upon one another, meaning there are certain things that have to be recognized within our belief and our power to ensure that we do things correctly. If we see the truth, it empowers us to create an IMPLICIT MEMORY that is operating from correct information about our self. If we do form implicitly a very healthy, truthful belief about our self, then our new memorized self, our auto-pilot of belief will have us experience life in a wonderful way, even when life throws its opposition our way.

Daily, constantly, we choose by our desires, our thoughts, and our actions whether we want to be blessed or cursed, happy or miserable. They say that in life suffering is mandatory, but misery is optional. We all have problems, but we also have choices. We can choose to be happy, or we can choose to be miserable. Being miserable requires effort, sometimes significant effort because you have to ignore a lot of things in order to stay so powerless.

— John Bytheway

Wherefore, men are free according to the flesh; and all things are given them which are expedient unto man. And they are free to choose liberty and eternal life, through the great Mediator of all men, or to choose captivity and death according to the captivity and power of the devil; for he seeketh that all me might be miserable like unto himself.

— Nephi

THE FINISH LINE IS IN SIGHT

When mapping the human genome, there were two messages that were decoded. The first message was the message of life. The DNA Code or sequencing of the 3.2 billion letters is the formula, or necessary information to produce proteins. Proteins are life and as a reminder we are comprised of about 250 thousand different proteins. The second message decoded was how the DNA is influenced in what proteins it will manufacture. In other words, there are biological controls built in to DNA performance and those biological controls are the choices we make in what we allow our cells to absorb.

What cells absorb influences the compositional medium of what cells bathe in and it is the compositional differences of proteins, enzymes and chemicals that influence DNA performance. This book is designed to have you understand that our thoughts are epigenetic signals of the environment which are absorbed by our cells. Our thoughts alter the compositional medium that our cells bathe in and therefore our own mindset will influence gene activity.

With this in mind, our work up to this point was to have you use the power of your mind, which is the power to observe, in determining if long-held beliefs about yourself were even accurate. As you came to honestly and intelligently observe that there were many distortions in your implicitly held belief about self, just seeing the distortions is not enough to get you to operate from a place of healthy-esteem. It is going to require that you repeatedly keep your mindset in a place of accurate views of yourself, even when life may bring challenges. Those accurate views are already part of your mind's knowledge and memory, but it will require your effort to bring these to the forefront, repeatedly, if you are going to create an IMPLICIT MEMORY that is the foundation of healthy-esteem. The three assignments of the Installing a Healthy Implicit Memory will teach you how to do so. You are approaching the finish line, it has come into view, but you have not reached it yet. The following three assignments are required to get you to cross the line

Being miserable has its degrees. Sometimes, minor irritations are readily manageable, while larger annoyances, discouragements and disappointments can have us react very negatively. Yet, anyone that has had an unhealthy view of them self would have developed the state or experience of being miserable more as a constant companion. They are burdened with greater negative emotional states, decreased ability to effectively rid themselves of their intrusive, negative feelings, and as such, continue to rely upon outward or external stimuli to notify them of whether they are okay or not.

With hyper focus on their emotions, individuals with unhealthy-esteem learn ways to manage the impact of negative feelings. Many of the strategies developed and used to ward off this constant negativity, instead, however, act in a way that actually increases the miserable experience. That is why I say that we can learn to be miserable.

Healthy-esteemed people have learned that reactive approaches to negative emotions, never really resolve the underlying belief that drives those undesired sensations. Instead, they focus on the truth of their identity and live in a way that supports that correct view of them self. Humans will never develop a secure sense of themselves from simply an intellectual view, however. Confident, secure living also requires that we act in accordance with our real self. The "PRACTICES" that I introduced act as a fundamental aspect of developing a more realistic and healthy view of our self. When these are absent, we will tend to experience a more negative, miserable view of our self and of life in general. However, when these become an integral part of how one operates in life, the individual experiences incredible optimism, confidence and hope in their life's journey, To remind you, those PRACTICES are:

1) The Practice of Living Consciously
2) The Practice of Self-Acceptance
3) The Practice of Personal Responsibility
4) The Practice of Self-Assertiveness
5) The Practice of Living Purposefully
6) The Practice of Integrity

This entire book has been organized around the first practice, The Practice of Living Consciously. It has so, because our mindset is recognized by our cells and any distorted or incorrect views of our self has largely been shaped and influenced by a negative or incorrect mindset. If you were going to begin to see yourself correctly, you had to begin to observe your internal conversation and what it was having you believe about yourself. While we have spent little time with Practices 2-6, when you complete the formal assignments outlined in this book, you will be introduced to the AfterCare Program, which will assist you in developing and/or strengthening these other PRACTICES within you. As a reminder, knowledge without experience is just philosophy. If healthy esteem is ever to be achieved it will require us doing something, not just knowing something.

Learning to be Miserable highlights the impact "our mental doing" has on self-perception. This assignment is to somewhat point out common approaches that miserable people incorporate that keep them from having better outcomes; and in contrast what happy people are doing differently.

Your homework is to read the following examples of what miserable individuals do; and if what you are reading resonates with your experience, meaning, "Larry is describing me," then in the space allotted I want you to complete the following assignment:

1) In your own words, write out what you think the lesson is
2) Provide three applications for how the concept being described is showing up in your life

Example:

**All or Nothing Thinking** – Misery can be experienced when we are not open to several options or possibilities. People that can only think in terms of "One or the Other" many times experience so many setbacks that those setbacks influence how they see themselves. All or nothing patterns of thinking can be experienced in terms of making something out to be all good or all bad. It's as if there is no in between. Perception is seen in black and white terms. "There is nothing to do" is a phrase for example children use when they feel down, upset, bored and unmotivated to change the situation. But it is the language that hinders reality for them. The statement is irrational but the thought rarely is challenged to support reality. The thought generates crummy feelings and the feelings then simply support the thought and the child becomes stuck. Since this is making sense to you can you begin to see other thoughts that fall into this category, e.g., "Nobody likes me," I'm the worst student in the school," "If I get an A on this test then I'm OK, but if I don't then I know I'm no good at all."

1) In your own words, write out what you think the lesson is:

I think the lesson is to be kinder to myself and quit trying to be so perfect in everything. Perfection is not the standard by which I should keep measuring my worth.

2) Provide three applications for how it is showing up in my life:

1- When I get less than an "A" on my tests, I feel like I failed
2- If I don't know the answer I think I am stupid
3- If I don't win at games I become angry


Happy people are open to being accepting of degrees. They are accepting of what went well, but they likewise don't dismiss their level of success if it did not fully come out the way they had hoped. Every Olympian would love to win the "Gold," yet many are so happy that they even got to compete no matter what the outcome was.

I have included boxes (☐) next to each category below. If you find that you struggle with any of the following items, please place a check-mark in the box. If you place a check mark in the box, then complete Items 1 and 2.

☐ **All or Nothing Thinking** – Misery can be experienced when we are not open to several options or possibilities. People that can only think in terms of "One or the Other" many times experience so many setbacks that those setbacks influence how they see themselves. All or nothing patterns of thinking can be experienced in terms of making something out to be all good or all bad. It's as if there is no in between. Perception is seen in black and white terms. "There is nothing to do" is a phrase for example children use when they feel down, upset, bored and unmotivated to change the situation. But it is the language that hinders reality for them. The statement is irrational but the thought rarely is challenged to support reality. The thought generates crummy feelings and the feelings then simply support the thought and the child becomes stuck. Since this is making sense to you can you begin to see other thoughts that fall into this category, e.g., "Nobody likes me," I'm the worst student in the school," "If I get an A on this test then I'm OK, but if I don't then I know I'm no good at all." If a situation falls short of perfect, it is viewed as a total failure. If one makes a mistake then that person is no longer a saint, but is a total sinner. This involves extreme pendulum swinging, i.e. all good or all bad, super smart or a complete idiot, etc. Other examples may include when an addict going through recovery may lapse and look at pornography again, but instead of getting back on track, he thinks that he may as well go for bust because he has blown it; or when a young woman on a diet ate a spoonful of ice cream, she told herself, "I've blown my diet completely." This thought upset her so much that she gobbled down an entire quart of ice cream.

1) In your own words, write out what you think the lesson is:



2) Provide three applications for how it is showing up in my life:

   1 –
   2 –
   3 –

Happy people are open to being accepting of degrees. They don't play in the extremes. They are accepting of what went well, but they likewise don't dismiss their level of success if it did not fully come out the way they had hoped. Every Olympian would love to win the "Gold," yet many are so happy that they even got to compete no matter what the outcome was.


☐ **Always and Never Thinking** – Misery can be experienced when we begin using limiting language, especially when that limiting language has us generalize one event or condition to many events or conditions. Generalizing is when we take one situation and let it define future situations. If it happened before, surely it will happen again. For example, a parent may become upset at a child for getting poor grades and the parent yells at the child. The child begins to interpret that any time his or her parents become upset that the parent is "always yelling at them." More realistically there are "times" the parent yells when upset, but not always. But again, the language sets in motion negative feelings, which simply reinforce the distorted thought. There are many examples of "always and never" thinking, e.g., "No one ever plays with me," "Everyone is always picking on me," "You never listen to me," "I will never have friends," "I am never lucky," "You always lie to me." Making sweeping statements such as "I can never control my temper" based on a minor incident, is an example of overgeneralization. A single negative event, such as a relationship break up, or being turned down for a job is seen as a never-ending pattern of being a loser. The favorite words for those who over generalize are, 'always' and 'never'.

1) In your own words, write out what you think the lesson is:

2) Provide three applications for how it is showing up in my life:

1 –
2 –
3 –

Happy people avoid limiting language. They use language that is more realistic such as, "There are times when you don't listen," or "I enjoy when others invite me to do things. I wish it would happen more often," or "I have not been very lucky at games of chance," or "At times........." or "It's frustrating when......" are also examples of more accurate language that does not give a false perception of being a victim.

☐ **Focusing on the Negative** – Misery can be experienced when we tend to focus on the negative of a situation. This occurs when your thoughts only see the bad in a situation and ignore any of the good that might or is happening. It is important, if you want to keep your mind healthy, to focus on the good parts of your life a lot more than the bad parts. Only focusing on the negative leads to depression and anxiety. Examples may include when we reject positive experiences by insisting they 'don't count,' or if you do a good job, you may tell yourself that it wasn't that good because anybody could have done it. Maybe you receive many positive comments about your presentation to a group of peers at work, but one of them says something mildly critical. You obsess about his reaction for days and ignore all the positive feedback. Discounting the positive takes the joy out of life because you won't take credit for a job well done, and it makes you feel unfulfilled and unrewarded. Picking out a single negative detail and dwelling on it exclusively, skews our vision and reality becomes darkened, like the drop of ink that discolors a beaker of water.

1) In your own words, write out what you think the lesson is:

2) Provide three applications for how it is showing up in my life:

1 –
2 –
3 –

Happy people know that how they think is important for good mental health. They know that focusing on the good parts of their life more than bad parts allows them to face everyday with optimism and hope. They are able to recognize and be thankful even for their smallest of blessings. They also are content with what they do have rather than complaining about what they don't. They graciously take a compliment and are happy when people recognize their talents, effort and contributions. In turn, they do the same for others. They sincerely recognize the good others have contributed. Because they recognize these things in others than certainly they can recognize them in them self.

☐ **Fortune Telling** – Misery can be experienced when people get in the habit of visualizing the worst; for example, predicting the worse possible outcome (self-fulfilling prophecy). An example may be that a child thinks, "I'm a lousy reader; the other kids will laugh at me." Because the child has this thought he or she becomes less involved. Being less involved the child begins to believe he or she is different. The child's anxiety increases and then when the teacher insists on the child's involvement, the child's anxiety interferes with their performance, resulting in some type of negative feedback. The feedback is seen as proof of the original thought, rather than recognizing how the original thought put into motion the entire defeating process. Fortune telling is depicted in predicting that things will turn out badly. You believe that the future is not going to turn out well. If you are going through a bad time, you may deduce that things will always be this way. Before a test you may say to yourself, "I'm really going to blow it" or "What if I flunk?" If you are depressed you may tell yourself, "I'll never get better."

1) In your own words, write out what you think the lesson is:



2) Provide three applications for how it is showing up in my life:

    1 –
    2 –
    3 –

Happy people know that the key to having better outcomes is facing the situation, practicing and preparation. Much of that preparation can be focusing on the positive outcomes. Doing what it takes to have the outcome desired is what happy people do.

☐ **Mind Reading** – Misery can be experienced when we believe we know what someone else is thinking. Assumptions create all sorts of difficulties, especially as it pertains to relationships. Examples of this type of thinking may look like, "So and so is mad at me," "So and so doesn't like me," or "So and so is talking about me," or "They are not calling me back because they didn't like me." Without checking it out, you arbitrarily conclude that someone is reacting negatively to you.

1) In your own words, write out what you think the lesson is:



2) Provide three applications for how it is showing up in my life:

    1 –
    2 –
    3 –

Happy people don't assume what others are thinking, they ask. If it is true that someone is not happy with them, they use assertiveness to work through the issue, thus improving trust with others. No one can read someone else's mind. Happy people always get more information before making a judgment or drawing a conclusion. Instead of predicting doom and gloom, they focus on what they can do to make things go right, i.e. be positive, demonstrate good judgment, act appropriately, etc.

☐ **Thinking with Your Feelings** – Misery can be experienced when we are run by our emotions or believing that our emotion are accurate. Emotional reasoning is when you believe something to be true because it feels like it is true. You assume that your negative emotions reflect the way things really are.  The language that detects this type of negative processing usually begins with "I feel..." "I feel like you don't love me," "I feel stupid," "I feel like a failure," "I feel like nobody will ever trust me." The very nature of the language creates strong feelings. Other examples may include, "I feel that I am not good enough to do my job," or "I feel hopeless. If I feel hopeless, I must be hopeless," or "I feel guilty. I must be a rotten person," or "I feel angry. This proves I'm being treated unfairly," or "I feel sad and lonely. I must not be good enough to be included.

1) In your own words, write out what you think the lesson is:


2) Provide three applications for how it is showing up in my life:

    1 –
    2 –
    3 –

Happy people know that every thought produces neurochemical releases that have us feel in correspondence to the thought, so happy people keep their untruthful, self-defeating thoughts in check. They grow more aware of their thoughts in order to regulate their emotion appropriately

☐ **Guilt Beatings** – Misery can be experienced when we take guilt beyond what it was designed for or confuse a "bad" feeling as guilt. Guilt is only beneficial if it causes someone to repent of a wrong doing. It is directly related to the breaking of a moral standard or code. "I should," "I must," "I have to," "I ought to," are signals that we are being driven through inappropriate guilt. Should statements directed against your self lead to negative feelings and frustration, i.e. 'I should have gotten up earlier with all that I had to do.' Another example, 'After playing a difficult piece on the piano, a gifted pianist told herself, "I shouldn't have made so many mistakes." This made her feel so disgusted that she quit practicing for several days. It appears that people that struggle with this kind of language believe that their acceptance is based upon their performance or they use such language to motivate themselves to perfectionism. In their mind, "If I am perfect, I have worth."

1) In your own words, write out what you think the lesson is:



2) Provide three applications for how it is showing up in my life:
   1 –
   2 –
   3 –

Happy people replace the "I should," "I must," "I have to," "I ought to," with honest statements, e.g., it would be beneficial to... I want to do this... It's in my best interest to..., Oh, I missed that opportunity, but there will be another time, etc. Changing your language to be more accurate, i.e. 'I wished I would have done that better,' or 'I was disappointed when I cheated on my diet, but I am happy that I have enough control not to binge;' when we begin to phrase statements in terms of the benefits of doing or not doing something, or the reason why we like or dislike something, then we are less likely to become burdened with feelings of inappropriate guilt, frustration and anger.


☐ **Labeling** – Misery can be experienced when we tend to meet the expectation of labels because the power of suggestion can easily cloud reality. Tell someone enough times that he or she is stupid and that person will likely begin to accept it as reality. At school, children with ADHD hear many labels, "loser," "pest," "clown" "idiot" "obnoxious", etc. Many times these labels become what the child says to him or herself and even aloud. Labeling is quite irrational because we are defining ourselves or redefining ourselves based upon a behavior. Some other examples; not getting a better grade (I'm stupid), Forgetting someone's birthday (I'm a horrible friend), Spending hours looking at pornography (I'm a loser), etc. Labels are useless abstractions that lead to anger, frustration and anxiety and a lack of healthy esteem. When you apply it to someone else, especially in a close relationship like in a family, it can often lead to a break down in communication. This is because you are making a judgment on someone's character, when more correctly, their thinking or behavior is what you have issue with. It is better to respond to what you like or dislike about the behavior or thoughts, as it provides information that can be built upon. Labeling limits information.

1) In your own words, write out what you think the lesson is:



2) Provide three applications for how it is showing up in my life:

   1 –
   2 –
   3 –


Happy people don't label themselves and they head-off other's attempts to label them. Instead they humbly take feedback about a certain way they do things that irritates others. They are open to hearing and trying to understand other people's perspectives rather than being defensive about their own view of things. They recognize there may be areas of improvement, but they focus on the improvement rather than creating a definition or label of themselves growing out of the underdeveloped area.

☐ **Blame** – Misery can be experienced when we are not willing to own up to what we need to own up to; e.g., not taking personal responsibility for what is ours. People that contribute to their own difficult circumstance have a strong tendency to blame others or external circumstances when things go wrong. Allowing the blame game creates in the person a sense of powerlessness – living life in a victim mode. Some examples, "My marriage is falling apart because my wife is so unreasonable," or "I don't do well in Language Arts because my teacher doesn't like me," or "I'm fat because of my genetics," or "It's my birth-orders fault," or "It's the government's fault." etc. They do not realize that if they could kick the person responsible for most of their troubles, they wouldn't be able to sit down for six months.

1) In your own words, write out what you think the lesson is:

2) Provide three applications for how it is showing up in my life:

   1 –
   2 –
   3 –

. Happy people keep a humble, happy attitude when they have ownership in something not going right. They may even poke a little fun at them self when taking ownership signifying that he or she recognizes every human can make mistakes. They know that the blame game is not a good place to be. While it relieves us of any responsibility for our outcomes, it does not provide the basis for us to live a more effective life. Happy people know it is better to focus on what they can control, or what they could have done differently in order to have a better outcome

☐ **Can't Statements** – Misery can be experienced when a person operates from a place of doubt. Have you ever heard of the old saying, If you say that you can or if you say that you can't, you are right." Starting off with definitive "can't statements" gives the individual permission to not try. This self-permission is simply a way to protect our own negative thoughts about ourselves. If we try and fail, then someone would think less of us and we don't want that; or, if someone else knew what I was really like they will not accept me. "I can't" words or phrases are coupled with power and when we use the words "I can't" we are giving ourselves permission to not even try, and as a result we "feel" reluctant to even do so. Some examples, "I can't swim," or "I can't understand what I am reading," or "I can't do it," etc. We use such patterns of irrational thinking in order to avoid the difficult or perhaps embarrassing thing.

1) In your own words, write out what you think the lesson is:

2) Provide three applications for how it is showing up in my life:

1 –
2 –
3 –

Happy people start from a place of belief in them self. They know that trying may end in failure, but they also know they can still learn even when something didn't go well. In essence, they don't worry about what others may think, they are simply interested in what they believe about them self. Happy people know that the "I cant's" are more likely the "I don't want to's." "I can if I keep at it long enough" is more realistic of human capability.

☐ **Magnification/Minimizing** – Misery may be experienced when you magnify the importance of a negative event, or lack of evidence for a positive event. You magnify your problems and minimize the importance of your blessings. Another form of minimizing is also used to avoid taking responsibility for your poor choices by magnifying someone else's behavior in relation to your own. For example, a young man watching his favorite team lose, then decides that he doesn't feel like going out with his friends after the game, or a young lady receiving her first paycheck, which is less than she expected due to taxes, grumbles about not being paid what she is worth, or a teenager being grounded by his parents when it is discovered that he is smoking pot says, "Why are you being so hard on me? I'm not using heroin like many of my friends at school."

1) In your own words, write out what you think the lesson is:

2) Provide three applications for how it is showing up in my life:

1 –
2 –
3 –

Happy people look for the good in events, which creates a more realistic view. For example, the young man that was disappointed in his team losing could have focused on being grateful that he was with friends and the fun they were having that evening. Likewise, the young lady, though disappointed in her net check, could still be grateful that she was employed and still had resources to improve her situation. The teenager would do better if he would not justify his poor choice simply because other people make worse choices.

☐ **Personalization** - Misery may be experienced when we take personal responsibility for an event that isn't entirely under our control. When you use hindsight to determine what you 'should have done' differently,' even though you could not had any way to know what that would have been before hand, you are personalizing. Some examples: "I should not have gone away on holiday then I would have been there when my father had the accident," or "If I had been a better mother then my daughter would not be having so many problems at school," or "If I was a better son my dad would not get drunk." As you can tell, 'personalizing' leads to guilt, shame, and feelings of inadequacy. Each of these feelings can become debilitating, especially shame. In each of the examples above, personalization stymies resolve of the issue.

1) In your own words, write out what you think the lesson is:


2) Provide three applications for how it is showing up in my life:

1 –
2 –
3 –

Happy people's focus is centered in what they can do to help the situation get better, what they can truly control, and what they can merely influence. By clearly delineating what is under our control or not gives us the ability to pinpoint our focus on what we can do and passes the appropriate responsibility to those that also contribute to the problem.


☐ **Using The Mind To Worry** – Misery may occur when we preoccupy our mind with worry. Worry is an outgrowth of fear and doubt. These people spend so much time trying to calm their anxiety that all it does is make anxiety a constant companion. They worry about what others may think of them, they excessively worry about their health, or things they can't control. They go through a process called "the worst case scenario" and when they finally can accept what may be the worse thing they settle their nerves, until the next worry arises. They are especially expert in worrying about their problems creating an ongoing burden that seems insurmountable.

1) In your own words, write out what you think the lesson is:


2) Provide three applications for how it is showing up in my life:

1 –
2 –
3 –

Happy people do not operate from a place of fear and doubt. They are realistic about what their mind is capable of, for example making a plan to get what they want, believing in what is true and acting in accordance with that truth, and being consistent at following the steps that will lead to preparedness. Happy people focus on what can be. They focus on their blessings. They believe they are in control and capable to make their life whatever they want it to be.

☐ **Woe Is Me** – Misery may occur when people believe that there is no power to change. Everyday they go around being acted upon and so nothing will ever change until others do. They give others power to tell them how they should feel, or how to think, or what to do. Everything is externally driven and that they are merely pawns to everything outside of them.

1) In your own words, write out what you think the lesson is:

2) Provide three applications for how it is showing up in my life:

   1 –
   2 –
   3 –

Happy people believe that change is an internal process. They believe in the power of the mind to change their lives by changing their perception. Even when externals do flex their muscle, they remain adamant and fixed in what they want to have happen in their life. They know that tough times are but for a season and so they stay the course. They know that change is up to them, not someone else.

☐ **Not Doing Anything** – Misery may occur when we choose a life of easiness, laziness, and procrastination. People that are not active, who are not exercising, who are not engaging in hobbies, who are not reading, who don't do the dishes, who don't get out of bed, take showers, get dressed, who don't put forth any real, consistent energy to make their life meaningful and accomplish things will create a life of being miserable. These people likewise fill their life with addiction, whether that is addiction to TV, computers, pornography, substances, sleep, whatever, it is because living a life of doing nothing disrupts the dopamine pathways. Instead of doing something to keep dopamine active, they choose a behavior like smoking or gaming to do the work.

1) In your own words, write out what you think the lesson is:

2) Provide three applications for how it is showing up in my life:

   1 –
   2 –
   3 –

Happy people look forward to everyday realizing it provides an opportunity for learning, achieving, building their dreams, and lifting others. An active day helps them fall asleep and stay asleep when their head does finally hit the pillow. They likewise feel good about them self at the end of the day and use relaxation as a balance in their life, not as the main way of living. They do not endlessly think about their problems, they solve their problems.

☐ **Not Being Content** – Misery may occur when people keep complaining about their blessings. They get upset because they can only afford a flip-phone instead of a Smart Phone. Their car is already two years old. Their house isn't four thousand square feet. The pizza they ordered was delivered a little bit late. Their 1080 HD TV does not have as nice a picture as the 4K TV. They were not able to get the seats they wanted at the premiere of the new Broadway play. They get upset when they have to wait to be seated at the restaurant. They can't believe they had to walk to school one day, etc.

1) In your own words, write out what you think the lesson is:


2) Provide three applications for how it is showing up in my life:

    1 –
    2 –
    3 –

Happy people recognize what an incredible gift it is to enjoy having a cell phone, no matter what. They are grateful that they have a reliable car. They keep and maintain their home and are grateful they are in a secure place every night. They understand that not everything goes perfectly and are flexible, patient and gracious. They simply enjoy having the ability to have entertainment available in their home. Happy people are simply thankful even for the smallest of blessings and are content with what the Lord has allotted them to this point in their life. That does not mean it is a bad thing to have nicer things, but they are never envious of others who do have nicer things.


☐ **Self-Centeredness** – Misery may occur when a person is mostly considering them self. They view relationships mostly in terms of what they can get from others or what others are doing to them. It is all about them! They have better relationships with things rather than people. They spend endless energy on what they can get and if they do spend any time thinking of others it is usually in terms of comparison. This is the way they assess how they are doing. Are they doing better than others? If they discover that someone else has an upper hand, they may spend time undermining that person or them self becoming bitter.

1) In your own words, write out what you think the lesson is:


2) Provide three applications for how it is showing up in my life:

    1 –
    2 –
    3 –

Happy people keep relationships as a priority. It is far less about what they are doing with others, just that they are with others. Happy people have discovered that when they contribute to someone else feeling uplifted, encouraged or hopeful in some way, they them self feel uplifted, encouraged and hopeful. Relationships are not about what they can get or what others are doing to them, relationships are about emotional connection, friendship, support and love, where there is much energy expended in giving as there is in receiving.

☐ **Not Learning From The Past** – Misery may occur when people use their past as evidence that they are a bad person. They review their bad memories over and over again, remaining stuck in time. These people believe that past mistakes define them, that they have done too much, that they are irredeemable, that if anyone were to find out about their past that no one would accept them. They forget that life was designed to have experience that we might learn.

1) In your own words, write out what you think the lesson is:

2) Provide three applications for how it is showing up in my life:

    1 –
    2 –
    3 –

Happy people know that poor choices were part of the plan of happiness. When they review their past mistakes they do so from a place of learning. They humbly express genuine sorrow, repair to whatever extent they are able the harm or damage that resulted from their mistake, they sincerely ask for forgiveness and then begin conducting their life in a positive manner as evidence of their learning. They let their mistakes go and hold on to the maturing development that came from appropriately handling the situation. They know God is pleased with their learning and that even He does not remember their past mistakes (Hebrews 10:17; D&C 58:42).

☐ **Self-Deprecation** – Misery may occur when people keep referencing themselves in devalued ways. Their ongoing put-downs occur both internally and externally. Internally, miserable people are experts at Automatic Negative Thoughts. Externally, they do not feel worthy of someone's approval. They divert attention away from sincere compliments. They make sure everyone knows that they do not have a friend in them. This has become a way to keep people paying attention to them, the problem is that people get exhausted being around them and so they have to keep the friend pool fresh.

1) In your own words, write out what you think the lesson is:

2) Provide three applications for how it is showing up in my life:

    1 –
    2 –
    3 –

Happy people are perfectly happy knowing, like every other human they are not perfect, but they do not sell themselves short. Happy people see themselves realistically. They tend to focus on the truth of who they really are. They graciously and humbly receive compliments and prefer attention from others because of their goodness, rather than receiving attention from being negative.

☐ **Grudge Holders** – Misery may occur when people hold onto or hold over people's heads grudges. It appears that grudge holder's understand the concept of "Justice" as they try to fill in the gaps of justice constantly. What they do not understand is the concept of "Mercy." The irony of grudge holding is that the only one truly burdened by it is the person that carries it. Grudge holders are easily offended, if you say something to them they take offense, if you don't say something to them they take offense. They are offended when someone offers to help; they are offended when no one offers to help. They are even offended when someone is trying to take accountability! As a result of all of this offense they become persuasive blamers, meaning that they are willing to tell anyone and everyone why they are right in holding the grudge. They will share their story over and over again as long as they have an audience of at least one.

1) In your own words, write out what you think the lesson is:


2) Provide three applications for how it is showing up in my life:

   1 –
   2 –
   3 –

Happy people are not easily offended and they in their own need for mercy are willing to extend mercy to others who may have caused some hurt or pain.

☐ **Questioning Motives** – Misery may occur when people assume that nice things done for them comes with a price. While it is true that others can use us for their own gain, going through life perpetually suspicious is exhausting. Those that go around on high alert do not allow themselves to become acquainted with good people.

1) In your own words, write out what you think the lesson is:


2) Provide three applications for how it is showing up in my life:

   1 –
   2 –
   3 –

Happy people are accepting of other's good gestures, kind words, and gifts. Like themselves, they know that others do good things simply because they love others. If it turns out that a kindness was part of being manipulative, the happy person sets appropriate boundaries around that one person, not the entire human population.

☐ **Happiness is Fleeting** – If you find yourself consistently saying, "I'll be happy when...." Then likely you are miserable. Misery may occur when people assign happiness to externals rather than just recognizing it is an attitude of choice. "I'll be happy when I move out of my parent's house," or "I'll be happy when I get that Chevrolet Camaro," or "I'll be happy when I get promoted," or "I'll be happy when my kids are out of the house," or "I'll be happy when I am retired, " etc. Miserable people always want more, because they use things or events to tell them that they are OK.

1) In your own words, write out what you think the lesson is:


2) Provide three applications for how it is showing up in my life:

    1 –
    2 –
    3 –

Happy people know that happiness is not based on what you have but who you are. Of course happy people want to get their own place, drive a fun car, do well at work, raise successful kids and be able to be financially secure, but they are happy during that whole journey not having to rely on things or events to give them permission to be happy.

☐ **Bad Attitude** – Misery may occur when we grow accustomed to focusing on the negative; and seeing first the bad of a situation and then walking around with a bad attitude. People with bad attitudes tend to be critical of other's beliefs, they complain about the other political party, they speak badly about leadership, they complain that their child did not do their chore perfectly; they yell at refs, they are always telling you what government does wrong, they are consistently cynical, complaining, and sarcastic. It's all doom and gloom and you know that person because you do all in your power to avoid them.

1) In your own words, write out what you think the lesson is:


2) Provide three applications for how it is showing up in my life:

    1 –
    2 –
    3 –

Happy people have learned, "If you can't say something nice then don't say anything at all!" These are the ones that saw what their child did well even if it wasn't perfect. These are respectful of other's opinions even if they disagree. These don't divide organizations by being critical of leadership. Happy people look for the good in others, they are grateful for rain even when it rains on their parade, and they are supportive of those over them.

☐ **Intellectually Stagnant** – Misery may occur when we do little to invest in our growing knowledge and experience. Reading good books, perusing research, getting out and exploring something new is not the experience of the miserable. Learning something new is seen as too much effort. They tend to fill their ears and minds with the mundane, the rerun, the Netflix binge, the things that appeal to the carnal (Moses 5:13; Alma 42:10). Miserable people don't stretch themselves, don't find hobbies, don't read, don't write and don't care.

1) In your own words, write out what you think the lesson is:


2) Provide three applications for how it is showing up in my life:

1 –
2 –
3 –

Happy people enjoy learning. They keep themselves informed. They challenge their intellect through discovery. They will attend lectures, purchase and use language learning programs, travel to other destinations, watch a cooking channel, ask questions, be found in museums, observing nature, developing new talents, and become involved in a new hobby. They know their mind is a terrible thing to waste!

☐ **Spiritual Spurting** – Misery may occur when we are not consistently taking care of the spiritual side of us (Job 32:8). Sporadic spiritual habiting prevents us from being in the top spiritual health. It is like those that have a gym membership and utilize its benefits every once-in-awhile. As discussed early on in this book, spiritual health is about developing and maintaining a really good relationship with Deity; as it is from the Divine that we receive all things necessary to fulfill the measure of our creation. Regular study of the scriptures, fervent and humble prayer, utilizing the Atonement, not just for forgiveness of sins, but also the sanctifying power that has us become like Him (D&C 11:30), properly preparing for the ordinances and service born out of love are all part of the spiritual lifting we do to keep our spirits in shape.

1) In your own words, write out what you think the lesson is:


2) Provide three applications for how it is showing up in my life:
1 –

Happy people have made it a priority to gain their own foundation through study, faith and prayer. By the small and simple things their spiritual understanding becomes great. In the process they do the right things for the right reasons. They even at times may miss a meeting at church because of the weightier matters (Matthew 23:23). Choosing the better part comes from spiritual healthiness. The evidence of such attending is that we become filled with His love (Moroni 7:47), which allows us to be connected to Him forever.

☐ **Misery Loves Company** – Misery may occur or be influenced by the company we keep. Just as "light cleaveth to light and intelligence cleaveth to intelligence" (D&C 88:40), so do shame filled people cleave to shame filled people. No one gets happy when everyone in the group is miserable. You know you are in a miserable group because when they speak, they do so in terms of faultfinding, gossiping, backbiting, complaining and murmuring. Miserable people live beyond their means and are entitled. They envy and covet, put-down rather than lift, are ungrateful, hold grudges and are jealous of others. Selfishness – "how everything affects me" is a tell-tale indicator that you are with a miserable person. Self-conceitedness, self-pity, worldly self-fulfillment, self-gratification, and self-seeking are the hallmarks of miserable people.

1) In your own words, write out what you think the lesson is:

2) Provide three applications for how it is showing up in my life:

    1 –

    2 –

    3 –

Happy people seek the company of those that lift, encourage, motivate and bring out the best in others. Environment influences each of us so happy people seek the companionship of those that are patient, kind, are grateful and can see beyond themselves and attune well to others. Happy people groups are active. They are out doing things. They are not just sitting around attached to their phones, their gaming systems, their Youtube channels, their snap-chats, twitters and instagrams. They actually put these things away and make real connections with one another, have real conversations, and create real memories from the activities they choose to do together.

☐ **Sleeping Their Life Away** – Misery may accompany those that sleep too much. A third of our life is already designated to sleeping, but the miserable try and go for two-thirds. The miserable say, "I sleep so much because I am tired." What they actually are experiencing is depression, but ironically the best cure for depression is activity.

1) In your own words, write out what you think the lesson is:

2) Provide three applications for how it is showing up in my life:
   1 –
   2 –
   3 –

Happy people know that a good's night rest is good for both physical and cognitive functioning, yet they also know that living with purpose, with goals, and with hope requires taking advantage of the day. Their theme song is, "Have I Done Any Good?" which says, "Then wake up and do something more then dream of your mansions above, doing good is a pleasure, a joy beyond measure...... and then they sleep well because they wore themselves out doing good.

☐ **Entitlement** – Misery may occur when we begin to believe that we are entitled to what life has to offer and someone else better hurry up and provide it for us. American culture trains entitlement! I lived a pretty, well-to-do childhood and therefore deserve a well-to-do rest of my life. Someone always took care of me growing up and now someone needs to step in and continue what I have grown accustomed to. It is unfair if I can't get what I want, when I want it, which is now. Wake-up people, I am pretty miserable over here.... You need to get busy in taking care of me.

1) In your own words, write out what you think the lesson is:


2) Provide three applications for how it is showing up in my life:

   1 –
   2 –
   3 –

Happy people recognize the connection between learning how to manage life's demands through one's own effort. Happy people believe in themselves. They know that life will pay them pretty much what it thinks they are worth, so they spend their formative years learning how to work, how to learn, and how to manage resources so that they can live a life that they dream of. Happiness is not something that is given it is an outgrowth from learning how to be self-sufficient.

☐ **Boring, Boring, Boring** – Misery may occur when a person does not go and experience new things, new foods, new friends, new adventures, new learning, new travels, new opportunities, new perceptions, new....... Well I think you are getting it. As life's difficult moments come it may not be as bad as it seems if we can look at it in a new way. Gaining a new friend may keep us laughing. Seeking adventure may inspire us and create wonderful memories. Learning how Quantum Theory explains how all of nature is influenced may give us hope that we can change our boring life by observing what an exciting life may consist of. Putting a little money down on a new company like Apple as part of managing their resources may pay huge dividends. Traveling to other countries may make them more interesting.

1)  In your own words, write out what you think the lesson is:


2)  Provide three applications for how it is showing up in my life:

1 –
2 –
3 –

Happy people know that if they are going to become someone new they have to do something new and so they do. Doing new things, changing perspective around adversity, meeting new people, learning new hobbies, saving to buy a new car, and getting outside of their comfort zone never allows room for the mundane and boring.


☐ **Isolation** – Misery may occur when we choose to live in a guarded manner, isolated, aloof, disengaged and withdrawn. When we spend so much time keeping ourselves safe from judgment, from others that will certainly never accept us, from the possibility of ever being hurt, or used by someone else, where we can do whatever we want when we want because we are our best friend and no one else is going to tell us how to live our lives.... And if for some reason someone puts forth the energy to perhaps become our friend, well we better make sure to test that person's true motive....... Yep, just as I thought....... They didn't really want to be my true friend. It had nothing to do with my being indifferent, codgidy, controlling or self-centered... a true friend would have accepted me for who I am....... therefore I will return to the safety of aloneness.

1)  In your own words, write out what you think the lesson is:


2)  Provide three applications for how it is showing up in my life:

1 –
2 –
3 –

Happy people know that it is not good to be alone, therefore the rewards of well-connected relationships, such as being listened to, creating memories, feeling close to someone, knowing someone likes them for who they are, someone who loves them enough to help them grow and become a better person, being with someone who has shared interests, having someone who in a moment's notice is there when we really need them, someone who in their old age has truly become a best friend, etc., happy people know that having wonderful relationships is a price beyond compare and so they put in the effort of being for others what they want others to be for them.

☐ **Being Anti=Responsible** – Misery may occur when individuals are not willing to become 100% responsible for their own lives. The hallmark characteristics of the anti-responsible are blaming others, rationalizing or justifying, making excuses, trivializing time-honored values and principles, hiding, covering up, running from or abandoning responsibility, denying or lying, rebelling, complaining or murmuring, finding fault and getting angry, making demands and entitlement, doubting, losing hope, giving up, quitting, indulging in self-pity, playing the victim, being indecisive, indifferent, procrastinating, run by fear and doubt, and enabling others to likewise be irresponsible.

1) In your own words, write out what you think the lesson is:


2) Provide three applications for how it is showing up in my life:

   1 –
   2 –
   3 –

Happy people know that being in control of their own lives is so much more peaceful, and empowering. It is a reflection of the virtue of living true to one's real identity. Happy people are charactered because of being honest, accountable, humble, adopting time-honored values and principles, not living the double-life, working hard and becoming self-sufficient, taking care of their own, being peacemakers, treating others with respect and allowing others to become responsible, demonstrating good judgment, and living by faith.


REVIEWING HOMEWORK ASSIGNMENT #9

We have just provided 31 ways or examples of learning how to be miserable, but we also pointed out what happy people are doing instead in each of those areas. When I am sitting with my client and they are reporting on what areas they struggle with, these being identified by the boxes they checked, I always ask them, "Well, what are happy people doing instead?" They then will accurately report the significant difference by reading the paragraph at the bottom of each example. I then ask them, "It sounds like what miserable people are doing is distinctly different than what happy people are doing – do you agree? Their answer is always "Yes!"

Sometimes a client will report that several of the things described above are exactly how they are doing life. The point of the assignment is not to make any one feel bad about them self, the point is to have them observe what happy people are doing instead. It doesn't matter to me how many things they resonate with, what I do every time is have them report what happy people are doing instead of what miserable people are doing. After their reporting I reinforce the distinction by asking, "It sounds like what miserable people are doing is distinctly different than what happy people are doing – do you agree? Eventually a smile or two will emerge as I insist on focusing their attention that happy people are doing something distinctly different than what miserable people are doing.

In my insistence that they observe what happy people are doing differently and after reviewing each of the areas they have recognized they struggle with, I offer an opinion with the end of the opinion having my voice go up as if it is a question, "It sounds to me like being miserable or being happy then is a choice?" If we can see so clearly the differences on how happy people are handling things in comparison to miserable people, then it really sounds to me like being miserable or being happy is a choice. What do you think? The answer comes as clear every time, being miserable or being happy is simply a choice.

When you, as the reader have come to the same conclusion, I then want to point out what this assignment is trying to help us understand. Up to this point I have been heavily focused on the power of AUTOMATIC NEGATIVE THOUGHTS. Those that have ongoing, repetitive AUTOMATIC NEGATIVE THOUGHTS will become miserable. However these 31 areas described above are not AUTOMATIC NEGATIVE THOUGHTS. These are incorrect ways people think about things or approach life by. The 31 areas described above are what are called THINKING ERRORS. People that incorporate THINKING ERRORS into their way of being will likewise experience misery. So, it is not just AUTOMATIC NEGATIVE THOUGHTS that lead to living miserably, but also THINKING ERRORS. The diagram below reinforces visually what is being said here:

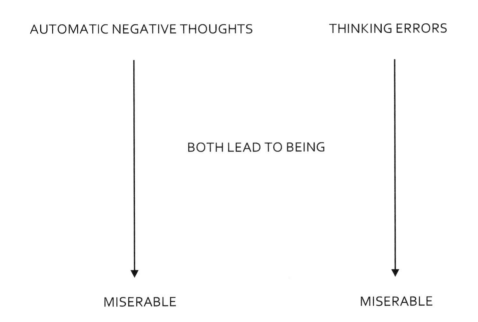

AUTOMATIC NEGATIVE THOUGHTS    THINKING ERRORS

BOTH LEAD TO BEING

MISERABLE    MISERABLE

Let me give you an example of a younger client I was working with who struggled with a THINKING ERROR. One night, Zach, a 15 year old client came into the office and plopped down on the couch. As he did so, you could hear the air coming out of the cushions, but you could also hear the air coming out of him, which was accompanied with these following words, "Well, that was a waste of a semester!"

I said to him, "Zach, it sounds like something didn't go the way you had hoped. Help me understand." Zach continued, "I got an 'A' in every single class except one, I got an A-Minus!" I am sure that you are saying in your mind, "Are you kidding? That is a great semester." But that is exactly my point. Zach had a THINKING ERROR which did not allow him to see things as you and I do.

To understand how this THINKING ERROR developed you have to get a bit of background about Zach's family. Zach had only one sibling, an older sister. Mom had a way, and I don't think it was intentional, but she had a way of constantly comparing Zach to his sister. It was done in the ebb and flow of life, so Zach would hear things like, "Zach, your sister seems to understand when dinner is ready and comes to the table without ever being told. Why do I have to ask you so many times;" or "Zach, get out of the house and go be with your friends. Your sister is always doing things with her friends;" or "Zach, please make your bed like your sister does everyday." This was Zach's ongoing environment.

Zach had one area though where he held an advantage over his sister and that was academics. His sister was a good student but she really had to work at it, but not Zach. Academics came pretty easy to him. However, herein lies the problem. This was the one area where he needed to show his mom that he was perfect, because if he could be perfect then his mother would not have room to compare. An "A-Minus" was not perfection and therefore to Zach it was a waste of a semester. If I can't be perfect, then my mom is right, I'll never be good enough at anything that my mother can be proud of me.

I would say that most formal therapy approaches at one time or another will delve into THINKING ERRORS and likely make it a significant part in helping their client live better lives. I don't think I need to spend a lot of time on THINKING ERRORS because I believe individuals are observant enough to recognize they have some, but also intelligent enough to evaluate the difference between what happy people are doing differently in those areas they find themselves struggling and begin to follow their example (3 Nephi 18:16).

Though I don't spend a lot of time on THINKING ERRORS my suggestion is that the boxes you checked above indicates that you have some work to do. I am not asking you to overwhelm yourself with having to fix every THINKING ERROR immediately. What I am suggesting is that you choose one or two of them, really focus on what happy people do differently in those areas and begin practicing those differences. Once you think you have got those licked, then choose a couple of more and begin working on ridding yourself of those. Keep working until you learn how to be happy by thinking about things correctly.

One thing I have come to understand is that THINKING ERRORS are much easier to rid ourselves of in comparison to Automatic Negative Thoughts. I know this to be true as I myself began to improve areas of my life by becoming aware of my own THINKING ERRORS. One of my problematic areas was in the realm of limiting language. When I read Albert Ellis' work on irrational thinking, I learned that words like 'always' and 'never' were accompanied by strong emotional responses. As is true in many relationships, I was guilty of using this type of language when confronting my wife about behaviors that brought me frustration. What I learned from Albert Ellis was that such language puts others in the position of not being able to do something differently. He suggested that such broad strokes of language skew reality and in doing so heighten hostility and conflict. I decided at that moment to bring high awareness of this type of language to my conversations with my wife. By replacing limiting language with more realistic language reduced the amount of conflict we experienced. It was that one time awareness that has remained with me ever since. That is why I know that THINKING ERRORS are much easier to change than Automatic Negative Thoughts.

I believe in you and I believe you are reading this book because you want to achieve healthy-esteem. I know that through the power of your awareness you can replace THINKING ERRORS with approaches that will increase your happiness. I am a regular at Harmon's Grocery Store because it is close to my office. I enjoy taking advantage of their soup and salad bar, There is one employee that I run into who seems to smile a lot. I reflected back to her that I noticed this about her, she replied by saying:

> "I finally figured out that happiness was a choice. It is a work that comes from the inside. I decided I would rather be happy."

Being happy or being miserable is a choice. If we will choose to eliminate both AUTOMATIC NEGATIVE THOUGHTS and THINKING ERRORS, happiness becomes a lock!

This was the first assignment of three of the INSTALLING A HEALTHY IMPLICIT MEMORY process. The two things I want the reader to walk away with are:

1) BEING MISERABLE OR BEING HAPPY IS A CHOICE
2) THINKING ERRORS, LIKE AUTOMATIC NEGATIVE THOUGHTS, IF NOT CORRECTED WILL LEAD TO BECOMING MISERABLE

ARE YOU AN INTELLIGENT BEING?

The power for creating a better future is contained in the present moment. You create a good future by creating a good present.

— Eckhart Tolle

The more you are positive and say, 'I want to have a good life' the more you build that reality for yourself by observing the life that you want.

— Chris Pine

"To be or not to be?' That is not the question. What is the question? The question is not one of being, but of becoming. 'To become more or not to become more' This is the question faced by each intelligence in our universe."

— Truman G. Madsen

HOMEWORK ASSIGNMENT #10: CREATING YOUR DAY -

Happy, confident people create their happiness and confidence. They use the power of their mind to create the outcomes they desire. They believe in their true self, which includes the power to achieve what they set their mind to. Irrespective of their current circumstances, they believe in themselves. They have identified what they want in life, they feed their mind with positive, correct information; they likely keep company with others that are likewise focused and they put forth the necessary effort that is required to seal in their happiness and confidence. It is this way of viewing that allows for the doors of opportunity to open.

Miserable people imprison themselves, creating walls and dead ends. Their perspective is shadowed with incorrect information. Their thoughts and attitudes have them play out the broken record of being acted upon. Their lives are filled with scarcity as they recall all the reasons why they haven't led a happier life. They just can't seem to get beyond their negative feelings. It is this approach that doesn't allow for change, because they can't think beyond their negative emotions, they just remain stuck. They are imprisoned by the unhealthy memorized self.

In the very beginning of this book I spoke about the emerging research and how the memorized self is formed. It is formed through our perceptions, manifested in a repetitive internal conversation, which becomes stored in IMPLICIT MEMORY. This type of memory is stored largely in two areas, the first being neural pathways in the brain and secondly in DNA. What wires to together plays heavily upon self-perception and what gets encoded onto DNA likewise seriously influences our view of self.

IMPLICIT MEMORY is comprised of unconscious cognitive and emotional patterns of relating to ourselves and others. It's the kind of memory you access without any high degree of awareness, because it has been learned so well. It's what makes you feel characteristically you. The area of IMPLICIT MEMORY this book has been largely focused on is how your IMPLICIT MEMORY has you see yourself and how this view of yourself has you experience all aspects of your life. The reason for this focus is because IMPLICIT MEMORY guides your ongoing experience, cognitively, emotionally and behaviorally; all on automatic drive, without thought or effort. You can think of IMPLICIT MEMORY as a set of instructions or *procedures* encoded in the brain and on your DNA. However, a procedure can't easily be described in words or contained in images; it forms as a general template where we continue to get our bearings. This template is below the threshold of awareness and so we are not fully conscious of the thoughts, meanings, and negative core beliefs that are driving that template. IMPLICIT MEMORY begins its formation early on in life. For the first 18 months of our lives the IMPLICIT MEMORY system is online establishing the basis of our character, yet if we were to truthfully expand that time frame it is from in-utero up to about seven years of age where most of our memorized self has taken shape.

When we begin by looking at the child's developing neural system, it should become evident quickly that these processes are not just coming together due to some genetic blueprint alone, no, it should be clear that the environment we are providing is acting on the development, sequencing, and strong associations being formed.

Because of the sequential development of the brain and its tremendous malleability early in life, early life experiences play a remarkable role in shaping how the brain functions; how IMPLICIT MEMORY functions. Early experiences create a cascade, or sequential set of cognitive, emotional, social, and physiological templates that we carry around with us, and use as we go through life. If you have traumatic experiences early on when the neural systems that are responsible for the fear response are developing, this will create pervasive hypersensitivity to threats, to challenges, to all kinds of things. We certainly know that high risk children, who come from chronic chaotic environment's literally change their baseline responsivity to every single cue. These patternistic responses form into IMPLICIT MEMORY that results in reactivity to any cue. These are state memories or cellularly stored memories not cognitive memories (i.e., pictures stored in the mind).

The developing neural associations that are occurring in our young children are a product of "signaling" that each of us is so sensitive to. Signaling is that process either genetically or environmentally that continues to impose itself on us throughout life and in doing so strengthens our self-concept or weakens it, depending upon how well we are observing the signals. Children lack the capacity to view things from a mature adult's perspective; hence the reason unhealthy personal belief about one's identity is so largely attached to the formative years. Children make too many incorrect observations of their experiences. Parents know this because many times as their children turn into adults and begin to share their perspective of their growing, developing years, parents are surprised by how their children perceived so many events differently than the parent did.

So much of what happens in relationships is about a process of resonance in which the emotional state of one person reverberates in that of the other. The Mirror neurons in our brains have the capacity to discern the intentions and emotions of another person. It is in the discernment that begins to shape a sense of "I" or self-perception. After an infant learns to identify their mother's face, voice, touch and smell, they learn how to communicate their needs to this "person", all based on trial and error. Successes and failures are recorded, with particular attention given to memories of interactions with caregivers, and gradually a patterned and predictable way of responding to the world evolves. If there appears to be a lot of unsuccessful emotional communication in these early, formative years an unhealthy template or IMPLICIT

MEMORY begins to become the companion of that child, which likely hangs on, even carrying well into adulthood.

This kind of memory is necessarily implicit because the newborn has no cognitive, conceptual or verbal ability like that of an adult and must depend on its inborn capacity to learn what it needs quickly and non-consciously, in an environment where survival itself depends on emotional connection. IMPLICIT MEMORY is *procedural*. This means IMPLICIT MEMORY, if it is going to be changed requires a strategic approach. That strategic approach is found in Quantum Theory. You just can't tell yourself, "Don't be stubborn" and hope this will change you permanently. This is like the left brain telling the right brain what to do. It is not going to happen this way. This is not how our brain works. It may take hundreds of hours of deliberate practice and constant repetition to turn a desired behavior; including the behavior of changing our self-talk into a habit. The Installing of a Healthy Implicit Memory, that part of the Program you are currently in, are the instructions on how to do things correctly.

Procedural memory, this memorized self is the basis for our character. The procedural memory system stores the instructions for our habitual responses. In other words it patterns how we do things. More profoundly, it is about who we are. Procedural memory is the basis of our identity and character, those aspects of our self that make us unique.

When we learn a behavior or an emotional response it becomes part of our procedural memory. Once it's been "programmed" into the procedural, implicit memory system we don't need to decide how to respond to a specific situation because it has now become automatic—after all, that's the whole point. You see these "over-learned" patterns are the "behind the scenes" kind of memory that frees up our attention for more important tasks. For instance, I can drive my car and carry on a conversation at the same time. The 'driving' behavior is encoded in procedural memory. Since I've over-learned the skills needed for driving I don't need to be conscious of every detail in order to keep my car on the road. We can form an unhealthy procedural memory of how we view ourselves, if we have practiced, for many years, a negative internal conversation. That negative internal conversation is what encoded an unhealthy view of our self into procedural memory.

When procedural memory kicks in, it's like being "on autopilot". Procedural memory is important in counseling because many of our emotions and behaviors that accompany them occur 'automatically' giving the therapist some insight to the underlying issues. In order to change behavior or any aspect of the negative internal conversation, we need to bring it into conscious awareness and 'out of procedure'. Forming a new "procedure" or IMPLICIT MEMORY takes a while to learn but once we can clearly see the distortions of the memorized self that are driving the patternistic struggles and then learn how to develop a healthy IMPLICIT MEMORY; it makes life a lot easier. If our IMPLICIT MEMORY is formed with a truthful and healthy view of self, of course it is going to make life incredibly easier.

An important feature of *procedural* or IMPLICIT MEMORY is that it tends to persist; it's resistant to change. This is a good thing because you don't want to have to keep re-learning behaviors or have to give high focus to everything you do. But this also means that you can't change a procedure, unless and until you pay attention to how and when it operates. And procedural patterns take a while to unlearn. I found this to bit a bit true when playing golf. I was a self-taught golfer. My swing, the way I held the club, my stance, and so on was developed to compensate for a slice. I had played golf like this for years. I finally decided to go and take some golf lessons and now I was up against it because I had learned my old swing so well, the change did not come automatically; it took concerted effort to learn the better way. The old neural pathways interfered with the new ones I was trying to create. It's hard to interrupt a well-established procedure. In fact, those original neural pathways, though weakened, may continue to show-up at times, until the new neural pathway becomes so well learned that the old learning dissipates. In other words, the new, regulated pathways will eventually override the old ones.

Once you unconsciously trigger very well established neural pathways, it's difficult to stop yourself from completing it. That is, it's difficult to interrupt the procedure. This explains why people repeat the same pattern in relationships even though these strategies clearly don't work. Once you understand how procedural memory, i.e. IMPLICIT MEMORY works you'll have a better handle on why people repeat ineffective, even self-defeating, behaviors. Once a procedure is initiated it acquires a forward momentum that is uncomfortable to stop. This is the source of the desire to continue the procedure. Procedural memory dances with our cortex which can always come up with a "rational" explanation or justification for our automatic patternistic struggles.

It takes many repetitions of a new internal conversation before it's ingrained, and once that procedure is established it, like the old memorized self, would be difficult to change. In fact, it will have fundamentally changed the original memorized self. I actually think that once a very correct view of our self is formed we will never go back to our old memorized self. For the same reason, we can't change our way of relating (i.e. implicit memory) simply by telling ourselves to feel differently. It requires special conditions for the change to occur. Our intelligence plays a significant part in why we would not go back to our old memorized self.

Quantum Theory is the science that assures us that we can change the organization of matter, by the energy our mind possesses. When we begin to observe our internal conversation and begin to connect how the procedural self was formed, we likewise are empowered to change any part of the unwanted, automatic, memorized, procedural self by seeing things accurately. Having our internal conversation reflect correct observation we then begin to introduce energy that will fundamentally alter the compositional medium, thus changing the organization of matter. Remember, our beliefs are organized as matter, but recall that all matter has potential, and so if our currently held beliefs continually have us experience undesired patterns of cognitive, emotional and behavioral responses, then through the power of the mind we can change or alter the matter to produce desired patterns.

The purpose of this assignment is to get you to go and interact with Quantum Theory and see if it is indeed the power that influences matter so that you can interrupt the memorized, procedural self, which is stored as matter. Before we get into the formal assignment, let's review what we do know about physiological functioning and how physiology acts as hardware which drives so much of our experience.

The mind is a part of us that allows us to observe. Observation will produce thoughts and every thought we have is so powerful that the electrical impulses resulting from thoughts will release a host of neuro-chemicals and it is these neuro-chemicals that influence heavily our perception. Our body and brain respond to each thought in myriads of ways. Some things to consider:

1) What, where, how and the length of time we give attention to something in life, along with our repetitive thoughts forms our neurological wiring. Concentrating on pain that exists within your body, sends electrical currents to your brain that continues producing the pain. We now know that thoughts create epigenetic differences upon the human epigenome, which in turn signals DNA functioning.

2) Repetitive thoughts create connections in the brain that quickly become iron clad. These thoughts move from conscious to unconscious ways of thinking and being. That is how we end up acting on auto-pilot.

3) The process of change requires forgetting what we know to discover new ways of being. Better observing practices accelerates the achievement of this goal and produce visible positive results.

4) Learning something new requires considerable energy and our undivided attention. Consider when you first learned to drive a car, the level of attention you possessed compared to that of an experienced driver who is primarily operating on auto-pilot.

5) We have the ability to alter who we are with every new piece of information that we learn. By combining this new information with practical application, a new experience is brought to life. We invoke greater levels of change, the more we repeat this process.

6) Our life-long repetitive negative thoughts are significant contributors to stress and disease within the body. Stress causes us to live in 'survival' state which negatively changes our internal state and exhausts our body, in turn, generating adverse responses including anger, depression, misery or confusion. These persistent emotional states lead to inflammation and inflammation is the leading cause to most health issues. When we are in this state, it can be likened to behaving like a bird trapped in a cage or a prisoner held captive, we fail to see the possibilities for our life. This is how people become 'stuck' for their consistent emotional state is highly addictive as a result of the production of neurochemicals generated by the thought that become the compositional medium in which our cells bathe.

As mentioned in Item 1 above, our formed neural pathways are not the only thing driving IMPLICIT MEMORY. Our epigenome impacts our ongoing view of our self, which likewise influences ongoing patternistic behavior or struggles. Both parental inheritance as well as epigenetic changes can and do shape self-perception. If that self-perception is faulty, it will be through highly observing and filtering epigenetic signals that will allow us to alter unhealthy views of self to healthy, truthful beliefs. Research demonstrates that we can produce positive changes. In 1942, Conrad Waddington introduced the term 'Epigenetics', which is the impact of genetics on development. Yet, it wasn't until the project of "Mapping the Human Genome," with the advanced technology that allowed a clear understanding that ongoing environmental signals really do affect DNA functioning.

Since epigenetic signals catalyze DNA function and expression, anyone that has achieved success in changing their IMPLICIT MEMORY, both in relation to neurological connections and DNA alterations did so by observing correctly what epigenetic signals they would allow their cells to absorb. Through correct observing, people develop new thoughts and create new ways of being, literally modifying genetic performance.

Visualization or Observation is a powerful tool used to stimulate the brain to generate strong mind-body connections. The brain is not the mind. The brain wires in correspondence to the mind. How the mind observes things is the very force of how the brain wires. Therefore, neural pathways may form which may contain incorrect information. Likewise, neural connectivity can also be filled with correct information. The difference is what the mind observes.

Our state of being, or memorized self consists of our repetitive cycle of our constant thoughts combined with the production of chemicals within our body which generates our emotions. This repetitive cycle has a direct impact on our behavior.

To change our reality and heal any ongoing negative pattern, both physically and emotionally is found in the secret ingredient in making up our mind to do so. We have the ability to fully recover and change our internal and external circumstances exactly like those patients who are told they would never walk again yet do so, sport stars who suffer from irreversible injuries yet fully recover, or those who have suffered a life-threatening cancer and a few months later it is no where to be found, or even those that no longer struggle with anxiety, depression or mood dysregulation. They understand the secret is having a powerful intention, believing they have the power to change their circumstances, loads of determination and the will to create what they want in life.

There is a partnership between acquiring knowledge and our life experiences. Our mind is supplied with the knowledge of eternity as we each existed for eons of time; and while there is a veil drawn over our mind of that past existence, yet eternal experience is written therein and can be regained to a considerable degree while here in mortality (John 14:26). We are deathless souls in a physical realm, each having a physical body, a physical-energy body to gain experiences here on earth. The body is the vessel used by the spirit (Job 32:8) that allows our eternal learning to continue, as there were many, many things we never could learn by remaining in the spirit form or as spirits only. Apparently, there is something important about that learning that requires us to forget our pre-earth life experience.

The most important memory to be regained while in our mortal sojourn is an understanding of who we really are. That memory cannot be accessed through knowledge alone; it also requires practicing the truth of that identity. 'Knowledge without experience is philosophy, and experience without any knowledge is ignorance. The interplay between the two produces wisdom'. Wisdom is sealed in us as a gift from the Holy Ghost.

Wisdom stems from one's intelligence to comprehend light and truth and live in it. Correct thoughts bring emotions of happiness, peace of mind, assurance, hope, love and joy. Such emotions encourage behaviors of cooperation with each other as we are part of one large family.

Anyone that experiences ongoing emotions of depression, fear, doubt, sadness, hopelessness, loneliness, cynicism, anger, and the like, or people who deal with ongoing relationship conflict, addiction, or can't find direction in their life is evidence that they don't know who they really are. To change your current identity or reality, you need to shift your state of mind by aligning your thoughts to the truth of who you are. The correct emotions that emerge from the new and correct thoughts coalesce in a way that increases confidence, hope, direction, better relationships and the rest.

Many of you readers are experiencing all sorts of patternistic struggles (hopefully a lot less by now), which may be a direct result of parental inheritance, but irrespective of your genes, it is possible to create a brand new you. Believe that you can and most importantly make up your mind with absolute conviction that what you want, though a process, will come to fruition.

So now let's return to something that was covered briefly in the very beginning of this book. Concerning implicitly held belief, the question was asked, "How do you change something that you can hardly even see?"

Quantum Theory provides us the answer to that question. Quantum Theory provides us information that has us begin to grasp what is occurring at microscopic levels, what influences energy and matter, and how to get the outcomes we are looking for. Let me review, Quantum Theory operates upon three laws and if we can understand these three laws, our whole perspective is changed on our existence. The three laws are:

1) The Law of Entanglement
2) All Matter has Potential
3) The Law of the Observer

Entanglement simply means that everything is connected, though some things have deeper or more well-defined association. The *Law of Entanglement* is to understand how one simple thing impacts another thing. When any subatomic particle (energy/matter) becomes Entangled with another subatomic particle, this highly developed association will have ongoing ramifications, meaning that as soon as one thing occurs in one subatomic particle, any other particle that has become highly associated with it, or Entangled, will too have an immediate response. This book has pointed out that our thoughts become highly associated with meanings, core beliefs, emotions and behaviors. The Law of Entanglement is explaining why IMPLICIT MEMORY is so powerful; it is because of these associations.

But what the Law of Entanglement is not saying is "Well since you have associated things incorrectly you are doomed." What it is saying is because of the long-term association that if you were to provide any part of that association with different information or energy it would immediately begin to impact all of the rest of the associations. This truth was demonstrated well when you began to see that behaviors formed from the Adult Ego State did challenge, made less true or even completely helped you overcome the Automatic Negative Thought. The Adult Ego State was different information or energy inserted into the Internal Conversation.

So, if we truly understand what the Law of Entanglement is suggesting, if through awareness we can change just one aspect of our long term associations, the other associated aspects will be impacted to likewise change. And if we no longer hold true the long-term associations would we then see our self differently? The answer is obvious and should give us hope that things can be different.

The second law of Quantum Theory is establishing a characteristic of the entire universe as well as our very own nature and that is that matter, all of it, has potential. It has potential to organize, in many ways and how it organizes is how we begin discerning what things are. Hydrogen, the most abundant element in the Universe is just one type of matter, but how it combines with other matter is why we can get so many different things. If it correctly bonds to

Oxygen we will get water, if it combines correctly with Nitrogen we get ammonia, or correctly entangles with Carbon we get methane gas. What I have said of hydrogen is true of all matter. So what gets matter to organize, shape or behave in any way that it does? What allows the elements to express itself in so many varied ways? What is the influencing power that acts on matter to get it to become? What allows matter to take on so many forms? The answer to that question is found in the *Law of the Observer*.

Quantum Theory states that matter becoming organized is influenced by energy found throughout the Universe. The mind is part of the Quantum Field of Energy that fills the Universe. Therefore, when matter is observed; observing being an attribute of the mind and an expression of energy will influence matter's organization. Therefore what begins to take shape and how that shaping is reflected in function is an outgrowth of our observation. By now, you likely notice some differences in how you see yourself, how you feel and how you are doing with life's stresses. Those differences are being experienced because you have fundamentally observed yourself differently, or in other words you have begun the process of changing how matter is organized within you. Your correct observing of yourself has created epigenetic changes at the DNA level and your brain wiring has also been changed. These changes are literally changes in matter and energy, which now has you experience yourself in a much better way.

The UNINSTALLING of an UNHEALTHY IMPLICIT MEMORY was utilizing Quantum Theory. By going through this program you have been observing what you had come to believe about yourself, even if some of that belief was incorrect. It was in your willingness to observe what had been stored IMPLICITLY and had become procedural that allowed you to find distortions, which have sat as a long time companion affecting how you were experiencing life in general. It is fundamentally from our view of our self that keeps shaping our ongoing experience.
As we have moved to the INSTALLING of a HEALTHY IMPLICIT MEMORY it will require correct observing to get the outcome you are seeking, meaning that you are able to develop a very healthy and truthful belief about yourself through correct observing. As you accomplish this highly aware and accurate observing it will then become engraven into IMPLICIT MEMORY. To reinforce the power of Quantum Theory, it is now time to get you to experiment with it to a degree that will enable you to see something about yourself, that has not been fully recognized up to this point. So, while we reviewed the laws of Quantum Theory and discussing their implications, we are still very much at an intellectual level. To this point, if nothing is acted upon, Quantum Theory is merely philosophy. Your goal in this assignment is to "go make the rubber meet the road," or to actually see if it works.

If it is going to work, then OBSERVATION is the KEY. The problem is that we are not very good at focusing. Our mind wanders constantly. It has been shown that we can lose attention six to ten times every minute. And yet here I am asking the reader to prepare him or herself to focus on one single entity well enough that such focus can change an entire day. Attentiveness is measured by specific brain waves and when these become the dominant wave in the frontal regions we are indeed focusing very well. One of those brain waves is called Beta. It has a frequency in its lower forms of 16 to 25 hertz and its higher forms 26-38 hertz. At its optimal levels, Beta wave frequency allows us to get things done. We get busy organizing contemplating, calculating, reading with interest and having better comprehension; reasoning and other aspects recognized as levels of focusing. Gamma waves are measured in hertz of 40 to 100. Gamma waves are still kind of new to neuro-research but it has been observed that

Gamma waves are critical in the process of learning, memory, and healthy cognitive functioning. People that meditate appear to be able to create these Gamma waves more consistently. Interestingly, those "Aha Moments," or those times of "Spiritual Attunement," meaning when we receive impressions or when doors of spiritual understanding are unlocked, Gamma waves are strongly correlated with such moments.

Paying attention and observation is a skill. It will improve with practice. There is no argument anywhere in research with that truth. The problem is that by nature the mind/brain connection appears to err on the side of laziness for self-preservation reasons. Being active supports increasing levels of Beta and Gamma waves. In practical terms, some of you are going to struggle with this assignment because you have erred way too long on the side of the lazy mind/brain connection. That long-term training is going to interfere as you go and prove that Quantum Theory is real. However if you will put forth the effort, you will experience the very power that comes from the mind's ability to observe.

There are varying opinions on what the mind is; what consciousness and awareness is. Deepak Chopra implies that consciousness is separate from the physical brain; or that consciousness appears to be integrated in the Universe and that the physical body, including the brain is an expression of that consciousness. On the other hand, in the strict models of science and research, consciousness is seen as an activity of the brain and in that model, the brain and the mind (consciousness) are seen as the same thing.

I have an opinion that is largely formed from my spiritual informing that may kind of bridge the gap. I want to emphasize here that there has not been much given in interpretation of some of the verses related to the term "INTELLIGENCE" in the scriptures. I don't want to go beyond what has been revealed and create some false doctrine. But as I studied what the recent research was suggesting, I couldn't help but have some of these obscure verses about INTELLIGENCE come into my mind as it appeared what has been revealed about this subject fit somewhat into what the research was uncovering.

Perhaps if we were to look at consciousness as non-local, which is what some of the most recent research is suggesting, we can begin to tie some of the scriptures with what the research is revealing. Larry Dossey, M.D. in his book, "The Science of Premonitions," states:

> My conclusion is that consciousness is not a thing or substance, but is a *nonlocal* phenomenon. *Nonlocal* is merely a fancy word for *infinite*. If something is nonlocal, it is not localized to specific points in space, such as brains or bodies, or to specific points in time, such as the present. Nonlocal events are *immediate*; they require no travel time. They are unmediated; they require no energetic signal to "carry" them. They are *unmitigated*; they do not become weaker with increasing distance. Nonlocal phenomena are *omnipresent*, everywhere at once. This means there is no necessity for them to go anywhere; they are already there. They are infinite in time as well, present at all moments, past present and future, meaning they are *eternal*.

When the scriptures suggests that God is God because all things are present before Him (Moses 1:6; D&C 38:2; 88:41; 130:7), and then we are given an insight that we too can progress and become as He is, for example, "For if you keep my commandments you shall receive of his fulness, and be glorified in me as I am in the Father; therefore, I say unto you, you shall receive grace for grace" (D&C 93:20; See Also D&C 84:38; Romans 8:16-17); "He that keepeth his commandments receiveth truth and light , until he is glorified in truth and knoweth all things" (D&C 93:28); or "That which is of God is light; and he that receiveth light, and continueth in God, receiveth more light; and that light groweth brighter and brighter until the perfect day" (D&C 50:24) it appears that intelligence is something that has the capacity to receive truth and light, and in doing so will one day take upon itself the character of the most intelligent being in the Universe (Abraham 3:19).

God's glory is "intelligence, or in other words, light and truth" (D&C 93:36). In the context of scriptural language, light is a law by which all things are governed. When adherence to the law is given, mans capacity to increase in knowledge and intelligence is activated. We are likewise informed that the fullness of light and truth is what constitutes God's power:

> The light which shineth, which giveth you light, is through him who enlighteneth your eyes, which is the same light that quickeneth your understandings. (D&C 88:11)

In His revelations to us, Christ reinforced that what He had revealed anciently:

> I am the true light which lighteth every man that cometh into the world (D&C 93:2; See Also John 1:4, 9, 12)

> This light, which "is in all things, which giveth life to all things," is "the law by which all things are governed, even the power of God who sitteth upon his throne" (D&C 88:13).

Perhaps in a poor analogy we might grasp how Light and Truth are being connected within the scriptural record. Light and Truth appear to be interchangeable words in describing the same thing (D&C 93:29, 40, 42; Ether 4:12). If you and I are in a dark room and we begin to navigate that that dark room, it is reasonable that we will find ourselves running into obstacles. However, if we begin to add light, let's say a very dim light like that of a match, we will be able to better navigate that room; yet because the light is so dim, we are still going to not see things clearly and will find ourselves coming upon obstacles that inhibit a completely successful journey across the room. However, if we increase that light, successful navigation across the room is easier to achieve. TRUTH IS LIGHT and as we obtain truth and begin to live by it we are increasing the light so that we can see the path to Eternal Life more clearly (D&C 88:7; 84:45). Increasing Light or Truth makes the journey more navigable, with decreasing chance of ever leaving the path. The scriptures indicate that while Light has the capacity to be added upon it likewise can be taken away through disobedience or rejecting Truth (D&C 93:39).

As attributes of God's nature, Truth and its Light are what constitute God's glory. Because of these attributes, God ".... comprehendeth all things, and all things are before him" (D&C 88:41). Further because He is the embodiment of all Truth and Light, ".... He is above all things, and in all things...." I find this revelation highly interesting in relation to what Dr. Dossey stated, "They are infinite in time as well, present at all moments, past present and future, meaning they are *eternal*."

This core intelligence, which was taken and organized into a spirit body by the Father, is a mystery to us. There has been very little revealed about it, as Joseph Fielding Smith cautioned:

> "Some of our writers have endeavored to explain what an intelligence is, but to do so is futile, for we have never been given any insight into this matter beyond what the Lord has fragmentarily revealed. We know, however, that there is something called intelligence which always existed. It is the real eternal part of man, which was not created nor made. This intelligence combined with the spirit constitutes a spiritual identity or individual" (Answers to Gospel Questions, comp. Joseph Fielding Smith Jr. [1963], 4:127).

We are expressly informed that this intelligence is co-eternal with God:

> Man was also in the beginning with God. Intelligence, or the light of truth, was not created or made, neither indeed can be. (D&C 93:29)

From this eternally existing intelligence, the Father organized Spirit Bodies, for the purpose of giving the eternally existing intelligence the capacity to increase in intelligence. Without a Spirit Body, advancement would have not taken place. Our spirit birth gave us godlike capabilities. We were born in the image of God our Father; He begot us like unto Himself. There is the nature of deity in the composition of our spiritual organization; in our spiritual birth our Father transmitted to us the capabilities, powers and faculties which He Himself possessed -- as much so as the child on its mother's bosom possesses, although in an undeveloped state, the faculties, powers, and susceptibilities of its parent. [Teachings of Lorenzo Snow, p.4] In order to continue obtaining light and truth a physical body likewise had to be incorporated, for there were things we would have never been able to gain or understand without it. As we continue, through obedience to His light and truth, "..... the day shall come when [we} shall comprehend even God, being quickened in him and by him" (D&C 88:49). It will be in that day we will clearly discern that Christ is "..... the true light that is in [us], and that [we] are in him, otherwise [we] could not abound" (D&C 88:50).

Bruce R. McConkie, an apostle, wrote: Abraham used the name *intelligences* to apply to the spirit children of the Eternal Father. The intelligence or spirit element became intelligences after the spirits were born as individual entities (Abraham 3:22-24). Use of this name designates both the primal element from which the spirit offspring were created and also their inherited capacity to grow in grace, knowledge, power, and intelligence itself, until such intelligences, gaining the fulness of all things, become like their Father, the Supreme Intelligence [*MD*, p. 387].

Brigham Young taught: The life that is within us is a part of an eternity of life, and is organized spirit, which is clothed upon by tabernacles, thereby constituting our present being, which is designed for the attainment of further intelligence. The matter composing our bodies and spirits has been organized from the eternity of matter that fills immensity. (Discourses of Brigham Young, p.49)

With this in mind, the secular language of "non-local" becomes interesting; and while Dr. Dossey states that consciousness is not substance, an idea that appears to be contrary to revealed truth (D&C. 131:7-8; 93:29); yet he appears to be tapping into something of the infinite or eternal nature of intelligence. As I have considered the research and the revealed word, I lean toward the idea that the mind is the core intelligence, as it received the inherited capacity to grow, being the off-spring of the Almighty. The intelligence has always existed, but its capacity is due to its organization. I am strengthened in that opinion by the words of the Prophet of the Restoration when he taught:

> *The mind or the intelligence which man possesses* is co-equal [co-eternal] with God himself.... I am dwelling on the immortality of the spirit of man.... The intelligence of spirits had not beginning, neither will it have an end.... There never was a time when there were not spirits; for they are co-equal [co-eternal] with our Father in heaven. (*History of the Church*, 6:302-317; Italics added for emphasis)

The mind then is the intelligent force that contains the power to observe. Through observance, learning or increasing intelligence is activated. The brain, both spiritual and physical is an instrument by which learning becomes stored. The mind has the capacity to eventually understand all things, but even in its limited states still has the capacity to create and be enlarged upon because of what it is. The brain is the instrument upon which the mind operates. Based upon what is observed, learned and/or believed, the brain will wire in correspondence to what the mind is observing. The mind is the process, it is consciousness. It is the basis of self-awareness, and it has the capacity to choose (D&C 93:30-31); which is the attribute of free-will we each are aware of.

To increase intelligence requires a dedicated focus of obtaining truth coupled with our obedience to it. Passivity will not allow us to advance. This is an interesting point to seriously consider as passivity is how most of us are going through life. The passive approach to existence is noticed because if our mind is paying attention to anything it is largely dedicated to three things, 1) Our Body; 2) The Environment and, 3) What Time It Is. These three things appear to occupy a considerable amount of our awareness and seem to drive so much of what we do. It is as if we are conditioned to them or that these three things dictate so much of how we spend our life activities. Consciousness allows us to walk away from these main three things and tap into other parts of our observation. Consciousness is the power that allows "light and truth" to be discovered. Consciousness is the power then to walk in the light of truth once it is discovered. For those whose mind is filled with worry is an illustration of those who lack awareness of truth that would eliminate such worry.

Our intelligence is heavily measured by our attitude and our attitude is largely measured by our thoughts, and our thoughts are largely measured by our investigation into truth and our obedience to it. The more truth we learn, the more positive and accurate our thoughts become. The thoughts we tell ourselves are powerful in shaping how we see ourselves, because these thoughts release neurotransmitters and chemicals within us that have us begin to feel in correspondence to our thoughts. If our thoughts adhere to truth about our identity, then we experience positive feelings and better attitudes, on the other hand, if our thoughts are delving into things that are not true about our self we will experience negative emotions and poorer attitudes.

For those that do not understand the connection between truthful thinking and their correspondent positive feelings or untruthful thoughts and their correspondent negative feelings can create an environment of self-defeatism. As you may recall from your work utilizing the Uninstalling Sheets, what got you to write a column was when you were experiencing a negative emotion. In time you learned that you were contributing to your negative emotions because of the thoughts you were saying to yourself, about yourself. But for those that have never understood the connection between thoughts and feelings, when they keep experiencing negative emotions, those negative emotions create a distortion in their identity. This distortion occurs because they have come to accept that the reason they are having the negative emotions is because they are somehow broken, or devalued in some way.

With their focus on the negative emotions being experienced, they begin to think negatively about themselves, but as you already know it is actually the thoughts that are producing the negative emotion and so such individuals create a loop where their body (emotions) becomes the master of their mind. In other words, their emotions are now in control of everything. When this occurs, intelligence is blocked. People become stuck.

Now that we have discussed the mind (Intelligence) as having always existed and that it has the capacity to be increased (D&C 88:40), then it becomes obvious that we want to keep the mind as the master of the body. It does so when it understands and is accepting of truth. We increase our mind's power when we are willing to walk away from Body, Time and Environment and begin to observe things as we want them to be. In other words, if we don't like the general negative identity we have come to believe about our self, we can change that identity when we engage the mind. We engage the mind through reflection, contemplation, reasoning and so forth. If we don't like our currently perceived self, we can ask our self some questions that have us tap into the power of the mind to see what we really want to be. For example, if I want to be something different then I can ask myself a question such as, "What would it be like to be a happy person?" Please don't too quickly answer this question. Take your time to answer that question. Recognize the thoughts that begin to emerge because of the power of the mind. Keep focusing on what you observe to be associated with happiness. You are going to be surprised how many answers you can provide to just this one simple question. Your consciousness, your power to observe is being engaged and your mind is providing you the answers you are writing. Your concentration and focus; your mental rehearsal is allowing you to see truth.

When you have exhausted that question, you can keep the power of the mind engaged by asking another question. You may ask, "Who do I know that is a happy person?" Again, don't too quickly move beyond the question until you have seriously considered how many people you recognize as having a general happy disposition. This may end up having several people becoming a part of your list. If you recognize that there are many that you know that are indeed happy, you can keep the power of your mind engaged by asking another question; "What are they doing differently than I am?" By staying focused on this question you can begin to record what your mind is observing those differences are. Your notes are growing; your insight is increasing as you purposefully give focus to these questions. When you have exhausted all that you can think of what these differences are you can increase the capacity to become happier when you engage the power of your mind by asking this question, "What do I have to do to become more like them?" Spend time answering this question, perhaps even more time as it will unlock the power to act upon those observances. Knowing something and then acting on it is necessary if we are going to grow in our intelligence.

The power of the mind is the power to observe and as you can tell from the example above, mental rehearsal is the key to obtaining truth that will have you advance. Mental rehearsal is all about the quality of the self-imposed questions we ask ourselves that stimulate consciousness. Mental rehearsal creates learning and if you remember my definition of learning it is when at least two neurons connect. Once learning has taken place that learning operates within us to become and to act. There was a research project that demonstrated the power of mental rehearsal and its role in learning. This research project utilized a piano as the means to create neural pathways simply through visualization or mental rehearsal. I like this research project because its duration was only 30 days long. The participants that qualified for the project did so because none of them had ever had any formal piano training. I know how to play "Turkey in the Straw" and "Heart and Soul" those songs that are pretty common during holiday get-togethers', but I never have had any formal piano lessons, so I would have qualified for the project.

After obtaining a large population, the group was broken up into four smaller groups. The first group was told to come to a location, Monday through Friday, two hours a day. They were going to sit down at a piano and there was a sheet of music and they were going to spend the time learning how to play that sheet of music. The instructions were simple. First they were provided a practice keyboard and note chart to put behind or above the piano keys and then they were taught "Every Good Boy Does Fine," or in other words they were taught how to read music. Using the practice keyboard and note chart as a reference, they were simply instructed to place a finger on the keyboard based upon where the note was displayed in the sheet music, in other words, "If you see a note on the 'D', then find the note on the keyboard and put your finger on it." That was the extent of their music instruction.

The second group was also told to come to the location Monday through Friday, two hours a day. They were going to sit down at a piano but there was no sheet music on their piano. This group was told they could do whatever they wanted to do for those two hours.

The third group was told to not show up at all. This was the control group.

The fourth group was told to come Monday through Friday, two hours a day; they were going to sit down at a piano where there was sheet music. This group was given the same instruments and instruction as the first group but they were told they could not put their fingers on the keys. They had to visualize what their fingers would like if they were on the keys.

A pre-scan and post-scan was taken of all of the participant's brains. In the first group the post-scan revealed a whole new region of the brain that was lighting up, that was not lighting up in the pre-scan. The only explanation for the difference is that learning had taken place. Neurons carry electrical currents which are visible in brain scans. It was apparent that new neurons had connected based upon the learning of playing a sheet of music on the piano.

The second group displayed no significant difference as the second group was not assigned to learn any thing. The third group showed no change at all since they never even showed up. But what about this fourth group, what do you think their post-scan revealed? It was almost identical to the first group, having us understand that mental rehearsal alone can create learning. Our mind's power to observe influences neural genesis and connectivity. Exactly what the Epigeneticists were helping us understand.

One of the interesting reports from those that were deeply involved in learning was that they had become so occupied in their rehearsal that they lost track of time and space. Some of them reported that the two hour session seemed like just a few minutes. Have you ever had that experience where you became so engrossed in something, before you even realized it time had flown? That is when you know you are engaging the power of observation, the power of the mind to become so highly focused that change is obvious.

Other conclusions from the research are, practicing anything will create learning; and that learning will operate in us even if that learning has come from mental practicing or rehearsing. Therefore if we go around observing ourselves as, or practicing being a victim because we see ourselves that way, then our ongoing experience is going to be seen in terms of suffering and no choice. On the other hand, if we go around observing ourselves as being in control, or practicing not being a victim or not seeing our self as a victim, we are going to see things very differently. Our ongoing mental rehearsal shapes our reality.

It used to be believed that the brain was static and hard-wired from birth; therefore our ongoing experience was determined by that wiring. Marie Diamond, a neuroscientist from California State University, Berkeley was given the opportunity to examine Albert Einstein's brain. In doing so she observed that he had more support cells in the brain than the average person. Now please consider Albert Einstein to the vast majority of the human population. This was a person that heavily used the mind's power to observe, to focus, to experiment, to reason and to theorize. Yet in his own words, this great scientist said:

> I have no special talent. I am only passionately curious. (The Collected Papers of Albert Einstein.; Vol I, The Early Years. Princeton University Press, 1987)

Based upon her research, Dr. Marie Diamond concluded that experience, stimulation and activity all impact the anatomy of the brain. There is a benefit to those that use the power of logic, reasoning, learning and observing. Our capacity to function well, meaning in a more positive way is improved when we engage in activities that increase learning. Impoverished environments likewise impact the brain's capacity in a negative direction. The term she coined for the changes occurring in the brain is "NEUROPLASTICITY." What she observed and later demonstrated many times is that the brain has plastic qualities. When you think about plastic in its liquid form, you can pour that plastic into any mold and when it cures it will take on that shape. Our mind has the capacity to create the mold and the brain has the capacity to wire based upon what we observe that mold to be. Those that are committed to life-long learning are constantly creating greater amounts of support cells; developing neural networks that have them live more optimistically.

Curiosity makes us smarter. Learning new things, like a language or how to play a musical instrument makes us smarter. Reading makes us smarter, and there are many other productive ways to gain knowledge, ensuring the strength of cognitive function. Stimulation of more support cells and neural pathways comes from learning. Learning is like food for the brain. It expands the power of brain function. This ongoing process is the basis for self-growth. It is the key to successful living.

While we have been talking about the mind in connection with the brain, I don't want us to lose sight of how the mind also impacts DNA. Since this whole book is about learning to see ourselves correctly, we must not forget that what is encoded upon DNA also heavily influences self-perception. Since we receive our DNA by inheritance, what is encoded upon our parent's DNA does operate in areas of self-perception. We inherit our parent's belief about them self and that belief can send signals that shape our own self-perception. But the power of the mind is also involved in self-perception and how that mind observes things will directly alter DNA expression and functioning. We have the power to overcome, for example, faulty signals inherited from parental belief and change the information encoded upon DNA by what we are doing, our own learning and the conclusions we are forming from our own focused observation.

If we are associating correctly we are developing learning and memory that has us see the truth of who we really are. Learning can come from observing others and it can likewise form through symbolic reasoning. Symbolic reasoning is how reading and comprehension is described. Every letter is a symbol and if we know the sounds the symbols make and how the symbols combined provide understanding of our environment then it is possible to learn from simply reading from someone else's experience or knowledge as they share it through symbolic structures. If I was in a classroom of let's say thirty third graders and asked them to please draw a picture of a chair, not one of those pictures would come back looking exactly the same, but the features of what a chair is would clearly be represented within each picture. That is a good example of symbolic reasoning.

However, learning is greatly enhanced through personal experience. The reason being is that when we are personally experimenting; when we are actually involved in the process we are utilizing all of the sensory system, whereas symbolic reasoning or merely observing others limit what senses are being used. The more senses utilized the more indelible the learning. The more senses being used the more neurochemicals being released that integrates learning. An example of what I am discussing is, you can read a book on how to fly a plane, but your learning is going to be more indelible when you get in the cockpit and actually work the controls.

Therefore, here is something to consider; since emotions are critical in learning, if we are merely operating from our addictive emotions; never experiencing new emotions, are we learning anything new? If we created such patternistic ways of handling ongoing life experiences and all we seem to do is to be controlled through our addictive emotional controls, how do we learn something new? The answer is that we have to do something new, whether that is changing a thought, making a conscious decision to look for the good, not defaulting to self-defeating behaviors, maybe developing a better relationship with our feelings instead of stuffing or ignoring them; or by increasing our study of God's perception. Doing something new will have us learn something new.

Those that use their emotions as the center of all that they do; those that hyper-focus on their emotions are going to become stuck in their development. Yes, even ignoring feelings is still evidence of being hyper-focused on them. Hyper-focus on emotions too many times has us conclude, "This is how I feel, and therefore, this is how I am. Addictive emotions are evidence of a time where we defined our self due to the emotion we experienced. There is room for a different identity if we do not like the present identity. That new identity will only become a reality when you can picture it. Can you see who you want to become?

To think greater than we feel is change. If you can only see yourself in terms of your negative emotions, if you cannot think greater than you feel then you are surviving. Survival is based in the idea that we believe that what is outside of us is more powerful than what is inside of us. Did you hear that definition? Read it again if you must.... SURVIVAL IS BASED IN THE IDEA THAT WE BELIEVE WHAT IS OUTSIDE OF US IS MORE POWERFUL THAN WHAT IS INSIDE OF US! With this understood, I would like you to consider the following question? Is God a survivor? Does God believe there is anything outside of Him that is more powerful than what is inside of Him? The answer is obvious! And since God is not a survivor then what is He? He is a creator because He is omniscient and omnipotent. Omniscience is the attribute of being all- knowing. There is nothing He does not know. Omnipotence is the attribute of being all-powerful. There is nothing He can not do. His knowledge and purity gives Him His unlimited power. Knowledge also acts as a precursor to new experiences. Increasing knowledge provides for new experience, new perspective, and increasing capacity. We are the Almighty's children, are we not then endowed with His capacity? The knowledge that we are intelligence both as a primal substance and then being organized when we became His offspring, such inheritance would have us understand that we have the capacity to grow in grace, knowledge, power and intelligence itself, until such intelligence gains its own fulness and we become like our Progenitor. We were born in the image of God our Father. There is a divine essence then within each of us, meaning based upon DNA inheritance our Heavenly Parents transmitted to us the very capabilities, powers and faculties, which They themselves possess, although in an undeveloped state.

As we increase in intelligence, or as we discover truth and act within its dictates, we modify our cells and enlarge the capacity of the Divine within us. Our increasing intelligence then has us become as He is. As Elder McConkie taught, "...men's bodies will reveal what law they have lived." If we have lived a celestial law, then our bodies will shine with perfection and glory and we will have filled the measure of our creation, becoming like our Father (D&C 88:67).

Since we have inherited His nature, we too have the capacity to Create. Creation is different than survival. Creation comes from the skill of observation (Abraham 4:18; 3:17) I would like to turn to a couple of thoughts on our power to create. The first comes from being an endowed member of the church. In the endowment, one thing that is presented as part of our instruction is the creative periods of this earth. In the endowment instruction, we hear the voice of Jehovah and Michael as they receive the ongoing direction of the creation. When the creation is complete, Michael is heard to acknowledge that the earth is beautiful. Jehovah echoes Michael's sentiment. That is one thing I would like my readers to take notice of, the act of creation will be accompanied by a sense of beauty. The second thing I would like to draw to our attention, that though the endowment focuses on Jehovah and Michael as being assigned the task of creation, Abraham 3:24 suggests that we were likely involved in creating this earth as well. That makes sense to me as we consider the following.

If you are familiar with the story of Job, it is recognized that Job is living a life filled with the blessings of a loving marriage, his house being filled with the voices of many children. The family is well-to-do. They appear to be living a life of industry and comfort. Not too long after Job's happy life is described, he begins to experience some significant reversals. He loses everything, his life-long spouse, his children, his wealth and eventually his health. One thing that remains in his experience are some supportive caring friends, but as Job continues to experience more and more negative set-backs, even these friends abandon him believing that Job has brought these curses upon himself due to some serious sin he has committed. It is at this point that Job's long term stresses have him become severely discouraged. He now feels all alone. Life's experiences are working against his previous perception and he is struggling. It is at this moment that the Lord comes to Job. The purpose of this personal visit is to have Job maintain the larger perspective. Job was losing perspective because of the ongoing discouraging events and the Lord wanted to remind him of a very important event, even though that event occurred in the pre-mortal realm:

> Gird up now thy loins like a man; for I will demand of thee, and answer thou me.
>
> Where wast thou when I laid the foundations of the earth? Declare, if thou hast understanding..... when the morning stars sang together and all the sons of God shouted for joy? (Job 38:3-4, 7)

Jehovah is reminding Job of an event that all of us participated in. It was a heavenly council in celebration of the earth being formed. The completion of the creation had the heavenly host singing and shouting. I ask, what is it that we were singing and shouting about? The first answer may be obvious. The creation of the earth allowed for progression. We could now enrobe our spirits in tabernacles of flesh, whereby we might continue the journey of progression. That is an obvious reason for the celebration, but I think there is quite another. Likely our response was due to the fact that we contributed to the creation itself. Like Michael, who acknowledged the beauty after the creation was complete, especially since he was an intricate part of it, we too were pleased with its outcome due to our own involvement. If Jehovah and Michael had the capacity to create as spirit sons of the Almighty, then it rings true that we had the same capacity. We have been creators for a very long time. Yet, our mortal experience has worked in a way where we have forgotten our true identity and many of us are merely surviving, not creating.

Now, one more thing I want to say about our pre-mortal experience. When the earth had been created there was no deception being practiced by our Heavenly Parents. They didn't try and create some rosy picture about what earth-life was going to be like. They were honest about the challenges, the difficulties and the, at times, immense opposition we would encounter here. We made our decision to come here based upon full-disclosure. We made the decision to move forward.

That is the intent of the Lord's conversation with Job is to provide correct perspective that keeps our bearings straight. Life has its way of dulling that perspective, I get it! If we have practiced for way too long being acted upon, it is time to remind ourselves that we have the power to act. We can create! Creation comes from the power of observing. Observing will entail using our mind to mentally rehearse that which we are trying to create.

Your assignment is to consider the Law of Quantum Theory that informs us that observing can influence the organization of matter and go out and create two days, each around a single entity. You are asking me, 'What is a single entity?" Let me give you some examples. Tomorrow I would like to create a day of:

1. friendship
2. productivity
3. service
4. fun
5. learning

6. holiness
7. compassion
8. improving relationships
9. developing talents
10. organization
11. character building
12. service
13. gratitude
14. happiness
15. healthiness

It doesn't matter to me what you choose. Again, the list above is just samples of what a single entity looks like. You may find something else you would like to create a day of. Once you have chosen a single entity, then the beginning of mental rehearsing or engaging the power of the mind to create is by asking this first question, 'What would a day of _____ even *look* like?" Do you see that word look? What is it you *observe* a day of _____ would consist of? Begin to write down the things that automatically appear in your mind. As you begin to record your ideas, it will stimulate even greater awareness of many ways that day would look like in context of your chosen entity. When you have exhausted yourself and believe you cannot think of a single thing more then ask yourself another question. For example, if you chose a 'day of friendliness' you may find your ability to expand your creative power by asking, "If I were to be friendly toward the stranger, what would that look like?' Again, just record what your mind is observing in relation to this more detailed question. You may then add something like, "If I were to be more friendly toward myself, what would that look like?' The question should promote even more ideas around the entity of "friendliness." 'What would it look like if I were to develop greater friendliness in my family?' 'What would it look like if I were to develop greater friendliness toward God?' 'What would it look like if I were to create greater friendliness to those I work with?' The self-imposed questions are what encourage mental rehearsing. The more time you put into mental rehearsing the greater power you develop to create.

Intentional mental rehearsal will likely create a list of so many things you would never be able to get it all in on one day. The point is not to try and accomplish everything that came to your awareness, the point is to create such improved awareness that you can go and create a day centered in that entity. Whatever day you go and apply your enhanced awareness to, please understand that the day will still be filled with all of things we have to do, i.e., eat, take showers, go to work or school, etc. But your focus is no longer on time, environment or body, but on this thing, this entity that you would like to develop as part of your experience within your normal day.

It is best to do the mental rehearsing the day or evening before the actual day you would like to create. Utilize your increased awareness of this single entity and see if you can't apply it to the next day. At the end of the day evaluate it.....'Was it a day of _____?' Part of the evidence that you did indeed actually create the day is what you sense at the end of the day. Was it a beautiful day? Was it a much better day than usual? Are you feeling happier, calmer; maybe more thankful? Are you more aware of what has been missing and how you want your life to be different?

Remember, you are creating two days, not one. The other day you create has to be created around a completely different entity than the first day. The reason for this is to demonstrate to you that you have the power to create what ever you put your mind to. The mind is the most powerful instrument in the Universe – learn how to use it effectively.

Before you get busy on the assignment I would like to address what it is that I am trying to help you understand because of this assignment. Our attitude is heavily influenced by our thoughts. Our collective thoughts resonate as attitude. Our thoughts carry incredible power because they produce cosmic waves in the universal sea of energy we live in. Our thoughts directly shape the matter we are made of and the energy coming off that matter. The power of a thought is a very potent form of energy that penetrates all time and space, so we need to be aware of our thoughts (Mosiah 4:30). With that let's consider the following:

James E. Faust stated:

> "I now turn to mastery of our own private thoughts. In this realm, conscience (observation, awareness) is the only referee that can blow the whistle when we get out of control. If not bridled, our thoughts can run wild. Our minds are a part of us that really require discipline and control. I believe reading the scriptures is the best washing machine for unclean or uncontrolled thoughts. For those who are eligible and worthy, the sanctity of the holy temple can lift our thoughts above the earthy." (The Power of Self Mastery, April 2000)

William James, a pioneering American psychologist and philosopher, wrote,

> "The greatest revolution of our generation is the discovery that human beings, by changing the inner attitudes of their minds, can change the outer aspects of their lives." (William James, in Lloyd Albert Johnson, comp., A Toolbox for Humanity: More Than 9000 Years of Thought (2003), 127.)

Thomas S. Monson taught:

> "So much in life depends on our attitude. The way we choose to see things and respond to others makes all the difference. To do the best we can and then to choose to be happy about our circumstances, whatever they may be, can bring peace and contentment." (Living the Abundant Life, Ensign January 2012)

Charles Swindoll—author, educator, and Christian pastor—said:

> "Attitude, to me, is more important than ... the past, ... than money, than circumstances, than failures, than successes, than what other people think or say or do. It is more important than appearance, giftedness, or skill. It will make or break a company, a church, a home. The remarkable thing is we have a choice every day regarding the attitude we will embrace for that day." (Charles Swindoll, in Daniel H. Johnston, Lessons for Living (2001), 29.)

Mahatma Ghandi:

A man is but the product of his thoughts – what he thinks, he becomes.

Neal A. Maxwell:

The human mind is remarkably retentive. We must be careful of what we allow in our mind for it will be there for a long time, reasserting itself at those very times when we may be most vulnerable. Just as harmful chemicals heedlessly dumped in a vacant lot can later prove lethal, so toxic thoughts and the mulching of the wrong memories in the vacant corner of the mind also take their toll.

Norman Van Horne:

When you're gifted with the power of thought
It is a wonderful thing in a way,
But it can also create problems
If your thoughts tend to go astray.
The power of thought brings things to light
That we tend to postpone
But now folks with the power of thoughts
Have today become quite known
So if you posses the power of thought
And don't know how to use it
Consult others who have the same quality,
But very seldom abuse it.
For the Lord gave us the power of thought
To do with as we choose
So hang on to it, always,
It is one power you don't want to lose!

Norman Vincent Peale:

Our happiness depends on the habit of mind we cultivate

When you expect the best, you release a magnetic force in your mind which by a law of attraction tends to bring the best to you.

Clint Eastwood:

You can work wonders with the power of thought. Through the instrumentality of thought, you acquire creative power.

Napolean Hill:

Success comes to those who become SUCCESS CONSCIOUS

Arnold Schwarzenegger:

> The mind is the limit. As long as the mind can envision the fact that you can do something, you can do it, but it will require some action to do it.

The purpose of this assignment is to have you become highly aware of the power of the mind to create the outcomes it can envision. When we use the mind in this manner, we are no longer surviving, we are creating. Why is this important? Life is still going to blow its winds at you. While we have less control of the wind, we do have the power to adjust our sails so that we can get the best outcome from the changing direction. Our thoughts and attitudes are what empower our sails to be stationed correctly.

REVIEWING HOMEWORK ASSIGNMENT #10

If you were my client returning to my office to report on this assignment you would be greeted with the following question, "Before we get into the details of your created days, generally speaking, what did you notice?" I can usually tell from the response whether or not much effort was put into the assignment.

When answers like:

1. Yeah, it was a little better, but I had a hard time keeping it going all day
2. Everything was fine until "such and such" negative thing happened that day
3. I had no problem in the morning but it fell apart in the afternoon
4. I didn't really notice any difference

These kind of answers are foretelling that little energy was expended in the mental rehearsal arena. On the other hand, when answers like:

1. That was the best day I can remember in a long time
2. Wow, that was much better
3. I want to do that more often. I don't think I had a negative feeling all day
4. People were wondering why I was so happy

These kind of answers are an outgrowth of really good mental rehearsal or observing.

In dealing with the first set of answers I ask my client to report on their mental rehearsing. Sometimes they look at me like, "What are you talking about?" I then review with them that the catalyst for mental rehearsal was directly influenced by the types of questions they were forming in order to get a visualization of what that day would look like. Usually such clients only asked them self one question. I can recall an example:

Me: So what day did you create?
Client: A day of being positive
Me: What did a day of being positive look like?
Client: I just told myself to be more positive

As stated before, IMPLICIT MEMORY is so powerful that trying to break it up will never occur by telling ourselves to "just be positive." Breaking up of IMPLICIT MEMORY must be much more intentional. The intention is demonstrated in the mental rehearsal. If using the same type of day, a person that mentally rehearsed, the conversation would look more like:

Me: So what day did you create?
Client: A day of being positive
Me: What did a day of being positive look like?
Client: I put several quotes around the house that inspire me, so whether I was in the bathroom, or going down the hall to get my kids up, or in the kitchen, I had these different quotes which helped me get my attitude going in the right direction first thing in the morning and throughout the day..

I then planned on finding 10 things in the morning that I was thankful for before I left the house.

I greeted my husband and children with smiling eyes. I told each one of them something I really admired about them and told them that I was lucky to be a part of their life.

I planned a breakfast that would give me energy

I made sure I did my morning devotional. I always have better days when I do.

I prayed and asked Heavenly Father to help me see things that day the way He sees them.

I played really great music as I was dropping the kids off to school. I was singing to it and my kids were laughing. I did this rather than let the school traffic bother me.

I met my girlfriends for a run. I made sure not to engage in any gossip. On the way home I went to the store to buy a new game I heard about so that later we could play as a family.

After showering, I went into our home office and took care of that stack on the edge of the desk, getting things recorded and filed.

I made a picnic basket and met my husband. We went to the park and talked. I thanked him for all that he does for me and our family. I told him there may be a surprise later!

I had selected two people that I knew might enjoy a visit. One of them I was not able to get a hold of, but the other was a young mother. While with her, she asked me for advice on certain things, but she told me that she was not very good at baking and so her and I spent some time in the kitchen and I showed her how to make a fruit pie. I also taught her a couple of tricks on how to get stains out of clothes. I told her that I thought she was doing a terrific job as a mother. She got a bit emotional.

On the way to school to pick up the kids, I called my parents to check in with them. I told them I was creating a day of being positive. They were interested in what I was doing.

When everyone was home from school, I prepared a dinner everyone liked. I encouraged the kids to get any homework done because after dinner we were going to play a game.

When dinner was over, I had everyone in the kitchen to clean-up together, getting it done quickly then shooed the kids off for showers.

We had family prayer and then played the game I bought earlier in the day. It was really fun.

When the kids were off to bed, I knelt and prayed and thanked Heavenly Father for a really nice day.

I gave my husband that surprise!

I hope you recognize the difference between the two examples. While these were just examples, it has been my experience over and over again that those that do take the time and mentally rehearse through asking and answering several self-imposed questions, that moment of engaging the mind to areas of awareness that are seldom exercised, brings about beautiful days.

As the client expresses how different those created days were, they recognize that the things days typically dictate to us were not experienced the same way. In other words, most of us go through our days having the day dictate to us when and where we are supposed to be, whether we even have time to prepare food, deciding instead we will just grab some fast food because we just don't have the time or energy to cook. We find ourselves maybe well intentioned, but easily distracted. We know things have to get done but then we reason that it can wait another day. We let others influence how we feel, sometimes dipping down to someone else's way of being. We minimally invest with others, finding it easier to play a game on our phone, stay too long in our social media; worry what the kid's homework is going to look like that day and all the rest. Those are the days we are surviving.

Yet in the day where things are still demanded of us, when creating, these demands do not have the same effect. In creating we find ways to change our perspective about the day, and when we do even those mundane daily duties are approached with a completely different attitude.

For the clients that come back with an obvious, uplifting experience, I chuckle a little bit just watching them enjoy the positive outcome of the assignment. So many are surprised by the empowerment they experienced when they decided to create what they wanted. I hear comments of commitment that they enjoyed the day so much they are going to continue doing it. And if you think I am kidding, I will get a text every now and then from a past client who will say, "Today I created a day of_____!;" usually accompanied with a smiley face emoji.

When the client is finished reporting on the significant difference in emotion, attitude and empowerment from creating their days, I ask them this question, "What allowed those days to be so much better?" The client answers every time, "Because I created it!"

KAYLA'S STORY

I had a very recent client who had spent a lifetime of surviving. Her name is Kayla. Though I cannot diagnose her mother, Kayla's description of events throughout her growing up years would certainly have anyone conclude that mother was and is a very toxic person. Kayla's

IMPLICIT MEMORY was highly associated with stress, worry, doubt, fear, etc. Kayla was going through life surviving.

When I met Kayla, she had recently returned to Saint George. Her relationship in another state was not going well. It too was filled with stress. Even though Kayla could not envision life without stress, she came to herself and wanted things to be different. Kayla began doing a few things, including therapy that would have her come to a better understanding of why she felt so stuck and defeated.

When I met Kayla, she was living at a friend's house. This friend was still living at home and Kayla had no room for herself. She slept on a hide-away in the front room. The parent's were heroin addicts and so you can begin to see the circumstances she found herself in trying to make a difference in her life. Not the best environment to do that. Because Kayla wanted to change, things began to change. She was offered a place to live from someone that came out of the blue. Her living circumstances allowed her to have her own bedroom, with no financial obligations at all to her living circumstances, but she was informed it would be only for a couple of months. She was encouraged to save her money so that she could get a place of her own.

During these two months, Kayla was attending therapy and progressing in the Program. Kayla was not religious, but she certainly was open to the idea that there was something out there greater than us; she just had no idea how to describe or really relate to it. She was accepting of some of my spiritual insights, but we kept our terms of this greater thing as the 'Energy of the Universe' or 'Universal Energy' It kind of reminded me of when Aaron says to the king of the land that the Spirit of the Lord had directed Ammon to go to the land of Ishmael (Alma 22:4). The king inquired about what this "Spirit of the Lord" was (Alma 22:5). Aaron counters with, "Believest thou that there is a God?" (Alma 22:7) The king's reply demonstrated some awareness of something greater, but it was obvious that he was not too familiar with or what a God is. However, the king did have a reference point historically about a "Great Spirit" (Alma 22:5-11). Aaron uses the king's reference point in helping him understand more. This was a little like Kayla, she had never had religion in her life, but she was open to there being something there and I leveraged her openness.

Like most people with unhealthy esteem, Kayla was very good at diversion, whether that was through addictive behaviors, being grandiose at times, or simply withdrawing from social opportunities, sometimes isolating her self for hours. Her phone was her life. On the weekend, sometimes she would sleep 15-20 hours a day. This was how she learned to survive. This was how she managed her intrusive, negative emotions.

Due to Kayla's depth of surviving, sometimes she would try and go through the motions of the homework assignments, but not really putting forth her best effort. This is pretty normal for clients that experience deeper shame. The homework requires clients to look at themselves and what they have come to believe about themselves, and when that picture is not so pretty, clients don't have the energy to intentionally look. They still implement the learned strategies of avoiding. I would encourage her at times to be more intentional in her homework so that she could learn from the assignments. As she became involved in the Uninstall Sheets, I think one of the things that surprised Kayla was the degree of her NEGATIVE INTERNAL CONVERSATION. Remember, shame-filled individuals focus more on their emotions, which keeps them stuck. As she began to use the Uninstalling of an Unhealthy Implicit Memory

Sheets, she was surprised at how often her IMPLICIT MEMORY defaulted to this negative self-talk, but now she was becoming aware that her negative emotions were being contributed to by her NEGATIVE INTERNAL CONVERSATION.

Her growing awareness of her IMPLICIT MEMORY helped Kayla begin to slow things down and even catch herself at times, telling herself to stop doing this. Early on in her use of the Uninstall Sheets, she asked me, "Since I now know that I am contributing to my own problems, why won't my negative emotions get under control when I do catch myself? Her being so early in the Program, I had to remind her that IMPLICIT MEMORY is powerful and is procedural. That procedure is so well engrained that it takes time to learn about it and then how to fully change it. I told her that while she can observe when she begins this procedure she still can't see what the distortions are that are driving her reaction. I encouraged Kayla that as she progressed in the Program she would see clearly what distortions were driving her memorized self, but it wouldn't be until then that she would find much improved control. I reminded her that the procedural, memorized self was so well established that simply being aware of the INTERNAL CONVERSATION would not be sufficient in changing it. You can't just say stop it and expect the procedural, memorized self to change.

When we completed the Uninstall Process it was evident that Kayla had been able to recognize the distortions in her IMPLICIT MEMORY. But like being in a new class, at times she was unable to more fully connect how these distortions were influencing her life experience. I simply replied that there was more for her to learn through the Install Process and then it would all make sense.

When we moved into the Installing a Healthy Implicit Memory part of the Program, I gave her the Learning to be Miserable assignment. When she returned to report on it, Kayla stated that not one of the Thinking Errors applied to her. She said she didn't do any of those things. Of course I challenged her and told her she was my first client in over 5-1/2 years that ever made that claim.

Behind the scenes, Kayla's life had become stressful The time had run out for her living arrangements, the new living plans fell through, she had not saved any money and so the old memorized self took over. Her procedural, memorized self had learned how to deny that there was anything wrong, which showed up in denying that she had any thinking errors. Nothing got better and now she was faced with homelessness, no place to sleep, to shower, or prepare food. Her facial affect took on a greater look of being tortured, which she was as her memorized self came back with a vengeance. Her addictive behaviors increased. Her body was filled with so much anxiety that it was visible as she would shake and not be able to sit still. She avoided her next appointment. When she did return to therapy she stated, "I changed my mind, I do have thinking errors. I found three of them." With this admission, I reassured her that being aware of THINKING ERRORS, like becoming aware of AUTOMATIV NEGATIVE THOUGHTS is vital if she wanted to have the power to change the procedural IMPLICIT MEMORY. For me, her admission of three was likely understated, especially with her level of shame, but I felt encouraged that she was willing to get back on track.

It was now time to give her this assignment, CREATING YOUR DAY. We reviewed Quantum Theory and heavily emphasized the power of the mind in its ability to envision, to observe, to go to places of awareness that very few of us spend any time and that by doing so we could change the outer aspects of our lives. Kayla returned the following week stating that she was having a hard time doing the assignment. For the reader, please don't forget about all of the stress she is experiencing. As pointed out earlier in this chapter, if our mind is paying attention to anything, when it is not going to deeper places of awareness, it defaults to our body, time, or the environment. These three things were consuming her. Her thoughts were driven to survival because of her situation. I simply encouraged her to try again. She returned the next time and was very down. She was tearful as she began to share how alone she felt and inadequate to meet the challenges she was facing. While she shared all of the reasons why she couldn't change, I was paying attention to the thinking errors she was using.

In my response to her venting, I first acknowledged the difficulty she was having and that based upon her perspective of things it was reasonable to feel all alone and defeated. I then took off my therapist hat and shared with her a little about my own personal life experience. I told her she had it easy, because at least she was young and single, which would make what she was trying to do much easier. I told her that her perspective was not much different than mine when I was her age. I came from a home environment that shaped shame and survival thinking. I told her that a big difference for me was that at her age I was married with children trying to not only take care of myself but others. I told her how stressful it was to be in college, working full time and trying to keep a roof over our heads. I told her that no one was helping me financially. I was paying for my own schooling. I told her how many times I became sad not being able to give more to my wife and children. I felt inadequate to the growing demands. I shared with her that she is not the only one that had to deal with unhealthy relationships. I said, the whole thing may have been easier for me to get through except that my wife appeared unable to take care of a home and deal effectively with children's emotions. Because of that I carried much of her responsibility as well.

Kayla heard me tell of how the increasing burdens forced me into improving my earnings by leaving school and finding employment that I thought would make life less stressful. I found out something, that the world paid me what it thought I was worth and without a degree it wasn't much. Eventually, I said to her, I decided to open my own business. I did so in the construction industry. I became a contractor and sought to develop a company that would take away the financial burdens. I told Kayla that I was so poor when I started this venture that I couldn't even afford to park in downtown Los Angeles. I told her that sometimes I would park in a neighborhood and walk one or two miles into the city and then spend the day there meeting with engineers, building owners, architects, developers and the rest trying to get work. One day, while I was walking into the city I said to myself that I was going to make the company that owned all of these parking lots my client so that I could park in downtown. I did that very thing. All of the persistence began to pay off. My reputation began to grow. Business eventually did well enough that we enjoyed vacations and a few other toys that allowed us to get away on weekends and such. I was able to return to school, complete my undergrad and then obtain my Master's.

I told her many more things about my own difficulties not shared in this book and then I said, "You cannot look at me and tell me I don't get it. I do!" I then told her that her biggest problem was herself. I pointed out all of the THINKING ERRORS she was using, giving herself permission to not take the hard road. I said life has its demands, the problem is you have never learned how to take responsibility for your life, only how to manipulate others to get them to take care of you. I said, "You tell me you have no money to get into college and so you have no opportunities to get ahead. There is no reason why you can't go get a second or maybe even third job to get yourself stabilized and begin to save for your tuition. These are the things we do. We may not like the journey, but the journey of hard decisions is what allows us to stop surviving. You complain about all of the reasons why you are a victim, but the only real reason why you see yourself that way is because of you. You are filled with anti-responsibility excuses, justifications and rationalizations." I asked her if she wanted to become like her mom. She became angry at the comment. I told her that her mom was so unhealthy and toxic because she too has spent a life time of blaming all of her problems on others. "Keep it up and you will become your mom!"

She didn't like any of this. You could see her growing angry, but this anger was occurring because what I was saying was true. She left the room without much to say.

Three days later she contacted me and told me that she went and got a second job. I commented by saying that she "heard" what I was saying as I provided her some of my own intelligence gained through adhering to truth. She told me she had become angry with me because of that truth but that she was now ready to face her challenges realistically. When she came back in, we reviewed the Creating Your Day assignment one more time. I had her practice mental rehearsing in the office and then sent her out. When she returned she reported, successfully, that she had created two days. What I was unprepared for was one of her experiences, she said, "Larry, I learned something by doing this assignment. What I learned, as I was mentally rehearsing was that my mind already has the answers. I never knew that because I was always surviving."

We spoke about this in greater depth and I told her that we are all connected to a Universal Energy that cares about us and if we will take the power of the mind and send out our desires and wishes to that Universal Energy that we will begin to see doors open, at times, almost magically. It returns to us in this manner because the Universal Energy wants each of us to know that we do matter, that we are loved, and that we are not alone.

Apparently Kayla took this idea to heart and she began to use her mind to send out signals of what she wanted. One of the things she did was reach out to her grandmother who paid for a hotel room for a week. During this week, she began to be more insistent with a friend who said he would like to find a place to share. Right at the end of the week, however, he backed out. We talked about it. I asked her what else she had done. I found out she had done several things, but none of them panned out. Finally, she made the decision to go to one of the local property management companies and got a list of available places. On the list was an apartment that would fit within her budget. She needed help though getting in and so she shared with her grandmother what she was doing. Grandmother provided her the money to secure the place. When she went to look at the place, it was as you can imagine a very run-down, disgusting apartment. I kidded with her and said, "Let me guess, the carpet is red." She laughed and said, "No, it is orange and it is filthy." I said, "Well, it's like walking two miles because you can't afford parking in downtown, but it is what is required right now."

Kayla was getting this "power of the mind sending out messages to the Universal Energy." She wanted something nicer, so her mind asked for it. She called the property management company and asked if there were any other units available. It turned out there was. She went and saw it and it was clean and nice. The carpet was new and the unit was a bit bigger than the first one she viewed and still the same price.

Then she came and addressed a problem in that the unit required a year lease. In her plans, she was thinking about changing some of her circumstances in six months. The lease requirement and her plans conflicted. I suggested that six months was still pretty far out and that many things could happen in that time. She came back and said that her mind sent the question out into the Universal Energy and that she felt that it was the right thing to take the apartment.

I took the time to review all of the recent changes she was experiencing and suggested to her that the changes were directly related to the power of her mind. I told her it was obvious that her mind was now positioned on what she wanted and what she could do. Because the mind contains the power to create, her intentions were creating changes in her environment. I told Kayla that I had learned something about this Universal Energy and that was to not forget to send out thoughts of thankfulness for the doors that were opening up. I asked her, "How can you demonstrate your gratitude in visible means?" She replied by saying that she would not get comfortable with her improving life and this time take the opportunity to really take control of her life. She likewise shared that she could take grandmother's gift and live in a way that would make her grandmother proud of her. I added that one of the best ways to show gratitude is to pay it back or pay it forward. Kayla smiled at this suggestion.

I am sure Kayla has been thankful in the past to those that have helped her, but being thankful is just the beginning of gratitude. Gratitude is demonstrated in the way we live because of our thankfulness. Kayla is learning about the Universal Energy and how to engage with it correctly. One of the ways we recognize we are correctly engaging with truth is the associated feelings that emerge within us. Feelings of hope, of vision, of assurance, of increasing confidence, of greater peace of mind, of happiness and just a rise in motivation and energy are all indicators that we are becoming more intelligent. Intelligence is the power of the mind to recognize truth and align with it. As we do so the power of faith increases within us, our capacity to become what we were designed increases; intelligence enlarges, resulting in greater views, and increasing intention.

This was the second assignment of three of the INSTALLING A HEALTHY IMPLICIT MEMORY process. The two things I want the reader to walk away with are:

1) QUANTUM THEORY IS THE SCIENCE OF SCIENCES AS IT EXPLAINS HOW ALL OF NATURE IS INFLUENCED
2) WE ARE NATURE AND OUR MIND HAS THE CAPACITY TO CREATE THE OUTCOMES WE ARE LOOKING FOR BECAUSE THE MIND IS THE POWER TO OBSERVE TRUTH AND ACT INTELLIGENTLY

Although difficult, change is always possible. What holds us back from making the changes we desire are our own limiting thoughts and actions.

— Satsuki

HOMEWORK ASSIGNMENT #11: LEARNING HOW TO DO THINGS CORRECTLY –

There is an important reason why I want my clients to implement the laws of Quantum Theory and discover that their mind has the power to create. The reason is that if life is going to continue down the right path then the client must stay *intentional* if they are going to create a whole new IMPLICIT MEMORY. Even though every client sees them self in a better, more realistic way by this point in the Program, to completely change out the old memorized, procedural IMPLICIT MEMORY requires much more repetitive, intentional observing. To completely discard the past of incorrect learning and replace it with a very healthy, truthful self-belief requires consistent attention to the truth of who we are.

Our cells are highly sensitive and susceptible to our intentions, whether those intentions are being driven IMPLICITLY or with FULL AWARENESS. While every person who has sincerely completed the homework to this point does have a better relationship with them self, in order to obtain an automatic response that has us live with confidence, hope and happiness will require that we develop an IMPLICIT MEMORY that will allow us to do so. Implicitly stored learning and memory is a wonderful design as long as the learning and memory stored is accurate.

Recall that IMPLICIT MEMORY is formed through only one method – repetition. I do not want to make it sound so simple, but repetition is the source of forming this type of memory within us. Once formed, it drives automatically, without having to pay high attention, our view of our self with all of its accompanying emotions and behaviors. Let me say clearly then, the 11 assignments you complete in this book is not enough repetition to have created a whole new IMPLICIT MEMORY filled with truth and healthiness, though it certainly has made you aware of your previously held distortions of self, freeing yourself to replace those distortions with things that are true and real about your identity. It will be in the working of the AfterCare Program where most of the repetition will take place. Yet, the purpose of this assignment is to get you to start doing things the right way, and if done repeatedly, will develop that wonderful memorized self.

Before I teach you how to do things right, you may be asking why I didn't start doing this at the beginning of the Program. My answer is simple; it would not have made a difference. Your old IMPLICIT MEMORY with all of its distortions would have interfered with you getting what this last assignment will teach you.

I have compared this to a software program that is already installed on the hard drive. As time goes on, software developers improve upon the original program, allowing us to upgrade to take advantage of the improvements. We do so by downloading the new and improved software program on our hard drive, yet if we do not first remove the old program we will receive error prompts telling us that the new version cannot be successfully downloaded until we remove the original program. This is very much how our physiology works in relation to

DNA and Neural Pathways. Our physiology is the hardware consisting of the Genome and the Neural Connections where learning is stored. What has been encoded on the Genome and wired in Neural Pathways is the current software program driving the outcomes of our ongoing experience. The UNINSTALL part of the Program was to have your mind observe correctly the distortions inherent in UNHEALTHY ESTEEM or your previously formed IMPLICIT MEMORY so that you could let those distortions go. As a reminder, here are the distortions:

1) In behavior the distortion is the controlling Parent Ego State and the Child Ego State. The reason these are distorted is because we have the capacity to see ourselves truthfully, meaning that each of us is a person of incredible value. When we correctly observe ourselves it empowers us to take better care of ourselves. When we have arrived at this correct perception, we then realize that everyone has this same value and likewise deserves to be treated with extreme care. Once introduced to the ADULT EGO STATE, you demonstrated the power of adjusting to it even while experiencing negative emotions. In your adjustment you came to realize that AUTOMATIC NEGATIVE THOUGHTS are challenged to the degree that you begin recognizing they are not even true.

2) The distortion of negative emotions is when we use them as evidence that somehow we are broken or devalued in some way. That is not the purpose of negative emotions. Negative emotions are designed in us to keep us on the right track of our identity. Negative emotions are pain, emotional pain. Pain is an indicator that something is going wrong and what is going wrong is that our cells are breaking as we give them incorrect information with our AUTOMATIC NEGATIVE THOUGHTS. The three chemicals that are given immediate rise in our bloodstream when we engage in AUTOMATIC NEGATIVE THOUGHTS are adrenaline, cortisol and neuroepinephrine. These chemicals are the chemicals of the 'Fight and Flight System." The Fight and Flight System is designed in us when there is a perception of harm or threat. It begs the question... Why is the Fight and Flight System activated when we talk to ourselves negatively? The only answer is that our cells must perceive such thoughts as harm. In other words, our cells already know who they are and this false information supplied to them in forms of AUTOMATIC NEGATIVE THOUGHTS is being registered as a threat to their true identity.

3) All three NEGATIVE CORE BELIEFS are distorted. Through a process of looking at evidence, it became clear that helplessness, unlovability and the body being a negative thing are complete falsehoods. We have to ignore a lot of evidence to continue to hang on to these distortions. Since these are the only three things in our human experience that drive the vast majority of negative emotions then our ongoing experience should be much more manageable as we recognize them for what they are. Capability, being Lovable and the complete Miracle of our Body are inherent in every one of us. It is who we are. It is how we were designed. It is evidence of the Divinity in each of us.

4) AUTOMATIC NEGATIVE THOUGHTS are distorted because not one of those thoughts is true in relation to what has been revealed about us. The only information available to us about who we are comes from the Father of us all. There is no other source that has us explore our true self, because no other source provides any incentive to do so. It becomes clear that only the revelations concerning our identity gives us the incentive to investigate as it provides an understanding of who we are and the purpose of our existence. Here it is belief begins to take shape as there is something tangible to believe in. The simple truth of being a child of God is revealed knowledge; and yet all of

creation supports the incredible truth that all living things have seed within itself to produce after its own kind. That seed is comprised of DNA. We are told that we are made in the likeness and image of God. That makes sense as we are His children. We have to ignore a lot of evidence to so easily dismiss this idea. In a world filled with disbelief comes the opportunity to examine a pearl of great price and weigh in the balance of all understanding and knowledge, how this singular idea compares in value.

As we began learning how to use the Uninstall Sheets so that we could learn how to LIVE CONSCIOUSLY, I started by asking if you had experienced any negative emotions in the past week. As you reported that you had, I asked what the context of those emotions appeared in. The context was recorded in the very first box of those columns, which box asked, "My Problem Is." The problem was THE EVENT. Now that you have learned how to LIVE CONSCIOUSLY you have recognized that THE EVENT does not predict the outcome. What predicts the outcome is how we evaluate or perceive THE EVENT. We evaluate by how we end up thinking about THE EVENT. Our thoughts about THE EVENT are what lead to the outcome of THE EVENT.

Thoughts are incredibly powerful as they result in a cascade of sequential responses within us:

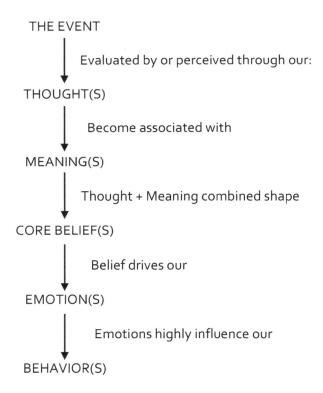

THE EVENT

↓ Evaluated by or perceived through our:

THOUGHT(S)

↓ Become associated with

MEANING(S)

↓ Thought + Meaning combined shape

CORE BELIEF(S)

↓ Belief drives our

EMOTION(S)

↓ Emotions highly influence our

BEHAVIOR(S)

The above diagram demonstrates the process that every human uses when experiencing life and its events. In this process, the most influential, the most vital component to increase our awareness around are the thoughts we place upon the events, because the thought is the mechanism for the sequential responses within us. If that thought is negatively directed toward ourselves then we end up shaping within us beliefs that are distorted which become procedural or automatic shaping and reinforcing an unhealthy view of ourselves. The formed perception will have ongoing ramifications on the quality of our life.

Since the thought is the most critical part of the process then we must develop the ability to filter our thoughts, related to THE EVENT, which will allow us to both develop and maintain a healthy view or perception of our self. There are actually three filters in forming thoughts, which if learned and utilized consistently will do just that. Please pay high attention to how each one is formed. They are as follows:

1) The Rational Thought – This type of thought is formed when we become the OUTSIDE OBSERVER, meaning that even though we are experiencing the unwelcomed or negative event, we remove our self and assess the event as if it were occurring to someone that we really care for. If this event were occurring to someone we have deep concern for, what is it that we would find our self saying to that person. Whatever that is, that becomes the RATIONAL THOUGHT. This develops the intervention to slow the memorized self down and use the power of the mind to change perception leading to better outcomes.

2) The Positive Thought – This type of thought is developed when we ask ourselves one of two questions related to the event.
    a. Is there anything in this event, no matter how small, that I can be thankful for?
    b. Is there anything I might learn or is there something God wants me to learn from this event?
   Whatever thought arises in relation to these questions forms the POSITIVE THOUGHT.

3) The Truthful Thought – This type of thought is formed when our thought is TRUTHFUL ABOUT OUR IDENTITY. These type of thoughts are the antithesis of the Automatic Negative Thoughts. An example may be, "I am capable," or "I can do this," etc.

Visually then, any event can be filtered through four different types of thoughts:

THE EVENT

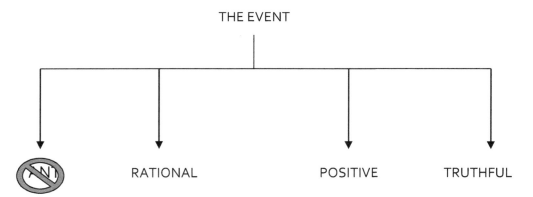

RATIONAL          POSITIVE          TRUTHFUL

The first of these thoughts is the AUTOMATIC NEGATIVE THOUGHT (ANT), but we already know the outcome of using this filter – it is not good, so I put the International Prohibition Symbol over that filter. Let's stop using it! What should become obvious in observing the above diagram is that there is a 3 to 1 ratio of perspectives or filters we can put life's events through. Amazing how many times we default to the only unhelpful one.

While all three filters will produce improved and more accurate perception, I would like to spend some time with the Positive Thought filter, especially as it relates to your true identity. When President Monson suggested that 'How we choose to see things can make all the difference in the world,' it is the Filter of Positive Thoughts that grants us so much power to do so. Let's look at how our perception can change when we ask ourselves the first question, 'Is there anything in this event, no matter how small, that I can be thankful for?"

One image that conjures up in my mind that teaches this line of thinking is when we see news coverage of natural disasters. I think of the reporter that is standing on the street where the day previous a tornado had ripped through a neighborhood. The images of houses being laid waste, rubble of bricks, two by fours turned into splinters; houses being completely ripped from their foundations. People's entire collection of worldly comforts, pictures and other memories wiped away in just a few minutes, and yet there we see the reporter standing next to the couple that owns that property and asking for their feedback. How many times do we hear people so devastated say, pointing toward the rubble, "This we can rebuild; we are just so *thankful* that no one lost their life!"

Knowledge of being children of the Highest can also help us maintain a thankful perspective. In a favorite Christian hymn we are reminded:

> When upon life's billows you are tempest tossed,
> When you are discouraged thinking all is lost.
> Count your many blessings; name them one by one,
> And it will surprise you what the Lord has done.
> (*Count Your Blessings*, Hymn 241, LDS Hymnbook)

Eternal perspective, meaning being able to see beyond the limits of mortality, has us recognize how blessed we really are. Such recognition should always have us reflect upon our circumstances from a place of thankfulness.

Another way we can begin to see things differently is through our thoughts that are formed when we ask ourselves the question(s); "Is there anything I might learn from this?" or "Is there anything God wants me to learn?" For those of us that have an understanding of the purpose of life, this question becomes one that perhaps we should pay more attention to. The Gospel is informing us that we came to earth to have experience so that we might *learn*. Since this is one of the main purposes of our sojourn it is interesting how our thoughts rarely entertain this perspective.

One of the things that I have noticed about the human experience is that at times people get stuck and sometimes stuck for extended periods of time. It seems that no matter how much reasoning they employ; how hard they try to make things different, they continue to experience ongoing roadblocks, hardships and discouragement. As I have observed this phenomenon I have recognized that, at times, the reason the season of difficulty remains is because the person has not learned yet what they were supposed to learn to have them become unstuck.

A general example of this found in the scriptural record when God reveals His truths to people and invites them to live according to His laws and commandments. As the people begin to do so they begin to prosper and be blessed. In time, some of these people begin to get the idea that their prospering and blessings are alone a result of their own industry. They become comfortable in their riches and decline in their diligence to keep the laws and commandments of God. I never mean to disrespect the written word when I paraphrase, but when the people begin to go against God and His revealed truth you hear God come to His servant the prophet and say, "My anger is kindled against them" followed by the annunciation that there awaits significant punishments if the people do not change (See As Examples: Moses 6:27-29; 2 Nephi 15:25; Isaiah 5:25; D&C 56:1). The prophet, as a type and shadow of the Holy One begins to mediate on behalf of the people and suggests that rather than destroy the people let him employ the sealing power, sealing the heavens from casting forth its moisture (See As Examples: 1 Kings : 17 and 18; Helaman 11:4-5). In time, the prophet reasons, that the people's food supplies will begin to dwindle and maybe then they might learn something. So set in motion is a period of time where the people, no matter how much reasoning they do, no matter how hard they try and change the circumstances themselves, eventually they realize they need help and many return to God, pleading with Him for that help. As they return to God, they learn that all of us are dependent upon Him. When correct perspective returns the heavens are then unsealed; and they begin to enjoy the growing blessings of prosperity as they have learned something about their relationship to God.

I once had a client who had experienced such a set-back. It seemed like no matter what he did to change his circumstances, things just remained stuck. Professionally he was an Insurance Agent. In the economic decline of 2008, there were several industries that were significantly impacted by that decline. One of the hardest hit was the insurance industry. My client had never known any thing else, I don't think he had to because he was able to provide well enough for his family. However as the economy dipped further and further into recession, my client found himself getting farther and farther behind financially, as many could no longer afford their policy premiums. As he tried to do something to stop the bleeding, he realized that without a degree he could only find low-paying jobs. Men tend to measure their value in large part based upon their ability to provide for their family and the economy was eroding the ability in my client. As he found himself unable to do so, my client began to become depressed, and began to give up. His wife recognizing the seriousness of their financial situation did whatever she could do to bring money in. This just further set him into a declining view of himself.

One day I offered on my radio show the opportunity for someone to go through my Program at no cost and the wife called in and claimed the prize. The husband had become stuck for years and his wife could see how his self-perception played out in all aspects of life. She could see clearly how her husband's view of himself was the real source for his inability to become unstuck.

Early on, I taught about Inherent Worth as a basis of beginning to operate from correct information. He stated to me that "intellectually" he could see that what I was presenting was true, but he added, "I have a hard time feeling it." His response was reasonable as he had been operating from incorrect information his entire life. He, like so many that deal with Unhealthy-Esteem do so because they confuse Self-Esteem with Inherent Worth. Such individual's train their cells to believe that worth is something to be earned and so when presented with correct information such a person can "intellectually" determine that what is being presented is correct, but their memorized self, meaning the incorrect belief formed in their implicit memory, is still sending signals that influence their incorrect belief.

As we continued working through the Program you could tell that while he was doing the homework he was not putting forth his best effort in doing so. It seemed that much of his reporting on what he was learning was purely reporting back "intellectually" what he could see as truth, but the emotional experience was somewhat absent. We finally came to the assignment, "Learning How To Do Things Correctly." I began to share with him my observation of people becoming stuck in their lives and things changing when they finally addressed the issue from the question, "Is there anything I can learn?" or "Is there something God wants me to learn?" This seemed to set in him a growing interest. He looked at his wife and their look was one of deep consideration. I could tell that what I just presented was of some significance to them. On the drive home, this couple began to discuss this perspective and she asked him, "What do you think God wants us to learn so that we can become unstuck?" He replied, "I don't know, but what I felt when he provided this perspective is that I need to address this with Heavenly Father." Chris made the decision to go and ask God what it was that He wanted him to learn. My client reported it had come clearly into his understanding that his worth was not based in what he could or could not do, but because he was God's son. In his own words, Chris told me what came to his mind in answer to his question: "Chris, I want you to know you are worth everything to me." My client began to feel his inherent worth. This was what God wanted him to learn. Within a week of that experience, my client received a call from a company offering more than double in an annual salary than what he had ever made previously in a year through residual income. Chris was now unstuck!

I think it is important for us to consider the benefit of increasing our awareness around this concept of becoming stuck and unlocking the doors through asking what we might learn or what God wants us to learn, especially since that is the primary reason for our mortal experience (D&C 98:12; Proverbs 1:5; D&C 131:6; Psalm 119:34). I am a personal witness of the strength that comes by filtering life through this positive filter of "What might I learn?" and even more so through the question of "What does God want me to learn?" There have been times in answer to such questioning that what comes seems a mile off of the radar of what I thought might come. Yet those moments have helped me improve my learning. I encourage all of my readers to implement this in their ongoing experience. Now back to the assignment.

The following homework assignment is going to look familiar in that it is organized just like the UNINSTALL SHEETS. But that is the point. Every human processes life events in exactly the same way, but these INSTALL SHEETS are designed to get you doing things the right way by utilizing one of the other filters we can place our thoughts through.

## RATIONAL, TRUTHFUL, POSITIVE THOUGHTS TO BEHAVIOR
## (Installing a Healthy Implicit Memory)

1. *Rational, Positive, and Truthful Thoughts* – develop from innate processes of critical thinking and becoming aware of our subconscious thoughts as they relate to our true identity and developing mental approaches that lead to supporting our true identity. Empowering our thoughts in this manner result in the development of positive core beliefs.

2. *Positive Core Beliefs* deal with reality and provide a sense of control over our environment. These Positive Core Beliefs are based upon evidence, and develop through humility and faith in time-honored values and principles, such as a strong work ethic, positive interactions in our relationships and taking care of our health.

   A. Capable core beliefs: I am adequate, I can succeed if I stick with it, I have the power to choose and act, I am safe, I feel like I have control
   B. Lovable core beliefs: I am likeable, I am wanted, I am inherently good, I have a realistic sense of my limitations, I am acceptable even when I make mistakes, I am attractive
   C. Positive body image: I am an absolute miracle, I am attractive to some and maybe not others, which is true of everyone, I have power to change many things about my body, I can improve my mental processes through practice

3. *Results:* Do my rational, positive and or truthful thoughts lead to better outcomes or do they lead to increasing problems.

## EXERCISES  EXAMPLE

| Date: | Date: | Date: |
|---|---|---|
| My Problem Is?<br><br>My husband forgot I had a meeting at church | My Problem Is? | My Problem Is? |
| My Rational, Positive, or Truthful Thought in My Mind Was?<br><br>I learned that I have really good support through my relationships at church<br><br>P-L | My Rational, Positive, or Truthful Thought in My Mind Was? | My Rational, Positive, or Truthful Thought in My Mind Was? |

| What Did My Thought Mean to Me? | What Did My Thought Mean to Me? | What Did My Thought Mean to Me? |
|---|---|---|
| That while creating a little stress by my husband's forgetfulness, I had others that were understanding and helped me. (1, 2)<br><br>Core Belief Option –<br>1. Capable<br>2. Lovable<br>3. Positive Body Image | Core Belief Option –<br>1. Capable<br>2. Lovable<br>3. Positive Body Image | Core Belief Option –<br>1. Capable<br>2. Lovable<br>**3. Positive Body Image** |
| My Emotional Reaction to the Thought<br><br>Grateful, Important | My Emotional Reaction to the Thought | My Emotional Reaction to the Thought |
| My Behavioral Response or Intended Behavior<br><br>I called a couple of my dear friends, explained what had happened and asked for help with some of the set-up. Told my 11 year old daughter to hold the fort down until her dad got home | My Behavioral Response or Intended Behavior | My Behavioral Response or Intended Behavior |
| Results of My Thoughts<br><br>✓Yes: Led to a Better Outcome<br><br>No: Led to Increasing Problem | Results of My Thoughts<br><br>Yes Led to a Better Outcome<br><br>No: Led to Increasing Problem | Results of My Thoughts<br><br>Yes: Led to a Better Outcome<br><br>No: Led to Increasing Problem |

Let's look at Item 1 in the big box at the top of these sheets. Please read what is written in Item # 1: *Rational, Positive and Truthful Thoughts*. After you finish reading Item #1 then return here.

The formation of RATIONAL, POSITIVE or TRUTHFUL thoughts is innate. That is the power of the mind to observe. You demonstrated the power of the mind when you did the CREATE YOUR DAY assignment. We have almost unlimited power to observe and if we train ourselves correctly, the mind becomes the master of the unwelcomed event, rather than have the event impose its own negative outcome.

Let's look at Item 2 in the big box at the top of these sheets. Please read what is written in Item # 2: *Positive Core Beliefs*. After you finish reading Item #2 then return here.

Item 2 states that the POSITIVE CORE BELIEFS of being CAPABLE, LOVABLE and having a POSITIVE BODY IMAGE are based in evidence. You were the one that collected the evidence as you went out and completed the assignments, "How would someone know they are capable," and "How would someone know they are lovable," and when we read how the body is designed, operates and is upheld by the Light of Christ. However, Item 2 is pointing out something else that helps develop and support a healthy view of ourselves and that is when through humility and faith we begin to accept time-honored values and principles.

Principles are natural human laws that mediate relationships, including the relationship we have with our self. For example, treating others as we would want to be treated is a principle. Likewise, being honest, working hard, service to others, etc are principles. Laws are discoverable and when we discover these principles and we realize that life is more enjoyable by abiding by them we take that principle and adopt it as a value. The reason they are referred to as "time-honored" is because they have been shown from time memoriam to be effective ways to live life better.

In spiritual vernacular the relationship between principles and values may be best explained in this way, "It is one thing to have the law written upon a tablet of stone. It is quite another to have the law written upon the fleshy parts of the heart." We can always avail ourselves to reading laws that have been written, but when we adopt them then we become the living law. The value of the principle has us conform to the law with joy. (Jeremiah 31:33; Romans 2:15; 2 Corinthians 3:3; Hebrews 8:10).

Developing humility in conforming to natural law or principles and exercising faith in them, meaning we actually act in accordance to what the law says, also works to us having us see our self for who we really are. For those that develop a very good work ethic, what might they learn about themselves? Would they not learn that they are capable? Or what if we were to treat others in a respectful loving manner, what might we learn about ourselves? Would we not also learn that we are lovable as those so treated in return demonstrate that same manner of interaction? Or what if we learn to take better care of our bodies through healthy eating habits, stretching, exercising and getting a good night's rest? Would we not improve our view of our bodies? The answer to all of these questions is obvious. Abiding by time-honored principles and valuing the positive results in doing so, would shape very POSITIVE CORE BELIEFS within us. These principles are written in the energy of the Universe, of which each of us is ENTANGLED. Our own energy, which each of us are made of will resonate more positively when we begin to accept the truths associated with these principles. This is how the gospel reinforces the truth of who we are. God our Father, through revelation, reveals to us these principles or laws. He then invites us to abide by them through covenant. As we do begin governing ourselves by these correct principles we assure ourselves of our own worth, our true self and our true potential. Harold B. Lee put it this way:

> Without experiencing a gospel principle in action, it is.... more difficult to believe in that principle. (Teachings of Presidents of the Church: Harold B. Lee 2000, 121)

Items 2A, 2B and 2C in the form above are representations of TRUTHFUL THOUGHTS we would find our self saying which would lead to shaping the POSITIVE CORE BELIEFS within us. Again, these are the antithesis of the Automatic Negative Thoughts. As in the Uninstall Sheets, the TRUTHFUL THOUGHTS represented in the INSTALL SHEETS are just a few examples of what lead to shaping POSITIVE CORE BELIEFS within us. These are not exhaustive, just samples. There can be many, many more.

Let's look at Item 3 in the big box at the top of these sheets. Please read what is written in Item # 3: *Results.* After you finish reading Item #3 then return here.

Item 3 is having us evaluate the thought we formed in whether it led to a better outcome or led to increasing problems. If you will recall in the UNINSTALL SHEETS we were evaluating our behavior, i.e. "Did my behavior in any way challenge, make less true or help me overcome my Automatic Negative Thought?" In the INSTALL SHEETS or PROCESS, we are trying to develop awareness around our thoughts in determining whether the power of the mind, if utilized correctly, can shape within us the POSITIVE CORE BELIEFS, allowing us to see ourselves correctly.

If you have already looked at the INSTALL SHEET above, you will recognize I included the same example used in the UNINSTALL SHEET when you first started learning the PRACTICE OF LIVING CONSCIOUSLY. The INSTALL SHEETS are still part of that practice as now you are being highly conscious of the ways we form better thoughts. You should find that they are easier to do because of your previous experience.

LIVING CONSCIOUSLY does more for developing a healthy sense of your self than any other PRACTICE. In fact, it likely leads to improved understanding of the other PRACTICES aforementioned in this Program and utilizing them more effectively.

As represented throughout this book, our thoughts are the most impactful environmental signal our cells absorb, which shapes our ongoing view of our self. The reason for the shaping is when you recall what the Epigeneticists are telling us. The DNA molecule has incredible capacity to be stored upon or encoded upon. Whatever is encoded upon that material broadcasts signals to the living organism. These signals influence how we see ourselves. Living consciously is the highly developed practice of becoming aware of our internal conversation and how effectively it contributes to our own healthy or unhealthy esteem. Quantum Theory states that all matter is influenced and shaped by how it is observed. This is the Creation or Organizing Principle. We are made of matter, which includes our Implicit Memory where belief is stored. By looking at our internal conversation, we can free ourselves from distortions that have developed through an incorrect, negative internal conversation and better yet, through high awareness, develop a very truthful, healthy internal conversation that fundamentally changes our physiology. Purposeful and sincere observations while living consciously teaches us how to evaluate life's ongoing experiences in a way that that shapes a very truthful and healthy self-perspective.

The thing that got you to write a column in the UNINSTALL SHEETS is the very thing that gets you to write a column in the INSTALL SHEETS and that is when you are feeling a negative emotion. But the INSTALL SHEETS are not having you spend any energy in finding the Automatic Negative Thought that led to the negative emotion. There is no reason at this point to do so. By now you know that we can talk to ourselves negatively. What I want you to spend your energy on is increasing your ability to form Rational, Positive and Truthful Thoughts, thus improving your Internal Conversation.

As the week brings its unwelcomed events; and you recognize the negative emotions that arise growing out of the perception of those events, go to the top box in the column, the "My Problem Is" box and record the context or background associated with those negative emotions. If you recall the example we used earlier, "This past Thursday, my husband knew I had to be to a meeting at church and he promised that he would not be late coming home from work. Well, he forgot and I had to call him. I was angry, disappointed and felt like I didn't matter."

Since we are now focused on using the filters of Rational, Positive and Truthful Thoughts, your homework consists in your finding a thought through one of the filters to place upon the event. Once that thought is recorded then go ahead and fill-out the boxes below as they relate to the thought you formed. In the example above in that box I placed the following, "I learned that I have really good support through my relationships at church." This thought was formed by asking the question, "What might I learn from this experience or what might God want me to learn?" Inside of this box is another small box in the lower right hand corner. In the first column where the example is being recorded you will see that there is a "P-L" in that box. Don't worry about that for now; I will explain later what that box is for.

The next box below is asking us to identify what the thought meant to us. If you will recall in the UNINSTALL SHEETS I would ask my client to write out a sentence describing that meaning and then at the end of the sentence put parenthesis and place within the parenthesis the numbers reflecting the Negative Core Beliefs they believed they were tapping into. That is what is expected in the INSTALL SHEETS as well. Please write out what that thought you recorded in the box above means to you and then in parenthesis place the numbers in correspondence to the POSITIVE CORE BELIEFS you sensed you were tapping into. In the above example it was stated, "That while creating a little stress by my husband's forgetfulness, I had others that were understanding and helped me." (1, 2) In this case the 1 represents the Positive Core Belief of being Capable and the 2 represents the Positive Core Belief of being Lovable.

When you complete the MEANING box, record your emotions in the box below, "My Emotional Reaction to the Thought" box. Do not record the original negative emotions that cued you to write the column, but the emotions you are recognizing by the thought you formed and what that thought means to you. In the example above, the emotions of being GRATEFUL and feeling IMPORTANT are recorded.

In the box below the Emotion Box is the Behavior Box. In that box just record the behavior you did or plan on doing based upon the Thought, Meaning, Positive Core Belief and Emotion you have just recorded. In the above example it was recorded in that box, "I called a couple of my dear friends, explained what had happened and asked for help with some of the set-up. Told my 11 year old daughter to hold the fort down until her dad got home."

The last box in the INSTALL SHEETS is the evaluation box. This time we are evaluating the thought our mind came up with as we focused on the three filters of Rational, Positive or Truthful thoughts. Our evaluation is simply assessing whether the thought we formed led to a better outcome or did it lead to increasing problems. A simple check mark by which ever one we decide is all that is needed. In the case of our example, the fictionary client marked or checked "Yes." An important aspect of evaluating is recognizing how the better thought kept you in touch with your real identity. The better outcomes being recognized are directly related to staying truthful about who we really are.

Before you get going on this assignment, please make sure to review the INSTALL SHEET above and how the first column is filled out in relation to the husband – wife scenario we used as an example. Recall that the first question that is asked prior to doing a column is, "Was there a recent time when you recognized you were experiencing negative emotions?" Negative emotions are the cue to fill out a column.

So here is your homework. In the coming week, I want you to complete ten of the columns found in the INSTALL FORM. Again, you can copy this form from the book or go to my website and download the form. Part of the requirement in completing the ten columns is to do a minimum of one a day. By now you should understand why I want you to look at your IMPLICIT PROCESS every day. I am training you to increase your awareness of the other filters our thoughts can be formed through. Your awareness has the capacity to become automatic through enough repetition, and that is what we are doing in this assignment, increasing your awareness more consistently around the thoughts that will lead to better outcomes and strengthening the truth of who you really are. It is without question one's ability to increase awareness of their implicitly held patterns and belief increase exponentially when they are trying to pay attention to it on a daily basis. Elder Boyd K. Packer explained:

> "It was meant to be that life would be a challenge. To suffer some anxiety, some depression, some disappointment, even some failure is normal. Teach our members that if they have a good, miserable day once in a while, or several in a row, to stand steady and face them. Things will straighten out. There is great purpose in our struggle in life" ("That All May Be Edified" [1982], 94).

I believe one of the great purposes for the struggles in life is to learn how to overcome (Revelation 2:7; 3:5; 21:7). We can stand steady and face these struggles when we teach ourselves to observe them correctly. If we will speak more truthfully to ourselves things straighten out much quicker. When I consider the example of Jesus Christ in the challenges presented to Him, it is apparent to me that His belief in Who He is strengthened Him and allowed Him to handle those challenges in an impressive meek manner. Elder David A. Bednar said concerning this attribute fully formed in our Savior:

> Meekness is a defining attribute of the Redeemer and is distinguished by righteous responsiveness, willing submissiveness, and strong self-constraint..... The Christ-like quality of meekness is misunderstood in our contemporary world. Meekness is strong, not weak; active, not passive' courageous, not timid, restrained, not excessive; modest, not self-aggrandizing; and gracious, not brash. A meek person is not easily provoked, pretentious, or overbearing and readily acknowledges the accomplishments of others. (Meek and Lowly, GC, April 2018)

Those of us that are pushed back so easily when challenges arise do not experience faith and hope. These feelings appear to be replaced with sorrow, fear and doubt. Such was the reply of the rich young man when in answer to his question, "What lack I yet?" the Savior invited him to sell what he had, give it to the poor and then follow Him (Matthew 19:20). Even though not recorded in the scriptural account, this rich young man evaluated that event through his thoughts. Those thoughts were obviously negatively directed toward himself as the account points out that he experienced negative emotions (Matthew 19:22). If the better and rewarding feelings of happiness, faith and hope are to be experienced they will do so when we accept the truth of who we are. Many of us lack the meekness to be accepting of our identity. Mormon said that faith and hope are developed through the attribute of meekness (Moroni 7:43). To experience greater faith and hope in the midst of life's challenges will occur when we respond correctly to the revelation that we are made in God's image.

## REVIEWING HOMEWORK ASSIGNMENT #11

Since you are not sitting in my office reviewing your columns personally with me, I am going to share with you what I have learned when reviewing these INSTALL SHEETS with others. For the most part clients appear to come up with better thoughts as this assignment's focus is to do so. These thoughts more likely lead to better outcomes as well. However, I find that most clients have not understood how they actually formed the thought. In other words, they were not highly focused on what I taught them in session of how the three different types of thoughts are formed, yet they were still able to come up with thoughts that led to better outcomes.

This is the purpose of the smaller empty box you find in the Rational, Positive or Truthful Thought Box in the INSTALL SHEETS. It is located in the bottom right-hand corner of that box. This is where I want you to evaluate your recorded thought and place in the empty box one of the following symbols, based upon how you believed you formed that thought:

R  - Stands for Rational Thought. A Rational Thought is formed when we become the Outside Observer

P-T – Stands for Positive/Thankful Thought. A Positive/Thankful Thought is formed when we ask ourselves the question, "Is there anything I can be thankful for?"

P-L – Stands for Positive/Learn Thought. A Positive/Learn Thought is formed when we ask ourselves the question, "Is there anything I can learn?" or "Is there something God wants me to learn?"

T – Stands for Truthful Thought. A Truthful Thought is formed when our thought is truthful in relation to our real identity.

In the example above, recorded in the Install Sheets, you will notice there is a P-L in the box as it is suggested from her thought that it was formed by asking "Is there anything I can learn" perspective.

Here are some examples of thoughts with their corresponding symbols:

1) I am acceptable even when I make mistakes: T
2) I think I am better off when I stop eating by 5 PM: P-L
3) I know everyone has bad days and I don't need to take everything so personal: R
4) I shouldn't doubt my impressions: P-L
5) I am glad that I live close by most things I need: P-T
6) I would much rather be looking for a new job already being employed: P-T

7) Don't get down, some things matter more than others: R
8) I believe in myself: T
9) Procrastination creates too much stress: P-L
10) I know I can get through this: T

If you will return to the "The Rational, Positive or Truthful Thought" Box and look at the thought you formed in each of your columns, please place in the box on the lower right hand corner the symbol representing the filter you used to develop that thought.

Most of you will recognize at this point that you were not so aware in the moment of forming that thought the filter you were using. For most of you this is being discovered in hindsight. I know this because most of the time when my client's come back to report and I ask them from what filter did they form their thought, they hesitate. My intent in this last assignment is to get you to become so incredibly aware of these filters that they become immediately available to you when you are faced with a challenge; that they become intentional and deliberate.

To assist you in increasing your awareness of these filters, I would like you to go back to your 10 completed columns and form a thought from every filter. And then complete the column based upon the different thoughts formed. If I were to use the example from the column it would look like this:

| My Problem Is? | My Problem Is? | My Problem Is? |
|---|---|---|
| My husband forgot I had a meeting at church | My husband forgot I had a meeting at church | My husband forgot I had a meeting at church |
| My Rational, Positive, or Truthful Thought in My Mind Was?<br><br>I learned that I have really good support through my relationships at church<br><br>P-L | My Rational, Positive, or Truthful Thought in My Mind Was?<br><br>I am capable<br><br>T | My Rational, Positive, or Truthful Thought in My Mind Was?<br><br>I too at times forget things. I'm sure that he did not forget intentionally<br><br>R |
| What Did My Thought Mean to Me?<br><br>That while creating a little stress by my husband's forgetfulness, I had others | What Did My Thought Mean to Me?<br><br>I can find others to help me (1,2,3) | What Did My Thought Mean to Me?<br><br>He is usually so good about these things. Overall I have a very supportive husband (1,2) |

| | | |
|---|---|---|
| that were understanding and helped me. (1, 2)<br><br>Core Belief Option –<br>1. Capable<br>2. Lovable<br>3. Positive Body Image | Core Belief Option –<br>1. Capable<br>2. Lovable<br>3. Positive Body Image | Core Belief Option –<br>1. Capable<br>2. Lovable<br>**3.** Positive Body Image |
| My Emotional Reaction to the Thought<br><br>Grateful, Important | My Emotional Reaction to the Thought<br><br>Calm, Focused | My Emotional Reaction to the Thought<br><br>Settled, Happy, Loved |
| My Behavioral Response<br><br>I called a couple of my dear friends, explained what had happened and asked for help with some of the set-up. Told my 11 year old daughter to hold the fort down until her dad got home | My Behavioral Response<br><br>I called a couple of my dear friends, explained what had happened and asked for help with some of the set-up. Told my 11 year old daughter to hold the fort down until her dad got home | My Behavioral Response<br><br>I called a couple of my dear friends, explained what had happened and asked for help with some of the set-up. Told my 11 year old daughter to hold the fort down until her dad got home |
| Results of My Thoughts<br><br>✓Yes Led to a Better Outcome<br><br>No: Led to Increasing Problem | Results of My Thoughts<br><br>✓Yes Led to a Better Outcome<br><br>No: Led to Increasing Problem | Results of My Thoughts<br><br>✓Yes Led to a Better Outcome<br><br>No: Led to Increasing Problem |

Your willingness to go back and form thoughts from all of the filters in relation to the same Event or Problem has you see the power of your mind to observe and perceive life's difficulties in ways that strengthen your true self, keeping your real self intact.

Our minds are the core of any increasing intelligence we develop. Intelligence is the ability to see truth, accept it and let it govern our lives. Knowing truth and not doing anything with it is not intelligence. Knowing truth and complying with it develops wisdom, strength and the power of faith. Each one of our cells will become an active partner in whatever we give them. Can you imagine what life would be like if you consistently gave them truth in the form of accurate thoughts about your self? Can you begin to see how your cells and the DNA within each one begins to respond to the information you are supplying them? Our mind and the thoughts it develops; and beliefs that become formed places controls on our genes. Our cells are programmable. The programming or controls are largely influenced by what we allow our cells to absorb. What is being absorbed, especially the consistent information we supply them acts upon the genetic blueprint. Whatever gets encoded upon the blueprint plays heavily upon our ongoing experience. Genes profoundly influence the life we experience.

Epigenetics is an emerging frontier of science that involves the study of changes in the regulation of gene activity and expression. Gene regulation involves changes, not to the sequence of DNA but to gene activity itself. Every gene has responsibilities, but how their responsibilities are being carried out can make a big difference in the life of the organism. Some genes are suppressing mutations, for example, but if that gene becomes deactivated then whatever it was suppressing may now emerge in the organism. These epigenetic signals, in this case meaning the thought patterns we produce can influence changes to histones (proteins, which DNA is wrapped in; i.e., the epigenome) and DNA methylation. These epigenetic changes can influence the growth of neurons in the developing brain as well as modify activity of the neurons in the adult brain. Together, these epigenetic changes on neuron structure and function can have a marked influence on our beliefs, emotions and behaviors.

The most recent research, which this book has been touting, is that our biochemical make-up is being driven by a blueprint called the Genome. The Genome is the basis for understanding who we are. However, at times the blueprint needs adjustments which are drawn by epigenetic or environmental signals. Through correct environmental signals, which the gift of agency allows, we can change the deceptive blueprint of survivor to the truthful blueprint of creator. Sometimes these environmental signals are related to diet and activity; sometimes to those we include in our relationships, our studying the gospel and praying with meekness influences cellular function, but as a rule our own thoughts are the most powerful and influential epigenetic or environmental signal our cells absorb. We are very powerful in finding the truth of who we each really are and then creating and unfolding the lives we lead in relation to who we are. Identity unveils purpose!

What flows through our minds can sculpt our brain in seemingly permanent ways. Our minds activate the nervous system. On a physical level these are the electrical waves and chemical releases occurring in relationship to our evaluation of life's events. We are rarely paying high attention to our evaluations because most of these have already been formed implicitly. As a thought travels through your brain, neurons fire together in distinctive ways based on the specific information being handled, and those patterns of neural activity actually change your neural structure. The more we reinforce the same wiring the more permanent it becomes. The only way we know how to alter these strong neural pathways is through observance of the thoughts we say to ourselves and the beliefs that have become registered as implicit. Please don't forget, our thoughts are likewise impacting gene expression. Whatever we tell ourselves the most will become encoded as belief upon the molecule of DNA. What we believe about ourselves is impacting what genes are activated and what genes are suppressed. All of our wiring and all of our DNA signaling is influencing and shaping our ongoing experience, therefore it is beneficial to make sure that we form healthy neural pathways and encode correct information on the epigenome.

Now that science has proven that choice is real and the incredible influence our choices have on our biochemical structures, this last assignment is a tool that will allow you to increase your awareness around the most influential of all epigenetic or environmental signaling. My invitation is to continue to use the Install Sheets until you have increased enough awareness around these filters that they begin to become more automatic. When you realize that you are beginning to transfer what you do on the Install Sheets to the immediate situation you are experiencing, then you know that you are forming Implicit Memory around your true identity.

## WHO BEARS THE RESPONSIBILITY FOR WHAT HAPPENS IN OUR LIVES

I had one client, when coming to report on this assignment, read through each column with agitation in her voice. I didn't respond to her attitude, but after reporting on each column, I had her go back and starting from the first column read the thought she recorded in the Rational, Positive, Truthful Thought Box. When she read it, I then asked her, "What filter did you use to form that thought?" She looked at me like, 'What was I talking about?' I said which filter did you use to form that thought – I then directed her to the instructions at the bottom of the second page on how to form each thought. She looked at them and said, "Positive." I then asked her, "Which Positive Category did you use, Thankful or Learning?" She replied, "I don't know Thankful!" It was actually a Truthful thought, which I then pointed her attention to how someone forms a Truthful Thought. We went from column to column and it was clear that her lack of effort in the assignment did not allow her to learn how to do things correctly. Her agitation was growing. I said to her, "The reason why I am being a stickler for this is because when we have developed high awareness on how to form these thoughts, then we have the resource to put ongoing experience intentionally through these better perspectives. In doing so, we maintain and strengthen our true self."

She stated that she had been doing this type of mental work for years and it doesn't work. I tried to be encouraging and reminded her mindfulness techniques or self-affirmations are not the same as correct perspective that grows within us using the different filters. I then asked her, "How do you form a positive thought? She said, "By saying something positive." I said, "No, a positive thought forms when we ask our self one of the following two questions in relation to the EVENT we are experiencing, "Is there anything I can be thankful for, no matter how small it is," or "Is there anything I can learn from this event, or is there something God wants me to know?" Her grandiosity on full display replied, "Just because I don't use the same language as you do, doesn't mean that I am not doing it."

Her attitude was not surprising. When she first started working with me she appeared to be super upbeat as she was going through the Program, especially the Uninstall Process. Here the assignments seemed manageable for her as she hoped by learning something new, she might experience something new.

She was a woman of 36 years of age. She was still living at home with her parents. She had never sought to improve herself through education. She had been married once and had other relationships, but she insisted that "all the men she met were unhealthy." She would go from job-to-job, insisting that every work environment she joined was "not what she had hoped it would be." It appeared that in time of any of her employment opportunities, the management or her fellow workers would provide her feedback, expressing concerns about her that she would take personal.  In response to their feedback she would just complain that she was worth more than what she was being paid and then quit.

Her home life seemed to be one of co-dependency where things were kept in a chaotic dance of despondency, not requiring the development of autonomy. She had been operating from UNHEALTHY ESTEEM her entire life. The roles of Victim and Grandiosity were so well learned, she could not see that she was the source of all that she complained about and here is the main reason why.

From the very beginning of the Program I emphasize a great truth about us as humans. HEALTHY-ESTEEM is a product of both KNOWING AND DOING. Confident, optimistic living occurs when we begin to organize our activity and efforts based upon the truth of who we are. In fact, without the effort of synchronistic behavior, we will not fully understand our true nature. Knowledge without experience is merely philosophy. One of the telling moments of sincerity is when a client recognizes the truth of who they are and begins to act in that truth. Likewise, one of the telling moments of insincerity is when a client recognizes that personal responsibility is a natural outgrowth of seeing one self accurately and that awareness results in the client becoming angry, resistant, and anti-responsible.

To compensate for the seemingly inability to live up to her potential with all of the accompanying negative emotions attached thereto, she began to rearrange her beliefs. For example, several times through the Program she indicated that she was LOVE because God was LOVE. Her interpretation of this perspective was that in the end, it would not matter what she did or did not do in this life. Whatever was found lacking, because God loves her, she would still receive all that He has (Alma 1:4; 2 Nephi 28:8)
:
To better deal with her inability to take care of her own self, she would complain that she was worth more than what employers were willing to pay her. She believed life was unfair and that if employers were not willing to pay her at least $15 an hour she would just move on. This was her justification for going from job-to-job.

To have her cope with her parent's criticism of her not being active in the faith she was raised in, she would find material on the internet that dismissed her religion as a fraud. In dismissing her religion, she likewise selectively held on to the verses in the scriptures she liked and dismissed the ones she did not like.

To explain why she never pursued any education, she rationalized, "Education is a big rip-off. They make you take classes you don't even need just so they can make more money." They make it too hard and expensive to get a degree.

To excuse herself from having any meaningful relationships, both friends and romantic she would grandiosely declare, "I am glad that I am independent."

 This last statement actually happened on the day we were reviewing this assignment. I challenged her claim that she was independent. I asked her where she was living. She said at her parents. I asked her if she was paying her parents for any of her living expenses. She replied "No." I asked her if she was employed, she stated she had just quit her new job. I said, "You are not independent, not even close and this is why you are so unhappy. You haven't learned how to do anything for yourself and in doing nothing have denied your true self. Your whole sense of insecurity and fear is realistic, because at any moment you may lose your support and you know that would expose you for how you are really trying to go through life, abdicating your responsibility for living life with faith and confidence. Your severe lacking of appropriate development at your age must be embarrassing, reinforcing your insecurity. I don't know, maybe you are waiting for your parents to pass away hoping they will leave you enough so you can go on avoiding responsibility. One thing I do know is that the only thing you have learned is how to get others to take care of you." She left my office in anger (1 Nephi 16:2).

People that live life like this client have a tendency to blame others or even God. Sometimes a sense of entitlement develops manifested by shifting responsibility to others, institutions or government programs for their welfare. Many change God insisting that He really doesn't care about our personal efforts to follow the laws He has instituted for our advancement. 'He will save us even if we refused to follow Him' they reason.

Misunderstanding God's plan, or denying God's plan will not change the plan. The path of anti-responsibility will claim her own. At the end of this path is a dead end where we find a congregation of those who achieved less – far less – than the full, divine potential inherent in each of us. In tonight's sky will be the reminder of this path, a moon whose light is so far less than the sun and stars that barely give any light at all. Those night time emblems are the tokens of moral relativism. Moral relativism presents itself as such an irony, because it is acceptance of the truth that each is endowed with agency, but it rejects the One who gave it as well as its intended purpose. Regardless, moral relativism states that we don't have to believe in something we don't like, even when that thing we don't like is an immutable truth. Resenting truth will not change the demands truth places on us.

This young deluded woman was so, because she would only accept half of what would allow her to become. She accepted that through agency she can learn and know something, but rejected the principle of personal responsibility in bringing into fruition what she was created to become. Both her temporal and spiritual life reflected her dead-end path. Assuming personal responsibility is likewise a gift that grows out of agency and is necessary to realize our full potential. Did she state that she knew her worth was inherent? Did she purposefully choose adult ego state behaviors and saw how in doing so challenged her negative thoughts directed toward herself? Did she recognize that negative emotions are manifestations in individuals that have lost to a degree the relationship with them selves? Did she observe she was capable, lovable and an absolute miracle? Did she believe what had been revealed about her true identity? Yes, she stated that she knew all of these things. Then why did she not improve during the Program? Because she resented and rejected the truth that agency demands personal responsibility.

The parable of the talents was provided by the Master Teacher that we might understand how one masters their life. Each of us has been given full agency, requiring full responsibility. So, the Master gave one five talents, another two, and another one, "every man according to his ability....

> Then he that had received the five talents went and traded with the same, and made them other five talents
>
> And likewise he that had received two, he also gained another two.

But he that had received one went and digged in the earth, and hid his lord's money." (Matthew 25:16-19)

After a lengthy period of time the Master asked for an accounting. In measuring their efforts, the first two were promised even more, while the last, who through fear did nothing, from him was taken that which he had been given and it was imparted unto one of the others.

While we are not all equal in experience, aptitude and strength, we all have the capacity to improve in each (D&C 78:18-19). That is what in large measure we are being gauged by – are we thankful for what we have been given and are we showing gratitude by improving with what has been given? God intends for us to act, not just know. Agency was given that we might choose to learn or not to learn and to become or not become. It is His plan and His will that we have the principle decision-making role in our mortal probation.

This was the third assignment of three of the INSTALLING A HEALTHY IMPLICIT MEMORY process. The four things I want my reader to walk away with because of this assignment are:

1) OUR THOUGHTS ARE THE MOST POWERFUL EPIGENETIC OR ENVIRONMENTAL SIGNAL INVOLVED IN SHAPING BELIEF, ESPECIALLY BELIEF ABOUT OUR OWN IDENTITY
2) WE HAVE A THREE-TO-ONE RATIO IN FORMING TRUTHFUL BELIEFS ABOUT OUR IDENTITY.
3) THE PRACTICE OF USING THE THREE FILTERS INTROCDUCED IN THIS ASSIGNMENT WILL ONE DAY BEGIN TO ACT AUTOMATICALLY. THE INCREASING AUTOMATIC USE OF THESE FILTERS IS EVIDENCE THAT A HEALTHIER IMPLICIT MEMORY IS FORMING
4) MORAL AGENCY REFLECTS IN BOTH LEARNING AND DOING

Healing may not be so much about getting better, as about letting go of everything that isn't you............

— Rachel Naomi Remen

We can only achieve quantum improvements in our lives as we quit hacking at the leaves of attitude and behavior and get to work on the root, the paradigms from which our attitudes and behaviors flow.

— Stephen R. Covey

THE AFTERCARE PROGRAM –

What you have learned from the 11 Assignments contained in this book is the foundation for permanent change. This book detailed accurately how a view of our self will continue to shape our ongoing experience. How we see our self will impact almost every other aspect of our life. It will impact how we handle stress, what types of relationships we will form. It will impact our emotions; our goals our dreams; whether we will do our homework or not, even the type of employment we will go after. It will highly influence our economic status, our behaviors and our habits. It will impact our view of the world, of existence in general; and whether we develop any real purpose. Our view of our self will persuade our political decisions, what we think of others and even impact what we believe others think of us. Our view of self will have ongoing ramifications in our life experience. It will shape our destiny.

This book likewise detailed how our physiology works in how belief is developed and registered within our cells. Cellular learning is real and what our cells absorb will influence what they learn. Some learning can be incorrect and that incorrect learning will continue to interfere with optimal living until we can become aware of the IMPLICITLY held learning and understand why the learning is incorrect. Once true distortions are discovered and dismissed, we improve cellular functioning and influence. Yet IMPLICIT LEARNING AND MEMORY requires significant repetition. Like cement, your new foundation has now been poured, but your newly formed belief is not yet IMPLICIT or completely cured or hardened. Curing of your new personal belief requires an ongoing, consistent awareness that has you repeatedly reinforce the truth of who you are. That is what the AfterCare Program is for. It is an instrument that provides the experience of regular observing of those parts you hardly pay attention to.

I want to state honestly that there is a significant difference between those that complete the AfterCare Program and those that do not. There are times I will receive a call from a past client indicating they need a "tune-up" because they are regressing. The first question I always ask to such clients is, "Are you doing your AfterCare Program?" The answer is always, "No I am not" or "Not consistently."  But for those that are willing to follow what the research indicates and stay active in the AfterCare Program find the power to transform their physiology and do a work of regeneration that changes neural circuitry and provides epigenetic footprints allowing for optimal gene expression and function. Here is a testament to the power of the AfterCare Program:

After having my life completely fall apart as a result of severe depression and anxiety, I have learned that most of the coping mechanisms people prescribe are Band-Aids to cover up the problem without really getting to the core of the issue. Depression and anxiety usually stem from some sort of childhood trauma, lack of self-confidence, or intense fear of failure. Once you get the "fruits" of the issue under control enough to start working on the "roots", you will really start to experience healing.

The neuro-pathways in your brain can be changed. Unfortunately, many people with depression and anxiety have engaged in certain thought patterns for years that have rendered a physiological reaction in their bodies that negatively impacts them. It's difficult to believe - especially with all the information out there about mental illness - but your thoughts really can change your life. The things that you tell yourself about yourself are literally having an impact on your body's physical makeup. We simply don't pay enough attention to the brain in our society and instead medicate all the external symptoms. Once you become aware of your thoughts and figure out why you think that way, you can start to have power over your life by changing the way that you think.

It's worth it to spend some time with yourself figuring out your past and why certain events trigger you. Even though it's easy to blame your circumstances on other people, YOU are the only one who can change your life. It's a difficult journey and it's not a quick one. But it's worth it. I still consider myself on the path to recovery, and it's been over two years since my massive life breakdown. But there really is hope and healing ahead - give yourself permission to feel your feelings and have the courage to face things head on. Neurofeedback can help your brain biologically be in a better place, and Larry's counseling can help you consciously work through your issues by changing the false beliefs that have formed because of your experience. The AfterCare Program was instrumental in having me reinforce the healthy beliefs I developed about myself through Larry's Program. Depression and anxiety do not have to be a way of life! (Heidi P)

Another past client wrote:

When I walked into Larry's office the first time I was broken. I was broken spiritually, emotionally and mentally. I was at a very low point in my life. I wasn't sure why because I was married and have 4 beautiful children. I was ready to end my 7 year marriage, I was giving up. I had very little hope. The first appointment was truly a blessing. EVERYTHING Larry said made complete sense to me. I knew I was in the right place at the right time in my life. I knew that if there was hope for happiness it was to be learned in his office.

Reflecting on the things that Larry taught me in his program, I would say the two most important principles are that I am not responsible for anyone's happiness except my own and that my worth is inherent. No matter what I do and what mistakes I make, my worth never changes in the eyes of my Heavenly Father.

My relationship with my husband was broken. I felt more alone when he was home than when he was at work. We needed help desperately. The more I met with Larry, the more I learned about love, joy and my worth. I absolutely have no doubt that he is an inspired man and his program was developed to change lives. It has changed mine. I am currently in the AfterCare Program and I am not the same person that walked into his office the first time. I can honestly say I am TRULY happy. I am the happiest I have ever been even among the many hardships I have recently faced.

I am the heaviest I have ever been, but the most confident I have ever been. In high school and as a young adult I was at a very healthy weight and extremely involved in sports. Even though I wasn't even close to being overweight, I was so ashamed of my body and was so embarrassed. I had absolutely no self esteem, no confidence and I was not happy with myself. I am so truly happy now!!! I cannot express how much my life has changed because of Larry and his program.

One of my biggest fears as a mother is seeing my children fall into the same pattern I did and to believe the lies I was told and things I believed about myself. I still fear that, but I now have the tools, confidence, healthy esteem and knowledge to stop the pattern that destroyed me and to teach them about their inherent worth and how loved they truly are. I am eternally grateful for the incredible impact Larry and his program has had and continues to have in my life and in the life of my family. (Shay D.)

Note: The person who wrote this testimony has actually dropped about 60 pounds. I saw her this past spring. She looks so happy!

The research is really clear now on what is required to transform old, unhealthy implicitly held belief into a healthy, truthful personal belief system. The time required is a year to two years of consistently reinforcing your awareness of those healthy beliefs. When I looked at the research I realized that if I was going to do my client a favor, I had to create the means by which his or her awareness would be reinforced. The AfterCare Program is the instrument that provides the basis to do so.

I have not included the AfterCare Program in this book. It is provided through my website for an additional cost. It can be purchased with a one-time payment of $100.00. I am hoping that your improved relationship with yourself will encourage you to trust the research and commit to the AfterCare process. Many people, when they believe they are doing better deceive themselves by thinking they are OK now. Simply telling yourself, 'You are OK now' is not effective in changing the memorized self. The procedural reaction of IMPLICIT LEARNING AND MEMORY is powerful and takes time and repetition to convert or recreate to a correct view of self.

"Ye shall have hope through the atonement of Christ"

— Moroni

## APPENDIX A – HELPING THE PROCESS

If you have read books that provide similar insight on the mind-body connection hopefully you have noticed one significant difference. I have not been directing people to turn to things like mindfulness, meditation, yoga, energy healing, the emotion code, essential oils, etc. to find the change they are looking for. Most of these approaches are focused on calming down the negative emotions one experiences when they have unhealthy esteem. The approaches mentioned above are focused on the wrong thing. The focus is on the negative emotions being the source of the problem. My research is saying that negative emotions are just a symptom of the source – the source being having an incorrect view of one's self. If we could see our self correctly the negative emotions would eventually resolve because we resolved the very source driving the negative emotions.

With that said, I have nothing against the approaches of trying to get one's emotions into a manageable place as part of the overall process of finding our true self. A good example of what I am saying can be seen when working with someone in overcoming ADHD. ADHD robs a person of the ability to stay engaged long enough to learn; at times to comprehend, and becoming more disciplined. However, if we provide that person with an intervention to help focusing improve then that individual is able to practice and strengthen attention thus resolving the condition.

The overarching struggle people have with ongoing intrusive negative emotions is that there Implicit Memory has already associated such feelings as evidence that one is broken or devalued in some way. That strong, though incorrect association has a powerful pull on perception and more than likely acts as a hindrance to establishing healthy esteem. It seems advisable then to suggest to anyone that is using this Program that if they see benefit in helping them self manage their negative emotions while implementing this Program they should do so. Here are a few of the interventions I am familiar with:

1. Neurofeedback
2. Biofeedback
3. Hypnotherapy
4. Mindfulness Techniques
5. Yoga
6. Meditation
7. Exercise
8. Essential Oils
9. Medication
10. Prayer and Scripture Study
11. EMDR
12. Reading from inspiring authors

I think it is crucial that we remind ourselves that some of the negative feelings that accompany our journey through mortality are designed in us to encourage us to improve and become better individuals. These feelings are directly related to our imperfections and weaknesses, our poor thoughts and choices; our susceptibility to the natural man tendencies in all of us (Alma 42:10). These seemingly undesirable feelings are wrapped up in the experience of emotion that accompanies going against that which we almost intrinsically recognize as being right. The innate, intrinsic recognition of what is right and what is wrong exists in us and is sustained in us through the Light of Christ. This Light is a real power that fills the immensity of space, including the space of our own cells. Each of us is connected to it. It is in all things and upholds all things, and its power strengthens or diminishes in us depending upon our use of agency. It strengthens in us when we choose the better part and it diminishes in us when we choose not to heed its invitation to walk in the paths of truth. This is what King Benjamin reminded us of (Mosiah 3:18-19) as he knew that Christ is literally the light of the world and as we learn how to follow Him we will not walk in darkness, but shall have the light of life (John 8:12).

As stated earlier in the Chapter dealing with Emotions, I don't think we ought to become upset, discouraged or self-condemning in dealing with these strategically designed responses. If viewed correctly, we might begin to see the feelings of guilt, being ashamed, feeling bad or sometimes embarrassed as incredible friends and benefactors. If we deal appropriately with them it will literally make saints of sinners as they drive and influence self-mastery. In our appropriate response to such feelings, like all adversity, these emotional experiences will be consecrated for our gain. In dealing with them appropriately, please accept that Godly sorrow and reviling ourselves are not the same thing.

FORGIVENESS AS AN EPIGENETIC SIGNAL

In light of Elder Bruce R. McConkie's statement 'that in the Day of Judgment men's bodies will reveal what law they have lived,' and Joseph Smith's teaching, 'we came to this earth that we might have a body and present it pure before God in the celestial kingdom;' that I gave particular attention to some very recent work in the field of Epigenetics. All the acts of men, including their thoughts are being etched into the epigenome of the cell (Alma 12:14). These are being stored as memory and influencing cellular function. These etchings or marks are likewise shaping personal identity or how one sees them self.

Shinya Yamanaka, a Japanese stem-cell biologist theorized that chemical marks present on genes function as a record of cellular differentiation or identity. In other words, the precursor to every specialized cell is a stem-cell, meaning that all cells *stem* from this pure cell. He wondered what would happen if he could erase these chemical markings. Working with adult skin cells, and after a decade's long search for identity-switching factors, Yamanaka and his team found a way to erase a cell's memory. The process required a cascade of events. But as the events unfolded they observed that the physical appearance of the cell changed. Its years of existing one way were reversed and the cell was brought back to its pure state. The metabolism of the cell was restored to youthful levels of energy. Epigenetic marks were erased and rewritten, resetting the landscape of cellular function.

I can't help but wonder if this is not some type and shadow of how our poor choices, etched and recorded in our cells are reversed to be made pure again. Forgiveness is the mechanism that erases these moral failings and mistakes. In order to unlock the power of forgiveness, we are given a cascade of events that we must do. These actions collectively are called repentance. We cannot skip any of these actions or events. Each one is necessary. These events include:

1. Godly sorrow for the moral violation (Alma 36:17; 42:29); i.e., recognition that one has moved away from the light and wholly desires to restore its strength and power.
2. Abandonment or forsaking of the sin
3. Proper and full confession of the wrongdoing
4. Restitution, as far as is in our power to make the wrong right, perhaps even doubling that which was taken away
5. Asking for forgiveness and accepting it
6. Strengthening one's self against sin by becoming more devoted to learning truth and abiding by it.

The attitude that drives a successful repentance process is a broken heart and a contrite spirit (2 Nephi 2:7; D&C 21:9). I think that forgiveness must be an actual, intelligent power and that it acts upon cells to reverse memory, bringing them back to a pure state. I am strengthened in that belief as the Lord revealed to us:

> Behold; he who has repented of his sins, the same is forgiven, and I, the Lord, remember them no more. (D&C 58:42; Isaiah 1:18; Jeremiah 31:34)

> [See Also: Jubilee Year that suggests that things be brought back to their original state; Atonement which suggests repairing of what had become injured, being brought back to its original state. The Atonement allows for the remission of sins, remission meaning no longer being able to detect; Kipur or Kaphar, the Hebrew word for Atonement, which suggests to cover or purge, to not be visible any more.]

His language suggest that memory of the sin is erased. While He is ready to forgive, many times we refuse to forgive ourselves. I suggest that when we choose not to forgive ourselves, that such approaches are still evidence that an individual does not see themselves correctly. In other words, they continue to act in the realm of Unhealthy-Esteem. Unhealthy-Esteem is manifest when an individual continues to define themselves by some sort of limitation, perhaps expressed in action. To a degree, unwillingness to forgive ourselves is likely related to an incomplete understanding of the Atonement. Our sins should trouble us but not unto self-condemnation but instead unto repentance (Alma 42:29). Our forgiveness of self is not a sideline event. The Lord has declared that it is part of the main event taking place on the field. His forgiveness to us and our forgiveness to others and ourselves are necessary if we expect to present ourselves pure before the Lord (D&C 64:10). Celestial beings forgive!

This book is providing some incredible insight to what has been discovered in the last ten years. For those that can understand the message are provided a means to gain a better and accurate relationship with themselves. But none of what is being presented is a substitution for the need of our Savior. The greatest intervening source to healing is the Atonement of Jesus Christ. As Elder Robert C. Gay pointed out:

> His love is always greater than our fears, our wounds, our addictions, our doubts, our temptations, our sins, our broken families, our depression, our

anxiety, our chronic illness, our poverty, our abuse, our despair, and our loneliness. He wants all to know there is nothing and no one he is unable to heal and deliver to enduring joy. His grace is sufficient. He alone descended below all things. The power of His atonement is the power to overcome any burden in our life. (General Conference, October 2018)

I find that many believers do not fully understand how to access the power of His gift to each of us and therefore prolong their suffering. There are three blessings that flow to us because of the Atonement. However, to access these blessings require us to do something to have the 'power of becoming' to be made manifest.

In His invitation to come unto Him "all ye that labour and are heavy laden" with a promise that He would give such rest (Matthew 11:28), is the invitation to access His power in overcoming all things that set us back and the power to become what each of us were designed to become. The Savior then addresses the process as follows:

> Take my yoke upon you, and learn of me; for I am meek and lowly in heart and ye shall find rest unto your souls. For my yoke is easy, and my burden is light. (Matthew 11:29-30)

To access the healing and becoming power found in His perfect gift requires that we yoke ourselves to Him. That yoking will require that what He has to offer to each of us will demand that we take upon ourselves the qualities and characteristics of meekness and lowliness. It will be only in these attributes and mindset that we will comprehend the lightness of our burdens and the easiness of being yoked. The imagery of becoming yoked has us recognize that the journey will still require effort and at times real arduous effort, but being yoked makes the required work easier because He too is carrying a good portion of the workload.

The reason why meekness and lowliness are required in us is because these two characteristics serve as facilitators in the development of all the holy characteristics necessary to fulfill the measure of our creation, or to become what we were created to become. One of the great human needs in the journey we are on is perspective, meaning having God's perspective. Without proper perspective we will lose stamina to follow the correct path. We will become easily and myopically distracted. Meekness and lowliness helps submissiveness. Submitting our will to His unfolds the great mystery in all of us – that we are not metaphorically children of God, but literally children of the Highest with capacity to become as He is. Meekness and lowliness are necessary elements to rid our selves of the distortions found in incorrect views of our identity. It is in the incorrect view of self where so much baggage and burden is carried. Elder Neal A. Maxwell speaking on this subject said:

> Thus overloaded, we then feel sorry for ourselves. We need not carry such baggage, but when we are not meek, we resist the informing voice......
> However, if we have sufficient meekness, we will have help to jettison unneeded burdens and keep from becoming mired in the ooze of self-pity.
> (Meek and Lowly, Pg 6)

As we further look at the imagery of being yoked then it becomes plain to see that while working together there are things we can and must do, while there are things only He can do.

This spiritually perceived mooring is demonstrated in several interactions the Savior has while ministering to others. The story of Lazarus has Jesus coming into Bethany after Lazarus had passed away. Jesus is greeted by Mary and Martha, sisters of Lazarus. In their greeting Him, they speak faithfully, "If thou hadst been here, [our ] brother had not died" (John 11:21). Jesus replies that their brother will rise again. The sisters respond that they know their brother will rise in the resurrection, but that is not what Jesus was saying. He says to them, "He that believeth in me, though he were dead, yet shall he live" (John 11:24-25). While there can be several layers of understanding to what Jesus just announced, certainly one of those layers was, because Lazarus believes in Him; Jesus is getting ready to bring Lazarus back to life. In doing so, Jesus asks others nearby, "Take ye away the stone" (John 11:39). Jesus could himself have removed the stone, but he did not. Why not? This is the principle; Jesus wants us to do the things we can do as part of our progressing pathway. But then the thing only He could do he does, crying with a loud voice, "Lazarus, come forth" (John 11:43).

> And he that was dead came forth, bound hand and foot with graveclothes: and his face was bound about with a napkin. (John 11:14)

As Lazarus appears at the entryway of the tomb, Jesus invites others to "Loose him, and let him go."  Jesus had the power to remove the grave clothes that held Lazarus bound, but He did not. Again, He allowed others to do the things they could do. In application, the blessings and power available to each of us through the Atonement of Jesus Christ require our yoking to Him. There are things that we can and must do to unlock the power and blessings (2 Nephi 25:23). This relationship is portrayed in the following manner:

BLESSINGS AVAILABLE THROUGH THE ATONEMENT

| BLESSING | OUR YOKE | HIS YOKE |
| --- | --- | --- |
| Resurrection | Keep our first estate | Power over the grave |
| Justification | Repentance | Power to be cleansed |
| Sanctification | Ask in faith | Power to become |

It seems that most believers focus mostly on the second blessing, that being Justification. However, there is an important association with the blessing of Justification and the blessing of Sanctification.

Sanctification is the power to become the 'Sons and Daughters of God' (D&C 11:30; 1 John 3:1-3). To become Sons and Daughters of God is a title bestowed on all those that have become "Like Him." However, the only way to become 'Like Him' is through the spiritual gifts and blessings transmitted by the Holy Ghost.  He, meaning the Holy Ghost, is the bearer of all spiritual gifts we currently do not possess, which are necessary to overcome the natural man and become perfect or completed (Ephesians 4:13; See Also: Mosiah 3:19). Perfection in the biblical verse comes from the Greek word *telios* which means complete or fully developed. Just as Christ did not receive this fulness all at once but went from grace to grace until He received the fulness, so too is our path to becoming completed (D&C 93:11-14, 19-20).

Grace is a means of Divine help. These are the helps administered through heaven's power not our own. Grace is an enabling power that we ourselves are not self-producing. This enabling power is unlocked as we keep ourselves clean (Justification) so that the Holy Ghost can dwell with us and administer the spiritual gifts that empower us to overcome the natural man and become perfected in Christ (Moroni 10:32-33).

The power of Sanctification is a real power and it is unlocked in our lives when we begin to ask, in faith, for those gifts that will remedy the imperfections in us. George Q. Cannon taught:

> If any of us are imperfect, it is our duty to pray for the gift that will make us perfect.... No man ought to say, "Oh I cannot help this; it is my nature." He is not justified in it, for the reason God has promised to give us strength to correct these things; and to give gifts that will eradicate them.... He wants his saints to be perfected in the truth. For this purpose He gives these gifts, and bestows them upon those who seek after them, in order that they may be a perfect people upon the face of the earth, notwithstanding their many weaknesses, because God has promised to give the gifts that are necessary for their perfection. (Millennial Star, 56 no. 17, p, 260-261)

I do not need to go into depth about this asking. In the chapter "The Power of Belief," I describe the manner of asking that is required to unlock this enabling power.

The recognition of the blessings and gifts being asked for becoming manifest in our lives is evidence of the Godhead's love for each of us. Our Father in Heaven wants us to know the truth about our real identity. Through meekness our hearts and minds are capable of having our true identity sealed in our Implicit Memory. When it has done so and we have organized around it, the negative emotions will disappear and like God we will have a certainty that there is no power outside of us that is greater than what is inside of us.

My invitation in your journey to find happiness, peace of mind, and emotional empowerment is to access the power of the Atonement by yoking yourself to the Savior. Of all the remedies that will get rid of distortions that drive ongoing negative emotions, the Atonement of Jesus Christ is the most powerful (3 Nephi 9:13-14).

Some people fight with each other for worldly thrones; mostly for the purpose of making others bow down to them. But I fight tirelessly to inspire my fellow humans to become Kings and Queens in their own worlds.

— Edmond Mbiaka

My brethren, all ye that have assembled yourselves together, you that can hear my words which I shall speak unto you this day; for I have not commanded you to come up hither to trifle with my words which I shall speak, but that you should hearken unto me, and open your ears that ye may hear, and your hearts that ye may understand, and your minds that the mysteries of God be unfolded to your view.

— King Benjamin

## APPENDIX B – A VIEW FROM ABOVE

Kings and Priests
Spencer W. Kimball
(February 15, 1966, *BYU Speeches of the Year*, 1966 3-18)

My beloved brothers and sisters, the title of my address today could be "Kings and Priests"; or it could be "A Tale of Three Contemporaries." This is a story of kings and queens, of priests and priestesses, of real and eternal royalty.

In June, 1894, three babies were born. Twins landed in Arizona, and the third, a man-child also, was delivered in England, where his birth was heralded on front pages of every newspaper of the realm, for he came to a royal home where town criers announced hourly the progress of the delivery. In pompous ceremony in the great cathedral, this little fellow was given the name of Edward VIII. His father was George V, the crown prince; his grandfather, Edward VII, King of England and Wales and Emperor of India.

Young Edward was born heir to an earthly kingdom of many centuries duration, and his destiny would bring him to the throne with crown and scepter, under the Divine Right of Kings. Divinely called by the Lord, supposedly, he would not be responsible to his subjects for his governing nor to any human court of appeal. Some thought that such a representative of God "could do no wrong."

As a child, Edward knew that, barring unforeseen circumstances, he would someday sit on the throne, wear a crown and hold a scepter, where now his grandfather, Edward VII, ruled and where later his father, George V, would reign. He learned that, in addition to being King and Emperor, he would also be the head of the Church of England-born to it, not called to it.

Across the sea in sunny Arizona, the twin boys were born the same day and month and year. The first to come into the world would be called John, and he who came fifteen minutes later would be called Peter. These names, John and Peter, were given them in the sacrament meeting by a proud father. There were no bulletins, no town criers, no hospitals, not even a doctor to deliver them. A midwife, experienced and kindly, assisted in the birth. Few luxuries did this family have. The father was a good, common country farmer and his wife, just a sweet, personable country girl; but both had character, ambition, and intelligence.

Humble their birth, lowly their circumstances, and goodly their parents, these twins were born "under the covenant" and were at once princes to heavenly kingdoms under the rule of the divine opportunity for kingship. Heirs they were to the same kind of kingdoms as their father and forefathers Jacob, Isaac, Abraham, Noah, Adam, and numerous others.

These permanent eternal kingdoms must be earned, not only be born to; but if attained, would never end and the glory would be most spectacular.

Early in their lives, they were likewise told of their destiny in Primary, Sunday School, seminary, sacrament meetings, stake conferences, and in their home by faithful parents.

They learned that they would not become kings merely by the death of an ancestor, but by living all of the commandments and having performed all the proper sacred ordinances.

They read the scriptures which said:

That . . . they might be washed and cleansed from all their sins, and receive the Holy Spirit by the laying on of the hands . . .

And . . .overcome by faith, . . . sealed by the Holy Spirit of promise, which the Father sheds forth upon all those who are just and true. **(D&C 76:52-53.)**

Peter and John came to know that such totally faithful people

. . . are they who are the church of the Firstborn.

. . . into whose hands the Father has given all things--

They are they who are priests and kings, who have received of his fulness, and of his glory;

And are priests of the Most High, after the order of Melchizedek, which was after the order of Enoch, which was after the order of the Only Begotten Son.

Wherefore, . . . all are theirs and they are Christ's, and Christ is God's.

And they shall overcome all things. **(D&C 76:54-60.)**

It must have been vague and complex to the little boys, but gradually they became aware that they could dwell in the presence of God and His Christ forever and ever and that they could be just men made perfect through Jesus the Mediator of the new covenant.

They eventually came to know they could become celestial, having a glory like that of the sun, even the glory of God, the highest of all.

The two little Arizona princes grew up on the farm; the English prince in Britain. He wore velvets and satins, attended school with guards at his side and the best tutors to train him. The twins wore overalls and sweaters and went to school in the "little red schoolhouse." No insignia was on their coats, nor were they pampered nor protected from the little fights and bloody noses of childhood.

The eventual royal role for them to play must have been far away and misty to the twins, whose kingship was farther removed; but Edward lived in a royal environment and saw kings and queens and princes from many lands and was immersed in the royal pageantry extravaganzas which would keep him conscious of his future.

The little farm boys were interested in kites and marbles and frogs, likes and ball games and spinning tops. It may have been to such as they the Lord addressed His scripture:

Verily, verily, I say unto you, ye are little children, and ye have not as yet understood how great blessings the Father hath in his own hands and prepared for you;

And ye cannot bear all things now; nevertheless, be of good cheer, for I will lead you along. The kingdom is yours and the blessings thereof are yours, and the riches of eternity are yours. **(D&C 78:17-18.)**

Years passed, as years are wont to do. The boys came to their midteens The twins were handsome, tall fellows, favorites on the athletic field, popular in school activities, alert in seminary and Church organizations where they were learning of their far-away destiny. They would soon belong to the royal priesthood and become eligible to incomparable and eternal kingdoms. They were now reading scriptures which were being unfolded, bringing into focus kings and priests and kingdoms, and principalities and powers and dominions.

As a matter of course, Edward was attending the Church of England in great splendor-the church of which he would someday be the head. Edward might come to his earthly throne regardless of his morals, or worthiness; the twins to theirs only through righteousness. Though Edward might rule for 35 or 40 years over millions of people, the twins properly qualifying could reign eternities over a posterity as numerous as the stars in the heavens. These promises were coming to have new glorious meaning to Peter, but less to John, who was now dating steady and becoming careless as to his duties.

At 17 the twins were finishing high school in a whirlwind of athletic, social and academic programs, while across the ocean there were important happenings: King Edward VII, Edward's grandfather, died, and the father, George V, came to the throne. Young Edward was now declared to be the Prince of Wales, the Earl of Chester, and the Duke of Cornwall, (July 13, 1911). (Encyclopedia Americana, 1946, Vol. IX, 706.)

The Prince was a likeable and friendly sort. All three of these boys served their countries in World War I and may have fought on the same battlefields, They all received medals for courageous service. Edward served with distinction for 18 months in France and Flanders and in the Mediterranean. Lord Kitchener protested the hazards in which fearless Edward found himself, and said: "Get killed if you must, but what happens if you are taken prisoner?" (Ibid.)

When the war was ended, the three were mission age. Peter had been an efficient proselyting missionary. John had not accepted a mission call. Now the three were in college: The Prince-Duke-Earl attended the finest of his country; the twins, their state university. Peter was active in institute activities. John was disinterested.

Encyclopedia Americana said of Prince Edward:

No crown prince in history ever had such thorough training for the throne as Edward received, and it is doubtful if a more popular crown prince ever lived. (Ibid.)

So loved and respected was he over the world that he was referred to as "Prince Charming."

He was called England's "super-salesman" and was a good-will ambassador for his country. Highly educated, with a delightful personality, the Prince Charming was now a world idol. Yet, he never married.

In college, John was a sport and playboy. Smart, handsome, personable and popular, he found the nonmembers of the Church less inhibited and made his friends and dated among them. His dating was not a real courtship. It degenerated gradually into a late-hour affair with all that goes with dark nights, lonely roads, abandoned canyons, and ended with an abrupt Las Vegas marriage. He had ignored his covenants.

Peter progressed in Church activities. His temple marriage was a solemn one. His twin, John, was not present, for he had no temple recommend.

Many years have passed. The three, now 42 years old, are successful with degrees and positions of importance and renown. Peter has a large family of bright, alert children from teen-age down. John has three sons, the eldest said to have been conceived out of wedlock.

Prosperous John was concerned with his earthly kingdom and he seemed to be a Midas, every venture turning into wealth. His family, including the three growing boys, concerned themselves with acquisition and social life and the things of this world. His sons, now in their teens, were growing up out of the Church, without auxiliary programs, seminary, or priesthood. This family golfed and skied, swam, hunted and fished on the Sabbath. Cocktails were on every social program. John was unrepentant and was moving farther and farther from his throne-it was so vague and misty, so dim and unreal to him now. It was as though he were moving into a fog and could see only those things immediately in front of him.

Like the children of Israel, he had hardened his heart and rejected the exalting program. He knew that without the ordinances of the gospel and the authority of the priesthood, "the power of godliness is not manifest unto men in the flesh; For without this no man can see the face of God, even the Father, and live." **(D&C 84:21-22.)**

In hot pursuit of pleasure, wealth, distinction, and the applause of men, these eternal things meant little to him now. Building his temporary, short-lived earthly kingdom, he had overlooked this important fact, that:

. . . they . . . whose names are not found written in the book of the law, or that are found to have apostatized, or to have been cut off from the church, in that day shall not find an inheritance among the saints of the Most High. **(D&C 85:11)**

But his worthy brother, Peter, and his large family were close to the Church. Family prayers, home evenings, attendance at meetings, tithing, Word of Wisdom, and all the standards of the Church were followed religiously; and here was the ideal home and family.

Of men like Peter the scriptures have said:

They who dwell in his presence are the church of the Firstborn; and they see as they are seen, and know as they are known, having received of his fulness and of his grace;

And he makes them equal in power, and in might, and in dominion. **(D&C 76:94-95.)**

Peter was on his way to kingship and godhood. The Psalmist had sung:

I have said, Ye are gods; and all of you are children of the most High. **(Ps. 82:6)**

And Peter was well on his way toward this glorious goal to become one of those who inherits positions, titles, powers beyond human understanding.

The latter-day Prophet Joseph Smith spoke of men like Peter:

They are they who are priests and kings, who have received of his fulness, and of his glory;

Wherefore, as it is written, they are gods, even the sons of God--

These shall dwell in the presence of God and his Christ forever and ever. **(D&C 76:56- 62.)**

In this eventful forty-second year, Edward's father, King George V, died (January 20, 1936) and Edward ascended to the throne of England and became "Edward, Duke of Windsor (formerly Edward VIII, King of Great Britain and Ireland and of the British dominions beyond the seas, Emperor of India." (Ency. Amer., op. cit, 706.)

With the government in the hands of competent men, the new King had time, freedom, and wealth to pursue his own desires. One early diversion was a yacht trip on the Adriatic Sea. Among the guests was a beautiful woman, Mrs. Wallis Warfield Simpson, the wife of a London ship broker, Ernest Simpson. She was an American, born in Pennsylvania. The cultured and attractive young socialite had her debut at 18 in Baltimore, and at 20 she married Earl W. Spencer, Jr., of the U. S. Navy, from whom she was divorced about 11 years later; and the following year she married Mr. Simpson, and then moved to London.

She had known King Edward earlier. Now five years later, this married woman was a guest of the King on the luxury yacht in the warm waters of the Adriatic Sea. This cruise was background for the revolutionary changes which were destined to rock the British Empire and shock the world. In this yacht developed a friendship which in a short time ripened into a romance that had repercussions throughout the Empire from one end to the other. (See Ibid. )

Newspapers in England and America were showing the King and the lady holding hands as they strolled along the decks.

That the couple were madly in love with each other was the implication in the newspaper stories. (Ibid., 707.)

Then, suddenly, like a bolt of lightning, came Mrs. Simpson's application for divorce from Simpson; and the gossip became thicker and traveled faster than anything had ever traveled throughout the kingdom for a long period.

Here was an unusual situation: an American divorcee, now a married woman, and the King of a vast empire in an illicit love affair!-a woman with a living husband and a King who was head of the great populous Church of England courting! How shocking!

The toppling Simpson marriage was doomed to end in short order. A King had stepped from the shadows.

The summer ended. The yacht cruise was over. The two principals returned to England and France. Short months were passing rapidly, and legally trained men were clearing the way for the divorce which was to rid her of a second husband and make way for a third, and it would be final in April, 1937, after six months.

The American papers were playing up the story. The British papers were keeping silence as near as possible.

Then the London Times of November 30, 1936, published an editorial which really was to shake the world:

. . . the Commons may well prove itself what the country has often required in similar times . . . a council of state . . . (to govern) in any crisis . . foreign or domestic. (Ibid.)

Then the storm broke.

The Bishop of Bradford spoke out in condemnation. All newspapers reported the Bishop's address, from which I quote:

Within a day or two the love affair of the King and Mrs. Simpson was first page news throughout the world . . .

The British public was thunderstruck. There followed much talk of the Constitution . . . the idea that the king who was also the head of the Church of England could for a moment contemplate marriage to a twice divorced woman was unthinkable in certain circles. (Ibid.)

October 20, 1937, Prime Minister Baldwin called on the King, urging resolution of the rumors and an end to them. Apparently, all British people were hoping it was only a rumor.

The report soon came that he was to marry her and would abdicate, if necessary.

The empire was rocking. No British King had ever voluntarily relinquished the throne. . . The public began to take sides. . .

Some insisted that the king should be permitted to marry whomsoever he pleased. Others . . . preferred abdication to marriage under the circumstances. . . . The Government belonged to the latter group, and it is also stated rather authoritatively that the queen mother, heartbroken, sided with the Ministry. . . .

At length, the Prime Minister Baldwin appeared before the House of Commons and tacitly admitted that the King wanted to marry Mrs. Simpson, morganatically if in no other way and then the Prime Minister added that from inquiries he had made he was satisfied that assent to a morganatic marriage would "not be forthcoming." (ibid.)

I consulted Webster, who informed me that a morganatic marriage is . . . a marriage where one of royal family marries one of inferior rank and wherein the wife, if inferior, does not acquire the husband's rank, and the children do not succeed to the titles, fiefs, or entailed property of the parent of higher rank.

Mrs. Simpson left England, went to France, and issued a statement that:

. . . she wished to avoid any action which would hurt or damage His Majesty or the Throne, and that she was willing to withdraw from a situation . . . both unhappy and untenable. (Ency. Amer., op. cit.)

The King had "let the cat out of the bag" when he first informed Baldwin of his intention to marry Mrs. Simpson whenever she should be free.

An Instrument of Abdication sent to Parliament by the King, December 10, 1936, read as follows, was accepted almost immediately:

I, Edward VIII of Great Britain and Ireland and the British Dominions Beyond the Seas, King, Emperor of India, do hereby declare my irrevocable determination to renounce the throne for myself and my descendants and it is my desire that effect should be given to this instrument of abdication immediately. In token whereof I have hereunto set my hand this 10th day of

December, 1936, in the presence of the witnesses whose signatures are subscribed. Edward, R. I. (Ibid.)

Albert, Henry, and George, his brothers, Duke of York, Duke of Gloucester, and the Duke of Kent, were the signed witnesses.

Baldwin said to the House of Commons he had talked to Edward, October20 and November 16, who had said, "I am going to marry Mrs. Simpson and I am prepared to go." (Ibid.)

It is claimed that this was the first voluntary abdication ever signed by a king of England. The phrase "By the Grace of God" was omitted from the instrument.

Had His Majesty followed custom, his instrument of abdication would have begun: "I, Edward VIII, by the Grace of God" of Great Britain, Ireland and the British Dominions Beyond the Seas, King, Defender of the Faith, Emperor of India . . . (Ibid.)

The House of Commons gave "effect" to the instrument of abdication, and it was passed by both houses of Parliament, December 11, 1936-one day later.

For 11 months Edward VIII had been King over a quarter of the earth's surface and population. In his speech of farewell to all his people, he said:

. . . I have found it impossible to carry the heavy burden of responsibility and to discharge my duties as King as I would wish to do without the help and support of the woman I love. (Ibid., 708.)

Speaking of his brother who would succeed him, he said:

. . . he has one matchless blessing, enjoyed by so many of you and not bestowed upon me, a happy home with his wife and children. (Ibid.)

He said, "I now quit, altogether, public affairs and I lay down my burden." (Ibid.)

That night, December 12, 1936, he left his country for Austria via France.

The new King immediately made the former King, Duke of Windsor. The new Duke of Windsor, Edward VIII, and Mrs. Bessie Simpson were married June 3, 1937.

More than three-score years and ten have sped by and much water has turned many wheels and run over many dams since that eventful day in June, 1894, when three male children had come into this world with such fantastic destinies. Let us review the status of these three contemporaries.

The Duke of Windsor, His Royal Highness, the ex-King, was in 1965 the feature actor in the play, A King's Story, filmed in England and France: "His vehicle a bitter-sweet recounting of his days from Victoria's time to the astonishing abdication that ended in his own short reign and shook the empire."

In the premiere film we shall see the picture of a king who abdicated his throne and let his infatuation for an attractive woman deprive him of his royal throne and scepter. Today, he is wrinkled; his hair is gray. Once a prince, a king, an emperor, head of the populous Church of England, he is now a private citizen, heir to no throne, earthly or heavenly. He may never return to the throne of England. He abdicated. Of course, he can still claim a heavenly crown if he is willing to pay the price. Unless there are early changes in attitude and interest, he may die an earthly duke but not a heavenly king, for precious time is passing. If he fails to qualify, he will be a single person in eternity-never the head of a family as he said he had craved; possibly no children, posterity or increase as he said he was deprived of. He will be a servant to a king, but never priest nor king.

The woman for whom he abdicated and gave up so much will also be single, neither wife nor mother, unless she meets the requirements. All three of her husbands will be strangers to her. And, she and the ex-King may both be servants forever-not rulers. Imagine, if you can, the ex-King and his charming wife as everlasting servants to others, yet that is their destiny unless something about it is done soon-servants, not rulers. The Lord has pronounced it. **(See D&C 132:1.)**

Perhaps a little differently from John, his contemporary, Edward, now only the Duke of Windsor, was exiled not only from England, but from exalted kingdoms. Not only did he relinquish the crown after 11 months and 21 days, depriving himself of his earthly kingdom, but he also deprived any children he might have the same throne, crown, scepter, and privileges. Did he have a right to deprive his possible children of life, opportunity, sonship, leadership, kingship? He gave up all this for the woman he said he loved, and in the act relinquished for eternity the very woman he thought he loved. In these later years the man Edward and his wife could investigate, accept, and magnify the gospel and have the same blessings as Peter. It is not likely he will avail himself of these matchless privileges, for one must be humble and courageous and spiritual and prayerful to merit these blessings.

The ex-King is a little like Atahualpa, the Inca. When in 1532 Francisco Pizarro brought his small Spanish army to Tumbes in the Andean region, he found a land of limitless wealth and a gullible people. Atahuapa, on the eve of being proclaimed Inca, the supreme god of his world, felt he had nothing to fear from a few mailed, helmeted horse-borne warriors. But with the cannon unknown to the Incas, and fear and superstition as their weapons, the Spanish subdued the Indians and Atahualpa was imprisoned. He offered a roomful of gold for his freedom. He was willing to give up all his gold for his life. But he lost his gold, then also his life.

A strange anomaly! When the King gave up his kingdom to get the woman he thought he loved, he lost his earthly kingdom and placed his wife in jeopardy for eternity.

As for John who was also born to greatness and trained toward the incomparable eternal goal, he had also lost his way. Once he was a prince and heir to greater dominions than an earthly empire, but it was evidently too vague and far away and demanding for him. He lived for the present and lost his way to the distant, glorious future. Against all the efforts of many people, he abdicated his future throne and relinquished his right to eternal royalty and kingship. He traded his birthright, as did Esau, for a mess of pottage, a mere few decades of fun and pleasure, public applause, comforts.

Last year he died. The funeral was spectacular. Many of the community folks were there. Mountains of flowers decorated the church which he had not entered many times in a half century. His body was finally back in the chapel of the Church he had abandoned. His wife had finally yielded to the pleadings of his aging, faithful parents.

Viewers had passed by the casket in the mortuary and noted that his head was still covered with curly locks of hair, now gray. The white shirt, the black tie, and the black suit in which his body lay gave him immaculate grooming, as throughout his lifetime. He could have been dressed in fine linen of pure white like the clothing spoken of by John the Revelator, who said of the bride of the Lamb, that

. . . to her was granted that she should be arrayed in fine linen, clean and white: for the fine linen is the righteousness of saints. **(Rev. 19:8)**

John could have been clothed in "white raiment" promised to all who are faithful and true, "that thou mayest be clothed, and that the shame of thy nakedness do not appear" (Rev. 3:18)

Many of his acquaintances returned to their offices, saddened with broken hearts, not for his death, but for the condition of his life and death. The family dutifully followed the remains to the grave. Great as were his wealth, his mansion on the hill, his Cadillac's, his stocks and bonds, his cattle, and his oil wells in Oklahoma, his casket, though elegant, like that of poor paupers, was only about seven feet long, two feet wide, and of shallow depth; and old Mother Earth who gave him his body-dear Mother Earth, which he had exploited for half a century; precious Mother Earth, which he might have had for an eternal inheritance-opened her mouth and loaned him her bosom for his body's resting place, perhaps willingly, perhaps grudgingly, the little space of about two cubic yards. Her bosom ached as her eyes watered at so promising a man having missed the mark so far. His extensive possessions and accumulations were soon in the courts with relatives quarreling over them. His spiritual destiny was not much to be coveted.

John had lost his way. He had abdicated his throne, his princehood, his kingship, his godhood, for who knows what? Let him now, today, as he looks down upon it all with sight no longer limited by poor physical eyes-let him now appraise his positions of prominence, his directorship, his managerships, his influence, his high honors. Let him now count his friends whom he may never see again. Let him now evaluate his influence. How many can he now employ? How much weight can he now throw around? To how many can he dictate? Let him now, today, clip his bond coupons, deposit his dividends, count his cattle, harvest his acres, balance his bank account. He failed to invest real capital. He spent it. It is not available to him now. The courts have it. In the vernacular of the street, he has had it. The good things of the earth he has lost. He has used them up. He has spent his capital. Spent or dissipated capital pays no dividends and no interest.

John's total family had missed the goal. They were deprived because of John. The wife was a worldly woman; and as for the sons and their families, they were strangers to the Church, with no missions, no temple marriages, no spiritual experiences and eternal accomplishments. The sons were banker, lawyer and physician and respected in their professions. John it was who led them off, who closed their doors, who will pay heavily for their deprivations. His total family knew the Church of the Lamb only historically. They were unacquainted with their God, their Christ, their Savior. They had little knowledge of His ways and requirements and blessings. And this limitation and deprivation was largely because of John, the dead man, John, their ancestor, who chose his and their ways of life.

This is the sad lot of many children of thoughtless, selfish parents, who choose the careless or evil way for their children. It reminds us of the sacred scriptures coming from Liberty Jail, from the great Prophet, who referred to such as the "servants of sin" and the "children of disobedience" themselves, who bring to themselves and their posterity bondage and death. **(See D&C 121:16-18.)**

Their basket shall not be full, their houses and their barns shall perish, and they themselves shall be despised by those that flattered them.

They shall not have right to the priesthood, nor their posterity after them from generation to generation **(D&C 121:20-21.)**

Bad enough it is to bring bondage to oneself; but criminal for one to set stakes or to make plans which might bring deprivation and death to their posterity.

John had lost not only himself but had led his posterity into the thicket of darkness from which they seemed unable to extricate themselves-many descendants left to wander aimlessly through life's maze.

Moses wrote of "visiting the iniquity of the fathers upon the children unto the third and fourth generation of them that hate me." **(Ex. 20:5)** The prophet Ezra also spoke of it:

These sought their register among those that were reckoned by genealogy, but they were not found: therefore were they, as polluted, put from the priesthood. **(Ezra 2:62)**

The stalwart and faithful Peter also died not long ago. His was a large funeral, also, and many people present had been blessed and helped on their way by him. Numerous were the stories of his goodness, his sacrifice, his devotion, his kindness to all whom he touched. His children were all prosperous people with excellent families, much honored. He left his small assets to the Church for missionary work since his wife had pre-deceased him.

In his casket, he was as radiant as a body can be after its spirit has gone. Or was it still around? He was immaculately dressed in his temple robes, white robes, made "white in the blood of the Lamb." (Rev. 7:14) He was prepared physically and spiritually for the trumpet sound when the graves will be opened. This great prince, holding the Royal Priesthood after the Order of the Son of God, was ready. He had received that . . peace, from him which is, and which was, and which is to come; . . .

And from Jesus Christ, who is the faithful witness, and the first begotten of the dead, and the prince of the kings of the earth. Unto him that loved us, and washed us from our sins in his own blood,

And hath made us kings and priests unto God and his Father; to him be glory and dominion for ever and ever. Amen. **(Rev. 1:4-6.)**

He knew this well:

And he that is a faithful and wise steward shall inherit all things. (**D&C 78:22**)

He had read from John the Revelator how the elders fell down before the Lamb with their harps:

And they sung a new song, saying, Thou art worthy to take the book, and to open the seals thereof: for thou wast slain, and hast redeemed us to God by the blood out of every kindred, and tongue, and people, and nation;

And hast made us unto our God kings and priests: and we shall reign on the earth.

And I beheld, and I heard the voice of many angels round about the throne and the beasts and the elders: and the number of them was ten thousand times ten thousand, and thousands of thousands;
Saying with a loud voice, Worthy is the Lamb that was slain to receive power, and riches, and wisdom, and strength, and honour, and glory, and blessing.

And every creature which is in heaven, and on the earth, and under the earth, and such as are in the sea, and all that are in them, heard I saying, Blessing, and honour, and glory, and power, be unto him that sitteth upon the throne, and unto the Lamb for ever and ever. (**Rev.5:9-13.**)

He knew and his loved ones knew that:

He that is ordained of God and sent forth, the same is appointed to be the greatest, notwithstanding he is the least and the servant of all.

Wherefore, he is possessor of all things; for all things are subject unto him, both in heaven and on the earth, the life and the light, the Spirit and the power, sent forth by the will of the Father through Jesus Christ, his Son.

But no man is possessor of all things except he be purified and cleansed from all sin.

And if ye are purified and cleansed from all sin, ye shall ask whatsoever you will in the name of Jesus and it shall be done. . . . as ye are appointed to the head, the spirits shall be subject unto you. (**D&C 50:26-30.**)

Now, you 10,000 priests and priestesses, where do you stand?

You are heirs to great fortunes, for eternal life is the greatest gift.

What will you do with it? You are entitled to a kingdom or a queendom. You are princesses and princes. Do you prize your inheritance? Will you abdicate and relinquish your heavenly rights to all that is your due? Do you but realize what the Lord has in store for you? Do you know what you could discard in a moment of carelessness and heedlessness? The Lord told his servants:

. . . Eye hath not seen, nor ear heard, neither have entered into the heart of man, the things which God hath prepared for them that love him. **(1 Cor. 2:9)**

The king's highway—the royal road to eternal joys and exaltation—is a hard road, full of sacrifices and restrictions and hard work. The way is narrow but it is straight, well-marked, and strongly-beamed. But if you get off course, the dot and dash tapping gets dimmer and fainter till it fades out entirely.

The permanent kingdom is yours, not for the asking, but for the earning.

Will you abdicate it? That is much easier than to claim it. Will you, like John, voluntarily renounce the throne? And through carelessness and heedlessness voluntarily relinquish your right to this powerful and blessed privilege? Will you forfeit your crown? Will you turn over your scepter to another? It follows easily. To do so, you need only to forget the Lord, ignore His commandments, become critical or bitter or inactive. Other things follow in turn and your kingship and queenship are in jeopardy!

John wanted the world. He got a good share of it for a few decades, but he paid a terrific price. It is as though he paid a million dollars for a door mat. He gave up an eternal kingdom for his considerable slice of this world for those few years.

He died. He left all of his things. He abandoned his nonmember wife. He had no right to die and leave her desolate, single, for eternity. He passed away. How cowardly for him to die and leave his posterity as it were in a Sahara Desert of barren sand when he could have left them in a watered garden-to leave them starving and cold and numbed when he could have left them fed and faithful, warmed and provided for. He had no right to die and leave them where he had placed them through his failures.

Serious enough to deprive himself far worse to dispossess his posterity of parents, leadership, kingship, and royalty.

John gambled. He placed his every effort, ability, interest on the table; and when the wheel quit spinning, the stakes were lost. He lost his family. He lost his little world, and was now "wretched, and miserable, and poor, and blind, and naked." **(Rev. 3:17)**

What are you going to do, my young friends? Your answer measures your degree of maturity.

Children grab what they want now. Adults can wait for the tree to grow and the fruit to ripen. Children spend their principal now. Adults can wait for interest and dividends. The immature are impatient for the good things today. The mature person can wait and save and enjoy indefinitely. The immature will do the thing which satisfies his immediate wants, his desires, his passions. The mature one will restrain himself, and wisely choose and plan for the ultimate good.

Edward gave up all for the woman he thought he loved. John gave up eternity for the world. Peter gave up all worldly trifles to live with the woman he really loved through eternity.

O, my beloved youth, I pray you, date faithful members, marry only in the holy temples of God, plan your course, chart your way, live righteously always, listen to your leaders, read the scriptures, think sanely, pray much and often, earn your eternal throne, claim your crown, hold tightly the scepter, keep your inheritance inviolate.

May you precious young people never abdicate your possible thrones, but become priests and kings of the most high throughout eternity, I pray in the name of Jesus Christ. Amen.

# BIBLIOGRAPHY

Albrecht-Bueler, Guenter (as quoted in) *Secrets of Your Cells: Discovering Your Body's Inner Intelligence,* Boulder, Colorado: Sounds True, 2013

Anderson, Neil L. *Whoso Receiveth Them, Receiveth Me*, General Conference, April 2016

Bach, Richard *Illusions: The Adventures of a Reluctant Messiah*, New York, New York: Delta Trade Paperbacks, 1977

Ballard, Melvin J. Conference Report, 1934

Barrett, Sondra *Secrets of Your Cells: Discovering Your Body's Inner Intelligence,* Boulder, Colorado: Sounds True, 2013

Bytheway, John *How to be Totally Miserable*, Salt Lake City, Utah: Shadow Mountain, 2007

Carver, George Washington *In His Own Words*, Columbia Missouri: University of Missouri Press, 1987

Denton, Michael *Evolution: A Theory in Crisis*, London: Burnett Books, 1985

Dossey, Larry *The Science of Premonitions*, New York, New York: Penguin Group, 2009

Dyer, Wayne *The Essential Wayne Dyer Collection*, Hayhouse Publishing, Inc., 2013

Engel, Beverly *It Wasn't Your Fault*, Oakland, California: New Harbinger Publications, 2015

Engelbreit, Mary *Life is Just a Chair of Bowlies*, Kansas City, Missouri: Andrews McMeel Publishing, 1993

Faust, James E. *The Power of Self-Mastery*, General Conference, April 2000

Gay, Robert C. *Taking Upon Ourselves the Name of Christ*, General Conference, October 2018

Ghandi, Mahatma *Mahatma Ghandi Quotes, Vol 2*, CreateSpace Independent Publishing, 2016

Goleman, Daniel *Emotional Intelligence,* New York, New York: Bantam Books, 1995

Grant, Heber J. *A Marvelous Growth*, Juvenile Instructor, December 1929

Hinckley, Gordon B. *Teachings of Gordon B. Hinckley*, Salt Lake City Utah: Intellectual Reserve, Inc., 2016

Holtz, Lou *Wins, Losses & Lessons*, New York, New York: Harper Collins Publishers, 2006

James, William *William James, in Lloyd Albert Johnson, comp., A Toolbox for Humanity: More Than 9000 Years of Thought*, Victoria, Cananda: Trafford Publishing, 2003

Jefferson, Thomas (as quoted in) *The Great Ones*, New Delhi, India: Abhinav Publications, 2003

Lee, Harold B. *Understanding Who We Are Brings Self-Respect*, October General Conference, 1973

Lewis, C.S. *The Quotable Lewis*, Wheaton, Illinois: Tyndale House Publishers, Inc., 1989

Madsen, Truman G. *Eternal Man*, Salt Lake City, Utah: Deseret Book, 2013

Mansfield, Katherine *On Love/Psychological Exercises: With Some Aphorisms & Other Essays.* Boston, Massachusetts: Weiser Books, 1998

Maxwell, Neal A. *Even As I Am*. Salt Lake City, Utah: Deseret Book, 1982
    *All These Things Shall Give Thee Experience*, Salt Lake City, Utah: Deseret Book, 1992
    *We Will Prove Them Herewith*, Salt Lake City, Utah: Deseret Book, 1982
    *Meek and Lowly,* Salt Lake City, Utah: Deseret Book, 1987

McConkie, Bruce R. *Mormon Doctrine, 2ⁿᵈ Ed*, Salt Lake City, Utah: Bookcraft, 1966
    *The Millenial Messiah*, Salt Lake City, Utah: Deseret Book Company, 1982
    *Who Hath Believed Our Report*, October General Conference, 1981

McGill, Bryant *Voice of Reason: Speaking to the Great and Good Spirit of Revolution of Mind*, Paper Lyon Publishing, 2017

Monson, Thomas *Living the Abundant Life*, Salt Lake City, Utah: Ensign January, 2012

Montaigne, Michael *Michael De Montaigne.* New York, New York: E.P Dutton & Company, 1911

Nuit, Natasa Pantovic *Mindful Being Towards Mindful Living*, Gizira, Malta: The Art of 4 Elements, 2016

Ogunlaru, Rasheed *Soul Trader: Putting the Heart Back Into Your Business*. Philadelphia, Pennsylvania: Kogan Page Limited, 2012

Peale, Norman Vincent The Power of Positive Thinking, New York, New York: Touchstone, 2003

Peterson, Wilfred Arlan *The Art of Living Treasure*, New York, New York: Simon and Schuster, 1977

Pilgrim, Peace *Peace Pilgrim: Her Life and Work In Her Own Words,* Santa Fe, New Mexico, 1982

Remen, *Rachel Naomi Table Wisdom: Stories That Heal*, New York, New York: Riverhead Books, 1996

Smith, Joseph Jr. History of the Church, Salt Lake City, Utah: Deseret News Press, 1951

Smith, Joseph Fielding, General Conference, April 1970

        *Doctrines of Salvation 2*, Salt Lake City, Utah: Bookcraft, 1956

        Answers to Gospel Questions, Salt Lake City, Utah: Deseret Book, 1963

Swindoll, Charles *Charles Swindoll, in Daniel H. Johnston, Lessons for Living,* Macon, Georgia: Dagali Press, 2001

Taylor, John *The Gospel Kingdom*, Salt Lake City, Utah: Deseret Book, 2002

Tolle, Eckhart *The Power of Now*, Vancouver, British Columbia: Namaste Publishing, 1999

Tolstoy, Leo *The Law of Love and The Law of Violence*, Mineola, New York: Dover Publications, Inc., 2011

Tracy, Brian *The Peak Performance Woman*, Jaico Publishing House, 2017

Twain, Mark *The Adventures of Huckleberry Finn*, Woodstock, Illinois: Dramatic Publishing, 1942

Woodruff, Wilford *The Discourses of Wilford Woodruff*, Salt Lake City, Utah: Bookcraft, 1946

Young, Brigham Discourses of Brigham Young, Salt Lake City, Utah: Deseret Book, 1954

CPSIA information can be obtained
at www.ICGtesting.com
Printed in the USA
LVHW101428070321
680809LV00026B/500